WINDOWS XP
PERSONAL

WINDOWS XP
PERSONAL TRAINER

CustomGuide, Inc.

O'REILLY®

Beijing • Cambridge • Farnham • Köln • Paris • Sebastopol • Taipei • Tokyo

Windows XP Personal Trainer

by CustomGuide, Inc.

Published by O'Reilly Media, Inc., 1005 Gravenstein Highway North, Sebastopol, CA 95472.

O'Reilly books may be purchased for educational, business, or sales promotional use. Online editions are also available for most titles (*safari.oreilly.com*). For more information, contact our corporate/institutional sales department: (800) 998-9938 or *corporate@oreilly.com*.

Editors	Tatiana Apandi Diaz and Nathan Torkington
Production Editor	Jamie Peppard
Art Director	Michele Wetherbee
Cover Designer	Emma Colby
Interior Designer	Melanie Wang

Printing History

November 2004:   First Edition.

 This book uses RepKover,™ a durable and flexible lay-flat binding.

ISBN: 0-596-00862-7

[C]

CONTENTS

INTRODUCTION

About the Personal Trainer Series

Most software manuals are as hard to navigate as the programs they describe. They assume that you're going to read all 500 pages from start to finish, and that you can gain intimate familiarity with the program simply by reading about it. Some books give you sample files to practice on, but when you're finding your way around a new set of skills, it's all too easy to mess up program settings or delete data files and not know how to recover. Even if William Shakespeare and Bill Gates teamed up to write a book about Microsoft Windows XP, their book would be frustrating to read because most people learn by doing the task.

While we don't claim to be rivals to either Bill, we think we have a winning formula in the Personal Trainer series. We've created a set of workouts that reflect the tasks you really want to do, whether as simple as resizing or as complex as integrating multimedia components. Each workout breaks a task into a series of simple steps, showing you exactly what to do to accomplish the task.

And instead of leaving you hanging, the interactive CD in the back of this book recreates the application for you to experiment in. In our unique simulator, there's no worry about permanently damaging your preferences, turning all your documents purple, losing data, or any of the other things that can go wrong when you're testing your new skills in the unforgiving world of the real application. It's fully interactive, giving you feedback and guidance as you work through the exercises—just like a real trainer!

Our friendly gym-themed guides can buff up your skills in record time. You'll learn the secrets of the professionals in a safe environment, with exercises and homework for those of you who really want to break the pain barrier. You'll have your Windows XP skills in shape in no time!

About This Book

We've aimed this book at Windows XP. Some features may look different depending on the updates you've downloaded from Microsoft. If our simulator doesn't match your application, check the version number to make sure you're using the right version.

Since this is a hands-on course, each lesson contains an exercise with step-by-step instructions for you to follow.

To make learning easier, every exercise follows certain conventions:

- This book never assumes you know where (or what) something is. The first time you're told to click something, a picture of what you're supposed to click appears in the illustrations in the lesson.

- When you see a keyboard instruction like "press Ctrl + B," you should press and hold the first key ("Ctrl" in this example) while you press the second key ("B" in this example). Then, after you've pressed both keys, you can release them.

Our exclusive Quick Reference box appears at the end of every lesson. You can use it to review the skills you've learned in the lesson and as a handy reference—when you need to know how to do something fast and don't want to step through the sample exercises.

Conventions Used in This Book

The following is a list of typographical conventions used in this book:

Italic

Shows important terms the first time they are presented.

Constant Width

Shows anything you're actually supposed to type.

Color

Shows anything you click, drag, or press.

NOTE *Warns you of pitfalls that you could encounter if you're not careful.*

TIP *Indicates a suggestion or supplementary information to the topic at hand.*

Indicates information about Windows XP Service Pack 2 updates.

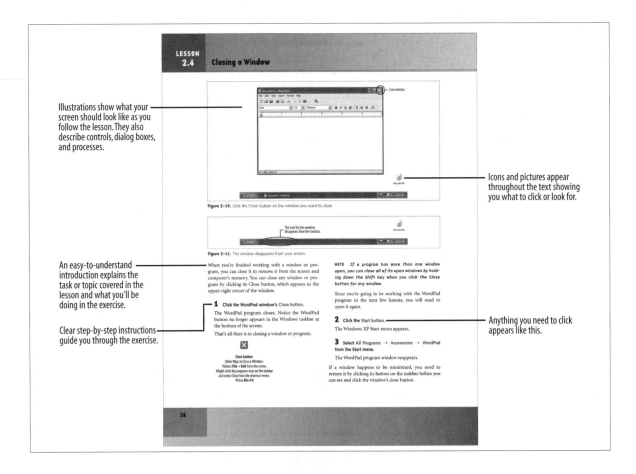

Illustrations show what your screen should look like as you follow the lesson. They also describe controls, dialog boxes, and processes.

Figure 2-10. Click the Close button on the window you want to close.

Figure 2-11. The window disappears from your screen.

Icons and pictures appear throughout the text showing you what to click or look for.

An easy-to-understand introduction explains the task or topic covered in the lesson and what you'll be doing in the exercise.

Clear step-by-step instructions guide you through the exercise.

Anything you need to click appears like this.

Using the Interactive Environment

Minimum Specs

- Windows 98 or better
- 64 MB RAM
- 150 MB Disk Space

Installation Instructions

Insert disc into CD-ROM drive. Click the Install button at the prompt. The installer will give you the option of installing the Interactive Content and the Practice Files. These are both installed by default. Practice files are also included on the CD in a directory called "Practice Files,"

which can be accessed without installing anything. If you select the installation item, the installer will then create a shortcut in your Start menu under the title "Personal Trainer," which you can use to access your installation selections.

Use of Interactive Content

Once you've installed the interactive content, placing the disc in your drive will cause the program to launch automatically. Then, once it has launched, just make your lesson selections and learn away!

How to Contact Us

We have tested and verified the information in this book to the best of our ability, but you might find that features have changed (or even that we have made mistakes!). As a reader of this book, you can help us to improve future editions by sending us your feedback. Please let us know about any errors, inaccuracies, bugs, misleading or confusing statements, and typos that you find anywhere in this book.

Please also let us know what we can do to make this book more useful to you. We take your comments seriously and will try to incorporate reasonable suggestions into future editions. You can write to us at:

O'Reilly Media, Inc.
1005 Gravenstein Highway North
Sebastopol, CA 95472
(800) 998-9938 (in the U.S. or Canada)
(707) 829-0515 (international or local)
(707) 829-0104 (fax)

To ask technical questions or to comment on the book, send e-mail to:

bookquestions@oreilly.com

The web site for *Windows XP Personal Trainer* lists examples, errata, and plans for future editions. You can find this page at:

http://www.oreilly.com/catalog/winxppt/

For more information about this book and others, see the O'Reilly web site at:

http://www.oreilly.com

CHAPTER 1

THE FUNDAMENTALS

CHAPTER OBJECTIVES:

What's new in Windows XP

Start and log on to Windows XP

Understand the Windows XP screen

Understand the new Windows interface

Use the mouse to: point, click, double-click, right-click, drag, and drop

Use the keyboard

Exit Windows and turn off the computer

Prerequisites

• **Windows XP must be installed on the computer.**

Welcome to Windows XP! If you're new to Windows, or to computers altogether, you're starting at the right chapter. This chapter covers the "bare-bones" basics about learning how to start your computer and load Windows XP. You'll learn how to operate the mouse by clicking, double-clicking, clicking and dragging, and right-clicking. You'll also learn about your computer's keyboard and what those cryptic-looking keys are used for. Finally, you'll learn how to exit Windows XP and shut down your computer.

Before we start, take a deep breath and relax. You may find this difficult to believe, but computers aren't nearly as difficult and complicated as you probably think they are. No matter what your previous experience with computers has been, this chapter assumes you're the most computer-illiterate person in the world and keeps everything as simple as possible. Actually, you're probably going to find that some of the lessons in this chapter are a little *too* easy. When you come across something you already know how to do, go ahead and skip the lesson (unless you're in a classroom of course—then go ahead and show everyone what a computer whiz you are!).

Ready? Did you take that deep breath? Then turn the page and let's get started!

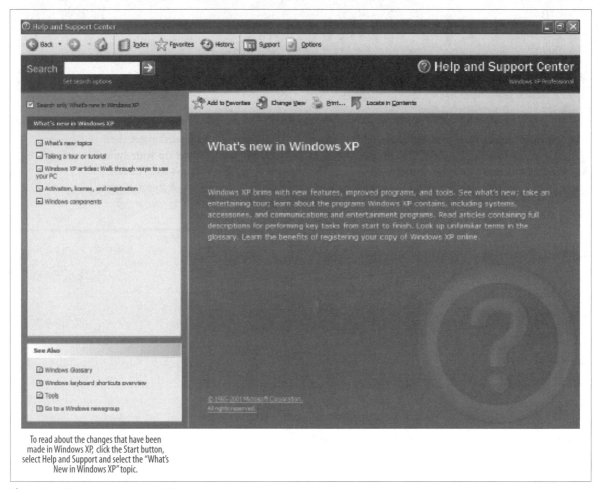

To read about the changes that have been made in Windows XP, click the Start button, select Help and Support and select the "What's New in Windows XP" topic.

Figure 1-1. The Help and Support Center window.

Before we start pointing and clicking, it helps if you actually understand what exactly Windows XP is. Windows XP is an *operating system*. Okay, so what's an *operating system*? An operating system is a software program that controls and runs just about everything on your computer. Here's what an operating system does:

- **Controls Your Computer's Hardware**

  Windows XP controls the different devices of your computer system. It's what makes your printer print, what makes graphics and text appear on your monitor, and what makes your mouse point and click. Actually, *you* make the mouse point and click, but Windows XP is what puts the mouse pointer on the screen and electronically connects it to your mouse.

- **Runs Your Computer's Programs**

  Windows XP is what runs all your programs. Without Windows XP, your word processor, Web browser

(Internet), and games wouldn't work. Windows XP lets your programs "talk" to your hardware, so, for example, your word processor can print things to the printer.

- **Organizes Files**

  Windows XP stores information in files and folders on your computer's local disk, just like you store files and folders in a filing cabinet.

Think of Windows XP as an orchestra conductor who makes sure all the parts of your computer—your hardware and programs—work together. Operating systems have been around for a long time; what makes Windows XP special is its ability to make computer operations easy. In the computer stone age (about 15 years ago), people had to type hard-to-remember, cryptic commands into their computer to make them do what they wanted. With Windows XP, all you have to do is point and click to do something.

So what's the difference between Windows XP and other versions of Windows, such as Windows 98 and Windows ME? Table 1-1 discusses some of the major differences.

Why Use Windows XP? Windows XP represents one of the most significant upgrades Microsoft has made to the Windows operating system since Windows 95. Windows XP is based on Microsoft Windows NT/2000 operating system, which means that it's much more reliable (read: doesn't crash or lock up as much) than previous versions of Windows. If your computer meets the minimum requirements, you should definitely consider upgrading.

If you do decide to upgrade, first make sure that you *can* upgrade. To use Windows XP, your computer should have at least:

- A Pentium II 300 MHz processor
- Minimum 128 MB of memory
- Minimum 1.5 GB free disk space

If your computer doesn't meet these requirements, you probably need to beef up your system before you make the switch to Windows XP. The features in Table 1-1 are just a few major new features. To read more about new features, go to *www.microsoft.com*, or go to Help and Support in the Start menu of Windows XP.

Table 1-1. What's new in Windows XP?

New Feature	Description
New Interface	The most obvious and controversial feature of Windows XP is a completely redesigned interface and Start menu that is easier to use and supposedly lets you find what you need more quickly. The jury is still out whether or not users will embrace this drastically new interface. If you can't stand the new Windows XP interface you can always switch to the Windows Classic interface of previous versions.
More Reliable	Windows XP is based on the same technology as Microsoft Windows NT and Windows 2000 business operating systems. This makes Windows XP more stable than Windows 95, 98, and ME, and greatly reduces the risk of your computer crashing.
Better File and Folder Management	Windows XP makes it easier to view and work with your files and folders. Thumbnail view lets you preview photos and images and the new File and Folder task pane lets you easily copy, move, rename, or delete any file or folder.
Better Help and Support	Windows XP makes it easier to access help and support with new features such as Remote Assistance, which allows you to contact a computer expert and let them fix a problem on your computer… even from hundreds of miles away!
Better Security Windows XP Service Pack 2	After years of worms, Trojan horses, and neverending Windows XP security patches, Microsoft has finally begrudgingly acknowledged and addressed many of the security problems in Windows XP with Windows XP Service Pack 2. Windows XP Service Pack 2 contains many dramatic Internet and network security improvements—make sure you visit Microsoft's Web site and download and install this critical update for Windows XP.
WiFi Support Windows XP Service Pack 2	Microsoft's new Windows XP Service Pack 2 includes new features and Wizards to support the new and growing wireless networking standards.

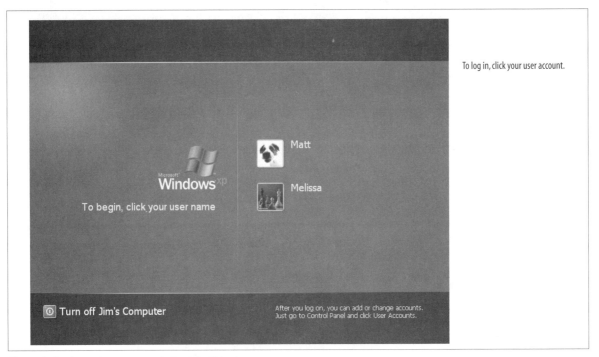

Figure 1-2. The Welcome screen is the default log in screen.

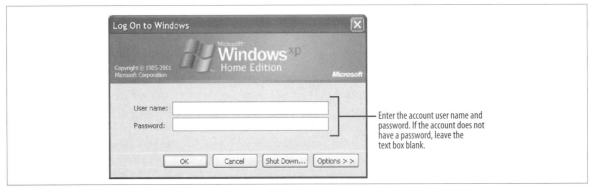

Figure 1-3. The Log On to Windows XP dialog box appears if the Welcome screen has been turned off.

After taking off your jacket and grabbing a cup of coffee, you probably begin your day by turning on your computer and starting Windows XP. Windows XP should automatically start after you turn on your computer. This lesson also explains what you need to do next.

The default login screen is the Welcome screen, as shown in Figure 1-2.

1 Click your account user name.

If your account has a password, you will be prompted to enter it.

NOTE *If someone has turned off the Welcome screen, logging in will be a little different, as shown in Figure 1-3.*

2 Enter your user name and password. If your account doesn't have a password, leave the text box blank.

Remember that when you enter your password, Windows XP will display a series of ••••••••s to protect your password from prying eyes.

3 Press Enter or click OK.

Windows XP logs in using your account settings.

QUICK REFERENCE

TO LOG ON TO WINDOWS XP HOME USING THE WELCOME SCREEN:

- CLICK YOUR ACCOUNT USER NAME. ENTER YOUR ACCOUNT PASSWORD IF PROMPTED.

TO LOG ON TO WINDOWS XP HOME WITHOUT THE WELCOME SCREEN:

1. ENTER YOUR USER NAME AND PASSWORD. IF YOUR ACCOUNT DOESN'T HAVE A PASSWORD, LEAVE THE TEXT BOX BLANK.

PRESS ENTER OR CLICK OK.

Figure 1-4. The Welcome to Windows XP dialog box.

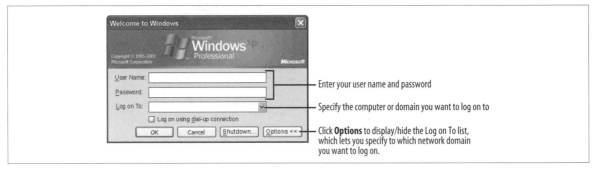

Enter your user name and password

Specify the computer or domain you want to log on to

Click **Options** to display/hide the Log on To list, which lets you specify to which network domain you want to log on.

Figure 1-5. The Welcome to Windows XP dialog box.

Logging on to a computer using Windows XP Professional is a little different because you are logging in to a network, not just a computer, so security needs to be tight.

The first screen is a defense against hackers or worms that might try to hack into your computer while you're not using it.

1 Press Ctrl + Alt + Delete.

The Welcome to Windows XP dialog box appears, as shown in Figure 1-5.

2 Enter your user name and password.

Remember that when you enter your password Windows XP will display a series of •••••••s to protect your password from prying eyes.

3 If necessary, click Options and click the Log on To list arrow to select the domain name that you want to log on to.

This setting probably won't ever change, but you should be aware that it is required to log in to the domain.

4 Press Enter or click OK.

Presto! You're logged on to Windows XP and are ready to get back to work.

QUICK REFERENCE

**TO LOG ON TO WINDOWS XP
PROFESSIONAL:**

1. PRESS CTRL + ALT + DELETE.

2. ENTER YOUR USER NAME AND PASSWORD.

3. MAKE SURE YOU ARE LOGGING IN TO THE CORRECT
   DOMAIN.

4. PRESS ENTER OR CLICK OK.

Figure 1-6. The major parts of the Windows XP screen. More items may appear on your computer, depending on how it is set up.

You might find the Windows XP screen a bit confusing and overwhelming the first time you see it. Nothing on the screen appears familiar to you—where do you even start? This lesson will help you become familiar with the main Windows XP screen, known as the *desktop*. There isn't a step-by-step exercise anywhere in this lesson—all you have to do is look at Figure 1-6 and then refer to Table 1-2 to see what everything you're looking at means. And, most of all, relax! This lesson is only meant to help you get acquainted with Windows XP—you don't have to memorize anything.

NOTE *If you're upgrading to Windows XP from previous versions, you may be surprised at the lack of icons and features on the screen. Don't be alarmed: My Documents, My Computer, and other useful functions are still around, they've just been moved under the Start button.*

Table 1-2. Major parts of the Windows XP screen

Item	Description
Desktop	This is the large background area of the Windows XP screen. You can customize the desktop by adding shortcuts to your favorite programs, documents, and printers. You can also change the appearance of the desktop to fit your mood and personality.
Recycle Bin	The Recycle Bin stores all the files you delete from your computer. You can use the Recycle Bin to retrieve files you've accidentally deleted. Create more disk space by emptying the Recycle Bin.
Taskbar	The Taskbar usually appears at the bottom of your screen and contains the famous Start button, which you use to start your programs. Whenever you open a program, document, or window, an icon for that program appears on the taskbar. This lets you see which programs are currently running and allows you to easily switch between them.

Table 1-2. Major parts of the Windows XP screen (Continued)

Item	Description
Start button	The Start button lets you quickly open your programs and documents. You can also use the Start button to find files and change the settings for Windows XP.
Quick Launch bar	The Quick Launch bar gives you quick access to your most frequently used applications. Internet Explorer, Outlook Express and the Windows XP desktop are included in the Quick Launch bar by default.

Don't worry if you find some of these things confusing at first—they will make more sense in the upcoming lessons, after you've actually had a chance to use them.

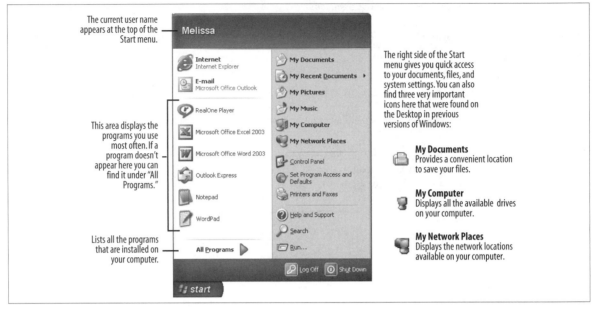

Figure 1-7. The new Windows XP Start menu.

You've probably already noticed that Windows XP's Start menu is drastically different than the Start menu in earlier versions. All the icons that were formerly stored on the desktop, such as My Computer and My Documents, are now on the Start menu, making it your single source for launching applications, finding documents, and changing computer settings.

The new Windows XP Start menu takes a lot of getting used to—especially if you're familiar with the Start menu in previous versions of Windows. Once again, there isn't a step-by-step exercise in this lesson—all you have to do is look at Figure 1-7 and then refer to Table 1-3 to see what everything in the new Windows XP Start menu does.

1 Click the Start button.

The Windows XP Start menu appears, as shown in Figure 1-7.

2 Keep the Start menu open and refer to Table 1-3 to find out what's new in the Windows XP Start menu.

The new Windows XP Start menu takes a *lot* of getting used to—especially if you're familiar with the Start menu used in earlier versions of Windows. Don't worry if you just *can't* get used to the new Windows XP Start menu—it's easy to change back to the classic Start menu that you're more familiar with—we'll cover that very topic in another chapter.

Table 1-3. Items in the Windows XP Start menu

Item	Description
All Programs	Opens your Internet browser.
All Programs	Opens your default e-mail software.
Recently Used Programs	Gives you quick access to the programs you use most often. If a program doesn't appear here you will have to look under "All Programs."
All Programs	Gives you access to all the programs installed on your computer, although you may have to wade through several submenus in order to find the program you're looking for.

Table 1-3. Items in the Windows XP Start menu (Continued)

Item	Description
My Documents	Provides a convenient location to save your files. In previous versions of Windows, My Documents was located on the Windows Desktop.
Recent Documents	Opens files you have recently worked on.
My Pictures	Provides a convenient location to save your photos and pictures.
My Music	Provides a convenient location to save your music files.
My Computer	Gives you access to the drives, folders, and files on your computer. In previous versions of Windows, My Computer was located on the Windows Desktop.
My Network Places	Access the drives, folders, and printers on the network. In previous versions of Windows, My Network Places was located on the Windows Desktop.
Control Panel	Opens the Windows Control Panel.
Connect To	Connects to the Internet or a network.
Set Program Access and Defaults	Sets the default programs that handle certain activities on your computer. (This replaces Connect To in SP2.)
Printers and Faxes	Shows installed printers and faxes. Also provides access to wizards that help install new printers and faxes.
Help and Support	Gets help on how to use Windows.
Search	Finds a file on your computer.
Run...	Runs a program.
Log Off	Logs off of Windows so that another user can log on to your computer.
Shut Down	Provides options for turning off or restarting your computer.

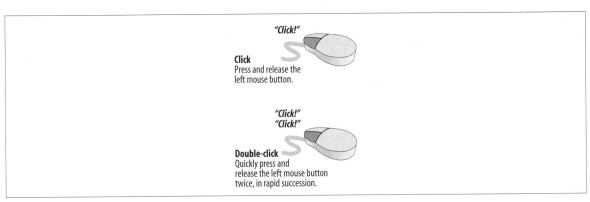

Figure 1-8. Clicking and double-clicking with the mouse.

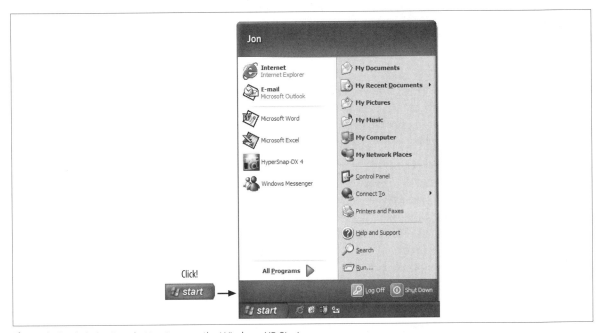

Figure 1-9. Click the Start button to open the Windows XP Start menu.

— Close button

Figure 1-10. Double-click the Recycle Bin icon to open it and display its contents.

Just like you control your television set using a remote control, you control Windows XP by using the mouse and keyboard. A mouse is a palm-sized device that lets you point at, select, and move objects on your computer screen. The mouse is linked to the pointer on your computer screen—when you move the mouse on your desk, the pointer moves on the computer screen. Think of the mouse as an electronic extension of your hand. This lesson shows you how to perform the two most basic mouse actions: clicking, and double-clicking.

1 Rest your hand on top of the mouse, then move the mouse and watch as the arrow moves across the screen.

The arrow (also called the cursor or pointer) follows the mouse as you move it across the desk or mouse pad.

Pointing is the most basic action you can do with the mouse. To point to something, simply place the mouse pointer over it by moving the mouse.

Mouse Pointer

2 Move the mouse pointer until the tip of the pointer is over the Start button. Leave the pointer there for a few seconds.

The message "Click here to begin" appears by the pointer after several seconds.

Clicking means pressing and releasing the left mouse button once. The mouse makes a clicking noise when-

ever you press and release one of its buttons, hence the term "clicking." The next steps will show you how to open the Start menu by clicking it.

3 Move the pointer over the Start button and click the left mouse button.

Start button

When you click the Start button, the Windows XP menu pops up, as shown in Figure 1-9. Congratulations! You've just made your first click!

NOTE *Most mice have two mouse buttons. Normally you will use the left mouse button (unless someone has changed the mouse options and reversed the buttons!). You can assume that you will use the left mouse button whenever you see the words "click" or "double-click." The right mouse button has its own purpose—and we'll discuss it in an upcoming lesson.*

You can close the Windows XP Start menu without selecting anything by clicking anywhere outside the menu.

4 Move the pointer anywhere outside the Windows XP Start menu and click the left mouse button.

Now that you're feeling comfortable with pointing and clicking, we'll move on to something a little more tricky: *double-clicking*. Just as it sounds, double-clicking means pressing and releasing the mouse button twice in rapid succession. You will usually open an object (such as a file, folder, or program) by double-clicking it.

5 Position your pointer over the Recycle Bin icon and double-click it with your left mouse button.

Recycle Bin

The Recycle Bin opens to reveal its contents, as shown in Figure 1-10.

NOTE *A lot of people have problems the first time they try double-clicking. If your double-click doesn't seem to work, it's probably because you're either not holding the mouse steady while you're* *double-clicking, or you're not double-clicking fast enough. If you click the mouse button too hard, you may accidentally slide the mouse before you've finished double-clicking, and your double-click won't register. If you're certain that you're holding the mouse steady while you double-click, you can adjust the double-click speed in the Windows XP Control Panel, which we'll talk about more in a later lesson.*

6 Close the Recycle Bin window by clicking its Close button.

Close button

Table 1-4. When to click and double-click

Click when you want to:	Double-click when you want to:
Select something.	Open a file.
Open a menu.	Open a folder.
Press a button on a toolbar or a control in a dialog box.	Display the properties or settings for an object (in certain programs).
Move to the area or field you want in a program or dialog box.	

QUICK REFERENCE

TO POINT:

- MOVE THE MOUSE SO THAT THE POINTER IS OVER THE OBJECT.

TO CLICK:

- POINT TO THE OBJECT AND PRESS AND RELEASE THE MOUSE BUTTON.

TO DOUBLE-CLICK:

- POINT TO THE OBJECT AND CLICK THE MOUSE BUTTON TWICE IN RAPID SUCCESSION.

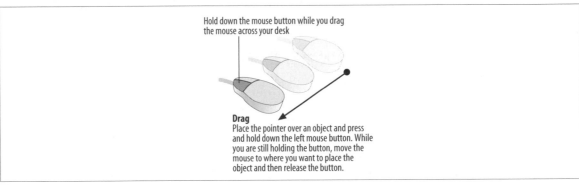

Figure 1-11. Clicking and dragging with the mouse.

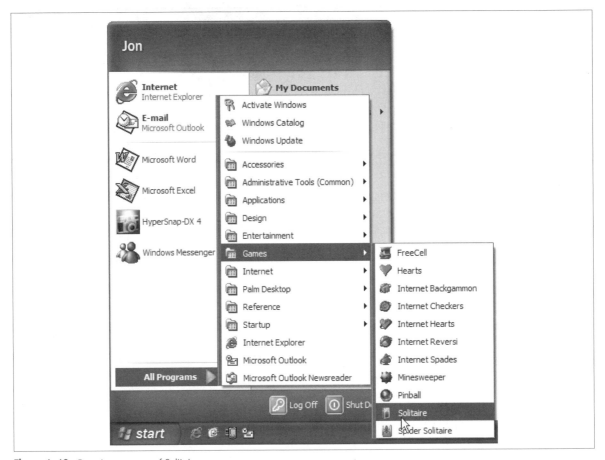

Figure 1-12. Opening a game of Solitaire.

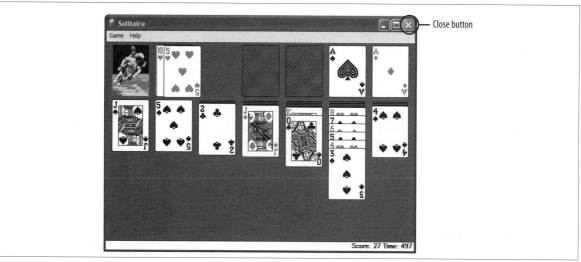

Figure 1-13. The Solitaire game.

You can move items around your computer screen by *clicking and dragging* them with the mouse. To click and drag something: (1) Move the mouse pointer over the object you want to move, then click and *hold down* the mouse button. (2) While you are still holding down the mouse button, move the mouse until the pointer is over the place you want to put the object. Then, (3) release the mouse button.

> **TIP**   *You may have trouble mastering click and drag right away. Don't get discouraged; this is a tricky task for beginners. Just keep practicing and you'll improve.*

This will probably be the most entertaining lesson in the book, because your assignment is to master clicking and dragging by playing a game of Solitaire! Microsoft included Solitaire with Windows XP to help people improve their mouse skills. You've probably noticed that some people never stop practicing these skills with Solitaire. Here's how to open Solitaire:

1 Click the Start button.

Close button

Remember that the Start button is located in the bottom-left corner of your screen. The Windows XP Start menu appears.

2 Point to the word All Programs.

The All Programs menu pops out to the right.

3 Point to the word Games.

Another menu, the Games menu, pops out, as shown in Figure 1-12.

4 Click the word Solitaire.

You're finally there! The Solitaire program opens, as shown in Figure 1-13.

5 Play a game of Solitaire and practice clicking and dragging the cards.

If you don't know how to play Solitaire, you can still practice your clicking and dragging. Just point to a card, click and hold down the mouse button, and move the card around the screen. Release the mouse button to drop the card. If you try dropping a card in an invalid location, the card will be whisked to its original pile.

6 Click the Close button located in the top right corner of the Solitaire program to exit the program when you've finished playing.

Start button

The Solitaire program closes.

Okay, there must be more to click and drag than cards! Although we'll be covering this stuff later on, Table 1-5 provides examples of when you can use click and drag.

Table 1-5. Things you can click and drag

You can do this:	By dragging this:
Move a window to a new location on the screen.	Drag the window by its title bar and drop it in a new location on the screen.
Move a file to a new folder.	Drag the file and drop it in the desired folder.
Change the size of a window.	Drag the borders or corners of the window.
Scroll a window to see something located off-screen.	Drag the scroll box (the little elevator) up or down the scroll bar and drop it in a new location.
Move just about anything on your computer's screen.	Point to the object, click, and hold down the mouse button, drag the object to a new place, and then release the mouse button.

QUICK REFERENCE

TO CLICK AND DRAG:

1. POINT TO THE OBJECT YOU WANT TO CLICK AND DRAG AND CLICK AND HOLD DOWN THE MOUSE BUTTON.

2. WHILE YOU'RE STILL HOLDING DOWN THE MOUSE BUTTON, DRAG THE OBJECT TO THE DESIRED LOCATION ON THE SCREEN.

3. RELEASE THE MOUSE BUTTON.

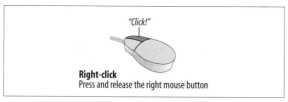

Figure 1-14. Right-clicking with the mouse.

Figure 1-15. The shortcut menu for the Recycle Bin.

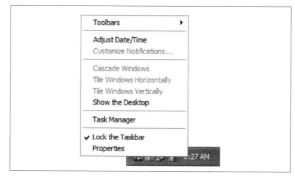

Figure 1-16. The shortcut menu for the clock.

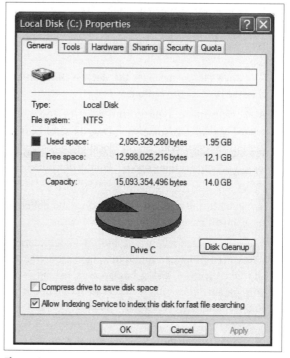

Figure 1-17. The Local Disk (C:) Properties dialog box.

You already know that the left mouse button is the primary mouse button, used for clicking and double-clicking, and it's the mouse button you will use over 95 percent of the time when you work with Windows XP. So what's the right mouse button used for? Whenever you *right-click* something, it brings up a shortcut menu that lists everything you can do to the object. Whenever you're unsure or curious about what you can do with an object, point to it and click it with the right mouse button. A shortcut menu will appear with a list of commands related to the object or area you right-clicked.

Right mouse button shortcut menus are a great way to give commands to Windows XP because you don't have to wade through several levels of menus to do something.

1 Move the pointer over the Recycle Bin icon and click the right mouse button.

A shortcut menu appears with a list of commands related to the Recycle Bin, as shown in Figure 1-15.

TIP *Right-click an object to open a shortcut menu of commands for the object.*

2 Point to and click the Empty Recycle Bin option on the shortcut menu with the left mouse button.

You still use the left mouse button to select menu items, even if they are found in a right-mouse button shortcut menu. A dialog box appears, asking you if you are sure you want to delete the contents of the Recycle Bin. Better play it safe and…

3 Click No with the left mouse button.

Next, you realize the clock displayed on the far right side of the taskbar is ten minutes fast. You can display the clock's properties by right-clicking the clock.

4 Move the pointer over the clock located on the far right end of the taskbar and click the right mouse button.

Windows Clock

Another shortcut menu appears with commands related to the Windows XP clock, as shown in Figure 1-16.

Notice one of the commands listed on the shortcut menu is Adjust Date/Time. Select this menu item if you need to adjust the date and/or time. But you don't want to adjust the date or time, so you can move on to the next step and close the shortcut menu without selecting anything.

5 Click anywhere outside the shortcut menu with the left mouse button.

The final object we'll right-click in this lesson is the computer's Local Disk drive. To get to the Local Disk The final object we'll right-click in this lesson is the computer's Local Disk drive. To get to the local Disk Drive you have to open My Computer.

6 Click the Start button. Click My Computer from the menu.

My Computer

The My Computer window opens, displaying the contents of your computer. You want to see how much space is left on your computer's local disk.

7 Right-click the Local Disk (C:) icon.

Local Disk (C:)
icon

A shortcut menu appears, with a list of commands related to the local disk.

8 Click the Properties option on the shortcut menu with the left mouse button.

A dialog box appears, showing a graph that illustrates how much space is left on your hard drive, as shown in Figure 1-17.

9 Click Cancel.

The dialog box closes.

You're done! You've learned all the actions you can perform with the mouse: pointing, clicking, double-clicking, clicking and dragging, and right-clicking. What an accomplishment!

QUICK REFERENCE

TO DISPLAY AN OBJECT'S SHORTCUT MENU:

• POINT TO THE OBJECT AND CLICK THE RIGHT MOUSE BUTTON. SELECT ITEMS FROM THE SHORTCUT MENU WITH THE LEFT MOUSE BUTTON.

TO CLOSE A SHORTCUT MENU WITHOUT SELECTING ANYTHING:

• CLICK ANYWHERE OUTSIDE THE SHORTCUT MENU WITH THE LEFT MOUSE BUTTON, OR PRESS THE ESC KEY.

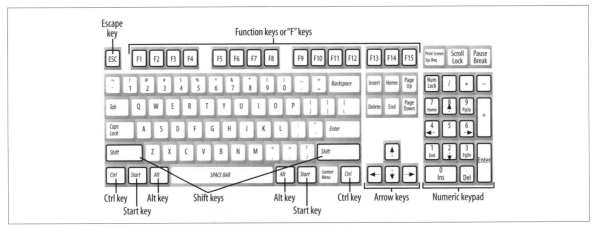

Figure 1-18. A standard keyboard (your computer may have a slightly different layout than the one pictured here).

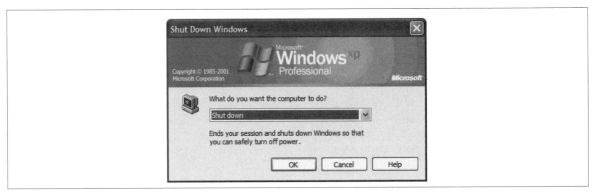

Figure 1-19. The Shut Down Windows XP dialog box.

Now that you've mastered the mouse, it's time to move on to the other device that you use to control your computer: the keyboard. The keyboard may seem more familiar and easy to use than the mouse at first, but don't be fooled! Computer keyboards sneak in some extra keys that are very useful. This lesson explains what these extra keys on the keyboard are and when to use them.

1 **Press and hold down the Alt key, press the F4 key, then release both keys.**

Pressing these keys commands the current program to close. Since you're using the Windows XP Desktop, the Shut Down Windows XP dialog box appears, as shown in Figure 1-19.

We're not ready to shut Windows XP down just yet. Follow the next step to back out of the Shut Down Windows XP dialog box without selecting anything.

2 **Press the Esc key.**

Pressing Esc does the same thing as clicking the Cancel button. The Shut Down Windows dialog box disappears and you're back at the Windows desktop.

Table 1-6 describes the Alt and Esc keys you just used, as well as some of the other confusing keys on the keyboard.

Table 1-6. Special Keys and Their Functions

Key(s)	Description
Alt	The Alt key doesn't do anything by itself—it needs another key to make things happen. For example, pressing the Tab key while holding down the Alt key switches between any programs that are currently running.
Ctrl	Just like the Alt key, the Ctrl key doesn't do anything by itself—you need to press another key along with it to make things happen. For example, pressing the X key while holding down the Ctrl key cuts whatever is selected.
F1	The F1 key is theHelp key for most programs. Pressing it displays helpful information about what you're doing and answers your questions about the program.
ESC	The Esc (Escape) key is the "wait, I've changed my mind!" key. Its function is the same as clicking Cancel in a dialog box. For example, if you click something and an unfamiliar dialog box appears, you can close it by pressing the Esc key.
Enter	The Enter key is the "carry out my orders" key. Its function is the same as clicking OK in a dialog box. For example, after you've typed the name of a program you want to run in a dialog box, press Enter to run the program. The Enter key also adds new lines and starts new paragraphs if you're entering text.
Tab	When you're in a dialog box, pressing the Tab key moves to the next field. When you're using a word processor, the Tab key works just like you'd think it would: it jumps to the nearest tab stop whenever you press it.
↑ ← ↓ →	The arrow keys move your computer's cursor on the screen.
Delete	Nothing surprising here. The Delete key deletes or erases whatever you select—files, text, or graphical objects. If you're working with text, the Delete key erases characters to the right of the insertion point.
Backspace	Use the Backspace key to fix your typing mistakes—it erases characters to the left of the insertion point.
Home	The Home key jumps to the beginning of the current line when you're working with text.
End	The End key jumps to the end of the current line when you're working with text.
Page Up	The Page Up key moves up one screen.
Page Down	The Page Down key moves down one screen.

QUICK REFERENCE

TO USE A KEYSTROKE COMBINATION:

- PRESS AND HOLD DOWN THE FIRST KEY, PRESS THE SECOND KEY, THEN RELEASE BOTH KEYS. FOR EXAMPLE, PRESS THE TAB KEY WHILE YOU'RE HOLDING DOWN THE ALT KEY.

TO USE THE SPECIAL KEYS ON THE KEYBOARD:

- REFER TO TABLE 1-6.

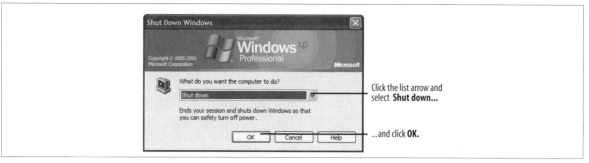

Click the list arrow and
select **Shut down...**

...and click **OK.**

Figure 1-20. The Shut Down Windows dialog box.

At the end of the day when you've finished using your computer, you need to shut down Windows before you turn your computer off. Shutting down gives Windows a chance to tidy up after itself, saving information in the computer's memory to the local disk, cleaning up temporary files, and verifying that you've saved any changes you made to any files you worked on.

Should I turn my computer off at all? One of the great computer debates is whether you should turn your computer off at all. Some people turn off their computer whenever they're finished with it, just like a television set. Others don't turn their computers off—*ever*. People who turn their computers off at night say that keeping the computer on 24 hours a day, 7 days a week wears out the computer's mechanical components and wastes electricity. Other people say that leaving your computer on keeps temperature fluctuations down, which is better for the computer's delicate internal components. Plus, most new computers enter a standby or hibernate mode after a period of time, so they don't really consume that much power. Which method is best? That's a decision you'll have to make on your own. Some people turn their *home* computer off when they finish using it and leave their *office* computer on 24 hours a day.

Whether or not you turn your computer off, you should *always* follow the next few steps when you shut down your computer.

1 Save all your work and exit all your programs.

Saving any files you've been working on is the most important step of all when you shut down your com-

puter. You should also consider backing up any vital information if you have a tape backup, Zip drive, or other backup device. You can also save any important files to a disk.

2 Click the Start button.

Start button

The Start menu appears.

3 Click the Shut Down button in the Start menu.

The Shut Down Windows dialog box appears, as shown in Figure 1-20.

4 Click the What do you want your computer to do? list arrow and select Shut down from the list. Click OK.

The computer's hard drive hums as Windows cleans up and shuts itself down.

NOTE *Leaving nothing to chance, Windows checks to make sure you've saved everything you've been working on, such as documents you created in your word processing program. If Windows notices you haven't saved a file, it asks if you want to save the changes you made to the file before it begins the shut down procedure.*

Windows shuts down and turns off your computer.

5 Make sure your computer and monitor are off.

Congratulations! You've completed the chapter and are well on your way to mastering Windows XP! You're probably wondering "What were those other Shut Down options for?" Table 1-7 explains them.

Table 1-7. Shut down Windows options

Shut Down Option	What it Does
Stand by	Use Stand by if you have a laptop and are going to leave your computer briefly but want to conserve as much energy as possible while you are away. After you return your computer to its original running state, you will be able to pick up exactly where you left off. (Make sure you save everything you were working on first!)
Shut down	Use this option if you want to turn your computer off. It saves your Windows settings and saves any information stored in memory to the local disk.
Restart	Saves any Windows settings, writes any information stored in your computer's memory to the local disk, and restarts your computer. Use this option if Windows or your Windows-based programs start acting flaky. You often have to restart your computer after installing new software.
Log Off As...	This option appears only if your computer is connected to a network. This option closes all your programs and disconnects your computer from the network, preparing your computer to be used by someone else.
Hibernate	Hibernate goes one step further than Stand by, allowing you to keep programs and documents open and shut off power. Hibernate saves your desktop status to the hard disk so the power can be turned off.

QUICK REFERENCE

TO SHUT DOWN WINDOWS:

1. SAVE ANY FILES YOU'VE BEEN WORKING ON AND EXIT ALL YOUR PROGRAMS.

2. CLICK THE START BUTTON AND CLICK THE SHUT DOWN BUTTON IN THE MENU.

   OR...

   PRESS CTRL + ALT + DELETE AND CLICK SHUT DOWN.

- CLICK THE WHAT DO YOU WANT YOUR COMPUTER TO DO? LIST ARROW AND SELECT THE SHUT DOWN OPTION FROM THE LIST. CLICK OK.

Chapter One Review

Lesson Summary

A Look at Windows XP and What's New

Be able to define an operating system.

Starting and Logging On to Windows XP Home

To Log On to Windows XP Home Using the Welcome Screen: Click your account user name. Enter your account password if prompted.

To Log On to Windows XP Home Without the Welcome Screen: Enter your user name and password. If your account doesn't have a password, leave the text box blank. Press Enter or click OK.

Starting and Logging On to Windows XP Professional

To Log On To Windows XP Professional: Press Ctrl + Alt + Delete. Enter your user name and password. Make sure you are logging in to the correct domain. Press Enter or click OK.

Understanding the Windows XP Screen

Be able to identify the main components of the Windows screen.

A Look at the New Windows XP Start Menu

Be able to identify the new components of the Windows XP Start menu.

Using the Mouse: Pointing, Clicking, and Double-Clicking

To Point: Move the mouse so that the pointer is over the object.

To Click: Point to the object and press and release the left mouse button.

To Double-click: Point to the object and click the left mouse button twice in rapid succession.

Using the Mouse: Clicking and Dragging

Point to the object you want to click and drag and click and hold down the mouse button. While you're still holding down the mouse button, drag the object to the desired location on the screen, and then release the mouse button.

Using the Mouse: Right-Clicking

To Display an Object's Shortcut Menu: Point to the object and click the right mouse button. Select items from the shortcut menu with the left mouse button.

To Close a Shortcut Menu Without Selecting Anything: Click anywhere outside the shortcut menu with the left mouse button, or press the Esc key.

Using the Keyboard

To Use a Keystroke Combination: Press one key while holding down the other key. For example, press the Tab key while holding down the Alt key.

Exiting Windows and Turning Off Your Computer

To Shut Down Windows: Save any files you've been working on and exit all your programs. Click the Start button and click the Shut Down button in the menu, or press Ctrl + Alt + Delete and click Shut Down. Click the What do you want your computer to do? list arrow and select the Shut Down option from the list. Click OK.

Quiz

1. Microsoft Windows is a (an):

   A. Word processing program.

   B. Database program.

   C. Operating System.

   D. Graphics program.

2. Windows uses only the left mouse button. (True or False?)

3. How do you move the pointer to another location onscreen?

   A. Press the arrow keys on the keyboard.

B. Move the mouse until the pointer points to that spot.

C. Move the mouse until the pointer points to that spot and then click the left mouse button.

D. Move the mouse until the pointer points to that spot and click the right mouse button.

4. A keystroke combination is:

A. Pressing two or more keys at the same time.

B. A way to lock your computer to prevent unauthorized access. To unlock the computer, simply retype your keystroke combination.

C. Using the keyboard in conjunction with the mouse.

D. A type of mixed drink.

5. To display a shortcut menu for an object, do the following:

A. Point to the object and press Ctrl + P.

B. Touch the object onscreen with your finger.

C. Click the object.

D. Right-click the object.

6. The F1 key displays help on whatever it is that you're working on. (True or False?)

Homework

1. Turn on your computer and start Windows XP.

2. Find, point to, and click the Start button, then close the Start menu without selecting anything.

3. Find and double-click My Computer.

4. Shut down Windows by selecting Shut down from the Start menu, verifying the Shut down option is selected, and clicking the OK button.

Quiz Answers

1. C. Microsoft Windows is an Operating System.

2. False. Windows uses both the left and right mouse buttons.

3. B. Move the pointer by moving the mouse until the pointer points to that spot.

4. A. A keystroke combination is when you press two or more keys at the same time. For example, pressing the Shift and Tab keys simultaneously.

5. D. Right-click the object.

6. True. Pressing the F1 key displays help on whatever it is that you're working on.

CHAPTER 2
WORKING WITH A WINDOW

CHAPTER OBJECTIVES:

Starting a program

Understanding the parts of a window

Minimizing, maximizing, and restoring a window

Moving and closing a window

Changing the size of a window

Switching between several programs

Tiling and cascading windows

Prerequisites

- **Know how to start and shut down Windows.**
- **Know how to use the mouse to click, double-click, drag and drop, and right-click.**

No doubt about it: computers are sophisticated, complex machines. To make computers easier to use, Microsoft designed Windows to operate similar to how you work at the desk in your office. When you work at your desk, you spread everything out, grab a piece of paper, work on it for a while, and then shuffle another piece of paper on top of it. That's how Windows works, except instead of working with papers, you work with *windows*—boxes that contain programs and information.

You can shuffle these windows around the screen just like you shuffle papers on your desk—which is why the main Windows screen is called the *desktop*. Just like your desk, if you're working with a lot of things at the same time, the Windows desktop can become messy and it can be very difficult to find things.

This chapter explains how to manage the windows and programs on your screen. First, you'll learn how to open a window. Next, you'll discover the parts that constitute a window (which are A LOT different than the ones on your house). Then you'll learn how to change the size of a window—*minimizing* it to a tiny little button that appears only on the taskbar and *maximizing* it so that it fills the entire screen. You'll also learn how to "shuffle" windows around, sending some to the background and bringing others up to the forefront. Let's get started!

Figure 2-1. Click the Start button to open the menu, and then point to All Programs to access the programs.

Figure 2-2. Click or point to Accessories to open the menu, and then click WordPad to start the program.

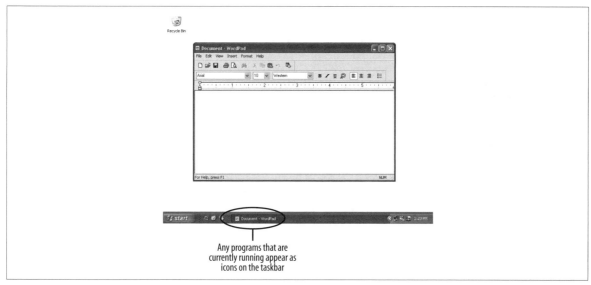

Any programs that are
currently running appear as
icons on the taskbar

Figure 2-3. The WordPad program.

To do just about anything with your computer, you need to run a program. A *program* is a complex set of instructions that tells your computer how to do something. Your word processor is a program, and so is the Solitaire game that comes with Windows. The easiest way to start a program is by clicking the Windows Start button and then selecting the program from the All Programs menu. This lesson explains one of the most basic operations you can do with Windows: starting, or *launching*, a program.

1 Click the Start button.

Start button

The Start menu pops up.

2 Click All Programs.

A menu listing the different program categories pops up above the Start menu, as shown in Figure 2-1.

3 Click the word Accessories.

Another menu, the Accessories menu, shoots out to the side of the All Programs menu, as shown in Figure 2-2. The program you want to load, WordPad, is in the Accessories menu. Can you find it?

4 Click the word WordPad.

The WordPad program appears on the screen in its own window, as shown in Figure 2-3. Notice that a button for the open application also appears on the taskbar.

WordPad is a simple word processing program that is included with Microsoft Windows.

NOTE *The All Programs menu is merely a list of the programs that should be available on your computer. When installed, programs should automatically add themselves to the Start menu. Occasionally, old MS-DOS programs or programs that are poorly written may not put themselves on the Start menu when you install them, and you will have to find and add the program to the All Programs menu yourself. You'll learn how to manually add programs to the Start menu in an upcoming lesson.*

Why do some programs appear on the left side of my Start menu? One of the biggest changes in Microsoft Windows XP is the personalized Start menu. As you use your computer, Windows keeps track of the programs you use most often. If Windows notices that you seem to be using the same program frequently, it may add it to the left side of the Windows Start menu so that you don't have to wade through the All Programs menu to find it.

QUICK REFERENCE

TO START A PROGRAM:

1. CLICK THE **S**TART BUTTON.

2. CLICK ALL PROGRAMS.

3. SELECT THE MENU AND ANY SUBMENUS WHERE THE PROGRAM YOU WANT TO RUN IS LOCATED.

4. CLICK THE NAME OF THE PROGRAM YOU WANT TO START.

Understanding the Parts of a Window

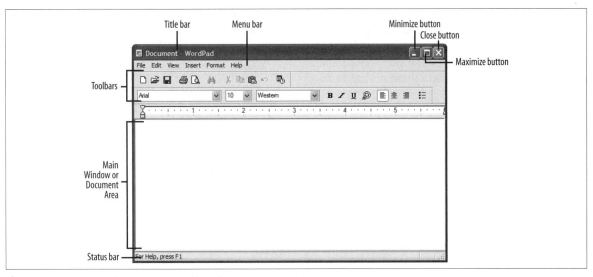

Figure 2-4. The parts of a typical program window.

Figure 2-5. The parts of a typical Windows XP window.

Windows contain buttons and menus to control the program and window. Because windows are used in most programs, you need to use these buttons, menus, and controls. Here's the good news: once you find your way around a window for one program, you'll be familiar with the windows for most programs since this window/menu/button concept appears in just about every Windows program.

There are no exercises or homework for you in this lesson—it's here to help you become familiar with the parts of a window. Just look at Figure 2-4 and then refer to Table 2-1 to identify what you're looking at.

Table 2-1. Parts of a window

Part	Description
Title bar	Displays the name of the program or window, and the name of the document or file that's being used.
Minimize button	Minimizes a window, hiding it from your screen but still running in your computer's memory, ready for quick use. You can minimize a program you're not using so that it is still running but is out of sight.
Maximize/Restore button	**Maximize:** Enlarges the window so that it fills the entire screen. This lets you see more of the window's contents. The Maximize button only appears when the window isn't maximized (does not fill the entire screen).
	Restore: When a window is maximized (fills the entire screen), clicking the Restore button returns the window to its previous smaller size.
Close button	Closes the window or program when you're finished working with it, removing it from the screen and the computer's memory.
Menu bar	Controls what the program does. The menus listed on the menu bar change from program to program, but the menu bar's location doesn't—it's always perched near the top of a window, right below the Title bar.
Toolbar	Some (but not all) windows and programs have one or more toolbars, which contain buttons you point and/or click to access frequently-used commands.
Main Window or Document Area	This is where the magic happens—where you work with whatever it is that you're working on. If you were using a word processor, this is where your letter would appear. If you were browsing the Internet, this is where the Web pages would appear.
Status bar	Displays information such as instructions, messages about the state of the computer, or your location in the window.
Address bar	Displays the location or path of the window being viewed.
Tasks	Displays common file and folder management tasks for the window.

Got everything down? Don't worry if you don't; this lesson is just a quick-guided tour of a typical window. The rest of the lessons in this chapter focus on how to use a window's controls, buttons, and menus.

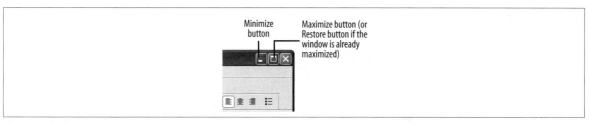

Figure 2-6. The Minimize, Maximize, and Restore buttons appear in the upper right corner of most windows.

Figure 2-7. A window in a restored state fills up only part of the screen.

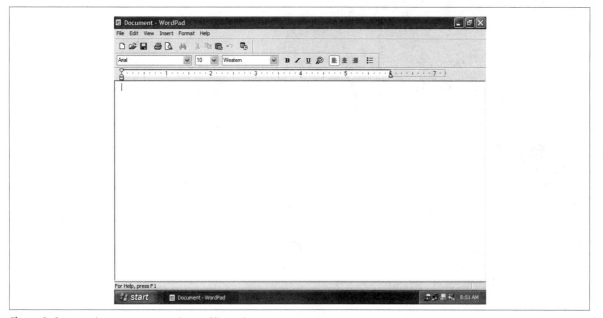

Figure 2-8. A window in a maximized state fills up the entire screen.

Figure 2-9. A window in a minimized state appears only as an button on the taskbar.

One of the benefits of Windows XP is that it enables you to open and work with several programs at the same time. To make working with several programs at once easier, you can change the size of the windows. You can *maximize*, or enlarge, a window so it takes up the entire screen; *minimize*, or reduce, a window so that it only appears as a button in the Windows taskbar; or size a window somewhere in between. This lesson explains how to change the size of a window by *maximizing, minimizing*, and *restoring*.

First, let's look at how to *maximize* a window. Some programs, such as word processors and Web browsers, are easier to work with when they fill the entire screen. To enlarge a window to fill your computer screen, click the Maximize button.

1 Click the WordPad window's Maximize button—the middle button in WordPad's title bar

Maximize button

The WordPad program maximizes, filling the entire screen.

You can change a maximized window back to its original size by clicking the Restore button. The Restore button appears in place of the Maximize button whenever a window is already in a maximized state.

2 Click the WordPad window's Restore button.

The window returns to its previous size.

Just like you can keep several papers on top of your desk, Windows can run more than one program at a time. For example, you can work on a letter with your word processing program while your Web browser is open and downloading a file from the Internet. There is a potential pitfall with running several programs simultaneously though—there isn't enough room for all of them to fit on your computer screen!

Luckily, you can tuck programs away—keeping them running and ready for use, yet out of view—by *minimizing* them.

Restore button
Other Ways to Maximize and Restore a Window:
• Double-click the title bar of the window to toggle between maximized and restored states.

3 Click the WordPad window's Minimize button.

Minimize button

The WordPad program shrinks to a button located on the taskbar. WordPad is still open and running—it's just hidden from view, tucked away and ready for future use.

It's important to note that minimized programs are still running. If a program is doing something, such as downloading a file from the Internet, it will keep going, even when the program is minimized.

It's easy to display a minimized program or window when you're ready to use it again.

4 Click the WordPad button on the taskbar.

The WordPad program springs back to life and appears on the screen.

It's important that you get all this maximize/minimize/restore stuff down, because it will help you to be more efficient when working with programs on your computer.

QUICK REFERENCE

TO MAXIMIZE A WINDOW:

- CLICK THE WINDOW'S  MAXIMIZE BUTTON.

OR...

- DOUBLE-CLICK THE WINDOW'S TITLE BAR.

TO RESTORE A MAXIMIZED WINDOW:

- CLICK THE WINDOW'S 🗗 RESTORE BUTTON.

OR...

- DOUBLE-CLICK THE WINDOW'S TITLE BAR.

TO MINIMIZE A WINDOW:

- CLICK THE WINDOW'S ▬ MINIMIZE BUTTON.

TO RESTORE A MINIMIZED WINDOW:

- CLICK THE WINDOW'S 🗗 BUTTON ON THE TASKBAR.

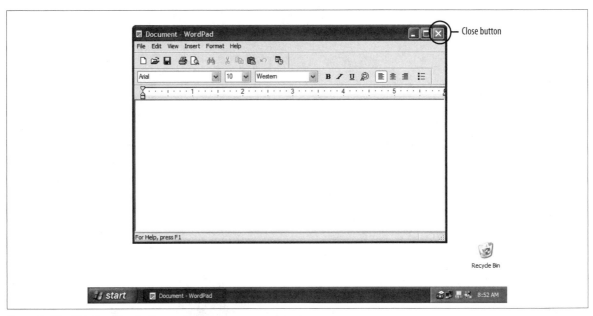

Figure 2-10. Click the Close button on the window you want to close.

Figure 2-11. The window disappears from your screen.

When you're finished working with a window or program, you can close it to remove it from the screen and computer's memory. You can close any window or program by clicking its Close button, which appears in the upper-right corner of the window.

1 Click the WordPad window's Close button.

The WordPad program closes. Notice the WordPad button no longer appears in the Windows taskbar at the bottom of the screen.

That's all there is to closing a window or program.

Close button
Other Ways to Close a Window:
• Select **File** →**Exit** from the menu.
• Right-click the program's icon on the taskbar and select Close from the shortcut menu.
• Press **Alt+F4**

NOTE *If a program has more than one window open, you can close all of its open windows by holding down the Shift key when you click the Close button for any window.*

Since you're going to be working with the WordPad program in the next few lessons, you will need to open it again.

2 Click the Start button.

The Windows XP Start menu appears.

3 Select All Programs → Accessories → WordPad from the Start menu.

The WordPad program window reappears.

If a window happens to be minimized, you need to restore it by clicking its button on the taskbar before you can see and click the window's close button.

QUICK REFERENCE

TO CLOSE A WINDOW:

- CLICK THE WINDOW'S  CLOSE BUTTON.

OR...

- SELECT FILE → EXIT FROM THE MENU.

OR...

- RIGHT-CLICK THE WINDOW'S BUTTON ON THE TASKBAR AND SELECT CLOSE FROM THE SHORTCUT MENU.

TO CLOSE ALL OPEN WINDOWS:

- HOLD DOWN THE SHIFT KEY AND CLICK THE CLOSE BUTTON OF ANY WINDOW.

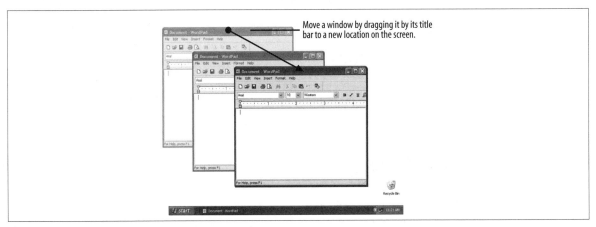

Move a window by dragging it by its title bar to a new location on the screen.

Figure 2-12. Moving a window to a new location on the screen.

If you have several programs or windows open, you may find that one window covers the other windows or other items on your screen. When this happens, you can simply move a window to a new location on the screen, just like you would move a report or folder to a different location on your desk.

Here's how to move a window:

1 Position the mouse pointer over the title bar of the WordPad program.

Remember that the title bar is the colored bar at the very top of a window or program. It displays the name of the program or window.

2 Click the title bar and move the mouse while still holding down the mouse button.

Yep, it's that drag and drop stuff you learned earlier. An outline of the window follows your mouse as you drag the window, as shown in Figure 2-12, showing you where you are moving it.

3 Release the mouse button to drop the window to a new location.

QUICK REFERENCE

- CLICK AND DRAG THE WINDOW BY ITS TITLE BAR. RELEASE THE MOUSE BUTTON TO DROP THE WINDOW IN THE DESIRED LOCATION ON THE SCREEN.

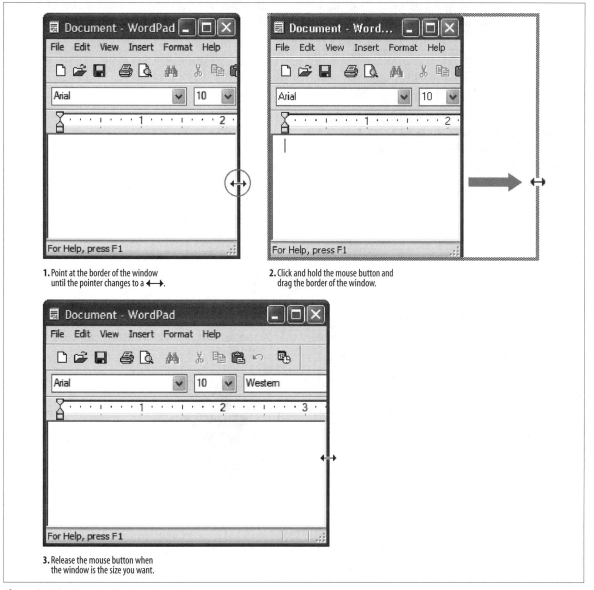

1. Point at the border of the window
until the pointer changes to a ↔.

2. Click and hold the mouse button and
drag the border of the window.

3. Release the mouse button when
the window is the size you want.

Figure 2-13. Changing the size of a window.

If you've been following the lessons in this chapter, you should already know how to change the size of a window or program by minimizing, maximizing, and restoring it. This lesson explains how to fine-tune the size of a window to meet your own specific needs.

1 Make sure the WordPad program appears as a window and doesn't fill the entire screen.

A window can't be maximized (fill up the entire screen) or minimized (a button on the taskbar) if you want to manually size it.

2 Position the mouse pointer over the right border of the WordPad window until it changes to a ↔, as shown in Figure 2-13.

The two arrows point in the directions that you can drag the window's border, in this case, left or right. Had you positioned the pointer over the top or bottom of the window, the pointer would have changed to a $\updownarrow$, indicating that you could drag the top or bottom of the window up or down.

NOTE *Windows is very picky where you place the pointer, and sometimes it can be tricky finding the exact spot where the pointer changes. It's there— just move the pointer slowly over the border until you find it.*

3 Click and hold down the left mouse button and drag the mouse to the right 1 inch.

Notice that the window stretches as you drag the mouse. When the window is the size you want, you can release the mouse button.

4 Release the mouse button.

The window is displayed in its new size.

This lesson explained how to resize a window by adjusting the right border of a window, but you can change a window's size by dragging its left, top, and bottom borders. You can also resize a window by dragging its corners just like you drag its borders.

QUICK REFERENCE

TO CHANGE A WINDOW'S SIZE:

1. POINT AT THE WINDOW'S BORDERS OR CORNERS UNTIL THE POINTER CHANGES TO A DOUBLE-HEADED ARROW $\leftrightarrow$.

OR...

- PRESS CTRL + L, TYPE THE WEB ADDRESS, AND CLICK OK.

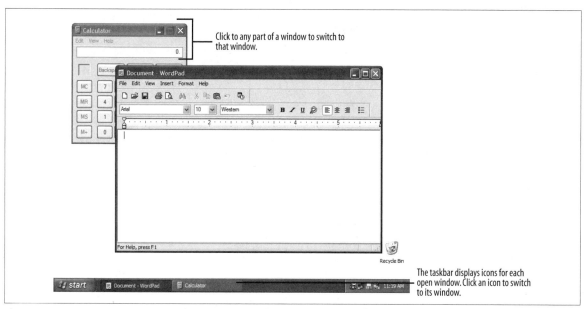

Figure 2-14. You can only work in one window at a time. Notice that WordPad appears in front and has a darker blue title bar.

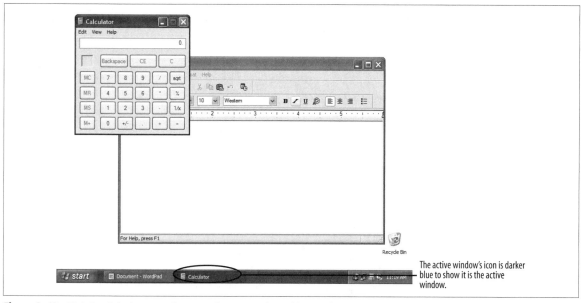

Figure 2-15. Click the Calculator window or its button on the taskbar so that it appears in front.

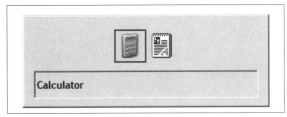

Figure 2-16. Pressing Alt + Tab lists all the windows that are currently open.

You can have several programs or windows open and running simultaneously, but you can only *work* in one window at a time. The window you're working with is called the *active window* and always appears on top of any other windows that you have open. If you think about it, you do the same thing at your desk. When you want to work on a piece of paper, you place it on top of everything else.

NOTE *When you're working with multiple programs, be careful not to accidentally run a second copy of the same program. This wastes memory and makes things confusing. For example, if you've been using the Calculator program and want to bring it back up, make sure you check the taskbar to see if it's already running (a Calculator button appears on the taskbar). If it is, use any of the methods you've learned in this lesson to switch to it. If a program is already running and you load it again from the Start menu, a second copy of the program opens and two buttons for the program will appear on the taskbar.*

This lesson explains how to switch between your open windows. There are actually several ways to switch between windows, and we'll cover all of them in this lesson. First, make sure you have several windows open …

1 Make sure the WordPad program is still open.

If it isn't open, click the Start button and select All Programs → Accessories → WordPad.

Next, open another program that comes with Windows XP—the Calculator.

2 Click the Start button and select All Programs → Accessories → Calculator from the menu.

The Calculator program window is active, appearing in front of the WordPad program window. A button

for the Calculator program also appears on the taskbar, next to the WordPad button.

You can make WordPad the active window by clicking its button on the taskbar.

3 Click the WordPad button on the taskbar.

The WordPad program window now appears in front, and its button on the taskbar is darker blue, indicating it is the active window. You can make another open window the active window by clicking on any visible part of the window.

4 Click any part of the Calculator window.

If you can't see the Calculator window at all, it's because the Calculator window is completely covered by the WordPad window. In this case, you will have to click the Calculator button on the taskbar.

Yet another way to switch between windows is using the keyboard: Alt + Tab.

5 Press and hold down the Alt key. Press and release the Tab key, but don't release the Alt key.

The task window appears, as shown in Figure 2-16. The task window lists all the windows and programs that are currently running.

Move on to the next step to see how you can active a program or window from the task window.

6 While still holding down the Alt key, press and release the Tab key until the WordPad program is selected, then release the Alt key.

When you release the Alt key, the selected window or program is activated and displayed in front of all other windows.

NOTE *Alt + Tab is especially useful when you use programs that fill the entire computer screen, such as MS-DOS programs and some games. When you can't see the taskbar or any part of another window, Alt + Tab is the only way you can switch between programs.*

Think you have a handle on switching between programs and windows? Good, because when you work with Windows, you'll find yourself switching between programs and windows a great deal throughout the day.

QUICK REFERENCE

TO SWITCH BETWEEN OPEN WINDOWS:

- CLICK THE WINDOW'S BUTTON ON THE TASKBAR.

OR...

- CLICK ON ANY PART OF THE WINDOW YOU WANT TO APPEAR IN FRONT.

OR...

1. PRESS AND HOLD DOWN THE ALT KEY AND PRESS THE TAB KEY TO DISPLAY THE TASK WINDOW. PRESS THE TAB KEY UNTIL THE WINDOW YOU WANT IS SELECTED, THEN RELEASE THE ALT KEY.

Figure 2-17. Right-click any empty area of the taskbar to display its shortcut menu.

Figure 2-18. Tiled windows allow you to view the contents of all your open windows at once.

Figure 2-19. Cascaded windows neatly overlap each other.

When you have several windows or programs open, you can have Windows automatically arrange them for you, instead of manually resizing and pushing them around yourself. Windows can organize your windows in two different ways by *tiling* and *cascading*. This lesson will show you both methods and how they work.

To demonstrate how to tile and cascade windows, we need to open yet another program.

1 Make sure the WordPad and Calculator programs are running.

These programs should still be running from the previous lesson. If they're not, open them by clicking the Start button and selecting them from the All Programs → Accessories menu.

The third window we'll load for this exercise is the My Pictures window.

2 Click the Start button and select My Pictures from the menu.

You can find My Pictures on the right side of the Start menu.

You're ready to have Windows arrange your windows.

3 Right-click an empty area on the taskbar.

A shortcut menu appears where you right-click. Be careful and make sure you right-click an empty area of the taskbar, otherwise the wrong shortcut menu will appear. Your shortcut menu should look like the one in the margin, or in Figure 2-17.

NOTE *Sometimes, especially when you have a lot of windows open, it can be pretty hard to find an empty area on the taskbar. There should always be an empty area just to the right of the last window button and to the left of the system tray (the area with the clock on it). Sometimes the empty area is a mere sliver, but it's still there!*

4 Select Tile Windows Vertically from the shortcut menu.

Windows organizes all the open windows by tiling them vertically on the screen, as shown in Figure 2-18. Had you selected the Tile Windows Horizontally option from the shortcut menu, the windows would have been tiled horizontally, giving each window equal space. Tiling windows is useful when you only have a few windows open and you want to view their contents at the same time.

Cascading windows is the other way to arrange your windows.

5 Right-click an empty area on the taskbar.

A shortcut menu appears.

6 Select Cascade Windows from the shortcut menu.

Windows organizes all the open windows by neatly overlapping them, as shown in Figure 2-19. Cascaded windows are useful when you have several windows open and want to quickly find all of them, without displaying their contents.

Guess what? Now you know everything there is to know about opening, closing, moving, sizing, switching between, and arranging windows. What an accomplishment!

QUICK REFERENCE

TO TILE WINDOWS ON THE DESKTOP:

- RIGHT-CLICK ANY BLANK AREA OF THE TASKBAR (USUALLY NEAR THE CLOCK) AND SELECT EITHER TILE WINDOWS HORIZONTALLY OR TILE WINDOWS VERTICALLY FROM THE SHORTCUT MENU.

TO CASCADE WINDOWS ON THE DESKTOP:

- RIGHT-CLICK ANY BLANK AREA OF THE TASKBAR (USUALLY NEAR THE CLOCK) AND SELECT CASCADE WINDOWS FROM THE SHORTCUT MENU.

Lesson Summary

Starting a Program

Start a program by clicking the Start button and selecting All Programs from the menu. Navigate through the list of programs by pointing to any menu or submenu. Once you find the program you want to run, click the name of the program.

Understanding the Parts of a Window

Be able to identify a window's title bar, menu, minimize, maximize, and close buttons.

Minimizing, Maximizing and Restoring a Window

Maximize a window so that it fills the entire screen by clicking its Maximize button, or by double-clicking its title bar.

Restore a window to its previous size by clicking its Restore button, or by double-clicking its title bar.

Minimize a window so that it only appears as an button on the taskbar by clicking the window's Minimize button.

Restore a minimized window by clicking its button on the taskbar.

Closing a Window

To Close a Window: Click its Close button, or select File → Exit from the menu, or right-click the window's button on the taskbar and select Close from the shortcut menu, or press Alt + F4.

To Close All Open Windows: Close all open windows by holding down the Shift key while you click the Close button of any window.

Moving a Window

Click and drag the window by its title bar. Release the mouse button to drop the window in the desired location on the screen.

Sizing a Window

Point at the window's borders or corners until the pointer changes to a double-arrow ↔. Click and hold down the mouse button and drag the border or corner to a new location until the window is the size you want.

Switching Between Windows

You can only work on one window at a time. The window you're working on is the active window and appears in front of all the inactive windows.

To Switch Between Open Windows: There are three ways to switch between open programs:1. Click on the window's button on the taskbar.2. Click on any visible part of the window that you want to appear in front.3. Press and hold down the Alt key and press the Tab key to display the task list. Press the Tab key until the window you want is selected, then release the Alt key.

Tiling and Cascading Windows

To Tile Windows on the Desktop: Right-click any blank area of the taskbar (usually near the clock) and select either Tile Windows Horizontally or Tile Windows Vertically from the shortcut menu.

To Cascade Windows on the Desktop: Right-click any blank area of the taskbar (usually near the clock) and select Cascade Windows from the shortcut menu.

Quiz

1. To start a program in Windows XP, do the following:

   A. Make sure the Program Manager is open, double-click the Program Group where the program you want to run is located, then double-click the Program.

   B. Click the Start button and select All Programs from the menu, navigate through the available programs, then click the name of the program you want to run.

C. Click the Start button, point to the Run menu, click the menu and any submenus where the program you want to run is located, and then click the name of the program you want to run.

D. None of the above.

2. The little bar found at the top of a program window is called the:

A. Windows bar.

B. Program bar.

C. Title bar.

D. Very-top-of-the-window bar.

3. You start your favorite word processing program to type a letter, but the program appears in a window that's too small to use. How can you maximize the window so that it fills the entire screen? (Select all that apply.)

A. Select Window → Full Screen from the menu.

B. Double-click the window's title bar.

C. Click the program's button on the taskbar.

D. Click the Maximize button located on the window's title bar.

4. You can open or restore a minimized window by clicking its button on the taskbar. (True or False?)

5. You can move a window to a different position on your computer screen by dragging it by its:

A. Title bar.

B. Status bar.

C. Move handle.

D. Tail.

6. You have several programs open at the same time—how can you switch between these programs? (Select all that apply.)

A. Restart the program.

B. Click the program's button on the taskbar.

C. Click on any visible part of the window that you want to appear in front.

D. Press and hold down the Alt key and press the Tab key to display the task list. Press the Tab key until the program you want is selected, then release the Alt key.

Homework

1. Open the Accessories menu.

2. Start the NotePad program.

3. Make the NotePad window a few inches bigger.

4. Minimize the NotePad window.

5. Restore the NotePad window to its previous size.

6. Move the NotePad window to a different location on the screen.

7. Open the Calculator program.

8. Tile both windows on the screen.

9. Close both windows.

Quiz Answers

1. B.

2. C. The little bar located along the top of the program window is called the title bar.

3. B and D. Double-clicking the window's title bar or clicking the window's Maximize button will maximize the window so that it fills the entire screen.

4. True. Clicking the button of a minimized program on the taskbar restores the window.

5. A. Move a window by dragging its title bar.

6. B, C, and D. You can use any of these methods to switch between open programs. Don't use A, which starts another copy of the program instead of switching to the already open program.

CHAPTER 3
WORKING WITH A WINDOWS PROGRAM

CHAPTER OBJECTIVES:

Use menus and toolbars

Fill out a dialog box

Enter and edit text

Save and open a file

Select, replace, and delete text

Use the undo function

Print a file

Cut, copy, and paste text

Format fonts and paragraphs

Get help

Save and open files in different locations

Prerequisites

- **Know how to start and shut down Windows.**
- **Know how to use the mouse to click, double-click, click and drag, and right-click.**
- **Know how to use the keyboard.**

Up until now, we've only been focusing on how to use the Windows XP operating system. In this chapter, you'll be working with a program. This chapter explains how to control programs using menus and toolbars. You'll also learn what a *dialog box* is (you'll see a lot of them in Windows), and how to fill one out.

Next, we'll get more specific. Every program is different, but the procedure for doing things in all programs is the same. This chapter explains these basic generic chores using the WordPad program. You'll learn how to enter, edit, and delete text; how to open, save, and print a file; and how to get help when you need it. Once you've learned these basic skills in WordPad, you can apply them to just about every other Windows program. This is one of the longest chapters about Windows XP, so we have a lot of ground to cover. Let's get started.

Figure 3-1. Starting the WordPad program.

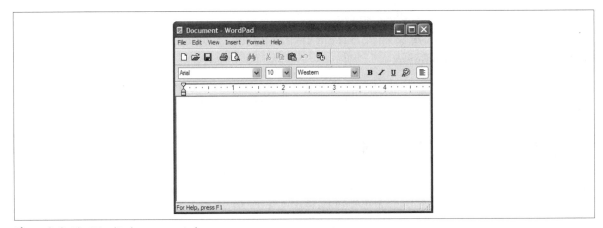

Figure 3-2. The WordPad program window.

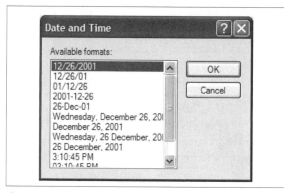

Figure 3-3. The Date and Time dialog box.

To make a program do your bidding, you give it commands. You can give commands to your Windows program several different ways: by using menus, toolbars, right mouse button shortcut menus, and keystroke shortcuts. This lesson explains the most common method of issuing commands to Windows programs—through menus. You can find a program's menu near the top of a window just beneath the title bar. In Figure 3-2, notice the words File, Edit, View, Insert, Format, and Help that appear near the top of the WordPad program. Those words indicate menus, and the next few steps will show you why they are there.

1 Click the Start button.

Start button
The Start menu appears.

2 Select All Programs → Accessories → WordPad from the Start menu.

That means you should click "All Programs," then click the word "Accessories" from the All Programs menu, and then click the word "WordPad" from the Accessories menu, as shown in Figure 3-1. The Word-Pad program appears.

3 Move the pointer to and click the word Insert on the menu bar.

A menu drops down under the word Insert.

The Insert menu contains a list of commands to insert things, such as the "Date and Time", which inserts the current date and/or time, and "Object," which inserts a file created in another program.

4 Point to and click the Date and Time option from the Insert menu.

The Date and Time dialog box appears, as shown in Figure 3-3, presenting you with several different date and time formats to choose from. You'll learn more about dialog boxes in an upcoming lesson.

5 Click the OK button.

The Date and Time dialog box disappears and the current date is inserted into the WordPad document.

Take a close look at the WordPad menu bar—do you notice that every word in the menu has an underlined letter somewhere in it? For example, the F in the File menu is underlined. Pressing the Alt key and then pressing the underlined letter in a menu does the same thing as clicking the menu with the mouse.

TIP *You can open menus by clicking the menu name with the mouse or by pressing the Alt key and the underlined letter in the menu name.*

6 Press the Alt key then press the F key.

The File menu appears. Once a menu is open, you can use the arrow keys on your computer's keyboard to navigate through the menus or press any other underlined letters in the menu.

7 Press the right arrow key → .

The next menu to the right, the Edit menu, opens.

If you open a menu and change your mind, it's easy to close it without selecting any commands. Just click anywhere *outside* the menu or else press the Esc key.

TIP *You can close a menu without selecting any commands by clicking anywhere outside the menu or by pressing the Esc key.*

8 Click anywhere outside the menu to close the menu without selecting any commands.

NOTE *The procedure for using menus and the general order/layout of the menu is usually similar in most Windows programs. So if you master the menus in one Windows program, you will be familiar with the layout and function of the menus in other Windows programs.*

Table 3-1 gives you a preview of some of the different menu items you will come across.

Table 3-1. Common Windows program menus

File	Description
File	Commands to open, save, close, print, and create new files.
Edit	Commands to copy, cut, paste, find, and replace text in a document.
View	Commands to change how the document is displayed on the screen.
Insert	Lists items that you can insert into a document, such as graphics, page numbers, and the current date.
Format	Commands to format text, paragraphs, tab stops, and so on. Strangely, the command to format the page (i.e., margins, etc.) is located in the File menu under Page Setup.
Window	Commands to display and arrange multiple windows (if you have more than one document open). WordPad doesn't have this menu since it can only have one file open at a time.
Help	Get help on the program you are using.

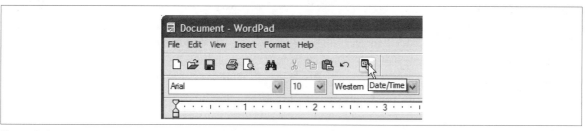

Figure 3-4. Move the pointer over a button and wait a few seconds for the button's description.

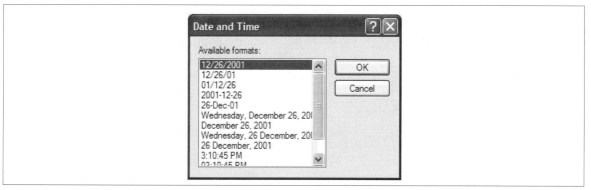

Figure 3-5. The Date and Time dialog box.

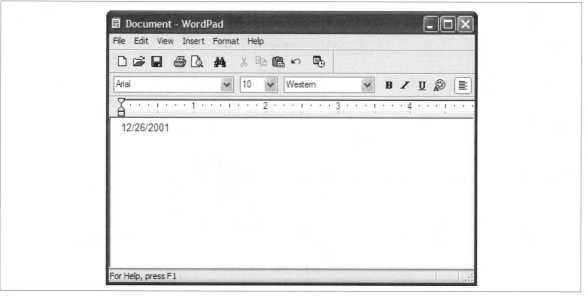

Figure 3-6. The WordPad document.

Toolbars are another common way to boss around your programs. While menus contain every conceivable command for a program, toolbars contain buttons for the commands you use most frequently. Instead of having to wade through several menus to do something, you can click a single button.

Two toolbars appear in the WordPad program—the Standard toolbar and the Formatting toolbar. The *Standard toolbar* appears on top and contains buttons for the most frequently used commands in WordPad, such as saving and printing a document. The *Formatting toolbar* is located right underneath the Standard toolbar and has buttons for quickly formatting fonts and paragraphs.

Toolbar buttons have small icons to indicate what they do. For example, a small picture of a printer appears on the Print button. If you still don't know what a button is used for, move the pointer over the button and wait a few seconds. Usually, a little window will appear with a brief description of the button.

1 Click after the date you entered in the last lesson and press the Enter key.

A new paragraph starts.

2 Point the mouse pointer over the Date/Time button on WordPad's Standard toolbar.

Date/Time button

A small window appears over the button, briefly identifying what the button is—in this case "Date/Time"—as shown in Figure 3-4.

3 Click the Date/Time button.

The Date and Time dialog box appears, as shown in Figure 3-5, presenting you with several different date and time formats to choose from.

4 Click the OK button.

WordPad inserts the current date and time in the WordPad document.

5 Press and hold the Backspace key to delete the date you just entered.

Only one date remains on your screen. You will learn more about deleting text in a later lesson.

Compare your screen with the one in Figure 3-6.

QUICK REFERENCE

TO USE A TOOLBAR BUTTON:

- CLICK THE TOOLBAR BUTTON.

TO SEE WHAT A TOOLBAR BUTTON DOES:

- POSITION THE POINTER OVER THE TOOLBAR BUTTON AND WAIT A SECOND. A SCREENTIP WILL APPEAR ABOVE THE BUTTON.

Filling Out a Dialog Box

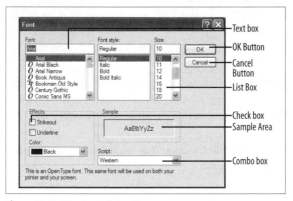

Figure 3-7. The Font dialog box.

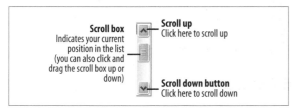

Figure 3-8. A scroll bar.

> **TIP** *You can select a control in a dialog box by clicking the control with the mouse or by pressing the Tab key until the control is selected.*

Some commands are more complicated than others. For example, saving a file is a simple process—all you have to do is select File → Save from the menu or click the Save button on the Standard toolbar. Other commands are more complex. Whenever you want to do something relatively complicated in Windows, you need to fill out a *dialog box*. Filling out a dialog box is not much different than filling out a paper form. Dialog boxes usually contain several types of controls, including:

- Text boxes
- List boxes
- Check boxes
- List arrows
- Buttons

This lesson will give you a quick tour of a more complicated dialog box and show you how to use the various dialog box components you will come across.

1 Select Format **from the menu.**

The Format menu appears.

Look at the items listed in the Format menu—Font, Paragraph, and Tabs are followed by ellipses (...). Whenever you see a menu item followed by ellipses, a dialog box is lurking just behind the menu.

2 Select Font **from the Format menu.**

The Font dialog box appears, as shown in Figure 3-7.

The Font dialog box is one of the most complex dialog boxes in the WordPad program and contains several types of controls. You have to select a control to use it. You can do this by clicking the control with the mouse. Or you can move to the control by pressing the Tab key to move to the next control, or Shift + Tab to move to the previous control, until the cursor appears in the control or it becomes highlighted.

First, let's look at text boxes. Text boxes are nothing more than the fill-in-the-blank boxes you've already used in many types of paper forms. Text boxes are incredibly easy to use—just type in the text you want.

3 Make sure the cursor is in the Font text box type `Arial`.

You've just filled out the text box—nothing to it.

The next stop in our dialog box tour is the list box. A list box puts several options together into a small box. Sometimes list boxes contain so many options that they can't all be displayed at once, and you must click the list box's *scroll bar* to move up or down the list. See Figure 3-8 for an illustration of a scroll box.

4 Click and hold the Font list box Scroll Down button **until Times New Roman appears in the list.**

5 Click the Times New Roman **option in the list.**

Our next destination is the list arrow. The list arrow is the cousin of the list box—it, too, displays a list of options. The only difference is that you must click the downward pointing arrow in order to display the list.

6 Click the Color **list arrow.**

A list of color options appears.

7 Select the blue color from the list.

Sometimes you need to select more than one item in a dialog box. For example, what if you want to add Strikeout formatting *and* Underline formatting to the selected font? Use the check box control when you're presented with multiple choices.

8 Click the Strikeout check box and click the Underline check box.

The last destination on our dialog box tour is the button. Buttons are used to execute or void commands. Two buttons can be found in every dialog box. They are:

- **OK:** Applies and saves any changes you have made and then closes the dialog box. Pressing the Enter key usually does the same thing as clicking the OK button.

- **Cancel:** Closes the dialog box without applying and saving any changes. Pressing the Esc key usually does the same thing as clicking the cancel button.

9 Click the Cancel button to cancel the changes you made and close the Font dialog box.

QUICK REFERENCE

TO SELECT A DIALOG BOX CONTROL:

- CLICK THE CONTROL WITH THE MOUSE.

OR...

- PRESS TAB TO MOVE TO THE NEXT CONTROL IN THE DIALOG BOX OR SHIFT + TAB TO MOVE TO THE PREVIOUS CONTROL UNTIL YOU ARRIVE AT THE DESIRED CONTROL.

TO USE A TEXT BOX:

- SIMPLY TYPE THE INFORMATION DIRECTLY INTO THE TEXT BOX.

TO USE A LIST BOX:

- CLICK THE OPTION YOU WANT FROM LIST BOX. USE THE SCROLL BAR TO MOVE UP AND DOWN THROUGH ITS OPTIONS.

TO USE A LIST ARROW:

- CLICK THE ARROW TO DISPLAY THE LIST OPTIONS. CLICK AN OPTION FROM THE LIST TO SELECT IT.

TO CLOSE A DIALOG BOX AND SAVE CHANGES:

- CLICK THE OK BUTTON OR PRESS ENTER.

TO CLOSE A DIALOG BOX WITHOUT SAVING CHANGES:

- CLICK THE CANCEL BUTTON OR PRESS ESC.

Entering Text in the WordPad Program

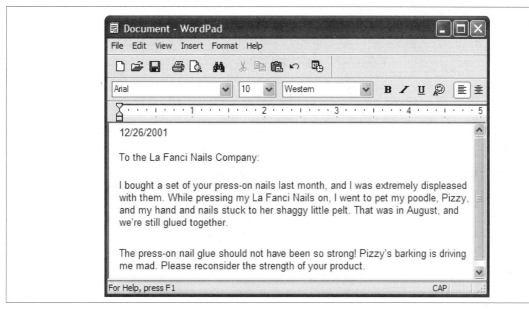

Figure 3-9. A simple letter created in the WordPad program.

This lesson explains how to create a document using the WordPad program. Actually, there isn't much to explain—all you have to do is type!

1 **If necessary, open the WordPad program.**

If you don't remember how to open WordPad, select All Programs → Accessories → WordPad from the menu.

Let's enter some text.

2 **Click in the WordPad window, and type** 9/29.

Good. Now we're going to write a letter.

3 **Press the Enter key twice.**

WordPad inserts a new paragraph, or new line, each time you press the Enter key.

4 **Type the following text:** To the La Fanci Nails Company:

As you type, notice that the insertion point (the small blinking vertical bar) moves to indicate where you are typing.

5 **Press the Enter key twice and type the following text:** I bought a set of your press-on nails last month, and I was extremely displeased with them. While pressing my La Fanci Nails on, I went to pet my poodle, Pizzy, and my hand and nails stuck to her shaggy little pelt. That was in August and we're still glued together.

The press-on nail glue should not have been so strong! Pizzy's barking is driving me mad. Please reconsider the strength of the product.

TIP *While you type, word-wrap continues text from one line to the next without making you press Enter.*

Make sure you press the Enter key twice to add a blank line between the two paragraphs. Don't press Enter when you reach the end of a line—WordPad will automatically move the text to the next line for you. This feature is called *word-wrap.*

When you're finished typing, compare your letter with Figure 3-9.

QUICK REFERENCE

TO ENTER TEXT IN WORDPAD:

1. PLACE THE INSERTION POINT IN WORDPAD BY CLICKING IN THE WORDPAD SCREEN.

2. TYPE YOUR TEXT.

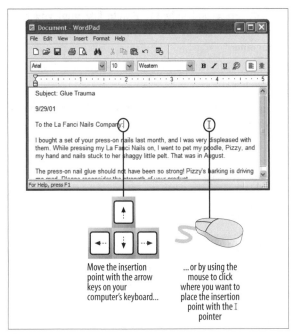

Figure 3-10. Use the keyboard or the mouse to move the insertion point in a document.

After typing a document, you will often discover that you need to make some changes to your text—perhaps you want to rephrase or even delete a sentence. Editing a document by inserting and deleting text is very simple. To insert text, move the insertion point (the blinking bar) to where you want to insert the text. You can move the insertion point using the arrow keys on the keyboard or by using the mouse to click where you want to move it, as shown in Figure 3-10. Once the insertion point is where you want it, just start typing.

There are a couple ways to delete text. One way is to place the insertion point immediately *after* the text you want to delete and press the Backspace key. Another way to delete text is to place the insertion point immediately *before* the text you want to delete and press the Delete key.

In this lesson, you'll get practice inserting and deleting text and revising the letter you created in WordPad.

1 Press the up arrow key ↑.

The insertion point moves up one line.

2 Press and hold the up arrow key ↑ to move the insertion point to the very top line in the document.

Now you need to move the insertion point to the beginning of the current line.

3 Press and hold the left arrow key ← to move the insertion point to the very beginning of the line.

4 Type Subject: Glue Trauma and press Enter twice.

The text and blank line is inserted at the insertion point, before the rest of the document. You've just learned how to insert text in a document—pretty easy, huh?

5 Move the insertion point immediately *after* the word extremely in the first body paragraph.

Here, you need to delete some text; delete the word "extremely."

6 Press the Backspace key several times, until the word "extremely" is deleted.

The Backspace key deletes one space to the left of the insertion point.

7 Type very.

You've just deleted the word "extremely" and inserted the word "very" to take its place.

You can also use the mouse rather than the arrow keys to move the insertion point instead of the arrow keys. Simply use the mouse to move the pointer where you want to place the insertion point and then click.

8 Click immediately after the word August in the sentence "That was in August and we're still stuck together."

The insertion point appears immediately after the word "August"—right where you clicked the mouse button.

You can also use the Delete key to delete text. Like the Backspace key, the Delete key also deletes text, but in a slightly different way. The Backspace key deletes text before, or to the *left* of the insertion point, while the

Delete key deletes text after, or to the *right* of the insertion point.

9 Press the Delete key.

The Delete key deletes text to the right of, or before, the insertion point.

10 Press and hold the Delete key until you have deleted the rest of the sentence "and we're still stuck together."

Great! You've learned how to delete text using the Delete key.

Compare your revised document with the one shown in Figure 3-10.

QUICK REFERENCE

TO MOVE THE INSERTION POINT:

- USE THE ARROW KEYS.

OR...

- CLICK WHERE YOU WANT TO PLACE THE INSERTION POINT WITH THE I POINTER.

TO INSERT TEXT:

- MOVE THE INSERTION POINT WHERE YOU WANT TO INSERT THE TEXT AND THEN TYPE THE TEXT YOU WANT TO INSERT.

TO DELETE TEXT:

- THE BACKSPACE KEY DELETES TEXT BEHIND, OR TO THE LEFT OF, THE INSERTION POINT.

- THE DELETE KEY DELETES TEXT BEFORE, OR TO THE RIGHT OF, THE INSERTION POINT.

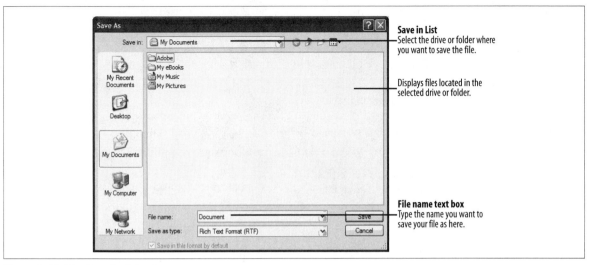

Figure 3-11. The Save As dialog box.

Save in List
Select the drive or folder where you want to save the file.

Displays files located in the selected drive or folder.

File name text box
Type the name you want to save your file as here.

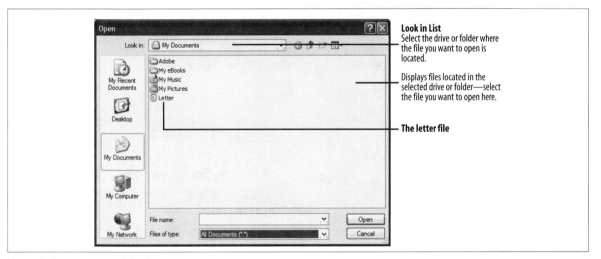

Figure 3-12. The Open dialog box.

Look in List
Select the drive or folder where the file you want to open is located.

Displays files located in the selected drive or folder—select the file you want to open here.

The letter file

Once you have created something in a program, you must *save* the file if you ever want to use it again in the future. When you save a file, you're transferring it from your computer's memory (which is erased when you close the program) to the computer's local disk (which is permanent and not erased when you close the program). In this lesson, you will learn how to save a file and then open, or retrieve it from the local disk.

1 Click the Save button on the Standard toolbar.

Save Button
Other ways to Save:
• Select **File→Save** from the menu.

The Save As dialog box appears, as shown in Figure 3-11. You must give your file a name and specify where you want to save it. First, tell the computer you want to save the file in your Practice folder.

2 Navigate to your Practice folder.

Your computer stores information in files and folders, just like you store information in a filing cabinet. To open a file, you must first find and open the folder where it's saved.

The Save As dialog box has its own toolbar, making it easy to browse through your computer's drives and folders. Two controls on this toolbar are particularly helpful:

- **Look in list:** Click to list the drives on your computer and the current folder, then select the drive and/or folder whose contents you want to display.

- **Up button:** Click to move up one folder level.

If necessary, follow your instructor's directions to select the appropriate drive and folder where your practice files are located.

3 Click the File name text box.

The File name box is where you give your file a name.

NOTE *File names can be up to 255 characters long and contain letters, numbers, and some symbols. You can't use the symbols " \ / : * | in a file name.*

4 Type Letter.

This will save the document you created in a file named "Letter".

5 Click Save.

Your computer saves the Letter file to the computer's hard disk.

Now that you've saved the file, you can safely close WordPad or even turn off the computer, knowing that your WordPad "Letter" file is stored and can be retrieved whenever you want to work on it again.

6 Close the WordPad program by clicking its Close button.

Close Button

The WordPad program closes.

Let's make sure the Letter document you created and saved in WordPad is still there.

7 Open the WordPad program again.

Once you have started WordPad, you can open the Letter document you saved.

8 Click the Open button on the Standard toolbar.

Open Button
Other Ways to Open a File:
• Select **File → Open** from the menu.

The Open dialog box appears, as shown in Figure 3-12. The Open dialog box is very similar to the Save As dialog box, except you specify the name and location of the file you want to open.

9 If necessary, navigate to your Practice folder.

The Open dialog box will display any WordPad files that have been saved in the Practice folder. Here's how to select a file you want to open.

10 Click the Letter file.

Shading appears over the Letter file, indicating that it is selected.

11 Click the Open button.

The Letter document appears in the WordPad window.

When you open a file, instead of selecting a file and clicking the Open button, you can save a half-second or so by simply double-clicking the file you want to open.

QUICK REFERENCE

TO SAVE A FILE:

- CLICK THE SAVE BUTTON ON THE STANDARD TOOLBAR.

OR...

- SELECT FILE → SAVE FROM THE MENU.

TO OPEN A FILE:

- CLICK THE OPEN BUTTON ON THE STANDARD TOOLBAR.

OR...

- SELECT FILE → OPEN FROM THE MENU.

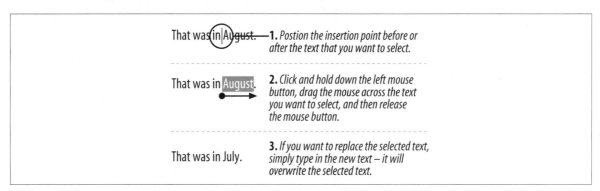

Figure 3-13. You can select and replace text.

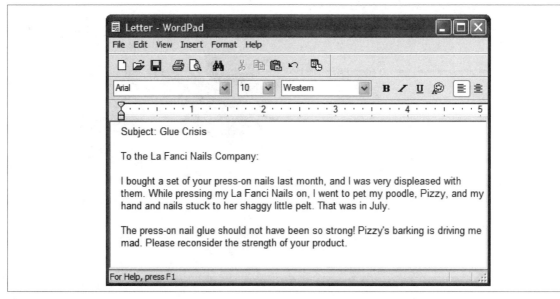

Figure 3-14. The updated letter.

This lesson explains how to select text. Whenever you want to edit more than one character at a time, you must *select* it first. A lot of editing and formatting techniques—such as formatting, cutting, copying and pasting text—also require that you select the text you want to modify. There are probably hundreds of reasons to select text in many Windows-based programs, so it pays to be an expert at it.

> **TIP** *To replace text, select the text you want to replace and type the new text you want to replace it with.*

1 Place the insertion point immediately in front of the word August in the last sentence of the first paragraph.

You learned how to move the insertion around using the mouse earlier in this chapter. Actually, you can place the insertion point before or after the text you want to select.

2 Click and hold down the mouse button and drag the mouse across the word August (the words should be highlighted). Release the mouse button when you're finished.

The word August should be highlighted in blue, as shown in Figure 3-13. Selecting text with the mouse can be a little tricky at first, especially if you're still a novice at using the mouse. When you select text, anything you type will replace the selected text.

3 Type July.

The word "July" replaces the selected text, "August." A quick way to select a single word is to double-click the word you want to select.

4 Double-click the word Trauma in the Subject line.

5 Type Crisis.

The word "Crisis" replaces the word "Trauma." You can also use the keyboard to select text if you don't like using the mouse. To select text using the keyboard, move the insertion point before or after the text you want to select, and then press and hold down the Shift key while you use the arrow keys to select the text.

6 Move the insertion point to the very end of the Subject: Glue Crisis line.

Try selecting text with the keyboard in the next step.

7 Press and hold down the Shift key and press and hold down the left arrow key ← until the Subject line is selected.

If you change your mind after selecting text, it's easy to deselect it. Just click anywhere else on the screen.

8 Click anywhere in the document to deselect the text.

The Subject line is no longer selected.

Another trick you should know is that you can delete any selected text by pressing the Delete key.

9 Select the date and press the Delete key.

The date is deleted.

And that's all there is to selecting text in Windows. Again, it's very important that you know how to select text. Knowing how to select text will make you much more proficient at using many Window programs.

Table 3-2. Shortcuts for selecting text

To Select This	Do This
A word	Double-click the word.
A line	Click next to the line in the left margin.
A sentence	Press and hold Ctrl and double-click the sentence.
The entire document	Press and hold Ctrl and double-click in the left margin.

QUICK REFERENCE

TO SELECT A STRING OF TEXT:

1. MOVE THE INSERTION POINT TO THE BEGINNING OR END OF THE TEXT YOU WANT TO SELECT.

2. CLICK AND HOLD THE LEFT MOUSE BUTTON AND DRAG THE INSERTION POINT ACROSS THE TEXT, THEN RELEASE THE MOUSE BUTTON ONCE THE TEXT IS SELECTED.

OR...

PRESS AND HOLD DOWN THE SHIFT KEY WHILE USING THE ARROW KEYS TO SELECT THE TEXT.

TO SELECT A SINGLE WORD:

- DOUBLE-CLICK THE WORD YOU WANT TO SELECT.

TO REPLACE TEXT:

- REPLACE TEXT BY FIRST SELECTING IT, THEN TYPING THE NEW TEXT.

TO DESELECT TEXT:

- CLICK ANYWHERE ON THE COMPUTER SCREEN.

TO DELETE SELECTED TEXT:

1. SELECT THE TEXT.

2. PRESS THE DELETE KEY.

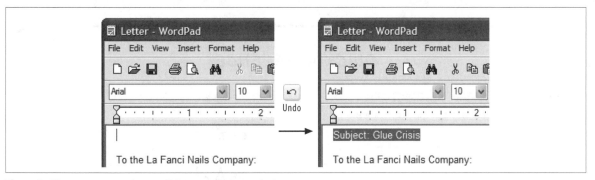

Figure 3-15. You can cancel a text deletion with the Undo feature.

You may not want to admit this, but you're going to make mistakes when you use Windows. You might accidentally delete a sentence in your word processing program that you didn't mean to delete, or paste something that you didn't mean to paste. Fortunately, Windows and most Windows programs come with a wonderful feature called *undo* that does just that—undoes your last action, making it as though it never happened.

Many people that are new to Windows or computers in general are often terrified of using computers because they are afraid they will make a mistake and seriously mess things up. First of all, it's more difficult to "mess up" your computer than you think it is. Secondly, you will learn how to use Undo, so even if you do make a mistake, you can easily cancel it.

1 Select the Subject: Glue Crisis line and delete it by pressing the Delete key.

Whoops! You didn't really want to delete that! Watch how you can undo your "mistake."

2 Click the Undo button on the Standard toolbar.

Undo Button
Other Ways to Undo:
• Select **Edit→Undo** from the menu.
• Press **Ctrl+Z**.

Poof! WordPad cancels your last action and the deleted text "Subject: Glue Crisis" reappears.

In most programs, Undo will only cancel your last action or change; if you don't catch your mistake right after you make it, Undo may not be able to help.

QUICK REFERENCE

TO UNDO YOUR PREVIOUS ACTION:

• CLICK THE UNDO BUTTON ON THE TOOLBAR.

OR...

• SELECT EDIT → UNDO FROM THE MENU.

OR...

PRESS CTRL + Z.

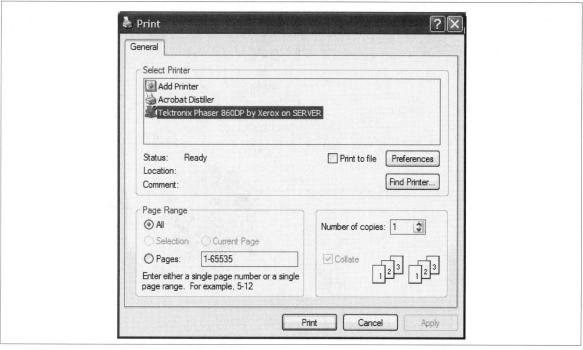

Figure 3-16. The Print dialog box.

This lesson will show you how to send whatever you're working on to the printer. Printing is one of the easiest things to do in Windows.

1 Select File → Print from the menu.

The Print dialog box appears, as shown in Figure 3-16. The Print dialog box may differ depend-ing on the program you're using, but it should usually contain the options listed in Table 3-3.

2 Click OK.

Windows sends the document to the printer.

Table 3-3. Print dialog box options

Print option	Description
Name	Used to select what printer to send your file to when it prints (if you are connected to more than one printer). The currently selected printer is displayed.
Properties	Displays a dialog box with options available to your specific printer such as printing on both sides of the page, selecting the paper size you want to use, printing in color or black and white, etc.
Page range	Allows you to specify what pages you want to print. There are several options: **All:** Prints the entire document. **Selection:** Prints only the text you have selected (before selecting the print command). **Pages:** Prints only the pages of the file you specify. Select a range of pages with a hyphen (for example: 5-8) and separate single pages with a comma (for example: 3,7).
Number of copies	Specifies the number of copies you want to print.

QUICK REFERENCE

TO PRINT A FILE:

- CLICK THE PRINT BUTTON ON THE STANDARD TOOLBAR.

OR...

- SELECT FILE → PRINT FROM THE MENU.

OR...

PRESS CTRL + P.

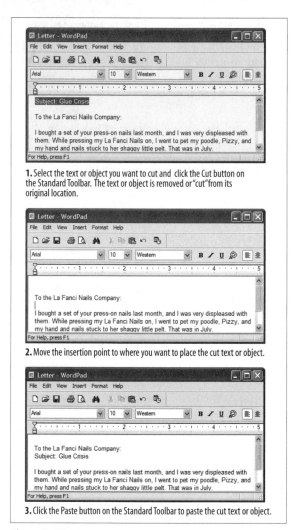

1. Select the text or object you want to cut and click the Cut button on the Standard Toolbar. The text or object is removed or "cut" from its original location.

2. Move the insertion point to where you want to place the cut text or object.

3. Click the Paste button on the Standard Toolbar to paste the cut text or object.

Figure 3-17. The steps involved in cutting and pasting text.

By now, you should already know how to select text in a document. Once text is selected, you can move it to another place in the document by cutting it and then pasting it elsewhere. Cutting and pasting text is one of the more common tasks you will use in your programs. Anything you cut is placed in a temporary storage area called the Windows *Clipboard*. The Clipboard is available to any Windows program, so you can cut and paste text between different programs.

1 Select the entire subject line.

Remember how to select text? Point to the beginning or end of the text you want to select, hold down the left mouse button, drag the cursor across the text, and release the mouse button.

Now you can cut the selected text to the Windows clipboard.

2 Click the Cut button on the Standard toolbar.

Cut Button
Other Ways to Cut:
• Select Edit→ Cut from the menu.
• Press **Ctrl+X**.

The selected text—the subject line—disappears from WordPad and is placed on the Windows *Clipboard*, ready to be moved to a new location.

NOTE *The Windows Clipboard can only hold one piece of information at a time. Every time you cut or copy something to the Clipboard, it replaces the previous information.*

3 Move the insertion point to the blank line immediately below To the La Fanci Nails Company:

This is where you want to paste the line you cut.

4 Click the Paste button on the Standard toolbar.

Paste Button
Other Ways to Paste:
• Select **Edit**→**Paste** from the menu.
• Press **Ctrl+P**.

Poof! The cut text, the subject line, appears at the insertion point.

Copying information is very similar to cutting information. Both commands put your selected information on the Clipboard where you can then paste it to a new location. The only difference between the two commands is that the Cut command deletes selected information when it copies it to the clipboard, while the Copy command copies the selected information to the clipboard without deleting it.

5 Select the entire document by holding down the Ctrl key and clicking the pointer in the left margin.

Now you can copy the selected text to the clipboard.

6 Click the Copy button on the Standard toolbar.

Copy Button
Other Ways to Copy:
• Select **Edit**→ **Copy** from the menu.
• Press **Ctrl+C**.

Nothing appears to happen, but the selected text has been copied to the clipboard.

One of the great things about Windows is that it allows you to share information between programs. For example, the information that you just copied to the Windows clipboard from WordPad can be pasted into another Windows program. To see how this works, you will need to open another Windows program—the Notepad.

7 Click the Start button and select All Programs → Accessories → Notepad.

The Notepad program appears. Notepad doesn't have a toolbar like WordPad does, so you will have to access the Paste command through the menu.

8 Select Edit → Paste from the Notepad menu.

The document you copied from the WordPad program is pasted into the Notepad program. You won't be using the Notepad program anymore in this chapter, so you can close it.

9 Click the Notepad program's Close button.

A dialog box appears, asking if you want to save the changes you made to the Notepad file. You don't need to save any changes, so you can safely click No.

10 Click No.

You should, however, save the changes you've made to your WordPad document.

11 Click the Save button on WordPad's Standard toolbar to save the changes you've made to the document.

WordPad saves your recent changes.

QUICK REFERENCE

TO CUT AN OBJECT OR TEXT:

1. SELECT THE TEXT OR OBJECT YOU WANT TO CUT.

2. CLICK THE CUT BUTTON ON THE STANDARD TOOLBAR.

OR...

SELECT EDIT → CUT FROM THE MENU.

OR...

PRESS CTRL + X.

TO COPY AN OBJECT OR TEXT:

1. SELECT THE TEXT OR OBJECT YOU WANT TO COPY.

2. CLICK THE COPY BUTTON ON THE STANDARD TOOLBAR.

OR...

SELECT EDIT → COPY FROM THE MENU.

OR...

PRESS CTRL + C.

TO PASTE A CUT OR COPIED OBJECT:

1. PLACE THE INSERTION POINT WHERE YOU WANT TO PASTE THE TEXT OR OBJECT.

2. CLICK THE PASTE BUTTON ON THE STANDARD TOOLBAR.

OR...

SELECT EDIT → PASTE FROM THE MENU.

OR...

PRESS CTRL + V.

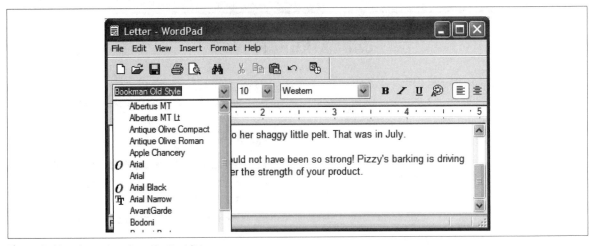

Figure 3-18. Select a font from the Font list.

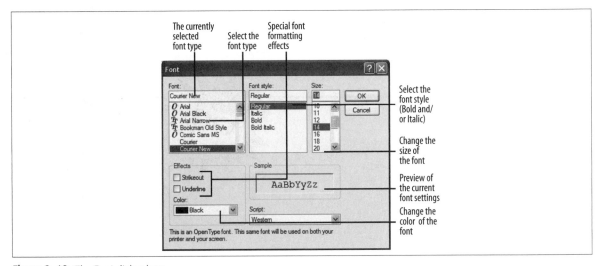

Figure 3-19. The Font dialog box.

In this lesson, you'll learn how to change the font or text size and style. Although you'll be working with the WordPad program, the basic procedure for changing the size and type of a font is the same in all Windows programs.

1 Move the insertion point the very end of the document and press Enter twice to add a blank line.

You are going to add your name to the document here, but first you want to use a different font to make it stand out.

2 Click the Font list arrow on the Formatting toolbar.

Font List
Other Ways to Change Fonts:
• Select Format→Font from the menu, select the font options you want from the font dialog box, then click OK.

A list appears with all the fonts that are available on your computer, listed in alphabetical order. Since there isn't enough room to display all the font types at once, you may have to scroll up or down the list until you find the font type you want.

3 Scroll up the Font list until you see the Bookman Old Style font, then click the Bookman Old Style font.

Anything you type at this point will appear in the selected Bookman Old Style font.

4 Type Jane Plain.

The name Jane Plain appears in the Bookman Old Style font. You can also select text and change it to a new font.

5 Select the line To the La Fanci Nails Company:.

In the next step, we'll change the selected text to Courier New font type.

6 Click the Font list arrow and select Courier New from the Font list.

The selected text changes to the Courier New font.

You can also change the size of a font and make it larger or smaller. Font size is measured in *points*: the bigger the point number, the larger the size of the font. 10 point and 12 point are the most commonly used font sizes. Changing the font size is similar to changing font types.

7 Make sure the To the La Fanci Nails Company: line is still selected, and click the Font Size list arrow.

Font Size List
Other Ways to Change Font Size:
• Select Format→Font from the menu, select the font
options you want from the font dialog box, then click OK.

A list of font sizes appears.

8 Select 14 from the Font Size list.

The font for the selected line is enlarged to 14 point.

So far, you've been using the Formatting toolbar to change the type and size of fonts. Another method of adjusting the type and size of fonts is to use the Font dialog box, which you can open using the menu. Since not all Windows programs have a Formatting toolbar, you should know how to format fonts with this method.

9 Select Format → Font from the menu.

The Font dialog box appears, as shown in Figure 3-19. Notice there are options for changing the font type and size, as well as other formatting options. After you've surveyed the Font dialog box, you can close it without making any changes by clicking the Cancel button.

10 Click Cancel to close the Font dialog box without making any changes.

Table 3-4. Examples of font types and sizes

Common Font Types	Common Font Sizes
Arial	Arial 8 point
Comic Sans MS	Arial 10 point
Courier New	Arial 12 point
Times New Roman	Arial 14 point

QUICK REFERENCE

TO CHANGE FONT SIZE:

- CLICK THE FONT SIZE LIST ARROW ON THE FORMATTING TOOLBAR AND SELECT THE POINT SIZE FROM THE LIST.

OR...

- SELECT FORMAT → FONT FROM THE MENU AND SELECT THE FONT SIZE IN THE FONT DIALOG BOX.

TO CHANGE FONT TYPE:

- CLICK THE FONT LIST ARROW ON THE FORMATTING TOOLBAR AND SELECT A FONT TYPE FROM THE LIST.

OR...

- SELECT FORMAT → FONT FROM THE MENU AND SELECT THE FONT TYPE IN THE FONT DIALOG BOX.

Using Bold, Italics, and Underline

Figure 3-20. WordPad's Formatting toolbar.

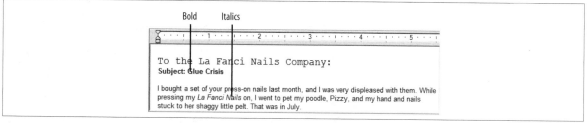

Figure 3-21. The document with bold and italics formatting.

In the previous lesson, you learned how to format characters in a document by changing their font type and font size. This lesson will show you how to emphasize text in a document by making the text darker and heavier (**bold**), slanted (*italics*), or by adding underlining.

1 Select the text La Fanci Nails, located in the first body paragraph of your document.

You can make the selected text stand out by formatting with Italics.

2 Click the Italics button on the Formatting toolbar.

Italics Button
Other Ways to Italics:
• Select Format→Font from the menu, select Italics from the Font Style box, and then click OK.

The selected text, La Fanci Nails, appears in italics. Notice that the Italics button is pushed down on the Formatting toolbar, indicating the text is formatted with Italics.

It's just as easy to format characters with bold or underline formatting.

3 Select the line Subject: Glue Crisis.

Now format the selected text with bold formatting.

4 Click the Bold button on the Formatting toolbar.

Bold button

The selected text appears in bold. To remove the bold style, repeat step 4.

5 Make sure Subject: Glue Crisis is still selected, then click the Bold button on the Formatting toolbar.

The bold style is removed from the selected text. You can remove italic and underline formatting from text by using the same method, except you would click the Italics or Underline button.

QUICK REFERENCE

TO FORMAT TEXT WITH BOLD, ITALICS, OR UNDERLINING:

- CLICK THE BOLD, ITALICS, OR UNDERLINE BUTTON ON THE FORMATTING TOOLBAR.

OR...

- SELECT FORMAT → FONT FROM THE MENU AND SELECT THE FORMATTING FROM THE FONT STYLE LIST.

OR...

- PRESS THE CTRL KEY AND:

  B FOR BOLD

  I FOR ITALICS

  U FOR UNDERLINING

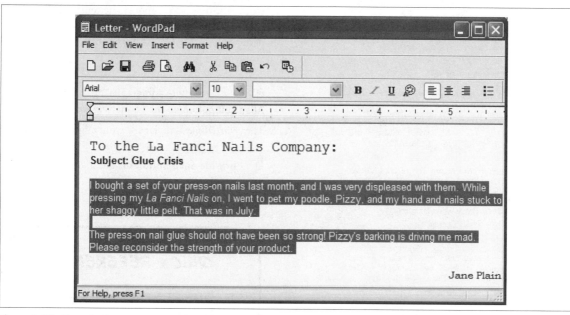

Figure 3-22. Place the insertion point in the paragraph you want to align, or select the paragraph(s).

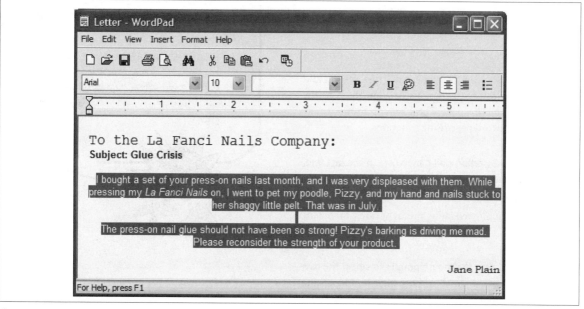

Figure 3-23. Clicking the Center button on the Formatting toolbar centers the selected paragraphs.

This paragraph is left aligned. This paragraph is left aligned. This paragraph is left aligned. This paragraph is left aligned. This paragraph is left aligned. This paragraph is left aligned. This paragraph is left aligned. This paragraph is left aligned.

Left Align

This paragraph is aligned right. This paragraph is aligned right. This paragraph is aligned right. This paragraph is aligned right. This paragraph is aligned right. This paragraph is aligned right. This paragraph is aligned right.

Right Align

This paragraph is center aligned. This paragraph is center aligned. This paragraph is center aligned. This paragraph is center aligned. This paragraph is center aligned. This paragraph is center aligned. This paragraph is center aligned.

Centered

This paragraph is justified. This paragraph is justified. This paragraph is justified. This paragraph is justified. This paragraph is justified. This paragraph is justified. This paragraph is justified. This paragraph is justified.

Justified

Figure 3-24. Left, right, centered, and justified paragraphs.

Align Left Button   **Center Button**   **Align Right Button**

This lesson moves on to paragraph formatting and explains how to justify paragraphs or align them to the left, right, or center of a page. These are common formatting tasks for all word processing programs.

1 Place the insertion point anywhere in the last line, Jane Plain, and then click the Align Right button on the Formatting toolbar.

The last line is aligned along the right side of the window.

2 Click and drag the mouse pointer to select the two body paragraphs, then click the Center button on the Formatting toolbar.

The selected paragraphs are centered on the page.

3 Press the End key to move to the end of the current line, then press Enter.

Notice the new paragraph will be centered like the one above it. That's because when you press Enter, the new paragraph "inherits" the formatting from the paragraph above it.

4 Select the two paragraphs again, and click the Align Left button on the Formatting toolbar.

The selected paragraphs are again aligned to the left.

5 Click the Save button on the Standard toolbar to save your work.

QUICK REFERENCE

TO CHANGE A PARAGRAPH'S ALIGNMENT:

- PLACE THE INSERTION POINT IN THE PARAGRAPH AND CLICK THE ALIGN LEFT, CENTER, OR ALIGN RIGHT BUTTON.

OR...

- PLACE THE INSERTION POINT IN THE PARAGRAPH, SELECT FORMAT → PARAGRAPH FROM THE MENU AND SELECT THE ALIGNMENT, FROM THE ALIGNMENT LIST.

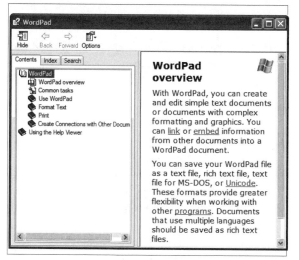

Figure 3-25. The Contents tab of the Help window.

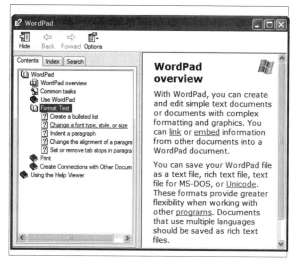

Figure 3-26. You can expand a Help Topic.

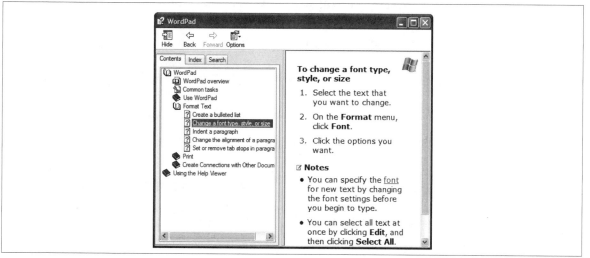

Figure 3-27. The displayed help topic.

When you don't know how to do something in Windows or a Windows based program, don't despair—most programs come with a built-in help feature. Help is one of the greatest—and sadly, one of the least used—features of most Windows programs. There is often more information about how to use a program under the *Help* feature than there is in the program manual! Many people actually learn how to use entire programs by simply using the Help feature of the program when they don't know how to do something.

Help allows you to try new, exciting things in programs all by yourself. It simply cannot be stressed how important and useful the Help feature is. There are several ways

you can get help in Windows—we'll look at them in the next couple of lessons.

For this lesson, imagine that you've seen several of your co-workers use different sized fonts in their WordPad documents. You decide it's time you learned how to change the size of fonts in WordPad, so you decide to use the help feature.

1 Make sure the WordPad program is open and press the F1 key.

TIP *The F1 key displays help on what you're doing.*

The Help window appears with the Contents tab in front, as shown in Figure 3-25. One way to get help is by going to Contents. Using Help's Contents is similar to using a book's table of contents. Help's Contents is a good way to get general information on a topic, especially if it's a subject you're not familiar with. The Help's Contents are organized in outline form. The book icons that appear to the left of a topic tell you there are sub-topics. To view this information, you have to open or expand the topic by double-clicking it.

2 Click the WordPad icon and then click the Format Text topic to expand it.

The topic opens and a list of sub-topics appear under it, as shown in Figure 3-26.

3 Click the Change a font type, style, or size topic (it has a question mark ? icon that appears to the left of it).

Information on text formatting appears in the right pane of the Help window, as shown in Figure 3-27.

You can easily print any Help topic.

4 Click the Options button at the top of the dialog box and select the Print... item.

Options Button

The Print Topics box appears. We just want to print one topic.

5 Select Print Selected Topic and click OK.

The Print dialog box appears, ready to carry out your print command. Since you already know how to print in Windows, save the paper and cancel the print job.

6 Click the Cancel button.

The Print dialog box closes and nothing is sent to the printer.

QUICK REFERENCE

TO GET HELP BY CONTENTS:

1. PRESS F1 OR SELECT HELP FROM THE MENU BAR, AND CLICK THE CONTENTS TAB IF NECESSARY.

2. SCROLL THROUGH THE LIST AND DOUBLE-CLICK THE HELP TOPIC YOU'RE LOOKING FOR.

3. DOUBLE-CLICK ANY HELP SUBTOPIC(S).

TO MOVE TO A PREVIOUS HELP SCREEN OR TOPIC:

• CLICK THE BACK BUTTON.

TO PRINT A HELP TOPIC:

• CLICK THE OPTIONS BUTTON AND SELECT PRINT TOPIC.

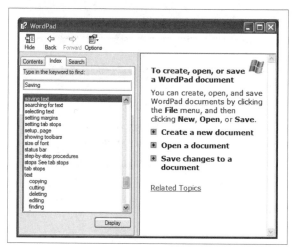

Figure 3-28. The Index tab of the Help dialog box.

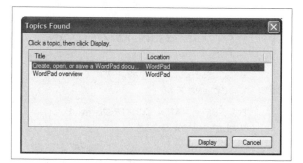

Figure 3-29. The Topics Found dialog box.

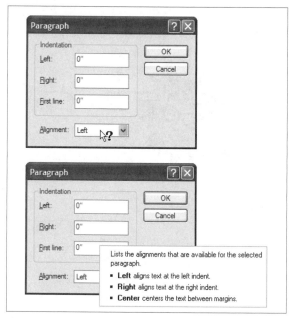

Figure 3-30. Using the "What's This?" button.

Two more methods of getting help are with the Help Index and Search. You use the Help Index just like you would use the index in the back of a book.

1 If the Help window isn't already open, press F1 to open it.

2 Click the Index tab.

The Index tab appears in front of the Help Window. This time, let's get some help on how to save files in WordPad.

3 Type Saving in the Type in the keyword to find box.

The Index topics list box displays all index entries that begin with the words "Saving", as shown in Figure 3-28. A help topic called Saving Text is listed—let's see what this topic is about.

4 Double-click the Saving Text topic.

The Topics Found dialog box appears, as shown in Figure 3-29. We need to choose a topic.

5 Double-click the Create Open or Save a WordPad Document topic.

Information on saving changes to a document appears in the right pane of the Help window.

The Search function is another way that you can search for Help topics. Search is much more specific and powerful than either Help's Contents or the Help Index. Search allows you to search for specific information.

6 Click the Search tab.

Next, you must specify what help you want to look for.

7 Type Save in the Type the word(s) you want to find box and click the List Topics button.

Both the words and topics lists are updated to show all help topics that contain the word "Save."

You can refine a help search by typing in more than one word.

8 Click after the word Save in the Type the word(s) you want to find box. Press the Spacebar and type File. Click Display.

Both the words and topics lists are updated and display only those help topics that contain both the words "Save" and "File" in them.

9 Double-click the WordPad Overview topic.

Windows displays the WordPad Overview help topic.

10 Click the Close button.

During your journey with Windows you will probably come across dialog boxes with a number of confusing controls and options. To help you find out what the various controls and options in a dialog box do, many dialog boxes contain a "What's This?" button, located right next to the Close button.

11 Select Format → Paragraph from the menu.

The Paragraph dialog box appears. Notice the Help button located in the dialog box's title bar just to the left of the dialog box's close button.

12 Click the "What's This?" button.

What's This
button

The mouse pointer changes to a ⟨?⟩, indicating you can point to anything in the dialog box to find out what it does, as shown in Figure 3-30.

13 Click the Alignment list arrow.

A window appears with a brief description of options in the Alignment list.

14 Click Cancel to close the Paragraph dialog box.

That's it—you're done learning the various ways to get help in Windows. If you know how to use a program's Help feature, you may never need to attend another computer class—everything you need to know is there, buried somewhere in Help. Make yourself a promise that the next time you have a question about how to do something in a program, you will try using the program's built-in Help feature before you reach for the manual or ask one of your computer-savvy friends.

QUICK REFERENCE

TO USE THE HELP INDEX:

1. PRESS F1 OR SELECT HELP FROM THE MENU AND CLICK THE INDEX TAB.

2. TYPE THE KEYWORD(S) THAT DESCRIBE THE HELP TOPIC YOU ARE LOOKING FOR.

3. DOUBLE-CLICK THE HELP TOPIC YOU'RE LOOKING FOR.

TO FIND A HELP TOPIC:

1. PRESS F1 OR SELECT HELP FROM THE MENU AND CLICK THE SEARCH OR FIND TAB.

2. TYPE THE KEYWORD(S) THAT BEST DESCRIBE THE TOPIC YOU ARE LOOKING FOR.

3. DOUBLE-CLICK THE HELP TOPIC YOU'RE LOOKING FOR.

TO SEE WHAT A CONTROL IN A DIALOG BOX DOES:

1. CLICK THE DIALOG BOX "WHAT'S THIS" BUTTON (LOCATED RIGHT NEXT TO THE CLOSE BUTTON).

2. CLICK THE CONTROL ABOUT WHICH YOU WANT MORE INFORMATION WITH THE ⟨?⟩ POINTER.

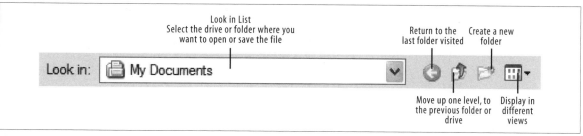

Figure 3-31. The Open/Save toolbar.

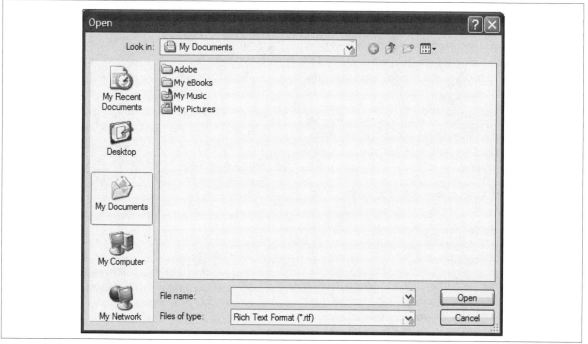

Figure 3-32. The Open dialog box for the WordPad program.

Open Button
Other ways to Open:
• Select **File→Open** from the menu.

By saving your files in related folders right away, you make them easier to find and don't have to do as much file management later. This lesson will show you how to save your files in different locations. You'll also learn how to save files in different file formats.

1 If necessary, open the WordPad program by clicking the Start button and selecting All Programs → Accessories → WordPad from the menu.

The WordPad program appears.

2 Click the Open button on the Standard toolbar.

The Open dialog box for the WordPad program appears, as shown in Figure 3-32. Before we open a file, first let's take a closer look at the Open dialog box. Notice the toolbar that appears near the top of the dialog box, as shown in Figure 3-31. If several of the buttons on the toolbar look somewhat familiar, they should—because they're the same toolbar buttons that you'll find in My Computer and Windows Explorer. When you're opening or saving a file you can navigate through the drives, folders, and files on your computer just like you do in My Computer and Windows Explorer.

3 Navigate to and open your practice folder.

Your computer stores information in files and folders, just like you store information in a filing cabinet. To open a file, you must first find and open the folder where it's saved.

The Open dialog box has its own toolbar that make it easy to browse through your computer's drives and folders. Two controls on this toolbar are particularly helpful:

- Look in: 🗀 Practice **Look In List:** Click to list the drives on your computer and the current folder, then select the drive and/or folder whose contents you want to display.

- 🔼 **Up One Level button:** Click to move up one folder.

If necessary, follow your instructor's directions to select the appropriate drive and folder where your practice files are located.

TIP *You can perform basic file management, such as renaming, deleting, moving, and copying files and folders from inside any Open or Save dialog box, just as if you were in My Computer.*

The Open dialog box reads the contents of the practice folder or disk and displays any Word for Windows (*.doc) files. Here's how you can view *all* the file types in the root directory on the drive—not just Word for Windows files.

4 Click the File of type list and select All Documents (*.*).

The Open dialog box is updated to display all the files in the root directory of the hard drive.

5 Double-click the Canada Meeting Memo file to open it.

WordPad opens the Canada Meeting Memo file. Normally, when you save an existing file, it's saved with its original file name in its original location or folder. There are times, however, when you will need to save a copy of a file in a new location, with a different file name, or in a different file format.

6 Select File → Save As from the menu.

The Save As dialog box appears.

Whenever you save or store files on a computer, try to save them in a related folder. For example, you might create a "Personal Letters" folder to store all your personal correspondence files and a "Business" folder for your business-related files. Selecting a folder to save a file in is easy—simply double-click the Create New Folder icon on the toolbar.

NOTE *If you don't specify a drive or folder when you're saving a file, the program will save the file in the current folder—the drive and folder that happens to be open at that time. This can often make the file more difficult to find in the future.*

7 Double-click the Trade Show folder.

The Trade Show folder opens—this is where you want to save the file.

Earlier in this chapter, you learned that computer programs save and open files in their own different types or formats, just like people from different countries speak different languages. But, just as some people can speak more than one language, many computer programs can open and save files using other file types or formats. WordPad normally saves files in Word for Windows (*.doc) format, but it's easy to save files in different formats.

8 Click the Save as type list arrow.

A list of different types of file formats appears.

9 Select Text Documents (*.txt) from the Save as type list.

One more thing before we save the file—we want to save it with a different name. If you clicked the Save button at this point, WordPad would save the file in the Trade Show folder with the original file name, "Canada Meeting Memo." To save the file with a different name, simply type the new file name in the File Name box.

10 Click in the File Name box and type Canada Letter.

11 Click Save and click Yes to confirm the loss in formatting.

WordPad saves the Canada Letter as a text file under the Trade Show folder.

12 Close the WordPad program.

QUICK REFERENCE

TO SAVE A FILE IN A NEW LOCATION:

• SELECT FILE → SAVE AS FROM THE MENU, OPEN THE DRIVE AND/OR FOLDER WHERE YOU WANT TO SAVE THE FILE AND CLICK SAVE.

TO SAVE A FILE IN A DIFFERENT FILE FORMAT:

• SELECT FILE → SAVE AS FROM THE MENU, SELECT THE FILE FORMAT FROM THE SAVE AS TYPE LIST, AND CLICK SAVE.

Lesson Summary

Using Menus

Open a menu by clicking the menu name with the mouse or by pressing Alt and then the underlined letter in the menu.

Using Toolbars

Click the toolbar button you want to use.

To See What a Toolbar Button Does: Position the pointer over the toolbar button and wait a second. A ScreenTip will appear above the button.

Filling Out a Dialog Box

Be able to identify text boxes, list boxes, check boxes, list arrows, and buttons.

Use a scroll bar to move up or down when a list or screen can't display all its information at once.

To Select a Dialog Box Control: Click the control with the mouse, or press Tab to move to the next control in the dialog box or Shift + Tab to move to the previous control until you arrive at the desired control.

To Use a Text Box: Type the information directly into the text box.

To Use a List Box: Click the option you want from the list box. Use the scroll bar to move up and down through its options.

To Use a List Arrow: Click the arrow to display the list options. Click an option from the list to select it.

To Save Changes and Close a Dialog Box: Click the OK button or press Enter.

To Close a Dialog Box Without Saving Changes: Click the Cancel button or press Esc.

Entering Text in the WordPad Program

To Enter Text in WordPad: Click in the WordPad screen to begin typing your text.

Editing Text

To Move the Insertion Point: Use the arrow keys on the keyboard or click where you want to place the insertion point with the I pointer.

To Insert Text: Move the insertion point where you want to insert the text and then type the text you want to insert.

To Delete Text: The Delete key deletes text after, or to the right, of the insertion point. The Backspace key deletes text before, or to the left, of the insertion point.

Saving and Opening a File

To Save a File: Click the Save button on the Standard toolbar or select File → Save from the menu.

To Open a File: Click the Open button on the Standard toolbar or select File → Open from the menu.

Selecting, Replacing and Deleting Text

To Select Text with the Mouse: Move the insertion point to the beginning or end of the text you want to select. Click and hold the left mouse button and drag the insertion point across the text, releasing the mouse button once the text is selected. Or double-click a word to select it.

To Select Text with the Keyboard: Move the insertion point to the beginning or end of the text you want to select and press and hold the Shift key while you use the arrow keys to select the text.

To Replace Text: Replace text by first selecting it, then typing the new text.

To Deselect Text: Click anywhere on the computer screen.

To Delete Text: Select the text. Press the Delete key.

Using Undo

To Undo Your Last Action: Click the Undo button on the Standard toolbar, or select Edit → Undo from the menu, or press Ctrl + Z.

Printing a File

Print a file by clicking the 🖶 Print button on the Standard toolbar, or by selecting File → Print from the menu, or by pressing Ctrl + P.

Select File → Print from the menu to display the Print dialog box, which allows you to specify printing options—such as printing specific pages or multiple copies.

Cutting, Copying, and Pasting Text

To Cut an Object or Text: Select the text or object you want to cut. Click the Cut button on the Standard toolbar, or select Edit → Cut from the menu, or press Ctrl + X.

To Copy an Object or Text: Select the text or object you want to copy. Click the Copy button on the Standard toolbar, or select Edit → Copy from the menu, or press Ctrl + C.

To Paste a Cut or Copied Object: Place the insertion point where you want to paste the text or object. Click the Paste button on the Standard toolbar, or select Edit → Paste from the menu, or press Ctrl + V.

Changing the Font Type and Size

To Change Font Size: Click the Font Size list arrow on the Formatting toolbar and select the point size from the list, or select Format → Font from the menu and select the font size in the dialog box.

To Change Font Type: Click the Font list arrow on the Formatting toolbar and select a font type from the list, or select Format → Font from the menu and select the font type in the Font dialog box.

Using Bold, Italics and Underline

Format text with bold, italics, or underlining by clicking the corresponding button (Bold, Italics, or Underline) on the Formatting toolbar or by selecting Format → Font from the menu and selecting the formatting from the Font Style list. You can also press the Ctrl key and: B for Bold I for Italics U for Underlining.

Changing Paragraph Alignment

Change a paragraph's alignment by placing the insertion point in the paragraph and then clicking the Align Left, Center, or Align Right button on the Formatting toolbar, or by selecting Format → Paragraph from the menu and selecting the paragraph alignment from the Alignment list.

Getting Help by Contents

Pressing the F1 key displays information on what you're currently doing.

To Get Help by Contents: Press F1 or select Help from the menu bar, and click the Contents tab if necessary. Scroll through the list and click the help topic you're looking for. Double-click any subtopics if necessary.

Click the Back button to move to the previous help screen or topic.

To Print a Help Topic: Click the Options button and select Print Topic.

Getting Help with the Help Index and Search

To Use the Help Index: Press F1 or select Help from the menu and click the Index tab and type the keyword(s) that describe the Help topic you are looking for. Double-click the Help topic that you're looking for.

To Search for a Help Topic: Press F1 or select Help from the menu and click the Search tab and type the keyword(s) that describe the help topic you are looking for. Double-click the Help topic that you're looking for.

Point to a control and click the ▣ "What's This" button to view an explanation of what a control does.

Saving and Opening Files in Different Locations

To Save a File in a New Location: Select File → Save As from the menu, open the drive and/or folder where you want to save the file and click Save.

To Save a File in a Different File Format: Select File → Save As from the menu, select the file format from the Save as type list, and click Save.

Quiz

1. You can open a menu in a program by: (Select all that apply.)

   A. Clicking the name of the menu with the mouse.

   B. Pressing Esc and then the underlined letter in the menu name.

   C. Pressing Alt and then the underlined letter in the menu name.

   D. Saying "Computer, open the (state the name of the menu here) menu".

2. How can you move the insertion point in WordPad? (Select all that apply.)

   A. By pressing the arrows keys on your computer's keyboard.

   B. By using the mouse and clicking where you want to place the insertion point with the I pointer.

   C. By selecting the Window → Move Insertion Point command.

   D. The insertion point is an immovable object and can't be moved.

3. Which key deletes text before, or to the left, of the insertion point?

   A. Page Up

   B. Page Down

   C. Delete

   D. Backspace

4. Typing overwrites, or replaces, any text that is selected (True or False?)

5. Which of the following statements is NOT true?

   A. You can undo the last action or mistake you made by clicking the Undo button on the toolbar or by selecting Edit → Undo from the menu.

   B. You can print the file you're working on by clicking the Print button on the toolbar or by selecting File → Print from the menu.

   C. You should save your work or file whenever you think about it.

   D. Files names can contain up to 8 characters.

6. The following will cut selected text or information and place it on the clipboard (Select all that apply.)

   A. Pressing Ctrl + X.

   B. Pressing Ctrl + Delete.

   C. Clicking the Cut button on the toolbar.

   D. Selecting Edit → Cut from the menu.

7. Unlike cutting, when you copy something you can't see it on-screen (True or False?)

8. Pressing F5 displays Help on what you're doing (True or False?)

Homework

1. Navigate to where your practice files are located.

2. Start WordPad. Open the Homework 3 file from your practice files.

3. Select File → Save As from the menu. Save the "Homework 3" file as "Memo" on the Practice CD in the D: drive, or in your practice files.

4. Move the insertion point to the end of the TO: line, press the Spacebar and type "All Staff."

5. Select the top three address lines.

6. With the top address lines still selected, click the Center button on the Formatting toolbar to center align them.

7. Select the top "North Shore Travel" line and change the font type to Times New Roman, the font size to 14 pt., and apply bold formatting.

8. With the top "North Shore Travel" line still selected, press the Delete key to erase the line. Click the Undo button on the Standard toolbar to undo the deletion.

9. Select the text "Sandra Willes, Communication Director" and copy it by clicking the Copy button on the Standard toolbar

10. Move to the very end of the document, press the Enter key to add a blank line, type "Sincerely," and press Enter four times to add several blank lines.

11. Click the Paste button on the Standard toolbar to paste the text you copied in Step 9.

12. Save your work and exit WordPad.

Quiz Answers

1. A and C. Clicking the menu name or pressing the Alt key and the underlined letter in the menu will both open a menu.

2. A and B. Either method will move the insertion point.

3. D. The Backspace key deletes text before, or to the left, of the insertion point. The Delete key deletes text after, or to the right, of the insertion point

4. True. Typing replaces any selected text.

5. D. MS-DOS files had an 8-character limit, but Windows XP file names can contain up to 255 characters.

6. A, C, and D. All of these three methods will cut selected text or information and place it on the clipboard.

7. True. Nothing visible happens when you copy something, but don't let this fool you! Anything you copy is placed behind the scenes on the invisible Windows clipboard.

8. False. F1 is the Windows help key.

WORKING WITH FILES AND FOLDERS

CHAPTER OBJECTIVES:

Understanding storage devices, folders, and files

Using My Computer to navigate through folders and files

Opening, creating, and renaming files and folders

Copying, moving, and deleting files and folders

Restoring a deleted file and emptying the Recycle Bin

Changing how information is displayed

Selecting multiple files and folders

Finding a file using the Search Companion

Using Windows Explorer

Prerequisites

• **Know how to use the mouse to click, double-click, click and drag, and right-click.**

• **Know how to use menus, toolbars, and dialog boxes.**

When you work at a desk, unless you make an effort to stay organized, all your papers and files begin to pile up and become disorganized. It takes a little more time, but the same phenomenon occurs when working with Windows—the files you create using your computer start to become cluttered, and are harder and harder to find.

In this chapter, you'll take your first step beyond the Windows basics and enter the world of *file management*. You'll learn how Windows stores information in files and folders, just like a file cabinet does. You'll find you will need to clean and organize your files and folders from time to time, just like you would the contents of a file cabinet. This chapter explains how to organize your computer by creating folders to store related information, how to move and copy files between folders, how to delete and rename files and folders, and how to retrieve a deleted file if you change your mind. You can perform file management using several different programs—My Computer, Windows Explorer, Files and Settings Transfer Wizard, and the Open and Save dialog boxes found in most programs.

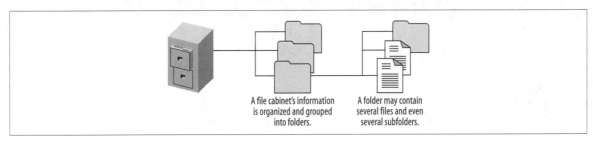

Figure 4-1. How information is stored in a file cabinet.

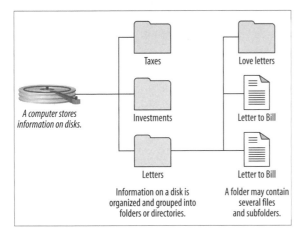

Figure 4-2. How information is stored on a disk.

In order to understand *file management*, you need to understand how your computer stores information. Filing cabinets store information in files, which are organized and grouped in folders and kept in big drawers. Computers also store information in files, which are also organized and grouped in folders, and stored not in big drawers but on *disks*. A *disk drive* is the part of the computer that reads and writes information onto disks, just like a tape recorder records and plays music on a cassette. There are four main types of disks and disk drives that computers use to store their information, as shown in the following table.

Table 4-1. Common computer disks/drives

Type	Drive Letter	Size	Description
Floppy Disk	A or B	1.44 MB	Floppy disks are the square plastic things that look like coffee coasters. Floppy drives can't hold a lot of information, but they're ideal for moving small files, such as word processing documents, between computers.
Hard Disk	C	Over 10 GB	Local disks, or hard disks, hide permanently inside your computer. Your computer's hard disk is its main filing cabinet—where it stores almost all of its programs and files.
CD-ROM	D or above	600 MB (CD)4.7 GB (DVD)	Compact discs, or CD-ROMs, look like the audio discs you play in your stereo. CD-ROMs are cheap and they can store a lot of information, which is why they're used to install software for games and programs with a lot of multimedia. DVDs are similar to CDs, but they hold even more information. DVDs are becoming the most common storage device for movies.
Removable Drive	D or above	Over 100 MB	Removable storage drives have features of both hard disks and floppy drives. Removable drives are like floppy drives because they read and write information on small, removable cassettes. They are like hard drives because each cassette can usually hold more than 100 MB and they are almost as fast as a hard drive.

Most computers come with a floppy drive, a hard drive, and a CD-ROM drive. However, many new computers omit the floppy drive and have a CD-ROM drive *and* a DVD drive instead. Your computer labels these drives with letters, as shown in Table 4-1.*s*

Just as liquids are measured in quarts and gallons, computers save their information in units called *bytes*. Unlike gallons, computers use the metric system, so 1,000 bytes make up a *kilobyte* and 1,000,000 (one million) bytes make up a *megabyte*, as shown in Table 4-2.

Table 4-2. How memory is measured

Term	Description	Size
Byte	A **byte** can store a single character, such as the letter "J" or number "8."	A single character
Kilobyte(K or KB)	A **kilobyte** (K) is about 1,000 bytes (1,024 to be exact). A kilobyte is equivalent to a page of double-spaced typing.	1,024 bytes
Megabyte(MB or MEG)	A **megabyte** (MB) is about one million bytes—about as much text as an average-length novel.	1,048,576 bytes
Gigabyte (GB or GIG)	A **gigabyte** (GB) is about one billion bytes—about as much text as several encyclopedia setsor a truckful of books.	1,073,741,824 bytes

Figure 4-3. My Computer displays the drives, folders (directories), and files that are in your computer.

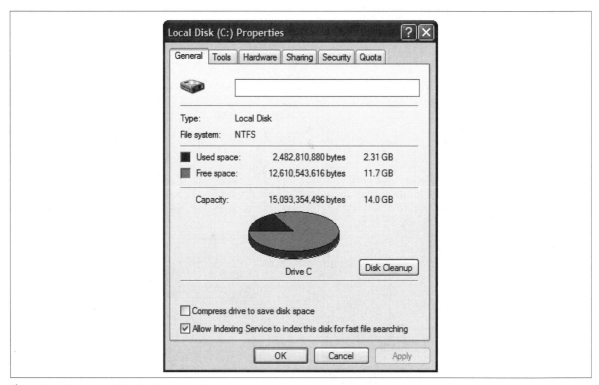

Figure 4-4. The Local Disk (C:) Properties dialog box.

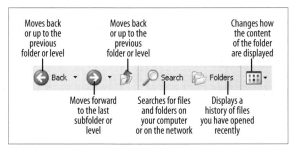

Figure 4-5. The My Computer toolbar.

When you want to see what's in a file cabinet, you simply pull open one of its drawers. You can view the information stored on your computer's drives in much the same way—by opening the drive you want to access. This lesson will show you how to look at the drives, folders, and files in your computer.

1 Click the Start button and select My Computer.

Start Button

The My Computer window appears, as shown in Figure 4-3. The main window lists all the drives on the computer. Since your computer may be set up differently, the contents of your computer may differ from those shown in Figure 4-3. Want to see what's inside something? All you have to do is double-click the drive, folder, or file you want to open.

My Computer

Notice that although it's not technically a program, My Computer appears in its own window, with its own buttons, scroll bars, and menus. The My Computer window works just like any other window you've been working with. You can move it, resize it, and minimize it.

2 Double-click the Local Disk (C:) icon.

Local Disk (C:)

The contents of the (C:) drive appear in the window. What do all those symbols in the window mean? Each item you see has an icon, or symbol, to help you identify what type of item it is. We'll take a look at what each of these symbols mean in an upcoming lesson.

To move back to the previous folder or level, click the Up button on the toolbar.

3 Click the Up button on the toolbar.

Up Button

You've moved from the (C:) drive back to My Computer.

Now that you know the procedure for displaying the contents of a drive, move on to the next step to display the properties of the Local Disk (C:) drive.

4 Right-click the Local Disk (C:) icon and select Properties from the shortcut menu.

The disk drive hums as Windows examines it. After a moment, the Local Disk (C:) Properties window appears, as shown in Figure 4-4. The Properties window displays the amount of used and free space on the disk in megabytes (MB) and gigabytes (GB). Refer to the previous lesson if you're unfamiliar with these terms.

5 Click the Properties dialog box Close button.

The Properties dialog box closes. Go ahead and close the My Computer window to complete the lesson.

6 Close the My Computer window.

Getting the hang of opening and exploring your computer? Good, because we'll be doing a lot more snooping inside the contents of your computer throughout the rest of this chapter.

QUICK REFERENCE

TO VIEW THE CONTENTS OF YOUR COMPUTER:

- CLICK THE START BUTTON AND SELECT MY COMPUTER.

TO VIEW THE CONTENTS OF A DISK DRIVE:

- FOLLOW THE ABOVE STEP TO OPEN MY COMPUTER AND THEN DOUBLE-CLICK THE DRIVE YOU WANT TO OPEN.

TO VIEW AN ITEM'S PROPERTIES:

- RIGHT-CLICK THE DRIVE, FOLDER, OR FILE AND SELECT PROPERTIES FROM THE SHORTCUT MENU.

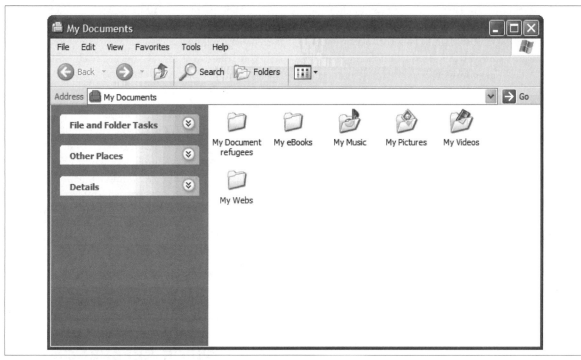

Figure 4-6. Double-click a folder to open it and view its contents.

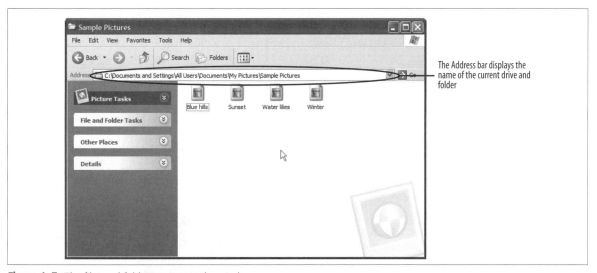

The Address bar displays the name of the current drive and folder

Figure 4-7. The files and folders appear in the window.

Your computer stores related files together in folders, just like you do with your file cabinet. In the previous lesson, you learned how to use My Computer to view the contents of your computer and open a disk drive and display its contents. In this lesson, we'll go a little bit further and show you how to open a folder.

Windows XP gives you your very own special folder named "My Documents" as a convenient location to store all your files. Here's how to open the My Documents folder (and any other folder).

1 Click the Start button and select My Documents.

The contents of My Documents appear in the window. The My Documents folder contains several folders, or *subfolders*. If you think about it, you probably do the same thing—keep several subfolders inside a larger folder—in your own file cabinet.

My Documents

2 Double-click the My Pictures folder.

My Pictures

The contents of the My Pictures folder appear in the Window. Notice the Address bar displays the current folder you are in: My Pictures.

Instead of clicking the Up button several times to jump back through several levels of folders, you can click the Address bar to quickly jump to the root directory of any drive on your computer.

NOTE *This is where the comparison we've been using between a file cabinet and a computer begins to break down a bit. When you file things in your file cabinet, you probably never have more than two, possibly three, nested folders (i.e. a folder inside another folder). Your computer's folders, on the other hand, can contain as many subfolders as you want, nested as deep as you want, so you can have a folder inside a folder inside a folder—ad infinitum.*

3 Click the Address list arrow.

A list of your computer's drives and the folder you are currently in appears. You can click any folder or drive to go to that folder or drive.

4 Select Local Disk (C:) from the list.

You return to the root directory of the (C:) drive. The Address bar is a fast way to select a drive, especially if you are in a folder that is nested several levels deep.

You can think of the Address Bar as your compass because even when you're exploring unfamiliar folders nested deep in the far recesses of your computer, it always tells you where you are. If you get really lost, you can always click the Address list arrow and jump back to the familiar (C:) drive.

All this moving around your computer and opening disk drives and folders is a little boring, but it's something you have to get used to if you want to have any degree of proficiency with Windows. Going back to our trusty file cabinet metaphor, imagine what would happen if you didn't know how to open the drawers and folders in your file cabinet. How would you find your tax returns if you were audited, or your insurance policy if you were in an accident? Opening disk drives and folders, and being able to navigate through the contents of your computer are among the most important Windows skills you can learn.

QUICK REFERENCE

TO OPEN A FOLDER:

• DOUBLE-CLICK THE FOLDER.

TO MOVE BACK OR UP TO THE PREVIOUS LEVEL OR FOLDER:

• CLICK THE UP BUTTON ON THE TOOLBAR.

OR...

• CLICK THE BACK BUTTON ON THE TOOLBAR.

OR...

• CLICK THE ADDRESS LIST ARROW ON THE TOOLBAR AND SELECT THE APPROPRIATE DRIVE OR FOLDER.

Creating and Renaming a Folder

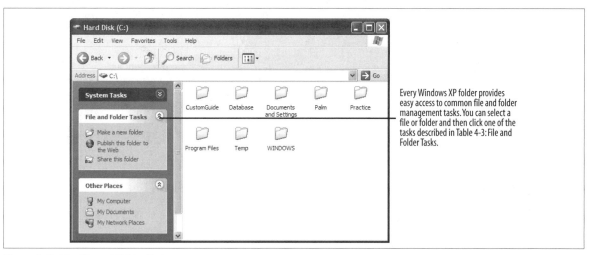

Every Windows XP folder provides easy access to common file and folder management tasks. You can select a file or folder and then click one of the tasks described in Table 4-3: File and Folder Tasks.

Figure 4-8. The File and Folder Tasks menu.

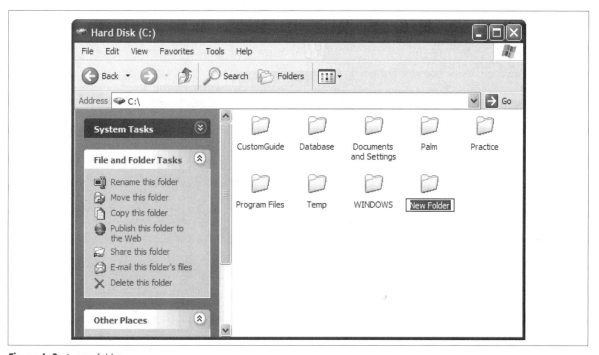

Figure 4-9. A new folder.

Windows XP comes with the My Documents folder which you can use to save your files in, but sooner or later you'll want to expand your horizons and create your own folders inside the My Documents folder or on the network to help you better organize your files. This lesson will show you how to create a new folder to hold and organize your files. You'll also learn how to rename an existing folder.

1 Click the Start button and select My Computer from the menu.

The My Computer window appears.

2 Double-click the Local Disk (C:) icon.

The contents of the (C:) drive appear.

Windows XP makes working with files and folders more efficient by listing the most common file and folder management tasks next to the folder contents.

NOTE   *You may have to resize the window to view these tasks.*

3 Make sure the File and Folder Tasks menu is expanded.

Let's use this menu to create a new folder.

4 Click the Make a new folder task in the File and Folder Tasks menu.

A new folder appears with a temporary name "New Folder" as shown in Figure 4-9. Now all you have to do is move on to the next step and give the new folder a name.

5 Type Practice Folder as the new folder name and press Enter.

Your new Practice Folder is located in the root directory, or top folder, of the (C:) drive. You can create a folder inside any existing folder the same way—by opening the folder and then repeating Steps 3-5. You can create as many folders as you like in order to develop your own filing system to help organize your files and folders. Open the Practice Folder to display its contents.

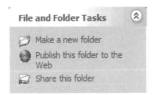

File and Folder Tasks menu
Other ways to Create a Folder:
• Right-click an empty area of the window and Select
New→Folder from the shortcut menu.

NOTE   *A file name can contain up to 255 characters, including spaces. File names cannot contain the following characters: \ / : * ? " |*

6 Double-click the Practice Folder to open it.

The contents of the Practice Folder appear in the window. That's right, there's nothing there. The Practice Folder is an empty folder, since you just created it.

Let's move back to the root directory.

7 Click the Up button.

You can easily change the name of a folder. Here's how:

8 Click the Practice Folder icon.

Now let's rename the folder. Here's how:

9 Click the Rename this folder task in the Files and Folders Tasks menu, type Temp Folder and press Enter.

The "Practice Folder" is renamed "Temp Folder."

NOTE   *Because you change the file path of all the files stored within a folder, be careful when you rename a folder. For example, a hyperlink that uses the file path C:\My Documents\Picnic to link to a file won't work anymore if the file path is changed to C:\My Documents\Picnic Project.*

Table 4-3. File and folder tasks

Task	Description
Make a new folder	Creates a new folder.
Rename this folder	Gives the selected file or folder a new name.

Table 4-3. File and folder tasks (Continued)

Task	Description
Move this folder	Moves the selected items to the destination you choose.
Copy this folder	Copies the selected items to the destination you choose.
Publish this folder to the Web	Transfers a copy of the selected items to a public Web page so that you can share them with other people.
Share this folder	Makes the selected folder available to computers on a network so that other people can access it.
E-mail this folder's files	Sends an e-mail message with copies of the selected items attached.
Delete this folder	Deletes the selected items and sends them to the Recycle Bin.

QUICK REFERENCE

TO CREATE A NEW FOLDER:

1. OPEN THE DISK OR FOLDER WHERE YOU WANT TO CREATE THE NEW FOLDER.

2. SELECT THE *MAKE A NEW FOLDER TASK* FROM THE FILE AND FOLDER TASKS MENU.

   OR...

   RIGHT-CLICK ANY EMPTY AREA IN THE WINDOW AND SELECT *NEW → FOLDER* FROM THE SHORTCUT MENU.

3. TYPE A NAME FOR THE FOLDER AND PRESS ENTER.

TO RENAME A FOLDER:

• CLICK THE FOLDER TO SELECT IT, SELECT THE *RENAME THIS FOLDER* TASK FROM THE FILE AND FOLDER TASKS MENU, TYPE A NAME FOR THE FOLDER AND PRESS ENTER.

OR...

• RIGHT-CLICK THE FOLDER, SELECT *RENAME* FROM THE SHORTCUT MENU, TYPE A NAME FOR THE FOLDER AND PRESS ENTER.

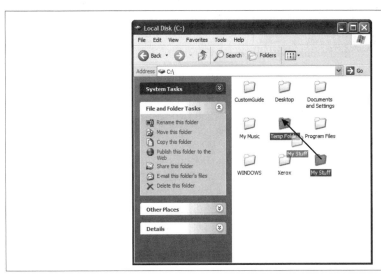

Figure 4-10. To move a folder, drag it to a new location on your computer (in this case to the Temp Folder).

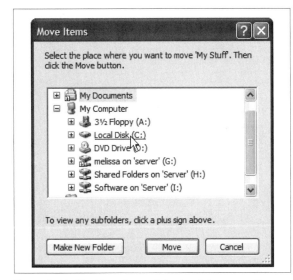

Figure 4-11. The Move Items dialog box lets you specify where you want to move or copy a file or folder.

You probably don't reorganize the folders in your file cabinet very often—and you probably won't need to move or copy the folders on your computer very often, either. When you find you *do* need to move or copy a folder however, you can do so by using one of two simple methods:

• Clicking and dragging.

• Using the File and Folder Tasks menu.

> **TIP** To copy a folder, hold down the *Ctrl* key as you drag the folder to the new location.

You'll learn how to use both methods in this lesson and how to delete a folder when you no longer need it.

1 Create a new folder called My Stuff **in your Local Disk (C:) drive.**

You learned how to create a new folder in the previous lesson.

2 Click and drag the My Stuff **folder to the** Temp Folder, **as shown in Figure 4-10.**

Already forgot how to click and drag? If so, here it is one more time: position the mouse over the My Stuff folder, click and hold down the mouse button as you move the pointer to the Temp Folder, then release the mouse button.

The My Stuff folder is moved inside the Temp Folder. Let's make sure it worked.

3 Double-click the Temp Folder **to open it.**

Yep, there's the My Stuff folder.

Here's another useful method for moving folders:

4 Click the My Stuff **folder to select it.**

Once you have selected the folder you want to move, go to the File and Folder Tasks menu.

5 Click the Move this folder **task from the File and Folder Tasks menu.**

The Move Items dialog box appears, as shown in Figure 4-11. This is where you tell Windows where you want to move the selected folder.

The Move Items dialog box displays the drives and folders on your computer in a *hierarchical* view. A plus symbol (⊞) or a minus symbol (⊟) beside a folder means a folder contains subfolders. Normally these subfolders are hidden. You can display the hidden folders within a folder by clicking the plus sign (⊞) beside the folder.

6 Click the My Computer ⊞ plus symbol.

My Computer expands and displays its subfolders.

The Local Disk (C:) is where you want to move the My Stuff folder.

7 Click the Local Disk (C:) icon and click Move.

The dialog box closes. Let's see if the folder really moved to the right spot.

8 Click the Up button on the toolbar to move up to the root directory.

The My Stuff folder is moved from the Temp Folder back to the root directory of the (C:) drive.

If you can move a folder you can copy a folder: to copy a folder, hold down the Ctrl key while you drag the folder.

9 Press and hold down the Ctrl key while you drag the My Stuff folder to the Temp Folder.

Although you can't see it, the My Stuff folder has been copied to the Temp Folder. Let's make sure.

10 Double-click the Temp Folder to open it.

The contents of the Temp Folder appear in the window. Sure enough, the My Stuff folder has been copied there.

11 Click the Up button to move back to the root directory.

Next, we'll delete a folder.

12 Click the Temp Folder to select it and then press the Delete key.

A dialog box appears, asking you to confirm the deletion.

13 Click Yes to delete the folder.

The Temp Folder and all its contents are deleted and disappear from the window. Windows places any deleted files or folders in the Recycle Bin in case you change your mind later on and decide you want to restore the file or folder. We'll discuss the Recycle Bin in an upcoming lesson.

NOTE   *Deleting a folder can be dangerous. Before you delete a folder, make sure it doesn't contain any important files. If you don't know what the contents of a folder are, you shouldn't delete it.*

14 Delete the original My Stuff folder by repeating steps 12 and 13 and then close the My Computer window.

We've worked on copying and moving folders to locations on the same drive, but you can also copy a folder to a different drive by dragging it to the drive icon where you want it copied. If you can't see the drive or folder where you want to move or copy something, you can open a second My Computer window and drag the folder from one window to the other.

QUICK REFERENCE

TO MOVE A FOLDER:

- DRAG THE FOLDER TO THE DESIRED LOCATION (YOU MIGHT HAVE TO OPEN ANOTHER MY COMPUTER WINDOW).

OR...

1. SELECT THE FOLDER AND CLICK THE MOVE THIS FOLDER TASK FROM THE FILE AND FOLDER TASKS MENU.

2. SELECT THE FOLDER OR DRIVE WHERE YOU WANT TO MOVE THE FOLDER AND CLICK MOVE.

TO COPY A FOLDER:

- HOLD DOWN THE CTRL KEY WHILE YOU DRAG THE FOLDER TO THE DESIRED LOCATION (YOU MIGHT HAVE TO OPEN ANOTHER WINDOW).

OR...

1. SELECT THE FOLDER AND CLICK THE COPY THIS FOLDER TASK IN THE FILE AND FOLDER TASKS MENU.

2. SELECT THE DRIVE OR FOLDER WHERE YOU WANT TO COPY THE FOLDER AND CLICK COPY.

TO DELETE A FOLDER:

1. SELECT THE FOLDER AND PRESS DELETE.

   OR...

   SELECT THE FOLDER AND CLICK THE DELETE THIS FOLDER TASK FROM THE FILE AND FOLDER TASKS MENU.

2. CLICK YES TO CONFIRM THE FOLDER DELETION.

Opening, Renaming, and Deleting a File

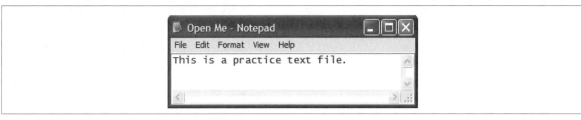

Figure 4-12. The Open Me file in the Notepad program.

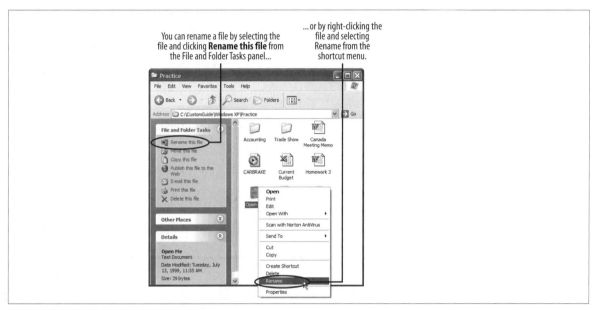

Figure 4-13. Select a file to display the File and Folder Tasks menu, or right-click a file to display a list of commands.

In the past few lessons, you've learned all about folders—how to open, rename, move, copy, and delete them. In the next couple of lessons we'll be working with the files that are stored in those folders. Working with files is very, very similar to working with folders. So similar, in fact, that the procedures for opening, renaming, moving, copying, and deleting a file are exactly the same as opening, renaming, moving, copying, and deleting a folder!

1 Click the Start button and select My Computer from the menu.

The My Computer window appears.

2 Navigate to and open your Practice folder.

Follow your instructor's directions to select the appropriate drive and folder where your practice files are located.

3 Find and double-click the Open Me file.

The Open Me file opens in the NotePad program—the program it was created in, as shown in Figure 4-12. You could review, make changes to, and then save the Open Me file if you wanted to at this point.

4 Click the Notepad program's Close button to close the program and the Open Me file.

The Notepad program closes.

You've already learned how to rename and delete a folder, so the next few steps should be really easy: files are renamed and deleted in exactly the same way.

5 Click the Open Me file to select it.

Now we can rename the Open Me file using the File and Folder Tasks menu.

6 Click the Rename this file task from the File and Folder Tasks menu. Type Text File as the new name for the folder, then press Enter.

Open
Explore
Search...
Sharing and Security...
Send To ▶
Cut
Copy
Create Shortcut
Delete
Rename
Properties

Other ways to Rename a Folder:
• Right-click the folder and select Rename from the shortcut menu.

The "Open Me" file is renamed "Text File,"

When you no longer need a file, delete it.

7 Click the Text File to select it, and then press the Delete key.

A dialog box appears, asking you to confirm the file deletion.

8 Click Yes.

The Text File is deleted and disappears from the window.

Deleting a file isn't quite as dangerous as deleting a folder, but you should always consider whether or not you might need the file again. Don't delete a file unless you're absolutely sure you will never need it again. And NEVER delete a file if you don't know what it is.

9 Close the My Computer window.

QUICK REFERENCE

TO OPEN A FILE:

- DOUBLE-CLICK THE FILE.

TO RENAME A FILE:

1. CLICK THE FILE TO SELECT IT, THEN SELECT THE RENAME THIS FILE TASK IN THE FILE AND FOLDER TASKS MENU.

   OR...

   RIGHT-CLICK THE FILE AND SELECT RENAME FROM THE SHORTCUT MENU

2. TYPE A NAME FOR THE FILE AND PRESS ENTER.

TO DELETE A FILE:

1. CLICK THE FILE TO SELECT IT AND SELECT THE DELETE THIS FILE TASK FROM THE FILE AND FOLDER TASKS MENU.

   OR...

   SELECT THE FILE AND PRESS THE DELETE KEY.

2. CLICK YES TO CONFIRM THE FOLDER DELETION.

Copying and Moving a File

Figure 4-14. To move a file, click and drag the file to the desired location.

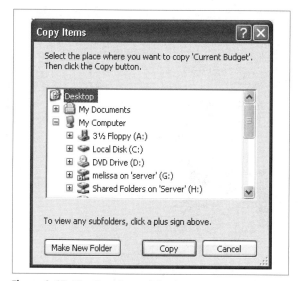

Figure 4-15. The Copy Items dialog box.

The procedure for moving and copying files is no different from moving or copying folders. This lesson about moving and copying files should be a refresher for you.

1 Click the Start button and select My Computer from the menu.

The My Computer window appears.

2 Navigate to and open your Practice folder.

When copying or moving files or folders, you may find it easier if you have two windows open at the same time: one window with the source file(s) and another window for the destination where you want to move or copy the file(s).

3 Click and drag the Current Budget file to the Accounting folder.

The Current Budget file is moved inside the Accounting folder.

Open the Accounting folder to make sure the file was moved.

4 Double-click the Accounting folder.

Sure enough, the Current Budget file has been moved to the Accounting folder.

To copy a file using the click and drag method, press the Ctrl key as you drag the file to a new folder.

5 Click the Current Budget file.

Now that the file is selected, you can move it to a different location.

6 Click the Copy this file task in the File and Folder Tasks menu.

The Copy Items dialog box appears, as shown in Figure 4-15. Now you can tell Windows where you want to move the selected file.

The Copy Items dialog box displays the drives and folders on your computer in a *hierarchical* view. A plus symbol (⊞) or a minus symbol (⊟) beside a folder means a folder contains several subfolders. Normally these subfolders are hidden. You can display the hidden folders within a folder by clicking the plus sign (⊞) beside the folder.

Now copy the file to the Desktop of your computer.

7 Select Desktop in the Copy Items dialog box and click Copy.

The Current Budget file is copied to your computer's Desktop.

NOTE *Some people save their most important files to the Desktop so that they won't lose them. Just make sure that you don't save too many files there—nobody likes a messy desktop!*

We don't want to clutter your computer's desktop with practice files, so let's delete the Current Budget files from the Desktop.

8 Click the Accounting folder window Close button.

The window closes, allowing you to view the Desktop and the copied Current Budget file.

9 Select the Current Budget file and press Delete.

A dialog box appears, asking if you really want to delete the file.

10 Click Yes.

The dialog box closes and the Windows deletes the file.

My Computer
Other ways to Move or Copy a file:
• Click the file to select it, select **Edit**→ **Move** to or Copy to from the menu.

QUICK REFERENCE

TO MOVE A FILE:

• DRAG THE FILE TO THE DESIRED LOCATION (YOU MAY HAVE TO OPEN ANOTHER WINDOW).

OR...

1. CLICK THE FILE TO SELECT IT AND CLICK THE MOVE THIS FILE TASK FROM THE FILE AND FOLDER TASKS MENU.

2. SELECT THE FOLDER WHERE YOU WANT TO MOVE THE FILE AND CLICK MOVE.

TO COPY A FILE:

• HOLD DOWN THE CTRL KEY WHILE YOU DRAG THE FILE TO THE DESIRED LOCATION (YOU MIGHT HAVE TO OPEN ANOTHER MY COMPUTER WINDOW).

OR...

1. CLICK THE FILE TO SELECT IT AND CLICK THE COPY THIS FILE TASK FROM THE FILE AND FOLDER TASKS MENU.

2. SELECT THE FOLDER WHERE YOU WANT TO COPY THE FILE AND CLICK COPY.

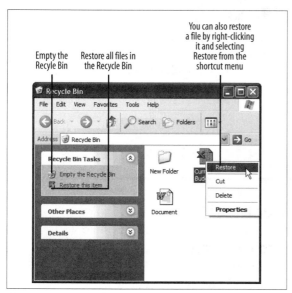

Figure 4-16. Restoring files and emptying the Recycle Bin.

Figure 4-17. The Recycle Bin shortcut menu.

Just like a wastebasket, the *Recycle Bin* stores all of the files and folders you have deleted. If you change your mind and decide you need a deleted file, it's easy to find and retrieve it. This lesson will show you how to open the Recycle Bin and see what's inside, restore a previously deleted file, and empty the Recycle Bin to free up some space on your hard disk.

Recycle Bin
containing deleted
items

NOTE *Be careful when emptying the Recycle Bin. Since Windows automatically erases the oldest files from the Recycle Bin, you shouldn't have to manually empty the Recycle Bin much at all. A lot of users empty the Recycle Bin just about every time they delete something—and then later kick themselves*

because they realize they needed the file they just permanently erased.

1 Double-click the Recycle Bin.

The Recycle Bin opens and displays all the files you have recently deleted. If you accidentally delete a file or folder, you can retrieve it from the Recycle Bin.

2 Select the Current Budget file.

Let's restore this file so it can be used again.

3 Click the Restore this item task from the Recycle Bin Tasks menu.

Restoring a file pulls it out of the Recycle Bin and puts it back in its original location.

4 Click the Recycle Bin window Close button.

Now make sure the Current Budget file is in its original location.

5 Verify that the Current Budget file has been restored to the Desktop.

Okay, you can delete the Current Budget file from the Desktop again, and this time we won't restore it.

6 Delete the Current Budget file from the Desktop.

There is theoretically a limit to how many deleted files and folders the Recycle Bin can hold. The maximum size of the Recycle Bin is normally set at 10 percent of the hard drive. For example, if you have a 10GB hard drive, the maximum amount of files the Recycle Bin could hold would be 1GB. When the Recycle Bin reaches its limit, Windows automatically starts deleting files from the Recycle Bin, starting with the oldest file.

You can adjust the properties for the Recycle Bin—so you could adjust its maximum size from 10 percent of the hard drive to 5 percent—by right-clicking the Recycle Bin and selecting Properties from the shortcut menu.

Usually it's best to let Windows automatically handle the Recycle Bin, but you can also manually empty the Recycle Bin if you need more free space on your computer.

7 Double-click the Recycle Bin.

The contents of the Recycle Bin appear.

8 Click the Empty the Recycle Bin task from the Recycle Bin Tasks menu.

A dialog box appears, asking you to confirm your deletion.

9 Click Yes.

All the files and folders are permanently deleted from your computer. Notice the Recycle Bin icon no longer holds any trash, indicating that it is empty.

QUICK REFERENCE

TO RESTORE A DELETED FILE:

1. DOUBLE-CLICK THE RECYCLE BIN TO OPEN IT.

2. SELECT THE FILE YOU WANT TO RESTORE AND CLICK THE RESTORE THIS ITEM TASK IN THE RECYCLE BIN TASKS MENU.

   OR...

- RIGHT-CLICK THE FILE YOU WANT TO RESTORE AND SELECT RESTORE FROM THE SHORTCUT MENU.

TO EMPTY THE RECYCLE BIN:

- CLICK THE EMPTY RECYCLE BIN TASK FROM THE RECYCLE BIN TASKS MENU.

OR...

- RIGHT-CLICK THE RECYCLE BIN AND SELECT EMPTY RECYCLE BIN FROM THE SHORTCUT MENU.

Figure 4-18. Files display different types of icons to help you identify what type of file they are.

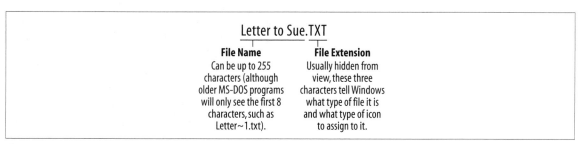

Letter to Sue.TXT

File Name
Can be up to 255 characters (although older MS-DOS programs will only see the first 8 characters, such as Letter~1.txt).

File Extension
Usually hidden from view, these three characters tell Windows what type of file it is and what type of icon to assign to it.

Figure 4-19. Every file has a three-letter extension, which is normally hidden from view, so Windows knows what type of file it is.

Figure 4-20. Files with their three-letter file extensions displayed.

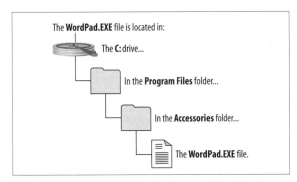

Figure 4-21. A file's path name is determined first by the drive, then by the folder(s), then by the file name.

In this lesson, we'll take a break from all that pointing, clicking, and dragging, and take a closer look at files. When you're viewing the contents of your computer, you've probably already noticed that everything has its own picture or icon to represent what it is. Folder icons almost always look like little manila folders. Files, on the other hand, come in a variety of types and icons.

> **TIP** A root folder, or directory, is the folder from which all the other folders branch. When you double-click the Local Disk (C:) icon, the window shows the contents of the root folder of the C drive.

There are two parts to every file: the *file name* (which you've already seen and are familiar with) and the *file extension*, which is three letters that tell Windows what type of file it is (see Figure 4-19). Since Windows assigns pictures or icons to the types of files it recognizes, it normally hides these file extensions from view. Whenever you open a file by double-clicking it, Windows automatically opens the file in the program it knows created the file. For example, Microsoft Word always adds the file extension DOC to its files, so when you double-click a DOC file, Windows knows it has to open the file in Microsoft Word.

The *path* of a file or folder is another common term. A *file path* is the drive and folder(s) where a file or folder is located—think of it as a street address. A path contains the drive letter, followed by a colon, followed by any folders (which must be separated by backslashes \), and last comes the name of the file. For example C:\Program Files\Accessories\WordPad.EXE (see Figure 4-21 for an illustration).

Table 4-4. Common file types

File Icon	Description
MS-DOS Program	MS-DOS programs are written for an earlier, more primitive operating system than Windows. MS-DOS programs don't have the fancy graphics, icons, and features of more advanced Windows programs. All Windows or DOS programs have .EXE, or sometimes, .COM, extensions. EXE stands for *executable*, meaning the file is a program that will run or execute when you open it.
Unknown File Type	Windows doesn't know what type of file this is, so you can't readily open it by double-clicking it. That doesn't mean the file isn't important – it's probably a very important file for Windows or a program. Leave these files alone unless you absolutely know what they are for.
Word Document	This is a document created in the word processing program, Microsoft Word. Word documents normally have a .DOC extension.
Excel Document	This is a spreadsheet created with the program Microsoft Excel. Excel spreadsheets normally have a .XLS extension.
Paint File (BMP)	This is a graphic file or picture, which was created in Paint or another graphics program. These files are also sometimes referred to as bitmaps. The extension for this particular type of graphic file is .BMP or bitmap. There are also other types of graphic files that use different extensions and icons.
JPEG File	Another very popular graphic file, most of the photographs you see on the Internet are JPEGs.
Text File	Text, or ASCII, files are simple files that only contain text – no formatting, graphics, or any fancy stuff. Text files usually have a .TXT extension.
Shortcut File	Shortcut files point to files and folders elsewhere on your computer so that you can quickly open that file, folder, or program without having to go to its actual location. All of the programs in the Start Menu and some of the items on your desktop are actually shortcuts that point to the program files, located elsewhere on your computer. Shortcuts only point to files or folders, so moving, renaming, or deleting a shortcut does not affect the original program or file in any way. You can tell the difference between a shortcut and an original file because the shortcut has an arrow ( ) in the lower left corner.
Setup Program File	Setup files are special executable (EXE) program files, except instead of running a program when opened, they install software programs onto your computer.

Since Windows assigns icons to help you distinguish between the different types of files, normally the three letter file extensions are hidden from view. You can tell Windows to display the extension, but we'll cover that when we learn how to customize Windows.

Changing How Information Is Displayed

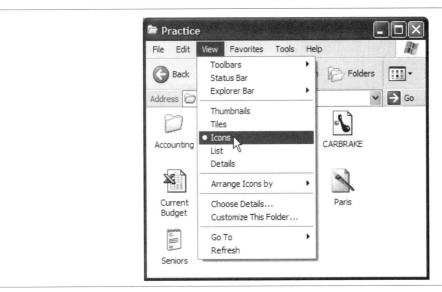

Figure 4-22. A bullet (•) *appears next to the current view.*

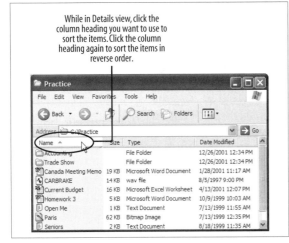

While in Details view, click the column heading you want to use to sort the items. Click the column heading again to sort the items in reverse order.

Figure 4-23. The window displayed in Details view.

When you work with files and folders on your computer, you may find that you need to change how you view information on the screen. This lesson will show you how to change the appearance of items using one of five view modes: Thumbnails, Icons, Tiles, List, or Details. Experiment to find the view that works best for you. You'll also learn how to change the order in which files and folders are sorted. You can sort the contents of files and folders by name, date (when they were created), size, and type (what type of file they are).

1 Click the Start button and select My Computer from the menu.

The My Computer window appears.

2 Navigate to your Practice folder.

Windows normally displays items as icons by default.

3 Select View → Icons from the menu.

You can display the most items in a window at a time by using List view. Try switching to List view now.

4 Select View → List from the menu.

The items are displayed as small icons in a list.

Details view displays information about each item, including the name, size, type of item, and when it was created or last modified.

5 Select View → Details from the menu.

You can sort items in a variety of ways: alphabetically by name, by size, or even by the date they were last modified or saved. If you're in Details view, all you have to do to sort the items is click the heading for the column you want to use.

6 Click the Name column heading to sort the items by name.

The list is sorted alphabetically by name. Clicking the heading again sorts the items in reverse order (Z–A).

7 Select View → Icons from the menu.

You can have Windows arrange and organize items so that they appear in neat columns and rows, instead of as a cluttered mess.

8 Select View → Arrange Icons by → Auto Arrange from the menu.

A check mark appears next to Auto Arrange when this feature is on. (You can skip step 8 if Auto Arrange already has a check mark.) Now, whenever you change the size of a window, or add, move, or delete a file, Windows will automatically rearrange the items.

9 Select View → Arrange Icons by → Name from the menu.

The list is sorted alphabetically by name.

Table 4-5. File and Folder Views

View	Description
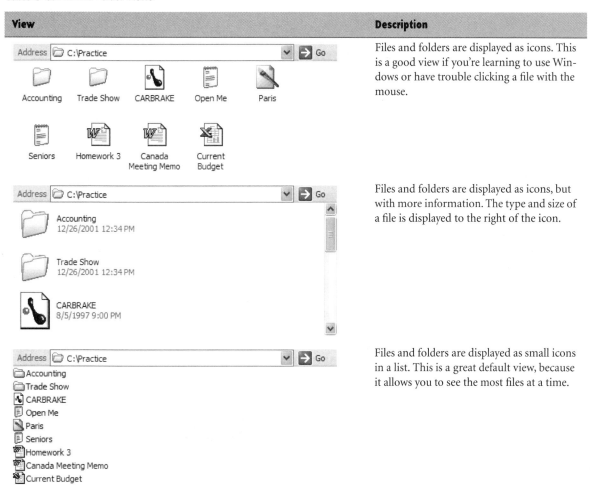	Files and folders are displayed as icons. This is a good view if you're learning to use Windows or have trouble clicking a file with the mouse.
	Files and folders are displayed as icons, but with more information. The type and size of a file is displayed to the right of the icon.
	Files and folders are displayed as small icons in a list. This is a great default view, because it allows you to see the most files at a time.

Table 4-5. File and Folder Views (Continued)

View	Description
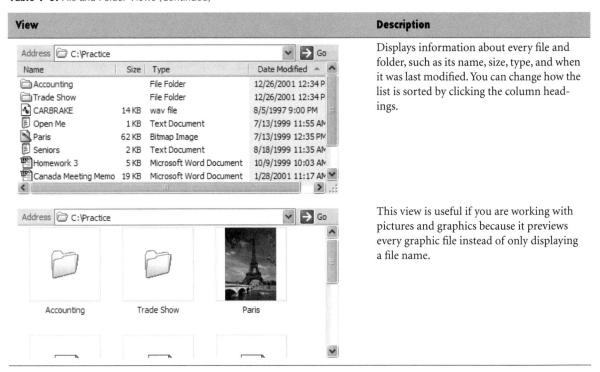	Displays information about every file and folder, such as its name, size, type, and when it was last modified. You can change how the list is sorted by clicking the column headings. This view is useful if you are working with pictures and graphics because it previews every graphic file instead of only displaying a file name.

QUICK REFERENCE

TO CHANGE HOW ITEMS ARE DISPLAYED:

- SELECT VIEW FROM THE MENU BAR AND SELECT ONE OF THE FIVE VIEWS (THUMBNAILS, TILES, ICONS, LIST, OR DETAILS).

OR...

- CLICK THE VIEW BUTTON LIST ARROW AND SELECT A VIEW FROM THE LIST.

TO ARRANGE OR SORT ICONS:

- IF IN DETAILS VIEW, CLICK THE COLUMN HEADING YOU WANT TO USE TO SORT THE WINDOW. CLICK THE COLUMN HEADING AGAIN TO SORT IN REVERSE ORDER.

OR...

- SELECT VIEW → ARRANGE ICONS BY AND CHOOSE AN ARRANGEMENT FROM THE MENU.

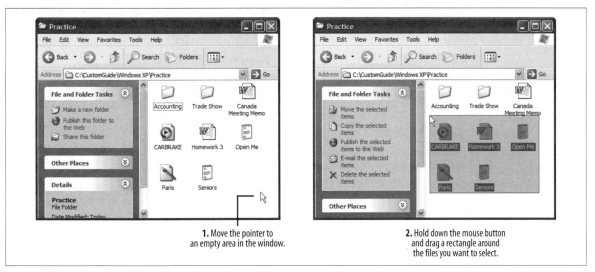

1. Move the pointer to an empty area in the window.

2. Hold down the mouse button and drag a rectangle around the files you want to select.

Figure 4-24. To select several files that are next to each other, hold down the mouse button and drag a rectangle around the files you want to select.

Shift | Click the first file you want to select, press and hold down the **Shift** key and click the last file you want to select.

Figure 4-25. When you want to select a group of adjacent files, select the first file you want to select, hold down the Shift key, and click the last file.

Figure 4-26. Use the Ctrl key when you want to select non-adjacent files.

By now, you know that you must select a file or folder before you can do anything to it, such as move or delete it. In this lesson, you will learn how to select more than one file and/or folder at a time, so you can move, copy, or delete a group of files simultaneously.

1 Navigate to and open your Practice folder.

First, let's review how to select a single file.

2 Click the Paris file to select it.

The Paris file is highlighted, indicating that it is selected. Now you could delete, move, or copy the Paris file. To deselect a file, just click in any empty area of the window.

3 Click any empty area of the window to deselect the Paris file.

The Paris file is no longer selected.

You can select more than one file or folder at a time, so you can delete, move, or copy a whole bunch of files at once. Like so many Windows functions, there are several methods to select multiple files. If the files you want to select are next to each other, you can move the mouse pointer to an empty area of the window, hold down the mouse button, and drag a rectangle around the files you want to select, as shown in Figure 4-24.

4 Move the pointer to any empty area in the folder window, click and hold down the mouse button, and drag a rectangle around several files, as shown in Figure 4-24.

The only problem with this method is that it only works when you want to select files that are next to each other.

5 Click any empty area of the screen to deselect the files.

Another method of selecting adjacent files and folders is to click the first file you want to select, hold down the Shift key, and then click the last file of the group of files you want to select.

6 Click the Carbrake file to select it, then press and hold the Shift key as you click the Paris file.

You've selected the Carbrake file, the Paris file, and all the files that are in between the two.

7 Click any empty area of the screen to deselect the files.

To select non-adjacent files and folders, hold down the Ctrl key and click each item you want to select.

8 Click the Carbrake file to select it, press and hold down the Ctrl key, click the Paris file and the Trade Show folder, then release the Ctrl key.

Remember, you can move, copy, or delete any selected files all at once. Holding down the Ctrl key also lets you click and deselect any selected files.

9 With the files still selected and the Ctrl key still pressed, click and drag one of the selected files (the Carbrake or Paris files, or the Trade Show folder) from the folder window to your Desktop.

All the selected files are copied to the desktop.

10 With the newly copied files still selected on your Desktop, press the Delete key.

The selected files are all deleted from the desktop.

To select all the files and folders in the window, select Edit → Select All from the menu.

11 Select Edit → Select All from the menu.

All the files in the window are selected.

12 Close the window to end this lesson.

QUICK REFERENCE

TO SELECT MULTIPLE ITEMS:

- IF THE ITEMS ARE NEXT TO EACH OTHER, YOU CAN CLICK AND DRAG A RECTANGLE AROUND THE ITEMS YOU WANT TO SELECT.

OR...

- IF THE ITEMS ARE NEXT TO EACH OTHER, YOU CAN CLICK THE FIRST ITEM YOU WANT TO SELECT, PRESS AND HOLD DOWN THE SHIFT KEY, AND CLICK THE LAST ITEM YOU WANT TO SELECT.

- IF THE ITEMS AREN'T NEXT TO EACH OTHER, YOU CAN SELECT NON-ADJACENT ITEMS BY HOLDING THE CTRL KEY AND CLICKING THE ITEMS YOU WANT TO SELECT.

TO SELECT ALL FILES AT ONCE:

- SELECT EDIT → SELECT ALL FROM THE MENU.

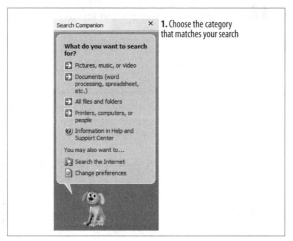

1. Choose the category that matches your search

Figure 4-27. The Search Companion guides your search by asking questions about your search.

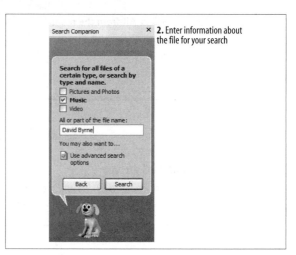

2. Enter information about the file for your search

Figure 4-28. Beginning a music file search.

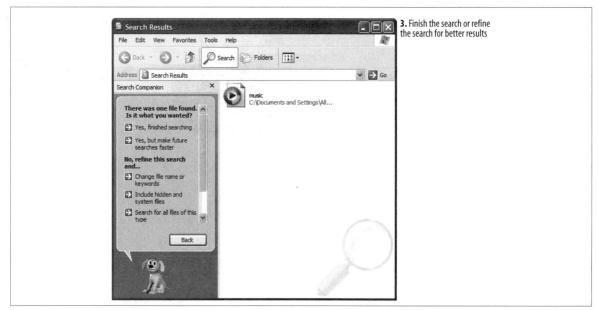

3. Finish the search or refine the search for better results

Figure 4-29. The search results window.

It's just as easy to misplace and lose a file in your computer as it is to misplace your car keys—maybe easier! Luckily, Microsoft has simplified the search process by introducing the Search Companion to Windows XP. A cousin of the Office Assistant, the Search Companion helps you organize your search by asking certain questions, such as what you want to search for (i.e., a picture or a file), which drive to search in, and the file name.

The Search Companion can search for files even when you can't remember the exact file name or location. You can search for a file by:

- The file name or any part of the file name
- The date the file was created or modified
- The type of file, such as a Microsoft Word document or graphic file
- The text within the file
- The size of the file

You can set one or several of these criteria to search for a file.

1 Click the Start button and select Search from the menu.

The Search Results window appears with the Search Companion, as shown in Figure 4-27.

The Search Companion will ask you different questions to help you with your search. For now, let's search for a music file.

2 Click the Pictures, music, or video option.

The next screen of the Search Companion appears, asking you for more details about your search.

3 Check the Music box. Click in the All or part of the file name text box and type David Byrne. Click Search.

The Search Companion begins the search and displays the names and locations of all the files that have the words David Byrne in their names. You can open any of these files by double-clicking them.

4 Double-click the music file.

The music file begins playing in the Windows Media Player.

5 Close the Windows Media program.

If you don't quite remember the file name, you can always search by when you last modified the file, or by the size of the file. We won't do a search using this criteria right now, but we can at least go ahead and figure out where these options are located.

6 To start a new search, click the Search button in the Search Companion.

The first screen of the Search Companion appears.

7 Click the All Files and Folders option.

A dialog box appears, giving options to search by file name, text within the file, location of the file, when it was last modified, size of the file, and other advanced search options to choose from.

8 Type Practice folder in the search options dialog box, and click Search.

The Search Companion searches for folder, and displays all finds in the results window.

9 Click the Search Results window Close button.

Table 4-6. Search options

Search For	Description
Pictures, music, or video	Search for pictures and digital photos (.jpg, .gif, and .bmp); music (.mp3); and digital video (.avi and mpeg) files.
Documents (word processing, spreadsheet, etc.)	Search for files created with a program, such as Microsoft Access (.mdb), Microsoft Excel (.xls), Microsoft PowerPoint (.ppt), Microsoft Word (.doc), or Notepad (.txt)
All files and folders	Search through all types of files and folders.
Computers or people	Search for computers on your network or the name of a person in your address book.
Information in Help and Support Center	Search for information in Microsoft Windows XP's built-in Help system.
Search the Internet	Search the Internet for information on a key word or phrase.
Change Preferences	Change your search preferences, such as whether or not you want to display an animated character or advanced search options.

QUICK REFERENCE

TO USE THE SEARCH COMPANION TO FIND A FILE:

1. CLICK THE START BUTTON AND SELECT SEARCH.

2. SELECT THE TYPE OF FILE YOU WANT TO SEARCH FOR.

3. ENTER PART OF THE FILE NAME OR TEXT WITHIN THE FILE. YOU CAN ALSO SEARCH FOR FILES USING THE DROP-DOWN LISTS AT THE BOTTOM OF THE SEARCH COMPANION.

4. CLICK SEARCH TO BEGIN SEARCHING FOR THE FILE(S).

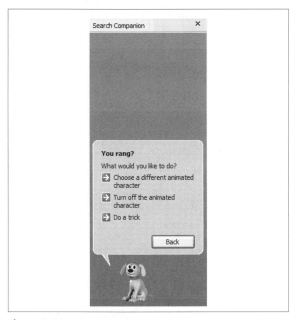

Figure 4-30. Choosing a different Search Companion.

Figure 4-32. Changing Search Companion preferences.

Figure 4-31. Click Back and Next to browse the different character options.

Based on the Microsoft Office Assistant, the animated character in the Search Companion does tricks as you perform your search. Whether your prior experience with animated characters has been charming or annoying, this lesson will teach you how to manage these new Microsoft darlings and how to change preferences in the Search Companion itself.

1 Click the Start button and select Search from the menu.

There's Rover, eager to help you with your next search! He's getting kind of old though, so let's find someone with new tricks.

2 Click Rover (the dog) and click Choose a different animated character.

Scroll through the different characters.

3 Click the Back and Next buttons to scroll through the different characters. Click OK to select a new character.

Rover disappears and the new character pops onto the screen.

Though the new character may be an improvement over Rover, you may want to hide the character altogether.

4 Click the **character** and click **Turn off the animated character.**

The character disappears but the Search Companion remains.

You can customize the Search Companion even more by changing its preferences.

5 Click **Change preferences** in the **Search Companion.**

You can change how the Search Companion works here. Refer to Table 4-7 for more information on these options.

Table 4-7. Search companion preferences

Preference	Description
With/Without an animated character	Hide or show the animated character in the Search Companion.
With Indexing Service (for faster local searches)	The Indexing Service extracts information from your files while the computer is idle, making searches faster.
Change files and folders search behavior	Choose between Default and Advanced: **Default:** Steps you through search options to help you define your search. **Advanced:** Manually enter your own search criteria. Recommended for advanced users only.
Change Internet search behavior	Search the Internet using the Search Companion, or using the classic Internet search without the Search Companion.
Show/Don't Show balloon tips	Toggle balloon tips in the Search Companion on or off.
Turn AutoComplete on/off	Toggle AutoComplete on or off.

QUICK REFERENCE

TO CHANGE THE SEARCH COMPANION CHARACTER:

1. CLICK THE CHARACTER AND SELECT CHOOSE A DIFFERENT ANIMATED CHARACTER FROM THE MENU.

2. CLICK THE NEXT OR BACK BUTTONS UNTIL YOU FIND A CHARACTER YOU LIKE AND CLICK OK.

TO HIDE THE CHARACTER:

• CLICK THE CHARACTER AND CLICK TURN OFF ANIMATED CHARACTER.

TO CHANGE SEARCH COMPANION PREFERENCES:

• CLICK CHANGE PREFERENCES IN THE SEARCH COMPANION.

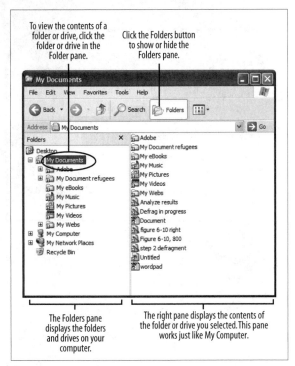

To view the contents of a folder or drive, click the folder or drive in the Folder pane.

Click the Folders button to show or hide the Folders pane.

The Folders pane displays the folders and drives on your computer.

The right pane displays the contents of the folder or drive you selected. This pane works just like My Computer.

Figure 4-33. The Windows Explorer window.

If you have been following the lessons in this chapter, by now you should know just about everything there is to know about file management. You learned that you can use My Computer to view and work with files and folders.

This lesson introduces how to use *Windows Explorer* to view and work with the contents of your computer. Windows Explorer displays the hierarchy of all the folders on your computer in the Folders pane, as shown in Figure 4-33. This is especially useful for when you want to copy and move files—you can drag the files from the Folders pane to the appropriate folder in the right pane. As a shortcut, you can also click the Folders button to view the Folders pane in any window. You would have to open two My Computer windows to accomplish the same thing.

If you're a Windows 95, 98, or NT user, this is the same as the Windows Explorer you're used to; but now you can click the Folders button any time you want to view or work with Windows Explorer.

1 Click the Start button **and select** All Programs → Accessories → Windows Explorer **from the menu.**

The familiar My Documents window appears but the Folders pane is also open, as shown in Figure 4-33. This is where Windows Explorer displays the hierarchy of files and folders on your computer.

You can see what's in a drive or folder by clicking it in the Folders pane.

2 Click My Computer **in the Folders pane.**

Windows Explorer displays the contents of My Computer in the right pane of the window. Move on to the next step to look at the contents of the hard drive.

3 Click Local Disk (C:) **in the Folders pane.**

Explorer displays the contents of your hard drive in the right pane of the window. The Folders pane displays the same drives and folders in a *hierarchical* view.

A plus symbol or a minus symbol beside a folder means a folder contains several subfolders. Normally these subfolders are hidden. You can display the hidden folders within a folder by clicking the plus sign beside the folder.

4 Click the Documents and Settings folder plus symbol **in the Folders pane.**

The Documents and Settings folder expands and displays all the folders within it.

Notice that the plus symbol changes to a minus symbol, indicating the folder is expanded and is displaying all the folders within it. Some of the Windows subfolders also have pluses by them, indicating that they, too, contain several subfolders.

5 Click the All Users **folder in the Folders pane.**

The contents of the All Users folder appear in the right pane of the Explorer window. Notice that the subfolders in the All Users folder are displayed in both the left and right panes.

You can collapse or hide folders to reduce the amount of information on the screen.

6 Click the Documents and Settings folder minus symbol **in the Folders pane.**

The Documents and Settings folder collapses and all its subfolders are hidden from view. The minus symbol changes to a plus symbol, indicating that all the subfolders in the Documents and Settings folder are hidden from view.

You can also adjust the size of the Folders pane.

7 Position the mouse over the right border of the Folders pane until the ⩘ pointer changes to a ↔, then drag to the right about a half-inch.

The Folders pane is now a bit wider.

Just like My Computer, you can change how information is displayed using the View menu.

8 Select View → Icons from the menu.

The contents in the right pane of Explorer are displayed in Icon view.

9 Select View → List from the menu.

The contents in the right pane of Explorer are displayed in List view.

It's important to remember that the right pane is still basically My Computer, so the procedures for creating, opening, renaming, moving, copying, and deleting files and folders are exactly the same.

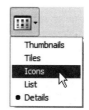

Other ways to Change Views:
• Click the view button list arrow and select a view from the list.

QUICK REFERENCE

TO VIEW WINDOWS EXPLORER:

• CLICK THE START BUTTON AND SELECT ALL PROGRAMS → ACCESSORIES → WINDOWS EXPLORER FROM THE MENU.

OR...

CLICK THE FOLDERS BUTTON IN A WINDOW TOOLBAR.

TO VIEW THE CONTENTS OF A DRIVE OR FOLDER:

• CLICK THE DRIVE OR FOLDER IN THE FOLDERS PANE–THE CONTENTS OF THAT DRIVE OR FOLDER WILL APPEAR IN THE RIGHT PANE.

TO DISPLAY OR HIDE A DRIVE OR FOLDER'S SUBFOLDERS:

• CLICK PLUS SYMBOL ⊞ TO DISPLAY ANY HIDDEN SUBFOLDERS, AND CLICK THE MINUS SYMBOL ⊟ TO HIDE ANY SUBFOLDERS.

TO RESIZE THE FOLDERS PANE:

• CLICK AND DRAG THE RIGHT BORDER OF THE FOLDERS PANE.

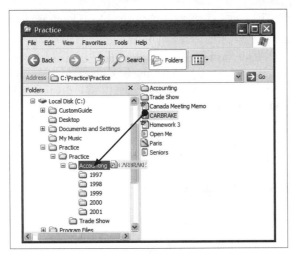

Figure 4-34. You can move and copy files using click and drag in Windows Explorer.

In this lesson, you'll learn how to perform basic file management in the Windows Explorer using the Folders pane. Specifically, you'll move a file and create a new folder. Again, although the Folders pane looks a little different than the rest of the My Computer screen, all the file management procedures you've learned still apply. If you've followed the other lessons, this should be a nice review of the chapter.

1 Make sure you have Windows Explorer open.

If you need to start Windows Explorer click, the Start button and select All Programs → Accessories → Windows Explorer from the menu.

2 Click the Local Disk (C:) icon in the Folders pane.

The contents of the (C:) drive appear in the right pane, and it expands in the left pane to show its sub-folders.

3 Click the Practice folder to display its contents.

The folder expands and displays all the files inside it, and the plus symbol (⊞) changes to a minus symbol. Since you can see all the files in the right pane, it's much easier to move and copy files and folders.

4 Hold down the Ctrl key while you click and drag the CARBRAKE file to the Accounting folder, as shown in Figure 4-34.

The Carbrake file is copied to the Accounting folder.

It wouldn't have mattered if you dragged and dropped the Carbrake file to the Accounting folder in the left pane or the right pane—it's the same folder. Move on to the next step and let's see if you can create a new folder while the Folders pane is displayed.

5 Create a new folder named 2002 in the root directory of the (C:) drive.

Need a refresher on how to create a folder? First, click the (C:) drive in the Folder pane to display its contents in the right pane. Next, click Make a new folder in the File and Folder Tasks menu, type 2002, and press Enter.

6 Click and drag the new 2002 folder from the right pane to the Accounting folder in the Folders pane.

Verify that the 2002 folder was moved inside the Accounting folder.

7 Click the plus symbol beside the Accounting folder.

The Accounting folder expands and displays all the folders inside it.

Try deleting a folder using Windows Explorer—you already know the technique.

8 Click the 2001 folder, press the Delete key, and then click Yes.

It doesn't matter if you use the left or right pane to select a folder—they're the same folder, and you can rename, copy, move, and delete folders in either pane of the window.

9 Close the Windows Explorer window to end this lesson.

Congratulations! You've just about completed what is probably the most difficult chapter in the book.

QUICK REFERENCE

TO MOVE A FILE OR FOLDER:

- DRAG THE FILE OR FOLDER TO THE DESIRED LOCATION IN THE FOLDERS PANE.

TO COPY A FILE OR FOLDER:

- HOLD DOWN THE CTRL KEY WHILE YOU DRAG THE FILE OR FOLDER TO THE DESIRED LOCATION IN THE FOLDERS PANE.

TO CREATE A NEW FOLDER:

1. CLICK THE DISK OR FOLDER WHERE YOU WANT TO PUT THE NEW FOLDER.

2. CLICK THE MAKE A NEW FOLDER TASK IN THE FILE AND FOLDER TASKS MENU.

3. TYPE A NAME FOR THE FOLDER AND PRESS ENTER.

TO DELETE A FILE OR FOLDER:

- SELECT THE FILE OR FOLDER AND PRESS THE DELETE KEY. CLICK YES TO CONFIRM THE DELETION.

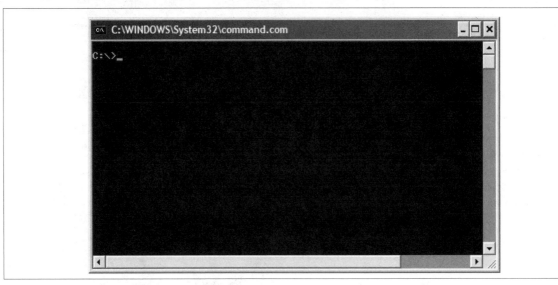

Figure 4-35. MS-DOS running inside a window.

Figure 4-36. The DOS prompt.

In the beginning, before there was Windows, there was MS-DOS. MS-DOS (Microsoft Disk Operating System) didn't have any windows, pointers, or icons—you ran programs, changed folders, and copied files by typing difficult commands. Windows has been around for a long time, so thankfully there aren't many DOS programs still around. Regardless, one day you might be on the phone with technical support and be told to go to an MS-DOS prompt. To prepare you for that day, here's a lesson all about MS-DOS.

1 Click the Start button and select Run.

The Run dialog box appears.

2 Type COMMAND in the box and click OK.

The MS-DOS Prompt window appears, as shown in Figure 4-35.

Yes, that stark, barren screen was all people had to work with to run programs, copy files, and navigate between folders in the old-fashioned days of the computer. Notice the DOS prompt, which tells you the current drive (C:).

Move on to the next step to see how you changed folders in MS-DOS.

3 Type CD WINDOWS and press Enter.

TIP   *The ★ (asterisk) is a wildcard character—use it as a substitution for any part of a file name in MS-DOS. For example, typing DEL ★.TMP would delete all the files with a .TMP extension in the current folder.*

The clumsy, hard-to-remember command you just typed brought you to the WINDOWS subfolder. Notice the DOS prompt changes to C:\ WINDOWS.

MS-DOS doesn't automatically display all the files and subfolders in the current folder like My Computer or Windows Explorer—you have to tell MS-DOS to display the contents of the current directory. Here's how:

4 Type DIR /W and press Enter.

The DIR (which stands for *directory*) command displays the contents of the current folder. The /W switch tells DOS to display the contents in wide mode—otherwise the contents of the current drive wouldn't fit on one screen and you wouldn't be able to view them all.

To run a program in DOS, go to the program's folder and type the program's name.

5 Type EDIT and press Enter.

The DOS-based EDIT program appears.

DOS programs aren't as standardized as their more advanced Windows successors, so even the most basic commands, such as how to exit a program, vary greatly between programs.

6 Press the Alt key then F (to open the File menu) then X (to exit the EDIT program).

You exit from the EDIT program and return to the desolate MS-DOS screen.

7 Type CD .. and press Enter.

This cryptic command changes to the previous parent folder. Let's return to the warm and user-friendly world of Windows.

8 Type EXIT and press Enter.

TIP *Most DOS commands have additional options called switches, which you specify after the DOS command, preceded by a /. Type /? after a DOS command to view all the switches or options for the command.*

The MS-DOS Prompt window closes.

Table 4-8. Common MS-DOS commands

Command	Syntax	Description
A: (Drive Letter)	[drive letter]	Change the current drive.
		Example: D: would change to the D: drive.
DIR	DIR	Displays the names of all the files and folders in a folder.
		Example: DIR /W displays the contents of the current folder in wide screen view.
COPY	COPY [source file] [destination]	Copies one or more files to another location.
		Example: COPY LETTER.TXT A: would copy the LETTER.TXT file to the A: drive.
XCOPY	XCOPY [source file] [destination]	XCOPY is a super-charged version of COPY.
		Example: XCOPY A:*.* C:\NEW would copy all the files in the A: drive to the NEW folder on the C: drive. If the NEW folder didn't exist on the C: drive, XCOPY would create the folder.
DEL	DEL [path] [filename]	Deletes one or more files.
		Example: DEL *.TMP would erase any files in the current folder with .TMP file extensions.
RENAME	RENAME [old name] [new name]	Renames a file or folder.
		Example: RENAME LETTER.TXT APPROVE.TXT would rename the LETTER.TXT file to APPROVE.TXT.
CD	CD [path]	Change the current folder. Type .. to change to the previous parent folder.
		Example: CD TEMP would change to the TEMP folder, CD .. would change to the root folder of the C: drive.
MD	MD [folder name]	Creates or makes a new folder.
		Example: MD DOCS would create a new folder named DOCS.
RD	RD [folder name]	Deletes a folder.
		Example: RD DOS would delete the DOCS folder.

QUICK REFERENCE

TO USE THE MS-DOS PROMPT:

1. CLICK THE START BUTTON AND SELECT RUN.

2. TYPE COMMAND IN THE BOX AND CLICK OK.

3. ENTER YOUR COMMANDS IN THE DOS PROMPT.

TO EXIT BACK TO WINDOWS:

• TYPE EXIT AND PRESS ENTER.

Creating and Using a Compressed Folder

A compressed folder
has a zipper on the folder icon.

Figure 4-37. A zipped folder in the Practice folder.

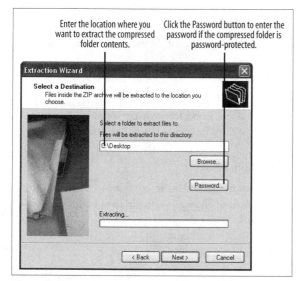

Enter the location where you want to extract the compressed folder contents.

Click the Password button to enter the password if the compressed folder is password-protected.

Figure 4-38. The Extraction Wizard.

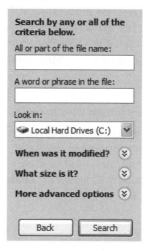

All Files and Folders Search Options

You can reduce the amount of storage a folder and its contents consumes on a drive by using a compressed, or *zipped*, folder. Compressed folders occupy less space on a drive, which also makes them easier to transfer and share with other computers. You can work with a compressed folder and its contents just as you would work with a regular folder.

1 Click the Start button and select My Computer.

The My Computer window appears.

2 Navigate to and open your Practice folder.

The contents of the (C:) drive appear.

3 Select File → New → Compressed (zipped) Folder from the menu.

A new compressed folder with a temporary name "New Compressed (zipped) Folder" appears in the drive.

4 Type Zip and press Enter.

The compressed folder is renamed, as shown in Figure 4-37.

You can save and move files and and folders saved in a compressed folder just like you would with a regular folder. Files and folders saved in a compressed folder are also compressed, but this doesn't change how you work with them.

5 Click and drag the Seniors file into the Zip folder.

Notice that a copy of the Seniors file still appears in the Practice folder. A compressed file is simply another version of the file, so instead of moving the original file into the compressed folder, a compressed *copy* of the file is created.

6 Double-click the Zip folder.

The Seniors file really is in the folder. You can view the compression ratio (compressed vs. uncompressed) by switching to Details view.

7 Click the Views button and select Details from the list.

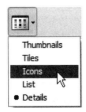

Other ways to Change Views:
• Click the view button list arrow and select a view from the list.

Notice the Packed size column and the Size column. The *packed size* is the amount of space the compressed file occupies. The *size* is the amount of space the uncompressed file occupies. As you can see from the Ratio column, the file has a compression ratio of 50 percent. Not bad!

Now let's make sure the file really hasn't changed, even though it has been compressed.

1 Double-click the Seniors file.

The Seniors file opens in Notepad. As you can see, the file opens just as it would from a non-compressed file.

2 Click the Notepad Close button.

The Notepad window closes.

Extracting is a term often used with compressed files. This is really just a technical term for decompressing files by moving them out of a compressed folder. You can extract a single file simply by moving it out of the folder. Or you can extract all the files from the compressed folder at the same time.

3 Click the Up button on the toolbar. Right-click the Zip folder and select Extract All from the shortcut menu.

The first screen of the Extraction Wizard appears

4 Click Next.

Select where you want the extracted file to be saved.

5 Click the Browse button. Click Desktop and click OK.

If the compressed folder is password-protected, click the Password button to enter the password.

6 Click Next.

The compressed files are extracted to the location you specified, as shown in the file path in the Extraction Wizard.

7 Click Finish.

A new window appears, letting you know the files have been extracted.

Some files may exhibit better compression ratios than others. For example, JPEG graphics files (which are already compressed) may actually become larger when compressed.

QUICK REFERENCE

TO CREATE A COMPRESSED FOLDER:

1. NAVIGATE TO WHERE YOU WANT TO SAVE THE COMPRESSED FOLDER.

2. SELECT FILE → NEW → COMPRESSED (ZIPPED) FOLDER FROM THE MENU.

3. TYPE A NAME FOR YOUR FOLDER AND PRESS ENTER.

TO EXTRACT FILES FROM A COMPRESSED FOLDER:

1. RIGHT-CLICK THE COMPRESSED FOLDER CONTAINING THE FILES YOU WISH TO REMOVE AND SELECT EXTRACT ALL FROM THE SHORTCUT MENU.

2. CLICK NEXT.

3. CLICK THE BROWSE BUTTON AND NAVIGATE TO WHERE YOU WOULD LIKE TO MOVE THE EXTRACTED FILES.

4. CLICK OK.

5. CLICK NEXT, THEN CLICK FINISH.

Chapter Four Review

Lesson Summary

Understanding Storage Devices, Folders, and Files

Computers store information on disk drives using files and folders, just like you store information in a file cabinet.

Know the following memory terminology and its corresponding size:

ByteA single character such as the letter j or number 8.

- Kilobyte (K or KB): 1,024 bytes – a typed page.
- Megabyte (MB or MEG): 1,048,578 bytes – a novel.
- Gigabyte (GB or GIG): 1,000,000,000 bytes – several encyclopedia sets.

Using My Computer to See What's in Your Computer

Click the Start button and select My Computer to view the contents of your computer.

Double-click a disk drive in the My Computer window to display the disk drive's contents.

To View the Properties of Something: Right-click the drive, folder, or file and select Properties from the shortcut menu. For example, right-clicking a hard drive and selecting Properties from the shortcut menu would display how much space is left on the hard disk.

Opening a Folder

Double-click a folder to open it and display its contents.

To Move Back or Up to the Previous Level or Folder: Click the Up button on the toolbar, click the Back button on the toolbar, or click the Address list arrow on the toolbar and select the appropriate drive or folder.

Creating and Renaming a Folder

To Create a New Folder: Open the disk or folder where you want to put the new folder. Select the Make a new folder task from the File and Folder Tasks menu, or, right-click any empty area in the window and select New → Folder from the shortcut menu. Type a name for the folder and press Enter.

To Rename a Folder: Click the folder to select it, select the Rename this folder task from the File and Folder Tasks menu, type a name for the folder and press Enter. You can also rename a folder by clicking the folder to select it, selecting File → Rename from the menu, typing a name for the folder and pressing Enter.

Copying, Moving, and Deleting a Folder

Move a Folder (Click and Drag Method): Move a folder by dragging it to the desired location, such as another folder or onto the desktop (you might have to open another My Computer window if you want to copy it to another folder).

Move a Folder: Select the folder and click the Move this folder task in the File and Folder Tasks menu, select the drive or folder where you want to move the folder and click Move.

Copy a Folder (Click and Drag Method): Hold down the Ctrl key while you drag the folder to the desired location (you might have to open another My Computer window if you want to copy it to another folder).

Copy a Folder: Click the folder to select it, click the Copy this folder task in the File and Folder Tasks menu, select the drive or folder where you want to copy the folder and click Copy..

To Delete a Folder: Select the folder and press the Delete key. Click Yes to confirm the folder deletion.

Opening, Renaming, and Deleting a File

Double-click a file to open the file in the program that created it.

To Rename a File: Click the file to select it, select the Rename this file task in the File and Folder Tasks menu, enter the file's new name and press Enter. Or, right-click the file, select Rename from the shortcut menu, type a name for the folder and press Enter.

To Delete a File: Select the file and press the Delete key. Click Yes to confirm the deletion.

Copying and Moving a File

You can copy and move files the same as you copy and move folders.

Move a File: Click the file to select it and click the Move this file task in the File and Folder Tasks menu. Select the drive or folder where you want to move the file and click Move.

Copy a File (Click and Drag Method): Hold down the Ctrl key while you drag the file to the desired location (you might have to open another My Computer window if you want to copy it to another folder).

Copy a File: Click the file to select it, click the Copy this file task in the File and Folder Tasks menu, select the drive or folder where you want to copy the file and click Copy.

Restoring a Deleted File and Emptying the Recycle Bin

To Restore a Deleted File: Double-click the Recycle Bin to open it. Select the file you want to restore and click the Restore this item task in the Recycle Bin Tasks menu. Or, right-click the file you want to restore and select Restore from the shortcut menu.

To Empty the Recycle Bin: Right-click the Recycle Bin and select Empty Recycle Bin from the shortcut menu.

A Closer Look at Files and Folders

There are two parts to a file: the **file name**, which can be up to 255 characters, and the **file extension**, which is three characters long and tells Windows what type of file it is.

The **path** of a file or folder is the drive and folder where a file or folder is located (its address).

Changing How Information is Displayed

To Change How Items are Displayed: Select View from the menu bar and select one of the five views, or, select a view from the View button list arrow on the toolbar.

The five view modes are Thumbnails, Tiles, Icons, List, and Details.

To Arrange or Sort Icons: Select View → Arrange Icons by and choose an arrangement from the menu, or, if you are in Details view, simply click the column heading you want to use to sort the window.

Selecting Multiple Files and Folders

By selecting multiple files and folders you can move, copy, or delete a group of files and folders all at once.

If the files are next to each other, you can click and drag a rectangle around the files you want to select. If you don't like that method, click the first file you want to select,

press and hold down the Shift key, and click the last file you want to select.

If the files aren't next to each other, you can select random files by holding the Ctrl key and clicking the files you want to select.

Select Edit → Select All from the menu to select all files at once.

Finding a File Using the Search Companion

To Find a File: Click the Start button and select Search from the menu. Select the type of file you want to search for and enter any part of the file name or text within the file. Use the Search Companion to enter information (file name, size, type, text within the file, date it was last modified, etc.) about the file you're searching for. Click Search to begin searching for the file(s).

Managing the Search Companion

To change the animated character, click the character and select Change the animated character from the menu. Click the Next or Back buttons until you find a character you like, then click OK.

To hide the character, click the character and select Turn off animated character from the menu.

To change search companion preferences, click the Change preferences option in the Search Companion.

Using the Windows Explorer

To View Windows Explorer: Click the Start button and select All Programs → Accessories → Windows Explorer from the menu. Or, click the Folders button in a window toolbar.

To View the Contents of a Drive or Folder: Click the drive or folder in the Folders pane—the contents of that drive or folder will appear in the right pane.

To Display or Hide a Drive or Folder's Subfolders: Click plus symbol (⊞) to display any hidden subfolders, click the minus symbol (⊟) to hide any subfolders.

To Resize the Folders Pane: Click and drag the right border of the Folders pane.

File Management Using Windows Explorer

To Move a File or Folder: Drag the file or folder to the desired location in the Folders pane.

To Copy a File or Folder: Hold down the Ctrl key while you drag the file or folder to the desired location in the Folders pane.

To Create a New Folder: Click the drive or folder where you want to put the new folder and click the Make a new folder task in the File and Folder Tasks menu. Type a name for the folder and press Enter.

To Delete a File or Folder: Select the file or folder and press the Delete key. Click Yes to confirm the deletion.

Using MS-DOS

To Use the MS-DOS Prompt: Click the Start button and select Run. Type COMMAND in the box and click OK, then enter your commands in the DOS prompt.

To Exit from the MS-DOS Prompt: Type EXIT and press Enter.

Creating and Using a Compressed Folder

To Create a Compressed Folder: Click the Start button and select My Computer from the menu. Navigate to and open the folder you want to compress, then select File → New → Compressed (zipped) Folder from the menu. Type a name for your folder and press Enter.

To Extract a File from a Compressed Folder: Right-click the compressed folder containing the files you want to remove and select Extract All from the shortcut menu. Click Next on the first page of the Extraction Wizard, then click the Browse button and select the folder you wish to move the extracted files to. Click OK when you're finished, click Next, then click Finish.

Quiz

1. Computers store information on which types of disks? (Select all that apply.)

    A. Floppy disks.

    B. Hard disks.

    C. Compact discs (CD-ROMs).

    D. Removable disks.

2. The purpose of your computer's folders is to: (Select all that apply).

    A. Lose your important files.

    B. Store related files and programs in the same place.

    C. Make it difficult to delete things unless you really know what you're doing.

    D. Organize related files and information on your computer.

3. .TXT, .DOC, and .BMP — these are all examples of:

    A. Three meaningless letters with a period in front of them.

    B. File extensions.

    C. Types of advanced degrees in computers.

    D. How confusing computers are.

4. Which program(s) can you use to view and manage the contents of your computer? (Select all that apply.)

   A. Netscape Navigator.

   B. My Computer.

   C. System Sleuth.

   D. Windows Explorer.

5. You open a file or folder by double-clicking it. (True or False?)

6. Do this to display the contents of a certain drive or folder:

   A. Right-click the drive or folder.

   B. Click the drive or folder while holding down the Alt key.

   C. Double-click the drive or folder.

   D. Triple-click the drive or folder.

7. To view an object's properties, right-click the object and select Properties from the shortcut menu. (True or False?)

8. When you're browsing the contents of your computer, do this to move back or up to the previous level or folder: (Select all that apply.)

   A. Click the Up button on the toolbar.

   B. Click the Back button on the toolbar.

   C. Press Ctrl + Z.

   D. Click the Address Bar on the toolbar and select the appropriate drive or folder.

9. Which of the following statements is NOT true?

   A. You can move a file or folder to a new location by dragging and dropping it.

   B. You can rename a file or folder by right-clicking it, selecting Rename from the shortcut menu, typing the new name, and pressing Enter.

   C. A plus symbol (⊞) next to a folder in Windows Explorer indicates the folder is locked and cannot be modified or deleted.

   D. Holding down the Ctrl key while you're dragging and dropping something copies it instead of moving it.

10. Delete a file or folder by clicking it, pressing the Delete key, and confirming the deletion. (True or False?)

11. Do this to select multiple files and folders: (Select all that apply.)

    A. Click and drag a rectangle around any adjacent files you want to select.

    B. Select File → Select Multiple Files from the menu, and then click the files you want to select.

    C. Click the first file you want to select, press and hold down the Shift key, then click the last file you want to select.

    D. Hold down the Ctrl key and click the files you want to select.

12. Which of the following statements is NOT true? (Select all that apply.)

    A. You can find a file on your computer by clicking the Start button, selecting Search, entering what you want to search for and clicking Search.

    B. Open Windows Explorer by clicking the Start button and selecting All Programs → Accessories → Windows Explorer.

    C. To save a file in a location other than the program's default folder, you have to save the file and then use My Computer or Windows Explorer to move the file to the desired location.

    D. You can display the contents of a drive or folder using Thumbnails, Tiles, Icons, List, or Details View.

13. The three-letter extension of a file is normally displayed in Windows XP. (True or False?)

Homework

1. Open My Computer.

2. View the contents of your Local Disk (C:).

3. Create a new folder in the root directory of your Local Disk (C:).

4. Name the new folder "Project Files."

5. Delete the Project Files folder from the (C:) drive.

6. Open the Recycle Bin and find the deleted Project Files folder. Do you know how to retrieve it?

7. Open Windows Explorer and view the contents of the (A:) drive.

8. Use the Windows Explorer View menu to display the contents of the (A:) drive in List view.

9. While you're still in List view, sort the files in alphabetical order.

10. Use the Start menu's Search feature to find all the files named "readme.txt" on your (C:) drive. Open one of these files by double-clicking it.

Quiz Answers

1. A, B, C, and D. Computers can store their information on any of these disk types.

2. B and D.

3. B. File extensions, which are used to identify the file type.

4. B and D. My Computer and Windows Explorer both display the contents of your computer and allow you to manage your computer's files and folders.

5. True. Double-clicking a file or folder opens it.

6. C. Double-click a folder to open it and display its contents.

7. True. Right-clicking an object and selecting Properties from the shortcut menu displays the properties of the object.

8. A, B, and D. Any of these will bring you back to the previous level or folder.

9. C. A plus symbol (⊞) next to a folder in Windows Explorer means the folder contains subfolders.

10. True.

11. A, C, and D. You can use any of these methods to select multiple files and folders.

12. C. You can easily save a file in a different location by opening the drive and/or folder where you want to save the file and clicking Save.

13. False. File extensions are normally hidden in Windows XP.

CHAPTER 5

CUSTOMIZING THE TASKBAR AND DESKTOP

CHAPTER OBJECTIVES:

Move, size, and hide the Taskbar

Customize the Start Menu

Work with the Quick Launch Bar

Open recently used files

Start a program with the Run command

Add shortcuts to the Desktop

Start a program when Windows starts

Prerequisites

- **Know how to use the mouse to click, double-click, drag and drop, and right-click.**
- **Know how to use menus, toolbars, and dialog boxes.**
- **Know how to view and navigate the contents of your computer (disk drives and folders).**
- **Know how to create, move, copy, and delete files and folders.**

When you turn on your computer and Windows loads and eventually pops to life on your screen, the first things you see are the *desktop* and *taskbar*. Not only are the desktop and taskbar the first things you see when you start Windows, they never leave your computer at all—unless you shut it off, that is. That's because the taskbar and desktop are two of the most important parts of Windows. The taskbar is the control center for Windows—where you start and manage all your programs. The desktop is your workspace—where you actually get your work done.

Because the taskbar and desktop are so important, this entire chapter is devoted just to them. In this chapter, you'll learn how to customize the taskbar and desktop so they work best for you. Customizing the taskbar and desktop is a lot like arranging furniture in an empty living room—there's no right way of doing it; just do whatever works best for you.

In this chapter, you'll learn how to move, size, and hide the taskbar; how to add and remove programs and folders to and from the Programs menu; and how to add shortcuts to the Windows desktop.

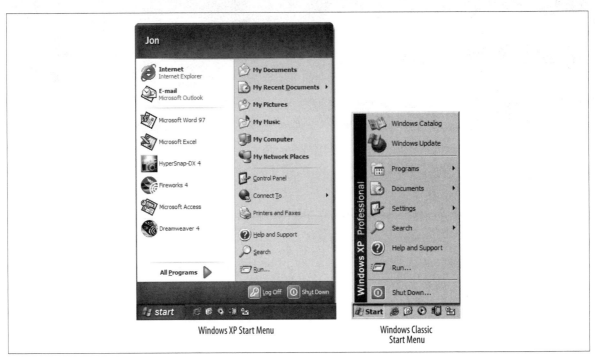

Windows XP Start Menu

Windows Classic
Start Menu

Figure 5-1. You can use the Start menu in either Windows XP mode or Windows Classic mode, both shown here.

Figure 5-2. The Start Menu tab of the Taskbar and Start Menu Properties dialog box.

Toolbars	▶
Cascade Windows	
Tile Windows Horizontally	
Tile Windows Vertically	
Show the Desktop	
Task Manager	
Lock the Taskbar	
Properties	

**Taskbar shortcut
menu**

It might take a while to become accustomed to the new Windows XP Start menu, especially if you're familiar with the Start menu used in earlier versions of Windows. Don't worry: if you don't like the new Windows XP Start menu, it's easy to change back to the more familiar Classic Start menu. Here's how to do it:

1 Right-click a blank area on the Windows taskbar.

A shortcut menu for the taskbar appears.

2 Select Properties from the shortcut menu.

The Taskbar and Start Menu Properties dialog box appears.

3 Click the Start Menu tab.

The Start Menu tab appears, as shown in Figure 5-1. You can choose how the Start menu looks and behaves by selecting one of the following two options:

- **Start menu:** Use the new Windows XP Start menu that gives you quick access to your documents, pictures, music, and recently used programs.
- **Classic Start menu:** Use a Start menu that has the same look and behavior as earlier versions of Windows.

4 Select the Classic Start menu option.

You can further customize the Start menu, such as what it shows or hides, by clicking the Customize button—although most of the Start menu options listed under the Customize button are rather inconsequential.

5 Click OK when you're finished.

That's it—you can now use the classic Start menu that you've grown to know and love.

QUICK REFERENCE

TO USE THE START MENU IN CLASSIC MODE:

1. RIGHT-CLICK A BLANK AREA OF THE WINDOWS TASKBAR AND SELECT PROPERTIES FROM THE SHORTCUT MENU.

2. CLICK THE START MENU TAB.

3. SELECT THE CLASSIC START MENU OPTION.

4. (OPTIONAL) CLICK CUSTOMIZE TO FURTHER CUSTOMIZE THE BEHAVIOR OF THE START MENU.

5. CLICK OK.

Figure 5-3. A window and desktop in Windows XP style.

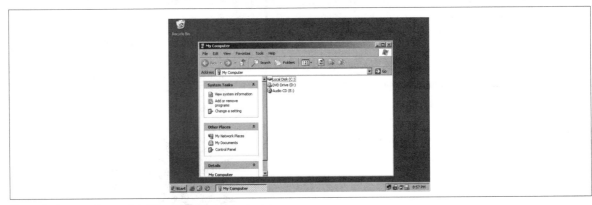

Figure 5-4. A window and desktop in Windows classic style.

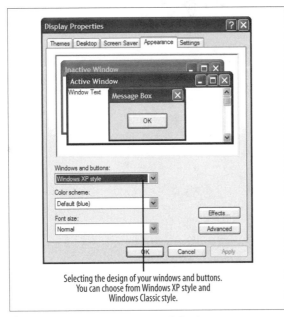

Selecting the design of your windows and buttons.
You can choose from Windows XP style and
Windows Classic style.

Figure 5-5. The Display Properties dialog box.

Don't like the bold new look of Windows XP? Give Windows the look of early, more serious-looking versions.

1 Right-click a blank area on the desktop, select Properties from the shortcut menu, and click the Appearance tab.

You have two choices:

- **Windows XP Style:** The radical new look and feel for Windows XP, with rounded corners, big buttons, and bright crayon-like colors.
- **Windows Classic Style:** The look and feel you're probably used to from previous versions of Windows, with square corners and a no-nonsense design.

2 Click the Windows and buttons list arrow and select Windows Classic style from the list.

That's it—all that's left is to close the Display Properties dialog box.

3 Click OK.

QUICK REFERENCE

TO SWITCH TO WINDOWS CLASSIC STYLE:

1. RIGHT-CLICK A BLANK AREA ON THE DESKTOP AND SELECT PROPERTIES FROM THE SHORTCUT MENU.

2. CLICK THE APPEARANCE TAB.

3. CLICK THE WINDOWS AND BUTTONS LIST ARROW AND SELECT WINDOWS CLASSIC STYLE FROM THE LIST.

4. CLICK OK.

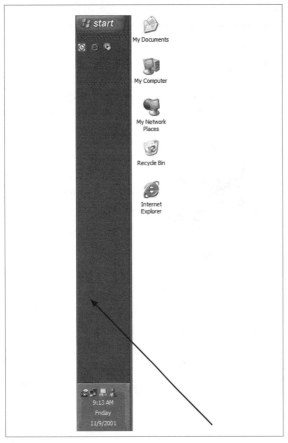

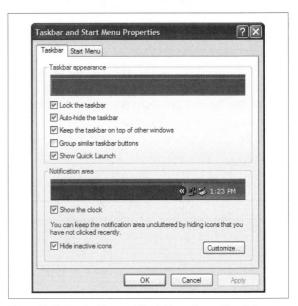

Figure 5-7. The taskbar and Start Menu Properties dialog box.

Figure 5-6. You can position the taskbar at the top, bottom, left, and right of the screen.

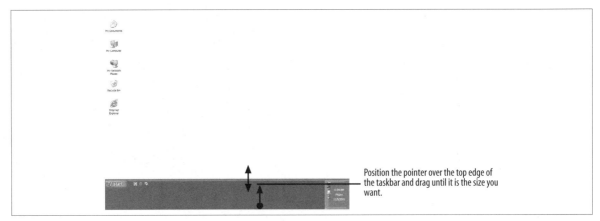

Position the pointer over the top edge of the taskbar and drag until it is the size you want.

Figure 5-8. You can resize the taskbar so it displays more information.

The taskbar is the command center for Windows, which is why it rests along the bottom of the screen, ready for use. Still, some people think the taskbar should be located in a different, more convenient location on the screen. Others don't like how the ever-present taskbar occupies a half-inch of valuable desktop space. This lesson will show you how to move the taskbar to a new location on the screen, how to change the size of the taskbar, and how to hide the taskbar to give you more room on the screen.

You will probably have to unlock the taskbar before you can move it. Here's how…

1 Right-click the taskbar and uncheck Lock the taskbar from the shortcut menu.

Now you're free to move the taskbar to a new location on the screen.

Taskbar shortcut menu

2 Position the mouse over a blank area of the taskbar and hold down the mouse button.

Move on to the next step and let's move the taskbar to a new location on the screen.

3 Drag the taskbar to the left of your screen and release the mouse button, as shown in Figure 5-6.

An outline of the taskbar appears to show where you're moving the taskbar. By dragging and dropping, you've moved the taskbar to the left side of the screen, as shown in Figure 5-6. You can move the taskbar to the top, bottom, left, or right edge of the screen.

4 Drag the taskbar back to the bottom of the screen.

You can also change the size of the taskbar to display more or less information.

5 Position the pointer over the top of the taskbar until it changes to a ↕.

6 Drag the taskbar up a half-inch and the release the mouse button, as shown in Figure 5-8.

The taskbar is resized.

7 Drag the taskbar back to its previous size.

You can also resize the taskbar so that it disappears entirely from the screen. If you can't find your taskbar, it has either been resized until it's almost off the screen (in which case you will need to resize it), or else the taskbar is hidden.

8 Right-click a blank area of the taskbar.

A shortcut menu for the taskbar appears.

9 Select Properties from the shortcut menu.

The Taskbar and Start Menu Properties dialog box appears, as shown in Figure 5-8.

10 Click the Auto-hide the taskbar check box and click OK.

The dialog box closes and the taskbar disappears. Don't worry—the taskbar is still there, it's just hidden.

11 Position the pointer over the bottom of the screen.

The taskbar reappears whenever the mouse pointer is near the bottom of the screen. When you move the mouse away from the bottom of the screen, the taskbar will disappear.

12 Right-click a blank area of the taskbar, select Properties from the shortcut menu, and click the Auto-hide the taskbar check box and click OK.

The Taskbar reappears on the screen.

QUICK REFERENCE

TO LOCK/UNLOCK THE TASKBAR:

- RIGHT-CLICK THE TASKBAR AND SELECT LOCK THE TASKBAR FROM THE SHORTCUT MENU. (IF THE OPTION IS CHECKED, IT IS LOCKED.)

TO MOVE THE TASKBAR:

- POSITION THE POINTER OVER A BLANK AREA ON THE TASKBAR AND CLICK AND DRAG THE TASKBAR TO THE TOP, BOTTOM, LEFT, OR RIGHT OF THE SCREEN.

TO RESIZE THE TASKBAR:

- POSITION THE POINTER OVER THE TOP EDGE OF THE TASKBAR UNTIL THE POINTER CHANGES, THEN DRAG THE EDGE UNTIL THE TASKBAR IS THE SIZE YOU WANT.

TO HIDE THE TASKBAR:

- RIGHT-CLICK ANY BLANK AREA OF THE TASKBAR, SELECT PROPERTIES FROM THE SHORTCUT MENU, CLICK THE AUTO-HIDE THE TASKBAR CHECK BOX, AND CLICK OK.

TO DISPLAY A HIDDEN TASKBAR:

- POSITION THE POINTER NEAR THE VERY BOTTOM OF THE SCREEN.

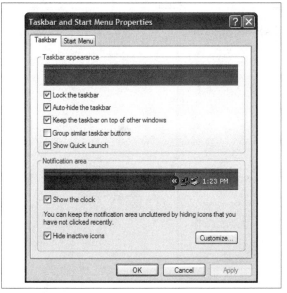 

Figure 5-9. The Taskbar tab of the Taskbar and Start Menu Properties dialog box.

Figure 5-10. The Start Menu tab of the Taskbar and Start Menu Properties dialog box.

Figure 5-11. The General tab of the Customize Start Menu dialog box.

Figure 5-12. The Advanced tab of the Customize Start Menu dialog box.

If you've gotten this far in the chapter, you've already learned the most important ways that you can customize the Windows Start menu and taskbar. This lesson deals with the remaining (but trivial) ways to customize the Start menu and taskbar. We won't actually be covering any of these trivial options (as there are quite a few of them), but we will at least show you how to access them. Let's get started!

1 Right-click the taskbar and select Properties from the shortcut menu.

The Taskbar and Start Menu Properties dialog box appears, as shown in Figure 5-9. The most common options for customizing the Windows Start menu and taskbar appear here. We won't be going through each of these options, but you can learn more about them in Table 5-1.

2 Click the Start Menu tab.

The Start Menu tab appears, as shown in Figure 5-10. This is where you can select the type of Start menu that you want to use by selecting one of the following two options:

- **Start Menu:** Use the new Windows XP Start menu that gives you quick access to your documents, pictures, music, and recently used programs.

- **Classic Start Menu:** Use a Start menu that has the same look and behavior as earlier versions of Windows.

You can further customize the Windows Start menu by clicking the Customize button.

3 Click Customize.

The General tab of the Customize Start Menu dialog box appears, as shown in Figure 5-11. Several options appear here:

- The icon size for the programs that appear in the Start menu.

- The number of frequently-used programs that appear in the Start menu.

- The Internet and E-mail applications that appear at the top of the Start menu.

Let's take a look at the Advanced tab.

4 Click the Advanced tab.

The Advanced tab of the Customize Start Menu dialog box appears, as shown in Figure 5-12. There are lots of advanced options that you use to further customize the Start menu and desktop. Almost all of these options are insignificant, so we won't go through any of them in this lesson.

5 Click OK to close the Customize dialog box.

The Customize dialog box closes and you're back to the Taskbar and Start Menu Properties dialog box.

6 Click OK to close the Taskbar and Start menu properties dialog box.

The Taskbar and Start Menu Properties dialog box closes.

To access the most common Start menu and taskbar options, simply right-click the taskbar and select Properties from the shortcut menu. Select from one or more of the options listed in the following table.

Table 5-1. Taskbar options

Option	Description
Lock the taskbar	Locks the taskbar at its current position on the desktop so that it cannot be moved to a new location. Also locks the size and position of any toolbar displayed on the taskbar so that it cannot be changed. This option is selected by default.
Auto-hide the taskbar	Hides the taskbar from view. To display the taskbar, position the mouse pointer near the bottom of the screen.
Keep the taskbar on top of other windows	Ensures that the taskbar is always visible, even when you run a program in full screen mode. This option is selected by default.
Group similar taskbar buttons	Displays taskbar buttons for files opened by the same program in the same area of the taskbar. This option is selected by default.
Show Quick Launch	Displays the Quick Launch bar on the taskbar. The Quick Launch bar is a customizable toolbar that lets you display the Windows desktop or start a program with a single click.
Show the clock	Displays a digital clock on the taskbar. This option is selected by default.
Hide inactive icons	Keeps the taskbar notification area from displaying unused icons. This option is selected by default.

QUICK REFERENCE

TO CUSTOMIZE THE TASKBAR AND START MENU:

- RIGHT-CLICK THE TASKBAR AND SELECT PROPERTIES FROM THE SHORTCUT MENU.

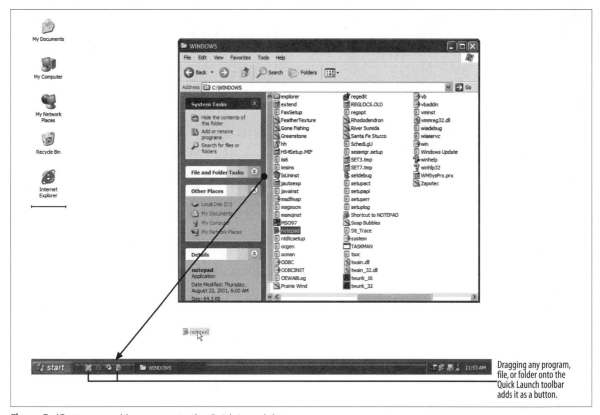

Dragging any program, file, or folder onto the Quick Launch toolbar adds it as a button.

Figure 5-13. You can add a program to the Quick Launch bar.

The *Quick Launch bar* lets you add buttons to the taskbar that you can use to start your favorite programs. Microsoft has already added several buttons to the Quick Launch bar to launch programs they think you will use frequently. Depending on who has used your computer, there may be a variety of icons on the Quick Launch bar. Some of the most common buttons include:

- **Microsoft Internet Explorer:** This launches your Web browser, letting you surf the Internet. If you use the Internet this is a great button to have.

- **Show Desktop:** Minimizes all the windows currently open so you can see the desktop.

- **Windows Media Player:** New in Windows XP, the Windows Media Player is a center for playing and organizing multimedia on your computer and on the Internet

Since the taskbar always appears at the bottom of the screen, the Quick Launch bar is probably the fastest and most convenient place to add shortcuts to your favorite programs. If the shortcut icons from Quick Launch start to crowd your taskbar, you can resize the Quick Launch bar by dragging its right border to the right or left. Some of the icons will "disappear" when you do this. To see them, simply click the ✧ arrows on the Quick Launch bar.

1 If your Quick Launch bar is visible on the left-hand side of your taskbar, skip to step 3. If the Quick Launch bar isn't visible, go on to the next step.

Let's track down that cute little Quick Launch bar.

2 Right-click an empty space on the taskbar and select Toolbars → Quick Launch from the shortcut menu.

The Quick Launch bar appears on the left-hand side of your taskbar and the toolbar menu closes.

As long as you can see the Quick Launch bar, you can add programs to it. Here's how…

3 Click the Start button and select My Computer from the menu.

TIP *Right-click a button on the Quick Launch bar to delete, rename, or modify it.*

The procedure of adding a program or file to the Quick Launch bar is almost the same as adding a shortcut to the desktop, so first you need to find the program you want to add.

4 Double-click the Local Drive (C:) icon. Double-click the Windows folder and display the folder's files if necessary.

Now find the Notepad program and add it to the Quick Launch bar.

5 Click the Notepad icon and drag it onto the Quick Launch bar.

Since there isn't a lot of room on the Quick Launch bar, you will probably have to resize it to see all of its contents. Again, here's how to resize the Quick Launch bar:

6 Click and drag the Quick Launch bar's grip handle to the right about a half-inch.

NOTE *The taskbar must be unlocked to resize the Quick launch bar; to unlock the taskbar, right-click an empty area of the taskbar and unselect Lock from the shortcut menu.*

You've just resized the Quick Launch bar. The only problem with making the Quick Launch bar bigger is that you make the rest of the taskbar smaller.

Try running Notepad from the Quick Launch bar.

7 Click the Notepad icon on the Quick Launch bar.

The Notepad program starts.

8 Close the Notepad program.

Of course, you can always delete a shortcut from the Quick Launch bar if it's no longer needed.

9 Right-click the Notepad icon on the Quick Launch bar and select Delete from the shortcut menu.

The Notepad shortcut is deleted from the Quick Launch bar.

If you, like many people, don't use the Quick Launch bar at all, you can hide it entirely and reclaim some valuable taskbar real estate.

10 Right-click any empty area on the taskbar and select Toolbars → Quick Launch from menu.

The Quick Launch bar disappears from view.

QUICK REFERENCE

TO HIDE-DISPLAY THE QUICK LAUNCH TOOLBAR:

- RIGHT-CLICK ANY EMPTY AREA ON THE TASKBAR AND SELECT TOOLBARS → QUICK LAUNCH FROM THE SHORTCUT MENU

TO ADD A PROGRAM TO THE QUICK LAUNCH BAR:

- ENSURE THE TASKBAR IS UNLOCKED, THEN DRAG AND DROP THE PROGRAM ONTO THE QUICK LAUNCH TOOLBAR.

TO RESIZE THE QUICK LAUNCH BAR:

- DRAG THE GRIP HANDLE OF THE QUICK LAUNCH BAR TO THE RIGHT OR LEFT.

TO DELETE A PROGRAM FROM THE QUICK LAUNCH BAR:

- RIGHT-CLICK THE PROGRAM'S ICON ON THE QUICK LAUNCH BAR AND SELECT DELETE FROM THE

Figure 5-14. The My Recent Documents menu keeps a list of the files you've used most recently.

Figure 5-15. The Customize Start Menu dialog box.

Windows remembers the files that you used most recently so you can quickly retrieve them without having to dig through several menus and/or windows. This lesson shows you how to use the My Recent Documents menu to open a recent file.

First, we need to create a document so Windows can retrieve it.

1 Use the Notepad program to create a simple text file (type whatever you want in it) and save it in the root directory of the Local Disk (C:) drive with the name Junk File. Close Notepad.

You learned how to save files in a previous lesson—just select File → Save from the menu and select the location where you want to save the file (the root directory of the (C:) drive).

You could retrieve the Junk File by opening Notepad and selecting File → Open from the menu. You could also retrieve the Junk File by opening My Computer or Windows Explorer, opening the (C:) drive, and double-clicking the file. Or…you could just select the Junk File from the My Recent Documents menu, as we'll see in the next step.

2 Click the Start button and select My Recent Documents from the menu.

The My Recent Documents menu appears, listing your recently-used files. Can you find your Junk File?

3 Select Junk File from the Documents menu.

The Junk File opens in Notepad, where you can review and make changes to the file.

4 Close the Notepad program.

Although there's really no need to, you can clear the list of recent documents from the My Recent Documents menu.

5 Right-click the taskbar and select Properties from the shortcut menu. Click the Start Menu tab and click Customize.

The Customize Start Menu dialog box appears.

6 Click the Advanced tab. Click the Clear List button in the Recent Document section.

It appears as though nothing has happened, but Windows has removed the list of files from the Documents menu.

7 Click OK, OK to close the dialog boxes.

Verify that the Documents menu has been reset and is empty.

8 Click the Start button and select My Recent Documents from the menu.

The My Recent Documents list is empty, for now. As you create and open files, they will appear in the My Recent Documents list.

QUICK REFERENCE

TO OPEN A RECENT FILE:

- CLICK THE START BUTTON, CLICK MY RECENT DOCUMENTS AND SELECT THE FILE YOU WANT TO OPEN.

TO CLEAR THE LIST OF RECENT DOCUMENTS:

1. RIGHT-CLICK THE TASKBAR AND SELECT PROPERTIES FROM THE SHORTCUT MENU.

2. CLICK THE START MENU TAB.

3. CLICK CUSTOMIZE.

4. CLICK THE ADVANCED TAB.

5. CLICK CLEAR LIST TO CLEAR THE LIST AND CLICK OK, OK TO CLOSE THE DIALOG BOXES.

Figure 5-16. The Run option in the Start menu.

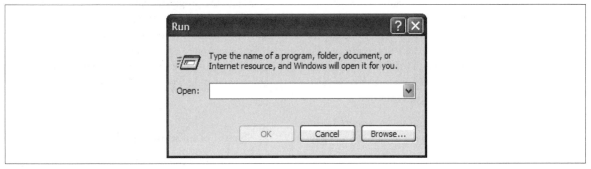

Figure 5-17. The Run dialog box.

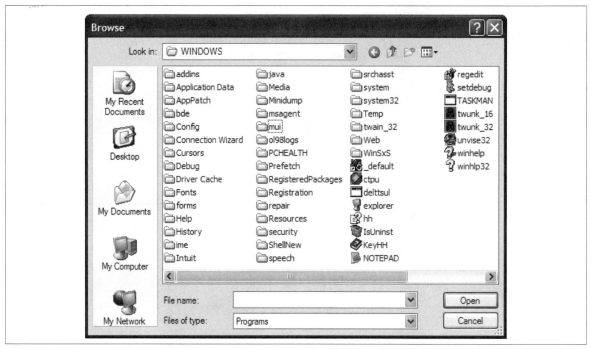

Figure 5-18. If you don't know the file path of the program, you can browse to find the program.

If you've gotten this far, you should already know at least a couple different methods of opening, or starting, programs. You can start a program by clicking the Start button, selecting All Programs, and then finding and clicking the program. You can also start a program by opening My Computer or Windows Explorer, finding the program (which can be tricky), and then double-clicking the program. In this lesson, you'll learn yet another way to start a program—by using the Run command.

The Run command is a more technical way to start a program, and hopefully you won't have to use it much—if ever. Still, just in case, here it is.

1 Click the **Start** button and select **Run** from the menu.

The Run dialog box appears, as shown in Figure 5-17.

If you know the program's file name and location, you can type it in the Open box. If you can believe it, this is how people used to run programs in the old MS-DOS operating system. MS-DOS didn't have any cute icons, windows, or pictures—there was nothing to point and click at all. People would start programs by typing the program's name and file path and pressing Enter. Yuck!

Using the Run command is very similar to using MS-DOS. To use it, you have to know the name of the program and the program's path (the drive and folders it's in). A path is like a street address, containing the drive letter, followed by a colon, followed by folders (which must be separated by backslashes \), and then the name of the program. For example, to run the Notepad program, you would type C:\WINDOWS\NOTEPAD.

Let's try it.

2 Type C:\windows\notepad **and click OK.**

The Notepad program opens.

3 Close the Notepad program.

Typing the program name and path is difficult, and impossible if you don't know the exact name of the file and folders. Isn't there an easier way to get the name and path of the program in the Run dialog box? Sure—you can find the program you want to run by browsing for it.

4 Repeat Step 1.

This time, instead of typing the program's name and path, let's browse for the Notepad program.

5 Click the Browse button.

The Browse window appears, as shown in Figure 5-18. Use the Browse window to help you enter the program's name and path.

6 Open the Windows folder, display the folder's files if necessary, then find and double-click the Notepad program.

The path to Notepad appears in the Run dialog box.

7 Click OK.

The Notepad program reopens.

8 Close the Notepad program.

You'll rarely, if ever, use the Run command to start programs. One instance where you might use the Run command is when you're installing a new program and the installation manual tells you to install a program by entering something like D:\SETUP.EXE. Now, when you run across instructions like that, you'll know how to do it

QUICK REFERENCE

TO START A PROGRAM WITH THE RUN COMMAND:

1. CLICK THE START BUTTON AND SELECT RUN.

2. ENTER THE PATH AND NAME OF THE PROGRAM YOU WANT TO RUN.

OR...

CLICK THE BROWSE BUTTON, FIND THE PROGRAM FILE, AND DOUBLE CLICK IT.

3. CLICK OK TO RUN THE PROGRAM.

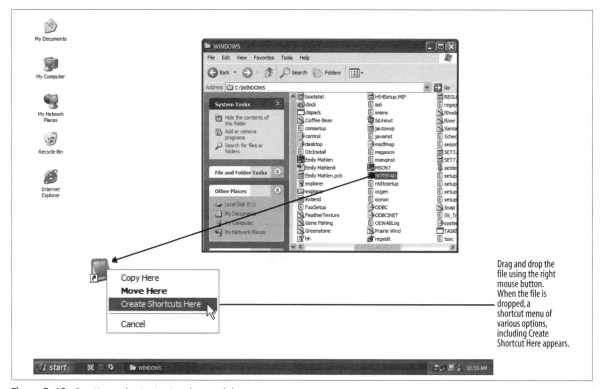

Figure 5-19. Creating a shortcut using drag and drop.

The Start menu makes it easy to find and open your programs. But sometimes the five seconds it takes to wade through the menu can be too long if you open the same programs or files over and over. A shortcut is a quick way to start a program or open a file or folder without having to go to its actual location. In fact, all of the programs in the Start menu are shortcuts that point to program files located elsewhere on your computer. And since shortcuts only point to files or folders, moving, renaming, or deleting a shortcut does not affect the original program or file.

NOTE *You can even create shortcuts to your favorite folders. For example, you could create a shortcut to a folder that contains your frequently used files on the Desktop.*

1 Click the Start button and select My Computer from the menu.

To create a shortcut, you need to find the program you want to create the shortcut to. In this exercise, create a shortcut to the Notepad program.

2 Double-click the Local Disk (C:) icon. Double-click the Windows folder, and display the folder's files if necessary..

The Notepad program is located somewhere in here.

3 Click the Notepad program.

There are a lot of programs and files in the Windows folder, so you will have to scroll quite a bit to find the Notepad program. Make sure the contents of the Windows folder are being sorted alphabetically by name—or you may never find it!

4 Using the right mouse button, click and drag the Notepad program from the window to your desktop.

Dragging items with the right mouse button causes a shortcut menu to appear when the item is dropped..

5 Select Create Shortcuts Here from the shortcut menu.

The Notepad shortcut appears on the desktop. The default names Windows gives to shortcuts usually aren't very meaningful, so you will usually want to rename them.

6 **Rename the** Shortcut to Notepad **shortcut** Notepad.

Remember how to rename files? Right-click the file, select Rename from the shortcut menu, rename the file, and press Enter. Now, try using your new shortcut.

7 **Double-click the** Notepad **shortcut.**

The Notepad program opens.

8 **Close the Notepad program.**

Since a shortcut only points to a program or file, deleting a shortcut does not delete the original file it points to.

9 **Click the** Notepad **shortcut and press** Delete.

To change the settings for a shortcut, such as what kind of window it starts in or if the location of the program changes, right-click the shortcut and select Properties.

QUICK REFERENCE

TO CREATE A SHORTCUT TO A FILE OR FOLDER:

- DRAG THE FILE OR FOLDER TO A NEW LOCATION WITH THE RIGHT MOUSE BUTTON. SELECT *CREATE SHORTCUT HERE* FROM THE SHORTCUT MENU.

OR...

- RIGHT-CLICK THE FILE OR FOLDER FOR WHICH YOU WANT TO CREATE A SHORTCUT, AND SELECT *CREATE SHORTCUT* FROM THE SHORTCUT MENU.

OR...

- RIGHT-CLICK AN EMPTY AREA OF ANY FOLDER OR THE WINDOWS DESKTOP AND SELECT *NEW →* *SHORTCUT* FROM THE SHORTCUT MENU. ENTER THE PATH AND NAME OF THE PROGRAM YOU WANT THE SHORTCUT TO POINT TO, OR CLICK THE BROWSE BUTTON, FIND THE FILE, AND DOUBLE-CLICK IT

Figure 5-20. The Startup folder in the All Programs menu.

If you use the same program each and every day, you can save five seconds or so by having Windows start the program automatically every time you turn the computer on. This lesson shows you how to automatically start a program when you start Windows, and how to stop programs from automatically starting. Let's get started!

1 Right-click the Start button and select Open (or Open All Users) from the shortcut menu.

The Start Menu window appears.

2 Double-click the Programs folder.

The Programs window appears. We want to open the Startup folder.

3 Double-click the Startup folder.

Programs in this folder will open when Windows starts. Here's how to add a program to it:

4 Click the Start button and select All Programs → Accessories.

Move on to the next step to add the Notepad program to the Startup group.

5 Position your mouse pointer over Notepad. Click the right mouse button and drag Notepad to the Startup window.

Dragging items with the right mouse button causes a shortcut menu to appear, listing copy and move options.

6 Select Copy Here from the shortcut menu.

You've successfully created a shortcut to the Notepad program in your Startup folder. Now Notepad will start every time you turn on your computer and start Windows. You don't need to restart your computer to see if Notepad will automatically open.

If you no longer want a program to start automatically, simply delete the program's shortcut from the Startup folder.

7 Click the Notepad shortcut and press Delete.

Close the window to end this lesson.

8 Click the Startup window Close button.

NOTE *Don't place programs in the Startup menu unless you really do use them every time you start Windows. Having too many programs open at the same time takes up memory and can really slow down how long it takes Windows to start.*

QUICK REFERENCE

TO START A PROGRAM AUTOMATICALLY WHEN WINDOWS STARTS:

1. RIGHT-CLICK THE START BUTTON AND SELECT OPEN OR OPEN ALL USERS FROM THE SHORTCUT MENU.

2. DOUBLE-CLICK THE PROGRAMS FOLDER.

3. DOUBLE-CLICK THE STARTUP FOLDER

4. ADD THEPROGRAM, FILE, OR FOLDER SHORTCUT TO THE STARTUP FOLDER.

Chapter Five Review

Lesson Summary

Using the Windows Classic Start Menu

Right-click a blank area of the Windows taskbar and select Properties from the shortcut menu. Click the Start Menu tab and select the Classic Start menu option. (Optional) Click Customize to further customize the behavior of the Start menu. Click OK.

Using the Windows Classic Appearance

Right-click a blank area on the desktop and select Properties from the shortcut menu. Click the Appearance tab. Click the Windows and buttons list arrow and select Windows Classic style from the list. Click OK.

Moving, Resizing, and Hiding the Taskbar

To Lock/Unlock the Taskbar: Right-click the taskbar and select Lock the taskbar from the shortcut menu. (If the option is checked, it is locked.)

To Move the Taskbar: Position the pointer over a blank area on the taskbar and click and drag the taskbar to the top, bottom, left, or right of the screen.

To Resize the Taskbar: Position the pointer over the top edge of the taskbar until the pointer changes to a ↕, then drag the edge until the taskbar is the size you want.

To Hide the Taskbar: Right-click any blank area of the taskbar, select Properties from the shortcut menu, click the Auto-hide the taskbar check box, and click OK.

To Display a Hidden Taskbar: Position the pointer near the very bottom of the screen.

Customizing the Start Menu

Right-click the taskbar and select Properties from the shortcut menu.

Working with the Quick Launch Bar

To Add a Program to the Quick Launch Bar: Drag and drop the program onto the Quick Launch bar.

To Resize the Quick Launch bar: Ensure the taskbar is unlocked, then drag the grip handle of the Quick Launch bar to the right or left.

To Delete a Program from the Quick Launch bar: Right-click the program's button on the Quick Launch bar and select Delete from the shortcut menu.

To Hide/Display the Quick Launch bar: Right-click any empty area on the taskbar and select Toolbars → Quick Launch from the shortcut menu.

Opening Recent Documents

You can open a recent document by clicking the Start button → My Recent Documents and selecting the file you want to open.

To Clear the List of Recent Documents: Right-click the taskbar and select Properties from the shortcut menu. Click the Start Menu tab, click Customize, and then click the Advanced tab. Click Clear List and then OK, OK.

Using the Run Command to Start a Program

Click the Start button and select Run. Enter the path and name of the program you want to run, or click the Browse button, find the file, and double click it. Click OK to run the program.

Adding Shortcuts to the Desktop

A shortcut is a quick way to open a file or folder without having to go to the actual location. Shortcuts always display an arrow (⬈) in the corner of the icon.

To Create a Shortcut to a File or Folder: Drag the file or folder to a new location with the right mouse button and select Create Shortcut Here from the shortcut menu. You can also create a shortcut by right-clicking the file or folder for which you want to create a shortcut and selecting Create Shortcut from the shortcut menu. Finally, you can create a shortcut by right-clicking an empty area of any folder or the Windows Desktop and selecting New → Shortcut from the shortcut menu and entering the path and name of the program you want the shortcut to point to.

Starting a Program Automatically when Windows Starts

Right-click the Start button and select Open from the shortcut menu. Double-click the Programs folder. Double-click the Startup folder. Add the program, file, or folder shortcut to the Startup folder.

Quiz

1. You can move the taskbar to any edge of the screen. (True or False?)

2. Which of the following statements is NOT true?

    A. You can change the size of the taskbar by dragging its top edge until the taskbar is the size you want.

    B. Move the pointer to the bottom of the screen to display a hidden taskbar.

    C. You can position the taskbar so that it floats in the middle of the screen.

    D. You can accidentally change the size of the taskbar so that it disappears almost completely from the screen – in which case you will need to resize it.

3. Which of the following statements are NOT true? (Select all that apply.)

    A. You can't add or remove programs from the Start menu.

    B. Most programs add themselves to the Start menu's All Programs menu.

    C. Deleting a program from the Start menu deletes the program from your local disk.

    D. You can open recently used documents by clicking the Start button, selecting My Recent Documents, and selecting the file you want to open.

4. You can create, rename, delete, and move folders and files in the Start menu, just like you would in:

    A. Windows Explorer.

    B. WordPad.

    C. A Macintosh computer.

    D. The taskbar.

5. You know a program is installed on your computer, but for some reason you can't find it in the All Programs menu. How can you start the program? (Select all that apply.)

    A. Click the Start button, select Run, click the Browse button, and find and double-click the file.

    B. Open My Computer, find the file, and double-click it.

    C. Open Windows Explorer, find the file, and double-click it.

    D. Wear a cactus as a hat and repeat the program's name thirty times while tapping your keyboard with a chicken bone.

6. Which of the following statements is NOT true?

    A. Shortcuts have a in the corner.

    B. When you delete a shortcut, it also deletes the file or folder it points to.

    C. You can create a shortcut by dragging the file or folder to a new location with the right mouse button and selecting Create Shortcut Here from the shortcut menu.

    D. The items in the Start menu's All Programs menu are actually shortcuts.

Homework

1. Position the taskbar at the top of the screen, then move it back to the bottom of the screen.

2. Display the Taskbar Properties dialog box.

3. Display a list of recently used files.

4. Create a new folder in the Programs menu named "Financial Programs."

5. Delete the Financial Programs folder.

6. Use the Start menu's Run command to start the NotePad program. (Hint: It's located in the C:\Windows folder).

7. Create a shortcut to the NotePad program on the desktop. Delete the shortcut when you're finished.

Quiz Answers

1. True. You can move the taskbar to any edge of the screen.

2. C. You can only move the taskbar to the edges of the screen.

3. A and C. You can easily add and remove programs from the Start menu—and deleting programs from the Start menu leaves the original program intact.

4. A. When you modify the Start menu, you're using Windows Explorer.

5. A, B, and C. You can start a program or open a file using any of these methods.

6. B. A shortcut only points to a file or folder elsewhere on the computer—deleting the shortcut, moving it, or renaming it in no way affects the original file.

CHAPTER 6

CUSTOMIZING WINDOWS

CHAPTER OBJECTIVES:

Changing the date and time

Adding wallpaper and changing the screen colors

Changing the screen resolution and color depth

Using a screen saver and desktop theme

Changing system sounds

Adjusting the mouse

Customizing how Windows looks and works

Prerequisites

- **Know how to use the mouse to click, double-click, click and drag, and right-click.**
- **Know how to use menus, toolbars, and dialog boxes.**
- **Know how to view and navigate the contents of your computer (disk drives and folders).**

In the old days, computers had two settings: on or off. Today, Windows lets you adjust your computer to work the way you do.

This chapter will show you how to customize Windows settings to suit your own personal needs and tastes. You'll learn how to adjust the date and time on your computer, the mouse settings so you can finally slow down that blasted double-click speed, and the sounds your computer makes. You'll also learn how to give your computer character by adding your own custom wallpaper, screensaver, desktop themes, and screen colors. Once you've decorated Windows with your personal theme, you'll want to make sure it looks as good as possible, so you'll learn how to adjust the screen resolution and number of colors that appear on the screen at once.

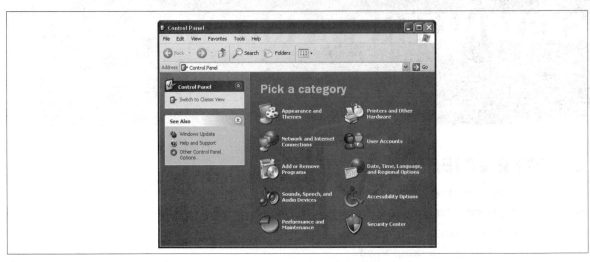

Figure 6-1. The Control Panel window.

Figure 6-2. The Printers and Other Hardware window.

**Windows XP
Service Pack 2**
Security Center is a new
Control Panel category in Service Pack 2.

The Control Panel is the place to go when you want to change the various settings of Windows. Since this chapter deals entirely with configuring your computer, you'll be seeing a lot of the Control Panel in the upcoming lessons. That's why this lesson is a quick introduction to the Control Panel. No exercises here—just a guided tour of the Control Panel to help you become familiar with it.

If you prefer the interface of the old Control Panel, click the Switch to Classic View task in the Control Panel menu. If you choose to switch to Classic View, the Control Panel will be quite a bit different, so make sure to pay attention to the margin notes in this chapter.

1 Click the Start button and select Control Panel from the menu.

The Control Panel appears.

Control Panel
Other Ways to Open the Control Panel:
• Open My Computer and click the Control Panel task in the Other Places menu.

If you've used earlier versions of Microsoft Windows, you'll notice that the Control Panel in Windows XP is quite different from earlier versions. The window is categorized by topic so it is easier to find the setting you want to change. Click on one of the categories to view all the Control Panel settings under a topic.

If you prefer the style of the previous control panel (and a lot of people do), you can always switch; simply click the Switch to Classic View task in the Control Panel menu,

2 Click the Printers and Other Hardware category.

**Printers and
Other Hardware**

The tasks and icons in the Printers and Other Hardware category appear.

If you know you want to perform a specific task, look under the "Pick a task" section. If you want to browse the options for a specific piece of hardware, click on its icon in the bottom half of the window.

Let's return to the main Control Panel window.

3 Click the Back button on the toolbar.

You've returned to the original Control Panel window.

4 Look at the various topic headings in the Control Panel and refer to 6-1 to see what they do.

If you want to see more, go ahead and click any of the icons or heading titles in the Control Panel to display the window that lives behind each one. Just don't touch anything beyond that window; you'll get your chance soon enough.

5 When you're finished, close the Control Panel.

Ready to start customizing your computer? Then move on to the next lesson and let's get started!

Table 6-1. What's in the Control Panel

Item	Description
Appearance and Themes	Customize the Start menu or taskbar, apply a theme or screen saver, or change items on the desktop. You can also change Windows' appearance from XP to classic style under this topic.
Network and Internet Connections	Configure network settings to work from home, create a small office or home network, connect to the Internet, or change modem, phone, and Internet settings.
Add or Remove Programs	Installs or removes programs and additional Windows components on your computer.
Sounds, Speech, and Audio Devices	Change the system's sound scheme or configure the settings for speakers and other sound equipment on your computer.
Performance and Maintenance	Increase space on your hard drive, schedule regular maintenance checks, or configure energy-saving settings.
Printers and Other Hardware	Change the settings for hardware such as the printer, keyboard, mouse, or camera.
User Accounts	Change settings and passwords for individual users.

Table 6-1. What's in the Control Panel (Continued)

Item	Description
Date, Time, Language, and Regional Options	Changes the date, time, and time zone information on your computer, the language to use, and region-specific display options for numbers, currency, time and dates.
Accessibility Options	Adjust settings for an individual user's vision, hearing, and mobility needs.
Security Center	Maintain the security settings for your computer, such as the Windows Firewall, and Automatic Updates to ensure your computer is protected. (This is an addition in SP2.)

QUICK REFERENCE

TO OPEN THE CONTROL PANEL:

- CLICK THE START BUTTON AND SELECT CONTROL PANEL.

OR...

OPEN MY COMPUTER AND CLICK THE CONTROL PANEL TASK IN THE OTHER PLACES MENU.

TO VIEW THE CONTROL PANEL IN CLASSIC VIEW:

- CLICK THE SWITCH TO CLASSIC VIEW TASK IN THE CONTROL PANEL MENU.

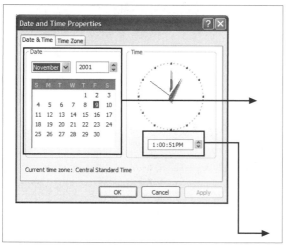

Figure 6-3. The Date & Time tab of the Date and Time Properties dialog box.

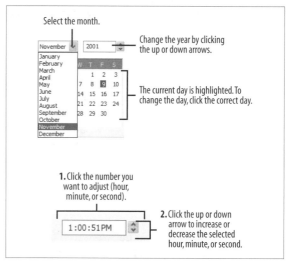

Figure 6-4. Using the time and dates control in the Date and Time Properties dialog box.

Figure 6-5. The Time Zone tab of the Date and Time Properties dialog box.

Your computer has its own built-in clock that serves many purposes, including determining when you created or modified a file. For this reason, you should make sure the date and time are set correctly in your computer. This lesson will show you how to set the date and time for your computer if you find it needs adjusting.

The far right area of the taskbar normally displays the time your computer thinks it is. To display the date, you merely need to move the pointer over the clock and wait a few seconds.

1 **Move the pointer over the clock on the taskbar and wait a few seconds.**

A small box that displays the date appears.

Display the Current Date

To change the date or time, double-click the clock on the taskbar.

2 Double-click the clock on the far right edge of the taskbar.

The Date and Time Properties dialog box appears, as shown in Figure 6-3. To change the time setting, click on the area of the clock you want to adjust and then adjust the settings using the up or down arrows.

3 Click the hour and click the clock's up arrow to advance the time one hour.

You could adjust the minutes the same way—by clicking the minute part of the time and then clicking the up or down arrows. You can also manually type the numbers using the keyboard.

You can change the date in the left area of the dialog box. Change the month and year by clicking their corresponding text boxes, located above the calendar.

4 Click the Month list arrow and select January from the list, then click the Year text box and click the up arrow to advance several years.

The calendar displays the days in the selected month, highlighting the current day. To change the day, just click the day you want.

5 Click on day 1 in the calendar.

If you use a laptop, you may need to adjust which time zone you're in. You can do this using the Time Zone tab of the Date and Time Properties dialog box.

6 Click the Time Zone tab.

The Time Zone tab appears in the front of the dialog box, as shown in Figure 6-5. You can click the Time Zone list arrow to select your current time zone from a list of all available time zones. Also, note the "Automatically adjust clock for daylight savings changes" box. When this box is checked, Windows will automatically adjust your computer's clock when daylight savings time changes, so you'll have one less clock to worry about.

7 Click Cancel to close the Date and Time Properties dialog box without applying the changes you've made.

The built-in clock in your computer should keep track of the date and time even when your computer is turned off. If your computer doesn't keep the proper time and date, it means there is probably something wrong with your computer's built-in clock.

QUICK REFERENCE

TO DISPLAY THE CURRENT DATE:

- POINT AT THE CLOCK ON THE TASKBAR FOR SEVERAL SECONDS.

TO CHANGE THE DATE AND/OR TIME:

1. DOUBLE-CLICK THE CLOCK ON THE TASKBAR.
2. ADJUST THE DATE AND TIME USING THE CALENDAR AND CLOCK CONTROLS AND CLICK OK.

TO CHANGE TIME ZONES:

1. DOUBLE-CLICK THE CLOCK ON THE TASKBAR.
2. CLICK THE TIME ZONE TAB, SELECT A TIME ZONE FROM THE LIST BOX, AND CLICK OK.

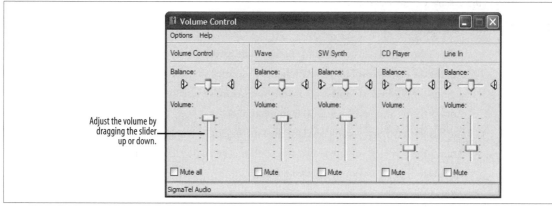

Figure 6-6. The Volume Control dialog box.

If your computer has a sound card that is working properly, you will be able to listen to sound and adjust the sound's volume. If you don't already have a volume dial on your speakers, this lesson will show you how you can adjust your computer's volume—something useful to know if you have someone in your home that uses the computer to play loud, annoying computer games!

For reasons unknown, Microsoft decided *not* to display the very useful volume control on the taskbar by default in Windows XP; no matter—it's easy to get put it back there.

1 Click the Start button and select Control Panel from the menu.

The Control Panel appears.

2 Click the Sounds, Speech, and Audio Devices category. Click Sounds and Audio Devices.

The Sounds and Audio Devices Properties dialog box appears.

3 Make sure the Place volume icon in the taskbar check box is selected, then click OK.

A small speaker icon should appear in the system tray of the taskbar.

NOTE *You may see a different screen than the Volume Control dialog box shown in Figure 6-6 depending on your sound card's software.*

Volume Control

4 Click the speaker icon in the taskbar.

The Volume control appears.

5 Drag the volume slider up or down to increase or decrease the volume.

The Volume control also contains a Mute check box. When the Mute box is checked, the computer's sound is turned off completely.

6 Click anywhere outside the Volume box.

The Volume control is usually all you will need to adjust your computer's volume. But if you're an audiophile, you can fine-tune the volume settings of your computer by double-clicking the speaker icon.

7 Double-click the speaker icon.

The Volume Control dialog box appears, as shown in Figure 6-6. The Volume Control dialog box has lots of volume and balance controls, just like an advanced, expensive stereo system. With the Volume Control dialog box, you can individually adjust the volume, balance between speakers, and input levels of your computer's sound system. The Volume Control dialog box for your computer may have different controls, depending on the capabilities of the sound card in your computer. See Table 6-2 for a description of the various controls in the Volume Control dialog box on the right side.

8 Close the Volume Control dialog box.

Table 6-2. Controls in the Volume Control dialog box

Control	Description
Volume control	Adjusts the overall playback volume of the sound card.
Wave	Adjusts the playback volume level of digitally recorded sounds, such as .wav files.
SW l	Adjusts the playback volume level of your sound card's music synthesizer and MIDI files.
Mic	Adjusts the recording volume level for a microphone.
Line-in	Adjusts the recording volume level for the Line-in jack.
CD player	Adjusts the playback volume level if you're playing an audio CD in your computer.
Video	Adjusts the playback volume level for a video.
PC speaker	Adjusts the playback volume level of just the speakers on your computer.

QUICK REFERENCE

TO DISPLAY THE VOLUME CONTROL ICON IN THE TASKBAR:

1. CLICK THE START BUTTON AND SELECT CONTROL PANEL FROM THE MENU.
2. CLICK THE SOUNDS, SPEECH, AND AUDIO DEVICES CATEGORY.
3. CLICK SOUNDS AND AUDIO DEVICES.
4. ENSURE THAT THE PLACE VOLUME ICON IN THE TASKBAR BOX IS CHECKED THEN CLICK OK.

TO ADJUST YOUR COMPUTER'S VOLUME:

• CLICK THE SPEAKER ICON LOCATED ON THE FAR RIGHT OF THE TASKBAR AND DRAG THE VOLUME SLIDER UP OR DOWN.

TO TURN THE VOLUME OFF:

• CLICK THE SPEAKER ICON LOCATED IN THE SYSTEM TRAY OF THE TASKBAR AND CHECK THE MUTE CHECK BOX.

TO DISPLAY THE VOLUME CONTROL DIALOG BOX:

• DOUBLE-CLICK THE SPEAKER ICON LOCATED IN THE SYSTEM TRAY OF THE TASKBAR.

Figure 6-7. The Appearance tab of the Display Properties dialog box and the default color scheme.

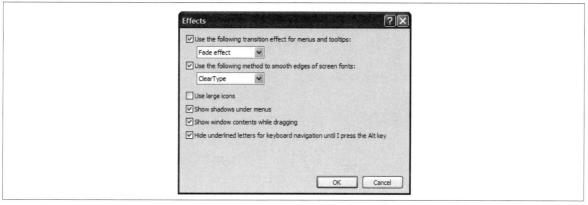

Figure 6-8. The Effects dialog box.

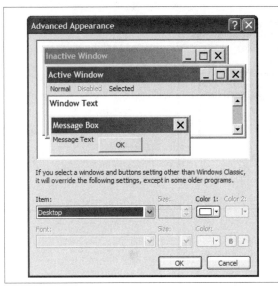

Figure 6-9. The Advanced Appearance dialog box.

Another way to personalize Windows is to change the screen colors. Windows' screen colors include all the basic parts of a window such as the title bar, the menu, and the scroll bars.

1 Right-click a blank area on the desktop, and select Properties from the shortcut menu.

The Display Properties dialog box appears.

2 Click the Appearance tab.

The Appearance tab appears in the Display Properties dialog box, as shown in Figure 6-7. This is where you can use a color scheme to change the appearance of many screen elements.

3 Click the Color scheme list arrow and select Olive Green from the list.

The preview area of the dialog box displays how your screen will look with the selected color scheme.

You can also click the Font list arrow to change the font size. If the default setting is difficult for you to see, you may want to switch to a larger font size.

Can't stand the bright new colors of Windows XP? You can easily restore the tried and true appearance of previous versions of Windows.

4 Click the Windows and buttons list arrow and select Windows Classic style from the list.

The preview area of the dialog box displays how your screen will look in classic style.

NOTE *This will only change the way windows and buttons are displayed in Windows; it will not convert everything back to classic style, e.g., the Start menu and the desktop.*

If you're really computer savvy, you can further customize how Windows looks by using the Advanced and Effects buttons.

5 Click the Effects button.

The Effects dialog box appears, as shown in Figure 6-8. We won't go through these options in this lesson, but you can find out what some of the more important settings do by looking at Table 6-3.

6 Click Cancel to close the Effects dialog box, then click Cancel again to close the Display Properties dialog box without saving your changes.

Table 6-3. Controls on the Display Properties Appearance tab

Control	Description
Windows and buttons	Lets you change Windows' overall visual design. You have two choices: **Windows XP Style:** The radical new look and feel for Windows XP, with rounded corners, big buttons, and bright crayon-like colors. **Windows Classic Style:** The look and feel you're probably used to from previous versions of Windows, with square corners and a no-nonsense design.
Color scheme	Lets you select a color scheme that changes the colors of many screen elements simultaneously. **NOTE:** Unless you have the Windows XP Plus software installed, you will limited to only a few color schemes.

Table 6-3. Controls on the Display Properties Appearance tab (Continued)

Control	Description
Font size	Lets you change the size of the fonts, or text, used throughout Windows. This option is useful if you have bad eyesight or a small monitor.
Effects	Click to open the Effects dialog box, shown in Figure 6-8, and select visual effects for Windows' menus, icons, and fonts.
	Use the following transition effect for menus and tooltips: Specifies whether to activate animations for menu commands and other Windows elements. Animations change how menus, lists, and tooltips open and close.
	Use the following method to smooth edges of screen fonts: Select Standard for desktop monitors; select ClearType for most laptop computers and other flat screen monitors.
	Use large icons: Specifies whether to use large icons to represent files, folders, and shortcuts on your desktop.
	Hide underlined letters for keyboard navigation until I press the ALT key: Specifies whether to suppress the underlined letters of keyboard shortcuts until you actually use the keyboard to navigate in Windows, generally with the ALT key.
Advanced	Click to customize the look of windows, menus, fonts, and icons, as shown in Figure 6-9. This option is only useful if you selected Windows Classic as your theme. Simply select the item you want to change (from the preview display or from the list) and then select a color for the object.

QUICK REFERENCE

TO CHANGE WINDOWS' COLOR SCHEME:

1. RIGHT-CLICK A BLANK AREA ON THE DESKTOP AND SELECT PROPERTIES FROM THE SHORTCUT MENU.

2. CLICK THE APPEARANCE TAB.

3. SELECT A COLOR SCHEME FROM THE COLOR SCHEME LIST AND CLICK OK.

TO CHANGE TO WINDOWS CLASSIC STYLE:

1. FOLLOW STEPS ONE AND TWO ABOVE TO GET TO THE APPEARANCE TAB.

2. SELECT WINDOWS CLASSIC STYLE FROM THE WINDOWS AND BUTTONS LIST.

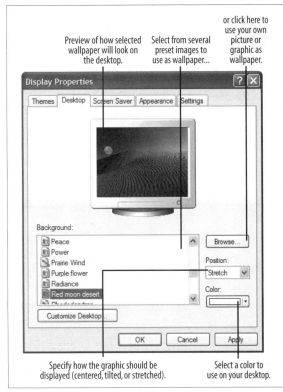

Preview of how selected wallpaper will look on the desktop.

Select from several preset images to use as wallpaper...

or click here to use your own picture or graphic as wallpaper.

Specify how the graphic should be displayed (centered, tilted, or stretched).

Select a color to use on your desktop.

Figure 6-10. The Desktop tab of the Display Properties dialog box.

Figure 6-11. Windows with the Red moon desert wallpaper.

Most of us don't work in a sterile work environment—we decorate our desktops with pictures, plants, and Dilbert calendars. Similarly, Windows lets you reflect your own personal tastes on your computer desktop. In this lesson,

you will learn how to personalize Windows by adding *wallpaper* to the Windows desktop. *Wallpaper* in Windows is a graphical picture you can stick to the desktop—the background area of the Windows screen.

1 Right-click a blank area on the desktop and select Properties from the shortcut menu.

The Display Properties dialog box appears.

2 Click the Desktop tab.

The Desktop tab appears in the Display Properties dialog box, as shown in Figure 6-10. This is where you can select a file to use as wallpaper.

3 Scroll through the Background list and click the Red moon desert option.

A preview appears of what your desktop will look like with the selected wallpaper. Notice the Position combo box—you can display your wallpaper using one of three different methods:

- **Center:** Centers the image in the middle of your desktop. Use this setting if you have a large picture you want to display, such as a scanned picture.

- **Tile:** Makes a repeated pattern from the image. Use this setting for small to medium sized pictures and for all the default files listed in the Wallpaper box.

- **Stretch:** Stretches the image so that it fills the entire screen.

4 Click the Position list arrow and select Center from the list.

You're ready to add your wallpaper.

5 Click Apply.

The Red moon desert background appears centered on your desktop. Notice that since you clicked Apply, the dialog box is still open.

If you want to use a picture that isn't listed in the Background section, such as a scanned picture of your family, click the Browse button.

To remove wallpaper from your screen, select (None) from the Wallpaper section.

6 Scroll up in the **Background** list and click the **(None)** option. **Click** OK.

The Display Properties dialog box closes, and the wallpaper is removed from the screen.

Here's one more wallpaper tip: if you're surfing the Web with Microsoft's Internet Explorer (the Web browser that comes with Windows XP) and happen to see a graphic or picture you like, you can use it as your desktop wallpaper. Just right-click the graphic and select the Set as Wallpaper option from the shortcut menu to save the image from the Internet and display it as wallpaper.

QUICK REFERENCE

TO CHANGE WALLPAPER:

1. RIGHT-CLICK A BLANK AREA ON THE DESKTOP AND SELECT PROPERTIES FROM THE SHORTCUT MENU.

2. CLICK THE DESKTOP TAB.

3. SELECT THE WALLPAPER YOU WANT TO USE FROM THE BACKGROUND LIST.

OR...

CLICK BROWSE AND SPECIFY THE NAME AND LOCATION OF THE PICTURE OR GRAPHIC YOU WANT TO USE AS WALLPAPER.

4. (OPTIONAL) CLICK THE POSITION LIST ARROW TO SELECT HOW YOU WANT THE WALLPAPER TO BE DISPLAYED (CENTERED, TILED, OR STRETCHED).

5. CLICK OK.

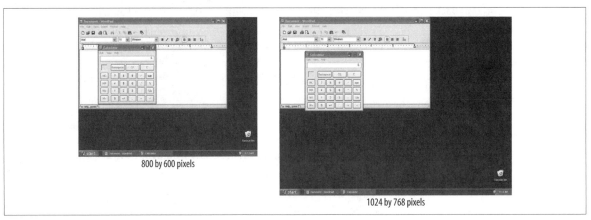

Figure 6-12. Lower resolutions (800 by 600) display larger images on the screen; higher resolutions (1024 by 768) display smaller images but let you see more information at once.

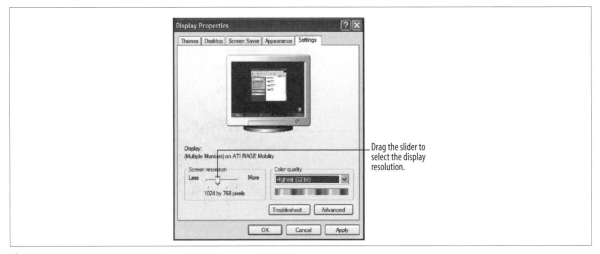

Figure 6-13. The Settings tab of the Display Properties dialog box.

Figure 6-14. Click Yes to keep the new resolution, click No to switch back to the original resolution setting.

Screen Resolution has to do with how much information can fit on the computer screen. Obviously you can't adjust how large or small your computer's monitor is (without buying a new one, that is), but you can make all the images on your screen larger or smaller so you can see more information at once.

1 Right-click a blank area on the desktop and select Properties from the shortcut menu.

The Display Properties dialog box appears.

2 Click the Settings tab.

The Settings tab appears in front of the Display Properties dialog box, as shown in Figure 6-13. The Screen resolution section is where you can change the resolution setting. Look at the numbers of pixels that are displayed—this is the current display resolution.

3 Slide the Screen resolution slider to the right or left to select the resolution you want to use.

The resolutions that are available depend on how much memory is installed on your computer's video card.

4 Click OK.

A dialog box, similar to the one shown in Figure 6-14, may appear, giving you 15 seconds to decide if you like the new resolution setting. If you do like it, click the Yes button, if you don't, click the No button. If you don't do anything, Windows assumes you don't like the new resolution setting, or your monitor can't display the new resolution, and switches back to the original resolution.

5 If prompted, click Yes to keep the new resolutions settings or No to return to the original resolution.

For a more complete description of the various resolution settings you can use, see Table 6-5. The highest resolution you can display depends on how much memory is installed on your video card. Most video cards have enough memory to display at least 800 by 600 resolution.

Table 6-4. Common screen resolutions

	Resolution	Description
640 by 480	640 by 480	**No longer supported in Windows XP,** 640 by 480 used to be the lowest resolution setting. Larger and newer monitors have made 640 by 480 resolution obsolete.
800 by 600	800 by 600	This has been the standard resolution setting for most computers, and is the lowest setting on newer monitors. 800 by 600 is quite confining for many new Windows applications, however. Unless you have poor eyesight or a 15-inch monitor, you will probably want to use a higher resolution.
1024 by 768	1024 by 768	The current standard, 1024 by 768 puts a lot of information on your screen,. Use this setting if you have a 17-inch or larger monitor, or when you want to see a lot of information at the same time, for example if you're working on a large spreadsheet, graphic files, or multiple windows.
1280 by 1024	1280 by 1024	Larger monitors have come down in price in recent years, and as a result, resolution standards have gone up. It's quite common now to find computers that use 1280 by 1024 and higher resolutions.
Higher Resolutions	Higher resolutions	Depending on how expensive the graphics card in your computer is, there may be several higher modes of resolution which continue to display more and more information and smaller and smaller images.

QUICK REFERENCE

TO CHANGE THE SCREEN RESOLUTION:

1. RIGHT-CLICK A BLANK AREA ON THE DESKTOP AND SELECT PROPERTIES FROM THE SHORTCUT MENU.

2. CLICK THE SETTINGS TAB.

3. SLIDE THE SCREEN RESOLUTION SLIDER TO THE RIGHT OR LEFT TO SELECT THE RESOLUTION YOU WANT TO USE.

4. CLICK OK

4 bits per pixel

24 bits per pixel

Figure 6-15. Change the number of colors displayed on your screen for more realistic images.

Display Properties

Change the color depth here

Figure 6-16. The Settings tab of the Display Properties dialog box.

Another change you can make in your display settings is the number of colors that are displayed on the screen at once, or the *color depth*. Why would you want to change the number of colors displayed on your screen? In the past, this was important, since the speed of your computer depended on how many colors it displayed. Now video cards are so advanced that it's almost impossible to see the difference between the available settings. Unless you do a lot with graphics, you probably don't have to worry about changing the color quality on your computer.

1 Right-click a blank area on the desktop and select Properties from the shortcut menu.

The Display Properties dialog box appears.

2 Click the Settings tab.

The Settings tab appears in front of the Display Properties dialog box, as shown in Figure 6-15. The Color quality list is where you can select the color depth you want to use. The Color quality list displays the current color depth setting.

3 Click the Color Quality list arrow and select the Color Depth setting you want to use.

The color depth settings that are available depend on how much memory is installed on your computer's video card.

NOTE *If only one option appears in the Color quality list, your video card is not properly installed. You'll need to reinstall the video drivers (software) that came along with your computer or video card.*

4 Click OK.

A dialog box may appear, giving you 15 seconds to decide if you like the new display settings. If you like it, click the Yes button, if you don't, click the No button. If you don't do anything, Windows assumes you don't like the new resolution setting, or your monitor can't display the new resolution, and switches back to the original resolution.

5 Click Yes to keep the new display settings or No to return to the original settings.

A dialog box may appear, asking you if you like the new display settings. Here again, click Yes if you want to keep the new settings and No if you want to switch back to the original color depth. If you don't do anything, Windows assumes you don't like the new display setting, or your monitor can't display it, and switches back to the original display settings.

For a more complete description of the various color depth settings you can use, see Table 6-6. The maximum color depth, or number of colors you can display at once, depends on how much memory is installed on your video card. Most video cards have enough memory to display at least 16 bit resolution.

Table 6-5. Common color depths

256 Colors

No longer supported in Windows XP, 256 colors was the standard color depth for Windows years ago, but most computers and video cards are fast enough to run with more colors without taking a performance hit, making this color depth obsolete in Windows XP

16 bit

Sixteen bit displays roughly 65,000 colors at once. This is the point where pictures become photo-realistic.

You have to really squint to see much difference between 16 bit and higher levels of color depth.

.

24 bit

Twenty-four bit and higher display millions of colors at once. Most newer computers use 24 or even 32 bit color depths.

32 bit and Greater

Thirty-two bit and higher display millions and millions of colors at once. Depending on how expensive the graphics card in your computer is, there may be several higher modes of color depth, which continue to display more and more colors on the screen.

QUICK REFERENCE

TO CHANGE THE SCREEN COLOR DEPTH:

1. RIGHT-CLICK A BLANK AREA ON THE DESKTOP AND SELECT PROPERTIES FROM THE SHORTCUT MENU.

2. CLICK THE SETTINGS TAB.

3. CLICK THE COLOR QUALITY LIST ARROW AND SELECT THE COLOR DEPTH SETTING YOU WANT TO USE.

4. CLICK OK.

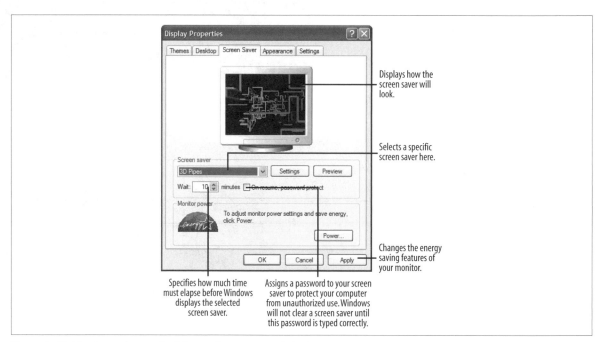

Displays how the screen saver will look.

Selects a specific screen saver here.

Changes the energy saving features of your monitor.

Specifies how much time must elapse before Windows displays the selected screen saver.

Assigns a password to your screen saver to protect your computer from unauthorized use. Windows will not clear a screen saver until this password is typed correctly.

Figure 6-17. The Screen Saver tab of the Display Properties dialog box.

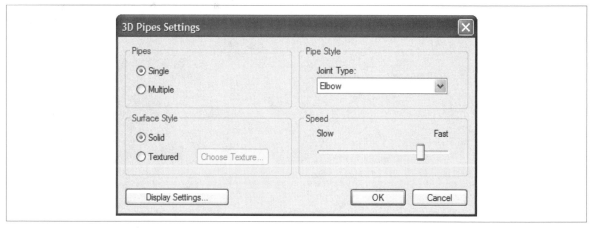

Figure 6-18. The 3D Pipes Settings dialog box.

A screen saver is a moving image that appears on the computer screen when you haven't used your computer for a while. Screen savers were originally used to protect screens from screen burn, which could occur when a static image was left on the screen for hours and hours. You don't have to worry about screen burn with today's monitors, but many people still like to use screen savers for entertainment and to personalize their computers.

TIP *Adding a password to your screen saver increases the level of security on your computer.*

This lesson will show you how to make a screen saver appear if your computer hasn't been touched for a while. You will also learn how to conserve power by having the monitor switch to a low-power standby mode or even turn off if the computer has been idle for a while.

1 **Right-click a blank area on the desktop and select Properties from the shortcut menu.**

The Display Properties dialog box appears.

2 Click the Screen Saver tab.

The Screen Saver tab appears in front of the Display Properties dialog box, as shown in Figure 6-17.

3 Click the Screen Saver list arrow.

A list of the available screen savers appears.

4 Select 3D Pipes from the list.

A preview of the 3D Pipes screen saver appears in the preview area of the dialog box. You can also preview the screen saver in full screen mode by clicking the Preview button. Change the settings for the selected screen saver by clicking the Settings button.

5 Click the Settings button.

A dialog box appears with settings for the selected screen saver, as shown in Figure 6-18. The options listed in this dialog box will vary, depending on the screen saver. There may be options for how many and what type of objects should appear on the screen, how fast the objects should move, or if you want to hear sounds when the screen saver is active—it all depends on which screen saver is selected.

6 Click Cancel to close the 3D Pipes Settings dialog box.

You can assign a password to your screen saver to protect your computer from unauthorized use by clicking the "On resume, password protect" check box. Windows will not clear a screen saver until this password is entered correctly.

You can easily change the amount of time it takes before Windows displays the selected screen saver.

7 Click the Wait box and type 15.

You can also click the Wait box up arrow until the number 15 appears. Now the screen saver will appear when you don't use your computer for 15 minutes.

Instead of using a screen saver, if you have an Energy Star compliant monitor you can conserve power by switching the monitor to a low-power standby mode or even have the monitor turn itself off if the computer hasn't been used for a while. Laptop users will also find energy-conserving settings here.

8 Click the Power button in the Monitor Power section.

The Power Options Properties dialog box appears.

NOTE *The Power Options dialog will have different settings, depending on whether you are using a desktop or laptop—or your computer may have its own unique power management software.*

9 Click the Turn off monitor list arrow and select After 30 minutes.

This setting will cause your monitor to turn itself off when the computer hasn't been used for 30 minutes. To turn the monitor back on, simply press a key on the keyboard or move the mouse—you don't need to push the monitor's on/off switch.

10 Click OK to close the Power Options Properties dialog box. Click OK to close the Display Properties dialog box.

QUICK REFERENCE

TO SET UP A SCREEN SAVER:

1. RIGHT-CLICK A BLANK AREA ON THE DESKTOP AND SELECT PROPERTIES FROM THE SHORTCUT MENU.

2. CLICK THE SCREEN SAVER TAB.

3. CLICK THE SCREEN SAVER LIST ARROW AND SELECT A SCREEN SAVER.

4. (OPTIONAL) SPECIFY HOW MUCH TIME MUST ELAPSE BEFORE WINDOWS DISPLAYS THE SELECTED SCREEN SAVER IN THE WAIT BOX AND CLICK THE ON RESUME, PASSWORD PROTECT CHECK BOX. WINDOWS AUTOMATICALLY ASSIGNS YOUR WINDOWS LOG IN PASSWORD TO THE SCREEN SAVER.

5. CLICK OK.

TO ADJUST THE ENERGY-SAVING FEATURES OF YOUR MONITOR:

1. FOLLOW THE PRECEDING STEPS 1 AND 2.

2. CLICK THE POWER BUTTON IN THE MONITOR POWER SECTION AND ADJUST THE INTERVAL AFTER WHICH THE MONITOR SHUTS OFF.

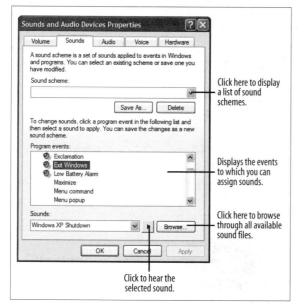

Figure 6-19. The Sounds and Audio Devices Properties dialog box.

Your computer can give you simple audio feedback, as long as you have a sound card and speakers. This lesson shows you how to assign sounds to events performed on your computer. An event is an action performed by you or a program. For example, when you press an incorrect key, the computer sometimes utters a simple beep. If you have a sound card, you can choose to play a sound rather than a boring beep whenever you press an incorrect key. You can also assign a sound to when you start or quit Windows.

1 Click the Start button and select Control Panel from the menu.

The Control Panel opens.

2 Click the Sounds, Speech, and Audio Devices category.

The Sounds and Audio Devices Properties dialog box appears.

3 Click the Change the sound scheme task.

This window displays the events to which you can assign sounds, and the sounds you can associate with the events.

NOTE Remember when Windows offered a plethora of sound schemes to choose from? Now, instead of

getting that bonus for free, you have to buy Plus! for Windows XP to install extra themes, games, and digital media. Microsoft must have some pretty high lawyer's fees...

Now you need to select the program event to which you want to add or change a sound.

4 Select Exit Windows in the Program events list.

You can listen to the sound that is currently assigned to any event by selecting the event and then clicking the play button located between the Sounds list and the Browse button in the dialog box. The sound assigned to the Exit Windows event (if one is assigned) appears in the Sounds box.

5 Click the Play button to the right of the Sounds box.

If you don't hear a sound, either the Exit Windows event doesn't have a sound assigned to it (you can check this by looking at the Sounds list), your computer doesn't have a soundcard and/or speakers, the volume is turned off, or the soundcard drivers are not installed correctly.

To assign a different sound to the selected event, click the Browse button to select the sound.

6 Click the Browse button.

The Browse window opens, listing all the different sounds you have to choose from. Select the sound you want to apply to the event.

7 Double-click Windows XP Startup.

The Windows XP Startup sound is now assigned to the Exit Windows event. You can listen to Windows XP Startup by clicking the play button at the bottom left corner of the window.

8 Click the Play button at the bottom left corner of the window to listen to Windows XP Startup.

Go on to the next step and close the Souds and Audio Devices Properties dialog box without making any changes.

9 Click Cancel to return to the Sounds and Audio Devices Properties dialog box.

QUICK REFERENCE

TO ASSIGN A SOUND TO A SPECIFIC WINDOWS EVENT:

1. CLICK THE START BUTTON AND SELECT CONTROL PANEL FROM THE MENU.

2. CLICK THE SOUNDS, SPEECH, AND AUDIO DEVICES CATEGORY.

3. CLICK THE CHANGE THE SOUND SCHEME TASK.D

4. SELECT THE EVENT FOR WHICH YOU WANT TO ASSIGN A SOUND FROM THE PROGRAM EVENTS LIST.

5. CLICK THE BROWSE BUTTON AND SELECT OR SPECIFY THE SOUND FILE YOU WANT TO ASSIGN TO THE EVENT. CLICK THE PLAY BUTTON TO LISTEN TO THE SELECTED SOUND.

6. CLICK OK TO APPLY THE SOUN

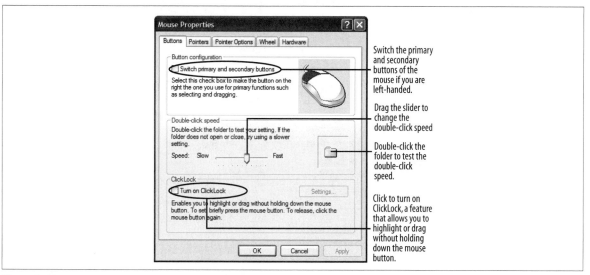

Figure 6-20. The Buttons tab of the Mouse Properties dialog box.

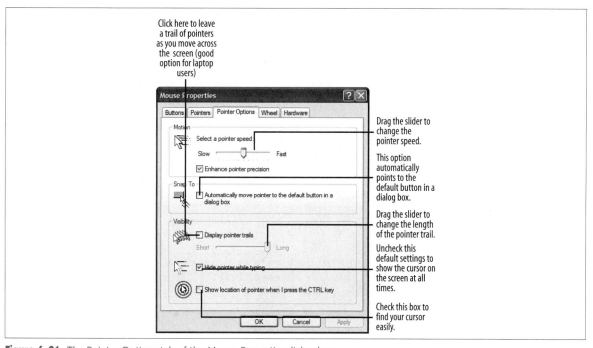

Figure 6-21. The Pointer Options tab of the Mouse Properties dialog box.

A common complaint many users have about Windows is they don't like how the mouse works. The mouse either is too slow or too fast, does not respond very well to your double-clicks, or worst of all if you're left-handed, its buttons are in the wrong places!

This lesson shows you how to adjust the mouse settings to make it easier for you to work with.

1 Click the Start button and select Control Panel from the menu.

The Control Panel opens.

2 Click the Printers and Other Hardware category and click Mouse.

Mouse icon

The Mouse Properties dialog box appears, as shown in Figure 6-20.

Many people complain that the double-click speed setting for Windows is too fast. To adjust the amount of time between clicks, drag the Double-Click Speed slider to the right or left. You can test the double-click speed by double-clicking the folder in the Test area box, located just to the right of the Speed slider.

NOTE *Your mouse dialog box and settings may appear completely different than those shown in Figure 6-20 depending on the type of pointing device and software installed on your computer.*

3 Drag the double-click slider to Slow, and then double-click the folder in the Test area.

The folder opens when you complete a successful double-click.

4 Drag the double-click slider to Fast, and then double-click the folder in the Test area.

It may be more difficult to open the folder when the speed is this fast.

You will have to experiment with the double-click slider, adjusting it to find a speed that suits your own personal preferences. Most people find that the double-click speed works best somewhere in the middle or on the slower side of the double-click speed bar.

5 Click the Pointer Options tab.

The Pointer Options tab of the Mouse Properties dialog box appears, as shown in Figure 6-21. Here you can also adjust how fast the mouse pointer moves across your screen when you move the mouse by dragging the Pointer Speed slider to the right or left. Refer to Table 6-7 for more information.

Now that you understand how to adjust the mouse to your liking, you can close the Mouse Properties dialog box to end the lesson.

6 Click Cancel to close the Mouse Properties dialog box without saving your changes.

Table 6-6. Mouse pointer options

Option	Description
Motion	
Select a pointer speed	Adjusts the distance that the pointer moves respective to the distance that the mouse or trackball moves. For example, to move your pointer across the width of your screen, you need to move your device further when the slider bar is set to Slow than when it is set to Fast.
Snap To	
Automatically move pointer to the default button in a dialog box	Specifies whether the mouse pointer snaps to the default button (such as OK or Apply) in dialog boxes. In some programs, Snap To may cause the pointer to automatically move to the center of the dialog box rather than to the default button.
Visibility	
Display pointer trails	Adds a trail to the mouse pointer, which makes it easier to see on Liquid Crystal Display (LCD) screens. To change the length of the pointer trail, drag the slider. The slider is dimmed until the check box is selected.
Hide pointer while typing	Hides the pointer when you type. The pointer reappears when you move the mouse or trackball.
Show location of the pointer when I press the Ctrl key	Shows the location of the mouse pointer when you press the Ctrl key.

QUICK REFERENCE

TO OPEN THE MOUSE PROPERTIES DIALOG BOX:

1. CLICK THE START BUTTON AND SELECT CONTROL PANEL FROM THE MENU.

2. CLICK THE PRINTERS AND OTHER HARDWARE CATEGORY AND THEN CLICK THE MOUSE ICON.

TO SWITCH THE LEFT AND RIGHT MOUSE BUTTONS:

- OPEN THE BUTTONS TAB OF THE MOUSE PROPERTIES DIALOG BOX, CLICK EITHER THE RIGHT-HANDED OR LEFT-HANDED CHECK BOX AND CLICK OK.

TO CHANGE THE DOUBLE-CLICK SPEED:

- OPEN THE BUTTONS TAB OF THE MOUSE PROPERTIES DIALOG BOX, DRAG THE DOUBLE-CLICK SPEED SLIDER TO A NEW POSITION, AND CLICK OK.

TO CHANGE THE POINTER SPEED:

- OPEN THE MOUSE PROPERTIES DIALOG BOX, CLICK THE POINTER OPTIONS TAB, DRAG THE POINTER SPEED SLIDER TO A NEW POSITION, AND CLICK OK.

TO CHANGE THE POINTER OPTIONS:

- OPEN THE MOUSE PROPERTIES DIALOG BOX, CLICK THE POINTER OPTIONS TAB, SELECT THE DESIRED POINTER OPTIONS, AND CLICK OK.

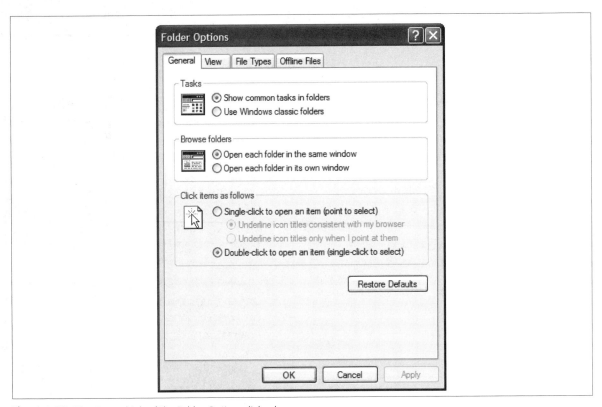

Figure 6-22. The General tab of the Folder Options dialog box.

In addition to the many options you can customize in Windows, you can also change how you work with folders and their contents. For example, by default Windows displays a list of common folder and file management tasks along the left side of the folder window. If you don't like this, you can view folders without the tasks. You can also change the way you click items. For example, instead of double-clicking to open something, you could single-click an item, like working with links on a Web page.

This is another self-guided lesson to help you become familiar with options for viewing your folders.

1 Click the Start button and select Control Panel from the menu.

The Control Panel appears.

2 Select Appearance and Themes and click Folder Options.

The Folder Options dialog box appears, as shown in Figure 6-22.

3 Refer to Table 6-7 for a description of each of the options. Click an option to see how it changes the icon to the left.

When you click an option, the icon to its left changes to preview how the change will effect a window.

Table 6-7. custom setting options

Option	Description
Tasks	
Show common tasks in folders	Specifies that hyperlinks to common folder tasks and other places on your computer are displayed in folders. These links appear in the left pane of the folder window.
Use Windows classic folders	Specifies that folder contents are displayed like classic Windows folders, which means that folder contents do not look and work like Web pages.
Browse folders	
Open each folder in the same window	Specifies that the contents of each folder open in the same window. To switch back to the previous folder, click the Back button on the toolbar, or press the Backspace key.
Open each folder in its own window	Specifies that the contents of each folder open in a new window. The previous folder content still appears in a different window, so you can switch between the windows.
Click items as follows	
Single-click to open an item (point to select)	Specifies that you want to open items in folders and on the desktop by single-clicking them, just as you would click a link on a Web page. To select an item without opening it, rest your pointer on it.
Underline icon titles consistent with my browser	Icon titles are underlined, just like links on a Web page.
Underline icons titles only when I point at them	Icon titles are underlined only when you point at them.
Double-click to open an item (single-click to select)	Specifies that you want to select files and folders by clicking to select an item and double-clicking an item to open it. This is how Windows normally works.

QUICK REFERENCE

TO CHANGE FOLDER OPTIONS:

1. CLICK THE **START** BUTTON AND SELECT CONTROL PANEL FROM THE MENU.

2. SELECT THE APPEARANCE AND THEMES CATEGORY AND CLICK FOLDER OPTIONS

3. REFER TO TABLE 6-7 AND MAKE THE DESIRED CHANGES.

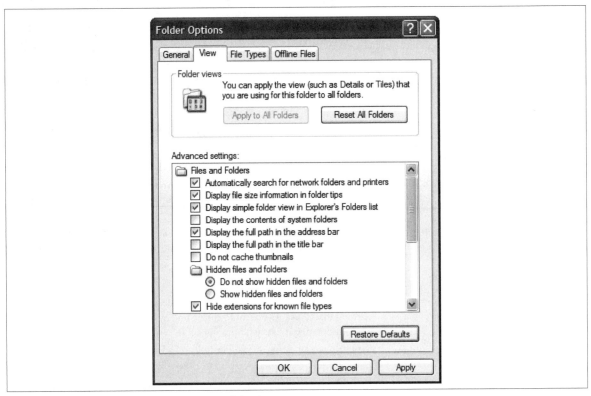

Figure 6-23. The View tab of the Folder Options dialog box.

Yet another lesson on folder options? Yep—in this lesson we will conclude our tour of how to customize how Windows looks and acts. This lesson explains how to change how information is displayed in a folder window. Remember the three-letter file extensions that are tacked on at the end of every file, such as .TXT? Normally Windows hides those extensions from view, but you can change this setting so Windows displays the file name *and* file extension, for example "Letter. TXT" instead of just "Letter."

This is another "look, but don't touch" lesson. We'll open the dialog box where you can change how the information is displayed, then you can look at Table 6-8 to see what everything means.

1 Click the Start button and select Control Panel from the menu.

The Control Panel appears.

2 Click the Appearances and Themes category and click Folder Options.

The Folder Options dialog box appears.

3 Click the View tab.

The View tab of the Folder Options dialog box appears, as shown in Figure 6-23.

4 Refer to Table 6-8 for a description of the more important folder options. Click Cancel when you're finished.

Table 6-8. Advanced folder options

Option	Default	Description
Display file size information in folder tips	✓	This displays the size of a file in the folder tips area.
Display simple folder view in Explorer's Folders list	✓,	In Windows Explorer, click the folder to display its contents and sub-folders. All folders are automatically closed when another folder is clicked. To hide or display a folder while it's still open, click on the plus or minus sign next to the folder.
Display the contents of system folders		System folders such as your C: drive, Program Files, Documents and Settings, and Windows, contain files your computer needs to run properly, and are usually hidden.
Display the full path in the address bar	✓	Displays the path of the folder in the address bar of the window, such as "C:\Windows\Program Files" instead of just "Program Files".
Display the full path in title bar		Displays the path of the folder in the title bar of the window, such as "C:\Windows\Program Files" instead of just "Program Files".
Do not cache thumbnails		When you store images in a cache file, Windows can reuse them instead of recreating them each time you open a folder. By disabling this automatic function, folders that contain thumbnails might take longer to open.
Hidden files and folders	✓,	Hides program or system files that should not be changed. Select this option to protect critical hidden files from accidentally being changed or deleted, and to reduce clutter in your folders.
Do not show hidden or system files		Specifies that both hidden and system files do not appear. Select this option to protect your hidden files from being accidentally changed or deleted, and to reduce clutter in your folder windows.
Show all files		Specifies that all files, including hidden and system files, appear in the list of files in this folder. Power Windows users like to use this option.
Hide file extensions for known file types	✓,	Hides the three-letter file name extensions for most files. For example, Filename.TXT would appear as just Filename. Click this option to reduce clutter in your folder windows.
Hide protected operating system files (Recommended)	✓,	Select this option to specify that files necessary to running your computer properly are hidden so they are not accidentally removed or changed.
Launch folder windows in a separate process		When you open a folder, this option specifies that it is opened as a separate part of memory. This can increase the stability of Windows, however it might decrease your computer's performance.
Remember each folder's view settings	✓,	Specifies that any folder settings you selected are retained whenever you reopen it. When this box is not checked, all folders return to their original state after you close them.
Show pop-up description for folder and desktop items	✓,	Shows a description of the selected item in a small pop-up window. If your folder is being displayed as a Web page, selecting this option has no effect, because the same information already appears in the left pane of the folder.

QUICK REFERENCE

TO CUSTOMIZE FOLDER VIEW OPTIONS:

1. CLICK THE START BUTTON AND SELECT CONTROL PANEL FROM THE MENU.

2. CLICK THE APPEARANCES AND THEMES CATEGORY AND CLICK FOLDER OPTIONS.

3. CLICK THE VIEW TAB.

4. SELECT THE DESIRED FOLDER VIEW OPTIONS AND CLICK OK.

Lesson Summary

A Look at the Control Panel

The Control Panel is where you can change the various settings of your computer and Windows.

To Open the Control Panel: Click the Start button and select Control Panel. Or, open My Computer and click the Control Panel task in the Other Places menu.

To View the Control Panel in Classic View: Click the Switch to Classic View task in the Control Panel menu.

Changing the Date and Time

To Display the Current Date: Point at the clock on the taskbar for several seconds to display the current date.

To Change the Date and/or Time: Double-click the clock on the taskbar, adjust the date and time using the calendar and clock controls and click OK.

To Change Time Zones: Double-click the clock on the taskbar, click the Time Zone tab, select a time zone from the list box, and click OK.

Adjusting the Computer's Volume

To Display the Volume Control Icon in the Taskbar: Click the Start button and select Control Panel from the menu. Click the Sounds, Speech, and Audio Devices category and click Sounds and Audio Devices. Ensure that the Place volume icon in the taskbar box is checked then click OK.

To Adjust Your Computer's Volume: Click the Speaker icon located on the far right of the taskbar, and drag the volume slider up or down.

To Turn the Volume Off: Click the Speaker icon located in the system tray of the taskbar and check the Mute check box.

To Display the Volume Control Dialog Box: Double-click the Speaker icon located in the system tray of the taskbar.

Changing the Color Scheme and Appearance

To Change the Color Scheme: Right-click a blank area on the desktop and select Properties from the shortcut menu, click the Appearance tab, select a color scheme from the Color scheme list, and click OK.

To Change Windows and Buttons to Classic Style: Select Windows Classic style from the Windows and Buttons list.

Adding Wallpaper to the Desktop

Right-click a blank area on the desktop and select Properties from the shortcut menu. Click the Desktop tab, and select the wallpaper you want to use from the Background list. You can also click Browse and specify the name and location of your *own* picture or graphic you want to use as wallpaper. Select how you want the wallpaper to be displayed (centered, tiled, or stretched) from the Position list and click OK.

Adjusting the Screen Resolution

Screen Resolution has to do with how much information can fit on the screen. Higher screen resolutions can display more information on the screen at one time, but at the price of making everything appear smaller.

To Change the Screen Resolution: Right-click a blank area on the desktop, select Properties from the shortcut menu, and click the Settings tab. Slide the Screen Resolution slider to the right or left to select the resolution you want to use, and click OK.

Adjusting the Screen Color Depth

Color depth has to do with how many colors are displayed on the screen at one time.

To Change the Screen Color Depth: Right-click a blank area on the desktop and select Properties from the shortcut menu, click the Settings tab, click the Color quality list arrow, select the Color Depth setting you want to use, and click OK.

Using a Screen Saver

To Set Up a Screen Saver: Right-click a blank area on the desktop and select Properties from the shortcut menu. Click the Screen Saver tab, click the Screen Saver list arrow, select a screen saver, and click OK.

To Adjust the Energy-Saving Features of your Monitor: You can adjust the energy-saving features of your monitor by opening the Screen Saver tab of the Display Properties dialog box, clicking the Power button in the

Monitor power section, and adjusting the interval after which the monitor shuts off.

Changing System and Program Sounds

To Assign a Sound to a Specific Windows Event: Click the Start button and select Control Panel from the menu. Click the Sounds, Speech, and Audio Devices category. Click the Change the Sound Scheme task. Select the event for which you want to assign a sound from the Program events list. Click the Browse button and select or specify the sound file you want to assign to the event and click the Play button to listen to the selected sound. Click OK to apply the sound.

Adjusting the Mouse

To Open the Mouse Properties Dialog Box: Click the Start button and select Control Panel from the menu. Click the Printers and Other Hardware category and click the Mouse icon.

To Switch the Left and Right Mouse Buttons: Open the Buttons tab in the Mouse Properties dialog box, select either the Right-handed or Left-handed option, and click OK.

To Change the Double-click Speed: Open the Buttons tab in the Mouse Properties dialog box, drag the Double-Click Speed slider to a new position, and click OK.

To Change the Pointer Speed: Open the Mouse Properties dialog box, click the Pointer Options tab, and drag the Pointer Speed slider to a new position, and click OK.

To Change Pointer Options: Open the Pointer Options tab in the Mouse Properties dialog box, select the desired pointer options, and click OK.

Customizing How Folders Look and Work

To Apply Custom Folder Settings: Click the Start button and select Control Panel from the menu. Click the Appearance and Themes category and click Folder Options, then make your selections in the Folder Options dialog box.

Customizing Folder View Options

Click the Start button and select Control Panel from the menu. Select Appearance and Themes, click Folder Options, click the View tab, select the desired folder view options and click OK.

Quiz

1. Used only for advanced networking settings, the Control Panel should never be touched by ordinary users. (True or False?)

2. Which of the following statements is NOT true?

    A. You can change the display style to Classic if you don't like XP style.

    B. You can change the colors for all Windows objects at once using a color scheme.

    C. Double-click the clock on the taskbar to adjust the time and date.

    D. You can only use preset patterns as your desktop wallpaper.

3. You can adjust your computer's volume by clicking Start → All Programs → Accessories → Entertainment → Volume Control. (True or False?)

4. 640 x 480, 800 x 600, 1024 x 768 are all examples of:

    A. Color depths.

    B. Dimensions for the three largest patios in the world.

    C. Screen resolutions.

    D. Multiplication problems that you would need to use a calculator to solve.

5. You're a huge fan of the early 1980's TV show, *The Dukes of Hazard*. Which of the following are ways you could customize your computer to show everyone your devotion to this forgotten show?

    A. Change the desktop wallpaper to a confederate flag, like the paint job on the Duke boys' car.

    B. Apply the "The Dukes of Hazard" desktop theme, which comes with Windows XP.

C. Add a system sound so that whenever someone turns on your computer they hear an engine sound.

D. Windows XP doesn't allow you to personalize your computer in such poor taste.

6. You can change the mouse's double-click speed in the Mouse Properties dialog box. (True or False?)

7. Double-clicking the desktop opens the Display Properties dialog box, which allows you to change any screen settings, such as colors, screen resolution, and desktop wallpaper. (True or False?)

Homework

1. Change Windows' wallpaper to Autumn, in center format.

2. Change Windows' screen colors to the Silver color scheme and then back to the previous color scheme.

3. Change Windows' Asterisk event to the TADA sound, and then back to the original sound.

4. Try out various screen resolutions to see which one you like best.

5. Adjust your mouse's pointer speed and double-click speed to suit your preferences.

Quiz Answers

1. False. The Control Panel is where you go to make changes to Windows and your computer. While there are a few technical areas in the Control Panel, most of it is straightforward and easy to understand.

2. D. You can use your own pictures and graphics as wallpaper in addition to Windows preset wallpaper settings.

3. True. You can also adjust your computer's volume by clicking the Speaker icon on the Windows taskbar.

4. C. These are all examples of screen resolutions.

5. A and C. Fortunately there isn't a Dukes of Hazard desktop theme that ships with Windows XP (or any titles, for that matter), but you can still personalize the other settings, such as the wallpaper and system sounds.

6. True. The double-click speed is probably one of the first things you should adjust if you're having trouble double-clicking with the mouse.

7. False. Right-click the desktop and select Properties from the shortcut menu to open the Display Properties dialog box.

CHAPTER 7

THE FREE PROGRAMS

CHAPTER OBJECTIVES:

Learn about WordPad

Learn about NotePad

Learn about the Calculator

Learn about the Sound Recorder

Learn about Paint and create a picture

Learn about Games

Learn about Character Map

Prerequisites

- **Know how to use the mouse to click, double-click, click and drag, and right-click.**
- **Know how to start programs in the Start Menu.**
- **Know how to use menus, toolbars, and dialog boxes.**
- **Know how to view and navigate the contents of your computer (disk drives and folders).**

Windows XP doesn't really do much by itself—you need to run a program whenever you want to do something with your computer. But before you rush off to the local computer store to buy a software program to let you type a letter or paint a picture, read through this chapter! Microsoft has included a handful of small, but useful, programs with Windows XP. You can find most of these programs—such as WordPad, Paint, NotePad, and Calculator—in the Accessories group of the Start Menu.

This chapter explores the programs that Microsoft tossed into the Accessories menu. You'll learn what all the "freebie" programs are, what they do, and if they'll work for your purposes.

If you're this far in the book, you should already have a good sense of how to work with a Windows program. Most of the lessons in this chapter are of the "guided tour" type and only a few of them have the usual step-by-step exercises. Don't worry—these programs are all very simple and easy to use, so you shouldn't have any trouble figuring them out.

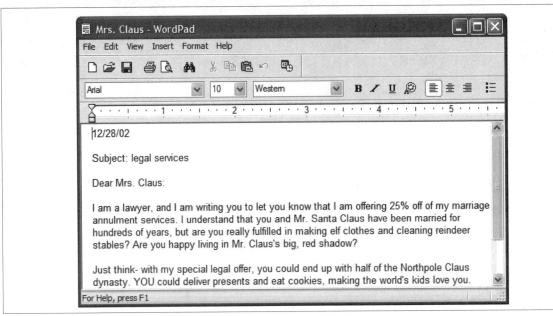

Figure 7-1. A simple word processor, the WordPad accessory allows you to create letters and documents.

WordPad is a "stripped-down" word processor and is one of the best freebies Microsoft tossed in with Windows XP. You can use WordPad to create letters, memos, and documents. You can format your WordPad documents with various font and paragraph styles. Here's how to open the WordPad program:

1 Click the Start button and select All Programs → Accessories → WordPad from the menu.

The WordPad program appears, as shown in Figure 7-1.

If you want, try typing some text in the WordPad and explore WordPad's menus.

2 Close the WordPad program.

Table 7-1. About WordPad

Description	Details
What it's for	A scaled-down word processing program you can use to create simple letters and documents
Type of file(s) used	Word files Rich Text files Text documents Write files
Features include	Font and paragraph formatting, bullets, tab stops, insert the current date, print preview, insert objects from other programs, and find and replace
Features don't include	Spell-checker, thesaurus, tables, headers and footers, many other advanced word processing features

Table 7-1. About WordPad (Continued)

Description	Details
Found under	All Programs → Accessories → WordPad

QUICK REFERENCE

TO OPEN WORDPAD:

- CLICK THE START BUTTON AND SELECT ALL PROGRAMS → ACCESSORIES → WORDPAD FROM THE MENU.

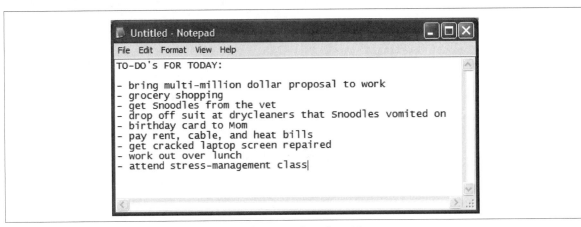

Figure 7-2. Use the Notepad program to jot down quick notes without formatting.

WordPad is one of the most full-featured free programs, while \Notepad is probably the simplest. You can use Notepad to create or edit simple notes or text files that do not require any type of formatting. Notepad opens and saves text in ASCII (text-only) format. Notepad can only open or read files that are smaller than 64K. If you need to create or edit a file that requires formatting or is larger than 64K, use WordPad. Let's take a closer look at Notepad.

1 Click the **Start** button and select **All Programs** → **Accessories** → **Notepad**.

The Notepad program appears, as shown in Figure 7-2. If you want, try typing some text in Notepad and explore Notepad's menus.

2 Close the Notepad program.

Table 7-2. About Notepad

Description	Detail
Notepad	📄 Text documents
Features include	Find text in any document, time/date stamp, word-wrap
Features don't inlcude	Formatting of any kind, can only work with text files under 64K
Found under	All Programs → Accessories → Notepad

QUICK REFERENCE

TO OPEN NOTEPAD:

- CLICK THE **S**TART BUTTON AND SELECT ALL
  PROGRAMS → ACCESSORIES → NOTEPAD FROM
  THE MENU.

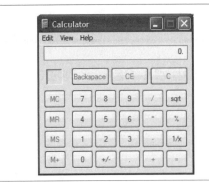

Figure 7-3. The Calculator program in Standard mode.

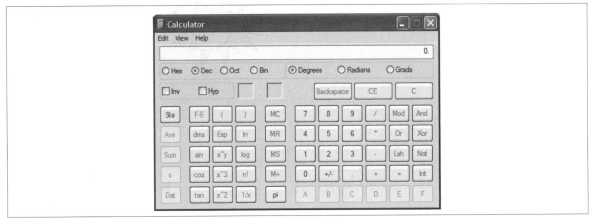

Figure 7-4. The Calculator program in Scientific mode.

The Calculator accessory is one of the more useful programs included with Windows. You use the Calculator just like you would use a calculator that's not on your computer. The only difference between the two is that instead of pressing the calculator's keys with your fingers, you click them with your mouse. You can also use the number keys or the numeric keypad on your keyboard to enter numbers into the Calculator program. Here's how to open the Calculator program:

1 Click the Start button and select All Programs → Accessories → Calculator from the menu.

The Calculator program appears, as shown in Figure 7-3.

If you want, try making some calculations with the Calculator. The Calculator program can be used in one of two modes: standard or scientific. Standard mode is adequate for most of us, but if you're an engineer, math teacher, student, or number freak, you might want to use the Calculator's scientific mode.

2 Select View → Scientific from the menu.

The Calculator appears in scientific mode, as shown in Figure 7-4. If you still remember your Trigonometry or Statistics, feel free to try out the expanded functions in scientific mode.

3 Select View → Standard from the menu to return to Standard mode, and close the Calculator when you're finished.

Table 7-3. About the Calculator

Description	Detail
Calculator	A computer version of a standard and scientific calculator you can use to make quick calculations on your computer
Found under	All Programs → Accessories → Calculator

QUICK REFERENCE

TO OPEN THE CALCULATOR:

- CLICK THE START BUTTON AND SELECT ALL PROGRAMS → ACCESSORIES → CALCULATOR FROM THE MENU.

TO SWITCH BETWEEN STANDARD AND SCIENTIFIC MODES:

- SELECT VIEW → SCIENTIFIC OR STANDARD FROM THE MENU..

Figure 7-5. The Sound Recorder program.

Figure 7-6. The Sound Recorder displays a waveform when it plays or records something.

Record Button   **Stop Button**   **Play Button**

To use the Sound Recorder program, you must have a sound card and speakers installed on your computer. If you want to record something, you will also need a microphone. If your computer system meets these requirements, then you can use Sound Recorder like a computerized tape recorder to record voice annotations or anything else you can think of.

1 Click the Start button and select All Programs → Accessories → Entertainment → Sound Recorder from the menu.

The Sound Recorder program appears, as shown in Figure 7-5. Try recording a sound.

2 Click the Record button, talk briefly into your computer's microphone, and then click the Stop button.

As you record your voice, a waveform should appear in the Sound Recorder window, as shown in Figure 7-6. If you don't see a waveform, your microphone is shut off or is plugged into the wrong jack in your soundcard, or there is something wrong with your soundcard (maybe you don't have one!).

3 Click the Play button.

Take some time to explore Sound Recorder's menus. Under the File menu, you can save a recorded sound or open a previously recorded sound. The Effects menu lets you do some cool things with your recordings, like adding an echo to it, reversing it, or adjusting its volume.

4 Close the Sound Recorder program.

Table 7-4. About the Sound Recorder

Descriptionr	Detail
Sound Recorder	Records voice annotations or other sounds and saves them to your computer.
Type of file(s) used	WAV files
Features Include	Record and playback, echo, reverse, increase/decrease volume
Features don't include	Advanced mixing features
Found under	All Programs → Accessories → Entertainment → Sound Recorder

QUICK REFERENCE

TO OPEN SOUND RECORDER:

- CLICK THE START BUTTON AND SELECT ALL PROGRAMS → ACCESSORIES → ENTERTAINMENT → SOUND RECORDER FROM THE MENU.

TO RECORD A SOUND:

1. CLICK THE RECORD BUTTON AND SPEAK INTO THE MICROPHONE.
2. CLICK THE STOP BUTTON WHEN YOU'RE FINISHED.

TO PLAY A SOUND:

- CLICK THE PLAY BUTTON.

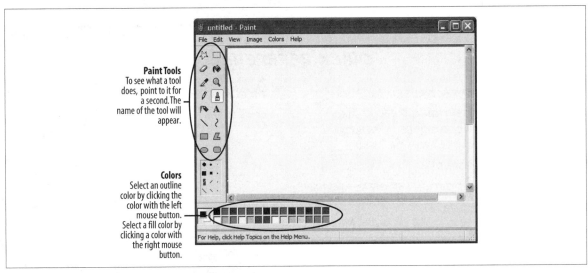

Figure 7-7. Create pictures and maps with the Paint program.

Paint is a drawing program that comes with Windows XP. You can use Paint to create and view pictures and graphics—including maps, artwork, and photographs.

1 Click the Start button and select All Programs → Accessories → Paint from the menu.

The Paint program appears, as shown in Figure 7-7. Paint includes a lot of tools to create pictures—see Table 7-6 for their descriptions.

Paint is the most complex of the free programs that come with Windows. If you want to learn more about how to use Paint, take a look at the tables in this lesson, then move on to the next lesson.

Table 7-5. About Paint

Description	Detail
Paint	Used to create, edit, and view pictures and graphics
Type of file(s) used	Bitmap (BMP) graphic files
Features Include	Draw shapes, add text, paint, use maximum number of possible colors (determined by your display's color depth settings)
Features don't include	Photo retouching, acquire from scanner, saving to many other graphic formats such as GIF as JPEG pictures
Found under	All Programs → Accessories → Paint

Paint provides a number of different tools to create pictures with. To see a tool's description, position the mouse over the tool button. After a moment, the name of the tool will appear. In addition, a brief description of the tool appears in the Status bar whenever the pointer is over it. The following table describes the Paint tools and their functions:

Table 7-6. The Paint tools

Tool	Name	Description
	Free Form Select	Use the mouse to draw a freeform outline around any shape to select it. Once you have selected an area, you can cut, copy, or move it.
	Select	Same as above except it uses a rectangle as the selection area.

Table 7-6. The Paint tools (Continued)

Tool	Name	Description
	Eraser	Erases portions of the current picture. You can choose from four different eraser sizes.
	Fill With Color	Fills area with the selected color from the color palette.
	Pick Color	Copies a color from one object to another.
	Magnifier	Zooms in or out of the current graphic.
	Pencil	Draw freeform objects, just as if you were using a real pencil.
	Brush	Paint freeform objects, just as if you were using a real paintbrush. You can choose from several different brush sizes and shapes.
	Airbrush	Applies color using an airbrush effect.
	Text	Inserts text into the picture.
	Line	Draws lines.
	Curve	Draws curved lines.
	Rectangle	Draws rectangles.
	Polygon	Draws polygons.
	Ellipse	Draws ellipses.
	Rounded Rectangle	Draws rectangles with rounded edges.

QUICK REFERENCE

TO START PAINT:

• CLICK THE START BUTTON AND SELECT ALL
PROGRAMS → ACCESSORIES → PAINT FROM
THE MENU.

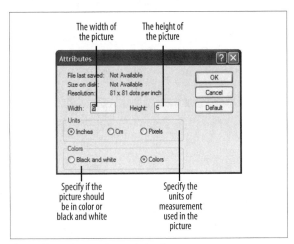

The width of the picture

The height of the picture

Specify if the picture should be in color or black and white

Specify the units of measurement used in the picture

Figure 7-8. The Attributes dialog box.

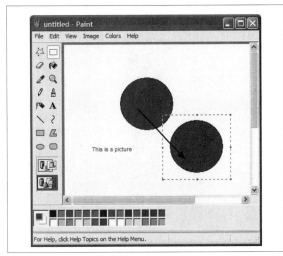

Figure 7-9. You can move a pasted object in Paint by dragging and dropping.

In the previous lesson, you were introduced to the Paint program; in this lesson, you'll get your hands dirty and actually create a simple drawing in Paint. Creating pictures in Paint is easy—simply click the tool you want, and your mouse pointer turns into that tool. To draw a rectangle, for example, click the rectangle button tool and then click and drag a rectangle in the Paint area of the window.

1 Make sure the Paint program is open.

TIP *To make a perfect circle or square, click the corresponding shape tool and hold down the Shift key while you drag the $+$ pointer.*

Pictures can be just about any size. Here's how to change a picture's dimensions or size:

2 Select Image → Attributes from the menu.

The Attributes dialog box appears, as shown in Figure 7-8. Here, you can specify how

large you want your picture to be, and if it should appear in color or black and white.

3 Click the Inches option in the Units section, set the Width to 6 inches and the Height to 6 inches, make sure the Colors option is selected, and then click OK.

Compare your Attributes dialog box with the one shown in Figure 7-8. Paint resizes the picture to your specifications. However, to make the actual Paint window bigger (not just the picture), you must resize it by dragging its lower right corner.

4 Click the Ellipse tool.

Text Tool

The Ellipse tool depresses and the pointer changes to a $+$, indicating that you can draw the selected shape. Also, notice that three fill options appear below the Paint tools. There are three options for any shapes you draw. They are:

- **Outline:** (Top option) Draws the outline of the shape.
- **Outline and Fill:** (Middle option) Draws the outline of the shape and fills the inside with the color currently selected from the color palette.
- **Fill:** (Bottom option) Draws a colored shape without an outline.

Fill Tool

5 Position the pointer in a blank area of the picture, then click and hold the mouse button and drag it down and to the right until you have a circle.

Here's how to add color to the circle you just created:

6 Click the Fill tool.

Select Tool

Now you need to select the color you want to use from the color palette.

7 Click the Blue color from the color palette at the bottom of the screen.

Now all you have to do is click inside the object. The pointer changes to a , indicating you can fill the object with the selected color.

8 Click inside the circle with the pointer.

The circle is filled with the blue color. You can also add text to your drawing.

9 Click the Text tool.

Elipse tool
To make a perfect circle or square, click
the corresponding shape tool and hold
down the Shift key while you drag the + pointer.

This time the pointer changes to a $+$, indicating that you can add text to your picture. Click where you want to add text to the picture.

10 Click a blank area of the picture.

The Text Toolbar should appear on the Paint screen, letting you select from several fonts and styles.

11 Type This is a picture.

You will probably have to adjust the text border so that the text fits. Actually, if you create a large enough rectangle by clicking and dragging with the $+$ pointer, you won't have to resize it.

12 Drag the text box's lower right border up and to the right until the text fits on a single line.

You can cut, copy, and paste objects in Paint, just as you can in most Windows programs.

13 Click the Select tool and select the circle object.

Fill Options

To select an object, position the pointer above the top-left corner of the circle, then drag a rectangle around the circle by clicking and dragging the mouse below the bottom-right corner of the circle and releasing the mouse button. A dotted rectangle appears around the circle.

14 Select Edit → Copy from the menu.

Now paste the picture.

15 Click a blank area of the picture to deselect the circle, and then select Edit → Paste from the menu.

The copied circle is pasted in the picture. Notice the pasted circle is selected. You can easily move any object while it is selected.

16 Move the selected circle by dragging it to a new position in the Paint window.

17 Exit the Paint program without saving your work.

QUICK REFERENCE

TO USE A PAINT TOOL:

- CLICK THE PAINT TOOL BUTTON. THE MOUSE POINTER TURNS INTO THAT SPECIFIC TOOL..

TO CHANGE THE SIZE OF A PAINT PICTURE:

- SELECT IMAGE → ATTRIBUTES FROM THE MENU. SPECIFY THE PICTURE SIZE AND CLICK OK

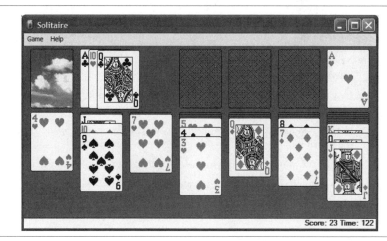

Figure 7-10. The Solitaire game.

Figure 7-11. The Minesweeper game.

TIP *Microsoft XP games can be strangely addicting! Don't get caught procrastinating with them!*

Windows XP comes with several simple games you can play when things get dull at the office. These games not only help you pass the time, but they're also a great way to improve your mouse skills. You can find these games under the Games menu.

Table 7-7. Games included with Windows

Game	Description
FreeCell	Solitaire card game. To win, you make four stacks of cards on the home cells: one for each suit, stacked in order of rank.
Hearts	Multi-player card game. The object of Hearts is to have the lowest score at the end of the game.
Internet Backgammon	New in Windows XP, Internet Backgammon lets you play a game of backgammon against another players on the Internet.
Internet Checkers	New in Windows XP, Internet Checkers lets you play a game of checkers against another players on the Internet.

Table 7-7. Games included with Windows (Continued)

Game	Description
Internet Hearts	New in Windows XP, Internet Hearts lets you play a game of Hearts against other players on the Internet.
Internet Reversi	New in Windows XP, Internet Reversi lets you play a game of Reversi against other players on the Internet.
Internet Spades	New in Windows XP, Internet Spades lets you play a game of Spades against other players on the Internet.
Minesweeper	Find all the mines on the playing field as quickly as possible without uncovering any of them.
Pinball	A classic pinball game that doesn't require any quarters to play.
Solitaire	The object of the game is to use all the cards in the deck to build up the four suit stacks from ace to king.
Spider Solitaire	An advanced solitaire card game.

QUICK REFERENCE

TO PLAY A BUILT-IN GAME:

1. CLICK THE START BUTTON AND SELECT ALL PROGRAMS → GAMES.

2. SELECT THE GAME YOU WANT TO PLAY

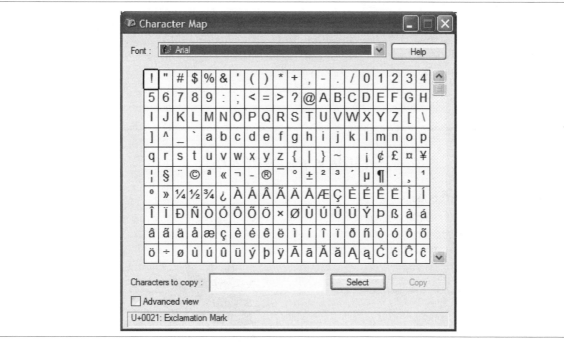

Figure 7-12. The Character Map program.

Believe it or not, you can enter many more characters and symbols into a document than can be found on the computer's keyboard. For example, you can insert the copyright symbol (©), foreign characters (£), silly characters (☺), and many, many more. In this lesson, you will learn how to insert special symbols with the Character Map program.

1 Click the Start button and select All Programs → Accessories → WordPad from the menu.

Now open Character Map to insert a special character into the WordPad document.

2 Click the Start button and select All Programs → Accessories → System Tools → Character Map from the menu.

The Character Map program appears, as shown in Figure 7-12.

NOTE *The Character Map program isn't always installed with Windows XP. If you can't find the Character Map program in the Accessories menu, it may not have been installed. You can install Character Map by opening the Control Panel, and choosing Add or Remove Programs → Add/Remove Windows Components → Accessories and Utilities*

→ *Details button* → *Accessories* → *Details button, checking Character Map, and clicking OK.*

3 Find and double-click the © symbol.

Emphasize the word *find* because you'll probably spend a few minutes looking for the tiny © symbol before you find it.

4 Click Copy.

The © symbol has been copied to the Windows clipboard.

5 Switch to WordPad and click the Paste button.

The © symbol is pasted into the WordPad document.

6 Close the WordPad and Character Map programs.

Table 7-8. About Character Map

Description	Found under
Description	Program that allows you to insert special characters into programs
Found under	Programs → Accessories → System Tools → Character Map

QUICK REFERENCE

TO OPEN CHARACTER MAP:

- CLICK THE START BUTTON AND SELECT ALL PROGRAMS → ACCESSORIES → SYSTEM TOOLS → CHARACTER MAP FROM THE MENU.

Lesson Summary

WordPad

WordPad is a simple word processor that supports font and paragraph formatting. The default file format for WordPad is Word 6.0 (DOC) files.

To Open WordPad: Click the Start button and select All Programs → Accessories → WordPad from the menu.

Notepad

Notepad is a simple text editor that can open and save text (ASCII) files that are smaller than 64K. No formatting of any kind is supported.

To Open Notepad: Click the Start button and select All Programs → Accessories → Notepad from the menu.

Calculator

Calculator is an on-screen calculator.

To Open the Calculator: Click the Start button and select All Programs → Accessories → Calculator from the menu.

To Switch Between Standard and Scientific Modes: Select View → Scientific or Standard from the menu.

Sound Recorder

Sound Recorder is a digital tape recorder you can use if you have a sound card and speakers installed on your computer. Sound Recorder saves its recordings as digital WAV files.

To Open Sound Recorder: Click the Start button and select All Programs → Accessories → Entertainment → Sound Recorder from the menu.

To Record a Sound: Click the Record button and speak into the microphone and click the Stop button when you're finished.

To Play a Sound: Click the Play button.

Paint

Paint is a drawing program that can use paint to create and view pictures and graphics. The default file format for Paint is bitmap (BMP) graphic files.

To Start Paint: Click the Start button and select All Programs → Accessories → Paint from the menu.

Creating Pictures with Paint

To Use a Paint Tool: Click the paint tool button. The mouse pointer turns into that specific tool.

To Change the Size of a Paint Picture: Select Image → Attributes from the menu. Specify the picture size and click OK.

Play Games

To Play a Built-in Game: Click the Start button and select All Programs → Games, and then select the game you want to play.

Character Map

The Character Map program lets you insert special symbols not found on the keyboard, such as © or J.

To Open Character Map: Click the Start button and select All Programs → Accessories → System Tools → Character Map from the menu.

Quiz

1. The WordPad program includes the following features: (Select all that apply.)

   A. Ability to use different fonts.

   B. A spell-checker.

   C. Ability to format paragraphs.

   D. A Thesaurus.

2. The NotePad program can open any text files of any size. (True or False?)

3. To record sounds with the Sound Recorder, you will need: (Select all that apply.)

   A. A sound card.

   B. A microphone.

C. A MIDI interface.

D. Speakers.

4. The Calculator program can be displayed using standard and scientific modes. (True or False?)

5. Which is NOT a game that comes along with Windows XP?

   A. Solitaire.

   B. Minesweeper.

   C. Starcraft.

D. FreeCell.

6. Which of the following statements is NOT true?

   A. You can play Spades against other people on the Internet.

   B. Paint is an advanced image program that you can use to touch up digital pictures.

   C. The Character Map program lets you insert special symbols not found on the keyboard.

   D. You can change the size of a paint picture.

Homework

1. Use Paint to create the following picture (and don't worry if yours doesn't turn out exactly the same):

1. Use the Calculator to find the square root of 12.

2. Open the "Seniors" text file in NotePad.

3. Start the WordPad program.

4. Copy all the text in NotePad and paste it into WordPad.

5. Insert a ☺ symbol anywhere in the WordPad document (Hint: You'll need to use the Character Map program).

Quiz Answers

1. A and C. WordPad can format fonts and paragraphs, but it doesn't come with a spell checker or a thesaurus.

2. False. NotePad can only open text files that are 64K or less. You'll have to use WordPad to open text files that are larger than 64K.

3. A, B, and D. You need a sound card and microphone to record sounds with Sound Recorder, and you'll need speakers if you want to hear what you recorded.

4. True. You can use the calculator in standard or scientific mode.

5. C. Starcraft doesn't come with Windows XP (although it is a great game!)

6. B. Paint is a useful, but very limited, drawing program. You probably won't want to use it to touch up your digital pictures.

CHAPTER 8

WORKING WITH PICTURES AND MULTIMEDIA

CHAPTER OBJECTIVES:

Transfer digital photos to your computer

View and manage your digital photos

Print your digital photos

E-mail your digital photos

Order digital prints online

Play a CD on your computer

Copy a CD to your hard drive

Create a playlist

Burn music CDs

Listen to Internet radio stations

Change skins

Play a DVD on your computer

Prerequisites

- **Know how to use the mouse to click, double-click, click and drag, and right-click.**
- **Know how to use menus, toolbars, and dialog boxes.**
- **Know how to view and navigate through the contents of your computer (drives and folders).**

If you are one of the millions of people who have discovered the advantages of taking pictures with a digital camera, or have been looking for a way to listen to the radio on your computer, then this chapter is right up your alley.

Even if you haven't jumped on the digital photography/multimedia bandwagon, this chapter demonstrates just how easy and efficient it is to manage your digital photos, copy a CD to your hard drive, and even watch a DVD on your computer, all using Windows XP. Windows XP offers a smorgasbord of programs and features to make life a little more fun...and other people jealous. Let's get started!

Figure 8-1. A digital camera.

Figure 8-2. A Web cam usually sits on top of a computer's monitor.

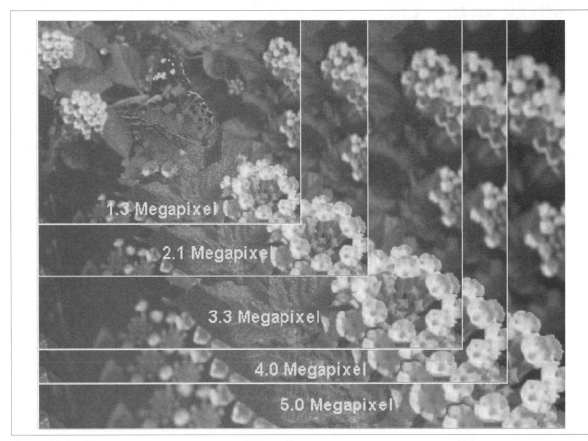

Figure 8-3. Cameras with more megapixels can take sharper and more detailed pictures.

TIP *A megapixel contains one million pixels.*

Have you ever developed a roll of film, only to find 6 of the 24 images appealing? Talk about a waste of money—and time. With a digital camera, *you* decide which photographs are printworthy and which ones you can do without. With Windows XP and the right hardware, you can take your digital images and then transfer them straight to your computer. Once you've transferred your pictures you can print them, insert them into a word processing document, or even send them in an e-mail message. You

can also edit digital photos, to remove such undesirable objects as redeye or an ex-boyfriend.

The quality of the pictures a digital camera takes depends on its resolution, which is measured in *megapixels*. One megapixel is equal to one million, or 1000×1000 pixels. The higher the number of megapixels, the clearer and more detailed the picture.

Digital cameras don't use film—they store their pictures on a type of removable memory called *flash cards*. Flash cards can store anywhere from a dozen to several hundred pictures, depending on how much memory they have. There are three different types or formats of flash cards out there:

• **CompactFlash:** Definitely the most common type of "digital film" out there, Compact-Flash cards can typically store anywhere from 8MB to 1GB.

• **Secure Digical :** Secure Digical (SD) and MultiMediaCard cards are undoubtedly the most popular flash memory format. SD and MMC cards look identical and, other than some small technical differences that you don't really need to worry about, are cmpatible with one another

• **Memory Stick:** Sony makes this type of memory card for use in its own products: Sony digital cameras, Sony PDAs, etc. Memory sticks are available in capacities ranging from 4 MB to 128 MB.

• **xD Picture Card:** The xD Picture Card is the newest memory card on the block. xD Picture Cards are amazingly small, but they don't skimp on memory: new Picture Cards have capacities of up to 1 GB.

Another popular toy you can add to your computer is a *Web cam*. A Web cam is a tiny digital video camera that usually sits on top of a computer's monitor. People use Web cams for videoconferencing and to send live images over the Internet.

Table 8-1. Comparison of megapixels

Megapixels	Image Size	Description
Under 1	640 × 480	Entry-level and obsolete digital cameras have a measly resolution of 640 x 480 pixels. These cameras are fine if you want to e-mail someone a picture or send someone a photo on a computer, but the quality of a printed image is terrible when printed as a4 x 6 inch photo.
1	1024 × 768	Supposedly 1024 × 768 resolution is enough to make sharp 4x6 inch prints. The truth is, at this point it depends more on the quality of the digital camera than the resolution. Many printed photos can still look "digital" or blurry at this resolution.
2	1600 × 1200	Two-megapixel cameras can take fine 4 x 6 inch prints and even respectable 8 x 10s, about what you'd expect from a low-end film camera.
3	2048 × 1536	Once you reach the three-megapixel bracket the quality of print is normally excellent up to 8 x 11 prints. If you're looking for a really good digital camera with strong features and good image quality, three megapixels is a good range to search in.
4	2272 × 1740	Four-megapixel cameras are starting to get into the "enthusiast" territory. They take exceptionally sharp photos and can print even larger prints than 8 x 11.
5	2560 × 1920 and greater	We're definitely in enthusiast-to-professional territory now. These cameras are even used by professional photographers to take really big prints.

QUICK REFERENCE

- A DIGITAL CAMERA LETS YOU TAKE PICTURES AND TRANSFER THEM TO A COMPUTER.

- THE QUALITY, OR RESOLUTION, OF THE PICTURES A DIGITAL CAMERA CAN TAKE IS MEASURED IN MEGAPIXELS, OR MILLIONS OF PIXELS (DOTS). THE MORE PIXELS, THE BETTER THE RESOLUTION.

- A WEB CAM IS A TINY DIGITAL VIDEO CAMERA THAT USUALLY SITS ON TOP OF A COMPUTER'S MONITOR. PEOPLE USE WEB CAMS FOR VIDEOCONFERENCING AND TO SEND LIVE IMAGES OVER THE INTERNET.

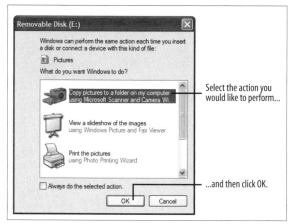

Select the action you would like to perform...

...and then click OK.

Figure 8-4. The Removable Disk dialog box.

You have just returned from a two-week vacation in Europe, and you can't wait to show all your family and friends the pictures you took with your digital camera. Transferring images from your camera onto your computer is fast and easy when using Windows XP.

Once you have connected your camera or adapter to your PC, you can use the Camera Wizard to download and save your images into the folder of your choice. Most cameras come with a USB cable that plugs directly into your PC. Windows XP includes and automatically installs drivers for many camera models, so you don't have to worry about manual setup. Let's get started!

TIP *If your camera is too old (pre-2000) to understand Windows XP's automated download features, you might need to buy an external card reader that plugs into a USB cable port.*

1 Connect your digital camera to your computer with the USB cable OR Memory Card Adapter.

The Removable Disk dialog box appears, asking you what you would like to do with the image files once they are transferred to your computer, as shown in Figure 8-4.

NOTE *If you have installed photo-management software, which most likely came with your camera, you will probably see a different dialog box.*

2 Click Copy pictures to a folder on my computer and click OK.

The Welcome page of the Scanner and Camera Wizard appears.

3 Click Next to continue walking through the Wizard, step by step.

You can also click the "Advanced users only" link to work with individual photo files in Windows Explorer. In our case, however, let's continue with the Wizard.

4 Select the photos you want to transfer to your computer on the Choose Pictures to Copy page.

You can manually select pictures to copy, or you can click the Select All button located below the image window to quickly select all pictures in the window. The buttons located to the left of the Select All button allow you to rotate pictures and view their properties.

NOTE *It is usually easier to transfer all of the images from your camera to your computer and then delete the ones you don't want afterwards.*

5 Click Next.

The Picture Name and Destination page appears. Now we need to give the group of pictures a name and designate the folder that we want them copied to.

NOTE *Check the "Delete pictures from my device after copying them" check box if you want to erase your camera or memory card after the transfer is complete.*

6 Name the group of pictures. Select the folder you want to copy the pictures to.

After you enter a name for your group of pictures, the Wizard automatically creates a folder for you. For example, if you named the group of pictures "Greece," the Wizard would automatically create a folder named "Greece" in the My Pictures folder.

If you do not want to save your pictures in the automatically created folder, click the Browse button or type a different path name.

7 Make sure the folder you selected is correct and then click Next.

The Copying Pictures page appears, showing you how far along the copying process is. This may take a few seconds, so be patient! If you want to cancel the copying process, all you have to do is click Cancel.

Once the Wizard has completed the transfer process, the Other Options page appears. This is where you will choose the next action you want to take with the pictures.

8 Select Nothing. I'm finished working with these pictures from the list and then click Next.

The last page of the Wizard appears. Here you can click the link to open the folder that contains your downloaded photos, or you can just click the Finish button to exit and close the Wizard.

9 Click Finish.

Ta-da! Now your images are stored safe and sound on your hard disk.

QUICK REFERENCE

TO TRANSFER DIGITAL PHOTOS TO THE COMPUTER:

1. CONNECT YOUR DIGITAL CAMERA TO YOUR COMPUTER WITH THE USB CABLE OR MEMORY CARD ADAPTER.

2. SELECT COPY PICTURES TO A FOLDER ON MY COMPUTER AND CLICK OK.

3. CLICK NEXT TO MOVE THROUGH THE CAMERA WIZARD, STEP BY STEP.

4. SELECT THE PHOTOS YOU WANT TO TRANSFER TO YOUR COMPUTER.

5. NAME THE GROUP OF PICTURES AND SELECT THE FOLDER YOU WANT TO COPY THEM TO.

6. CLICK NEXT UNTIL YOU ARE FINISHED WORKING THROUGH THE CAMERA WIZARD.

7. CLICK FINISH TO CLOSE THE CAMERA WIZARD.

Figure 8-5. A folder in Filmstrip view.

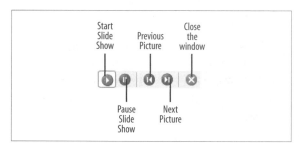

Start Slide Show — Previous Picture — Close the window

Pause Slide Show — Next Picture

Figure 8-6. When viewing your pictures as a slide show, use the onscreen toolbar to scroll through your pictures.

> **TIP** *To use an image as your desktop background, select the image and then click the "Set as desktop background" task from the Picture Tasks menu.*

Once you have transferred pictures to your computer from a camera, scanner, or Internet download, you can view them on your computer screen and organize them to meet your specific needs. For example, you can view your images as a slide show, change the orientation of an image, rename image files, or group images into new folders.

Windows XP's official storage location for digital images is the My Pictures folder. This doesn't mean you can't store your images elsewhere, but My Pictures is extremely easy to locate and open, and it is also the default storage location for many programs and wizards.

My Pictures offers many options for viewing and managing digital images. What are you waiting for? Let's take a closer look at those pictures!

1 Click the **Start button** and select **My Pictures** from the menu.

The My Pictures window appears, displaying its contents.

2 Double-click the folder containing your images.

A preview of all the files appears.

Let's switch views.

3 Click the **Views button** and select **Filmstrip** from the list.

Views button list

The first image appears enlarged on your screen with all other images displayed as thumbnails below it, as shown in Figure 8-5.

Use the buttons below the image to view another picture.

4 Click the Next Image (Right Arrow) button.

The next picture in the filmstrip appears.

You can also view the images in an automatic slide show, starring your pictures.

5 Click the View as a slide show task from the Picture Tasks menu.

A self-advancing slide show of the images in the folder begins on your screen.

6 Move your mouse.

Notice that a small toolbar appears in the upper-right corner of the screen as shown in Figure 8-6. You can use the toolbar to navigate through your images, in addition to the left and right arrow keys on the keyboard.

Let's stop the slide show.

7 Click the Close the window button on the toolbar.

The slide show closes and you are back in the folder window.

8 Click the Views button and select Icon.

One of the most annoying things about digital photographs is that they are saved under pesky serial numbers that are difficult to remember and understand. You can change this by renaming the files.

9 Right-click the image you want to rename and select Rename from the shortcut menu. Type a new name for the image file and press Enter.

And that's all there is to it. Now you won't confuse yourself with all those random serial numbers. Repeat this step for every image you want to rename.

NOTE *If you are in Filmstrip view, right-click the thumbnail image to rename the file.*

If you want to organize your images, you can move them into specific folders.

10 Select the image you would like to move. Click the Move this file task from the File and Folder Tasks menu.

The Move Items dialog box appears. To find the folder you want to move the file to, click the ⊞ plus button to display all items hidden inside a drive or folder, or click the ⊟ minus button to collapse them.

If you can't find the folder you're looking for, or you're just not happy with any of the existing folders, create a new one.

11 Select the drive or folder where you would like the new folder to reside. Click the Make New Folder button, then type a new name for your folder.

Now you're ready to move your items into the new folder.

12 Make sure the new folder is selected and then click Move.

Your file has now been moved from its original location and into the new folder.

QUICK REFERENCE

TO VIEW DIGITAL PHOTOS:

1. CLICK THE START BUTTON AND SELECT MY PICTURES FROM THE MENU.

2. DOUBLE-CLICK THE FOLDER CONTAINING YOUR IMAGES.

3. CLICK THE VIEWS BUTTON AND SELECT A VIEW FROM THE LIST.

TO RENAME AN IMAGE FILE:

• RIGHT-CLICK THE IMAGE YOU WANT TO RENAME AND SELECT RENAME FROM THE SHORTCUT MENU.

TO MOVE AN IMAGE FILE:

1. SELECT THE IMAGE YOU WANT TO MOVE AND CLICK THE MOVE THIS FILE TASK FROM THE FILE AND FOLDER TASKS MENU.

2. SELECT THE DRIVE OR FOLDER WHERE YOU WANT THE FILE TO RESIDE AND CLICK MOVE.

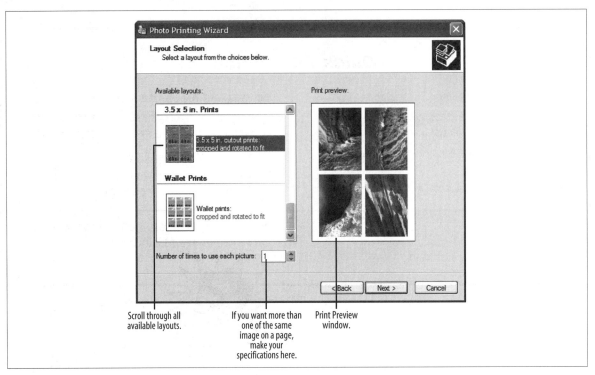

Scroll through all
available layouts.

If you want more than
one of the same
image on a page,
make your
specifications here.

Print Preview
window.

Figure 8-7. The Layout Selection page of the Photo Printing Wizard.

Now that you have all of your digital images downloaded and saved onto your computer, it's time to show them off!

With Windows XP's Photo Printing Wizard, you can print off as many photo-quality prints as you want—without leaving your home or office. And, by printing multiple photos on a single page you can save yourself a lot of money on expensive photo paper—not to mention photo lab fees.

> **TIP** *You must have a printer installed or connected to your computer to complete this lesson.*

1 Click the Start button and select My Pictures from the menu. Double-click the folder containing the pictures you want to print.

The pictures in the folder appear in the folder window.

2 Click the Print Pictures task in the Picture Tasks menu.

The Photo Printing Wizard appears.

3 Click Next.

The Picture Selection page shows you all the photos in the folder.

To narrow the number of pictures, select the pictures you want to print before clicking the Print Pictures task.

4 Click the check box next to images you don't want to print.

The checkmark is removed from the box, indicating that the image will not be printed.

If it's easier, you can also click the Clear All button and click the check box next to images you *do* want to print.

5 Click Next.

Now we need to select a printer.

6 Click the What printer do you want to use? list arrow and select a printer from the list.

Once you've selected the right printer, make sure its settings are ready to print pictures.

NOTE *If there are no computers listed in the printer list, you are not connected to a working printer or there was an error installing the printer. Click Install Printer to open the Add Printer Wizard.*

7 Click the Printing Preferences button.

Set up the paper tray, color, and resolution options. For the best results in color quality, try printing with glossy photo paper. Since all printers are different, check your printer handbook for more detailed instructions involving paper setup.

8 Change the Printer Preferences. Click OK.

The Printer Properties dialog box closes.

9 Click Next.

Now specify how you want your photos arranged on the page. Choose from nine different layouts and preview the outcome in the Print Preview window.

10 Scroll down the Available layouts list and select a layout. Click Next when you're finished.

The pictures are sent to your printer.

11 Click Finish to close the Photo Printing Wizard.

As you can see, it is extremely easy to print digital photos from your own computer.

Of course, the appearance of your images will depend on the type of printer and the quality of paper used. Dye-sublimation printers produce beautiful prints, but most people choose the more common inkjet printer. When it comes to photo paper, weight and surface texture are two of the main factors in determining photo quality. Online user groups and mailings for inkjet printers are great sources for hints and tips when it comes to choosing the right supplies.

As you get more comfortable with the process, try experimenting with different layouts, surface papers, and even inks. The following table describes how to choose the right photo paper for your pictures.

Table 8-2. Types of photo paper

Photo paper	Description
High-gloss	Produces the richest and most colorful prints.
Semi-gloss	Produces a lower contrast and is often used for portraits.
Matte	Produces the lowest contrast of all and is excellent when used for black and white prints.

QUICK REFERENCE

TO PRINT DIGITAL PHOTOS:

1. CLICK THE START BUTTON AND SELECT MY PICTURES FROM THE MENU. DOUBLE-CLICK THE FOLDER CONTAINING YOUR PHOTOS.

2. CLICK THE PRINT PICTURES TASK IN THE PICTURE TASKS MENU. CLICK NEXT.

3. MAKE SURE THE PHOTOS YOU WANT TO PRINT ARE CHECKED. CLICK NEXT.

4. SELECT A PRINTER FROM THE PRINTER LIST. CLICK NEXT.

5. CHOOSE A PRINTING LAYOUT. CLICK NEXT.

6. CLICK FINISH TO CLOSE THE WIZARD.

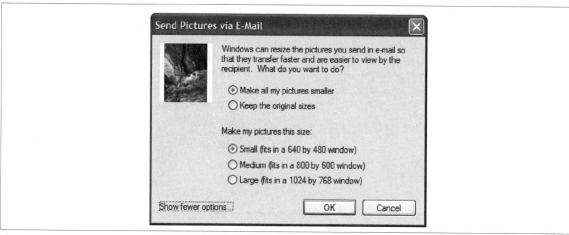

Figure 8-8. Adjust file settings in the Send Pictures via E-mail dialog box.

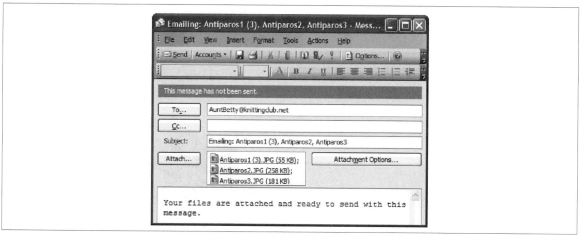

Figure 8-9. The e-mail window.

TIP *Windows compresses bitmap (.bmp) and TIFF (.tif) files before resizing them. GIF (.gif) and JPEG (.jpg) files are already compressed, so Windows XP resizes them without any more compression.*

Aunt Betty in North Carolina *really* wants to see the pictures you took on your recent trip abroad. Only problem is, you (and your pictures) live in California. Before you break the bank and buy a plane ticket across the country, why not send the pictures via e-mail? With Windows XP you can forget about extraneous expenditures—sending pictures via e-mail is fast, easy and cost-efficient.

1 Click the Start button and select My Pictures from the menu. Double-click the folder containing the images you want to send via e-mail.

Now you need to select which images you want to send.

2 Select the image you want to send.

Press and hold down the Ctrl key to select more than one image.

3 Click the E-mail this file task from the File and Folder Tasks menu.

The Send Pictures via E-mail dialog box appears.

You may have trouble sending photos if your (or your recipient's) mail service bounces attachments larger than 1MB or 2MB. Windows XP offers several image-shrinking tools in order to combat this problem.

4 Click Show more options.

The default settings compress and resize images to 640 x 480 pixels, which is just fine for on-screen viewing. A larger size shows more detail, but a smaller size ensures the photos will be received *and* available to view without a lengthy download process.

5 Select a picture size and click OK.

Windows XP automatically opens your e-mail program, creates a new message, and attaches the compressed files. All you have to do is type the recipient's e-mail address, add your own message (if desired), and send away!

6 Type the recipient's e-mail address in the To... field. Click Send.

Now you *and* Aunt Betty can reap the benefits of sending photos via e-mail.

QUICK REFERENCE

TO E-MAIL DIGITAL PHOTOS:

1. CLICK THE START BUTTON AND SELECT MY PICTURES FROM THE MENU. DOUBLE-CLICK THE FOLDER CONTAINING THE IMAGES YOU WANT TO SEND.

2. SELECT THE IMAGE(S) AND CLICK THE E-MAIL THIS FILE TASK.

3. CLICK SHOW MORE OPTIONS.

4. SELECT A PICTURE SIZE AND CLICK OK.

5. ENTER THE RECIPIENT'S E-MAIL ADDRESS IN THE TO... FIELD AND CLICK SEND.

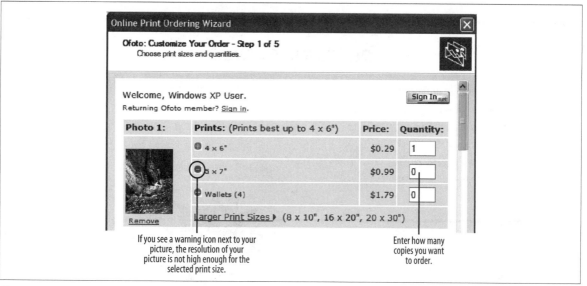

Figure 8-10. The Online Print Ordering Wizard.

Don't have a photo-quality printer? Don't feel like going to the photo lab? No problem! You can still enjoy your digital images in printed format by ordering them off the Web.

The Online Print Ordering Wizard walks you through the process step-by-step, while you call all the shots. You select the photos to be uploaded to an online photo processor (Ofoto, Fujifilm, or Shutterfly), what size to print, and how many. Prices will vary, but your new prints will be shipped right to your front door and should arrive in about a week.

1 Click the Start button and select My Pictures from the menu. Double-click the folder containing the pictures you want printed.

The pictures in the folder appear in the folder window.

2 Click the Order prints online task in the Picture Tasks menu.

The Online Print Ordering Wizard appears.

3 Click Next.

Next you need to choose the image(s) you want to order.

4 Click the check box next to images you don't want to print.

The checkmark is removed from the box, indicating that the image will not be printed.

If it's easier, you can also click the Clear All button and click the check box next to images you *do* want to print.

5 Click Next.

The Select a Printing Company page appears.

6 Select the company you want to order your prints from. Click Next.

Information from the selected vendor appears. Specify print size and quantity of each of your pictures.

NOTE *If a warning icon appears next to a print size, the image's resolution is too low to produce a high-quality print.*

7 Select the print size and quantity for each image, then click Next.

You are now prompted to enter all shipping and billing information.

8 Follow the instructions to complete the Wizard. When you're finished, click Finish.

The Wizard closes, and your photos are off and running to the printer.

QUICK REFERENCE

TO ORDER PRINTS ONLINE:

1. CLICK THE **START** BUTTON AND SELECT MY PICTURES FROM THE MENU. DOUBLE-CLICK THE FOLDER CONTAINING YOUR PHOTOS.

2. CLICK THE **ORDER PRINTS ONLINE** TASK IN THE PICTURE TASKS MENU. CLICK NEXT.

3. MAKE SURE THE PHOTOS YOU WANT TO PRINT ARE CHECKED. CLICK NEXT.

4. SELECT A PHOTO PROCESSOR. CLICK NEXT.

5. SELECT THE PRINT SIZE AND QUALITY. CLICK NEXT.

6. FOLLOW THE INSTRUCTIONS AND CLICK FINISH.

Introduction to the Windows Media Player

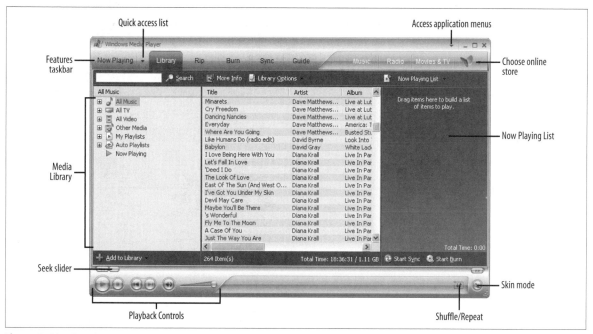

Quick access list

Access application menus

Features taskbar

Choose online store

Now Playing List

Media Library

Seek slider

Skin mode

Playback Controls

Shuffle/Repeat

Figure 8-11. The Library window of the Windows XP Media Player.

Windows Media Player is Microsoft's free multimedia program that plays digital music files, videos, CDs, and DVDs. The Media Player acts as your own digital jukebox, helping you to find and organize digital media files. You can also listen to online radio stations, rip tracks from audio CDs to your hard drive, create custom CDs, download songs to your portable music player, and more.

1 Click the Start button and select All Programs → Windows Media Player from the menu.

The Media Player window appears, as shown in Figure 8-11.

Table 8-3. The Features Taskbar

Taskbar Button	Description
Now Playing	View a video, visual, or information about the media file that is playing.
Library	Organize media files into playlists of your favorite songs and videos.
Rip	Play a CD or copy tracks from a CD to your library.
Burn	Burn your own music CDs from the tracks stored on your hard drive.
Sync	Synchronize your digital files to a portable device.
Guide	Go online to WindowsMedia.com, updated daily with links to the latest movies, music, and videos.
Music, Radio, Movies & TV	Access digital music, radio, and video through a selected content provider.

QUICK REFERENCE

TO START THE WINDOWS MEDIA PLAYER:

- CLICK THE START BUTTON AND SELECT ALL
  PROGRAMS → WINDOWS MEDIA PLAYER FROM
  THE MENU.

TO EXIT THE WINDOWS MEDIA PLAYER:

- CLICK THE CLOSE BUTTON.

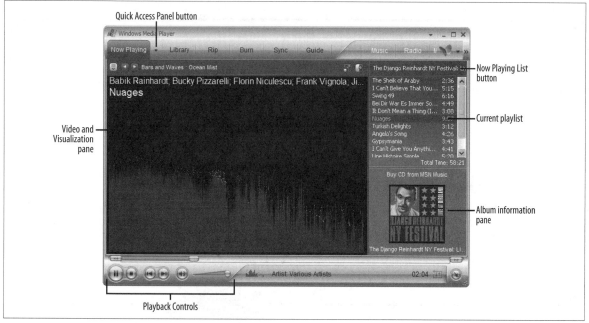

Quick Access Panel button

Now Playing List button

Current playlist

Album information pane

Video and Visualization pane

Playback Controls

Figure 8-12. The Now Playing window of the Media Player.

Now that you've familiarized yourself with the Windows Media Player and all it has to offer, let's try it out!

1 Insert a music CD into your computer's CD drive.

Since we already have the Media Player open, the CD should start playing automatically. Playing a CD on your PC doesn't interfere with any other programs you have open, and it's very easy to use and manage.

If the CD doesn't start playing automatically, you can quickly start the CD using the hidden menu bar.

2 Click the Quick Access Panel button in the Features taskbar.

A menu of drives and libraries appears. The title of the CD in your computer should appear next to your CD drive in the menu.

3 Select the CD Drive where your CD is inserted.

The CD begins to play.

To see more information about the CD, click the Now Playing button on the Features taskbar.

4 Click the Now Playing button on the Features taskbar.

The artist, title, and track information of the CD is displayed with visualization effects.

Media Player plays through the playlist in order, unless you specify otherwise.

We're finished listening to our CD, so let's eject it using the hidden menus.

5 Click the Access application menus button. Select Play → Eject from the Media Player menu.

The CD drive opens.

Playing music on the Media Player is very easy, especially if you have used a CD player before.

QUICK REFERENCE

TO PLAY A MUSIC CD:

• INSERT THE CD INTO YOUR COMPUTER'S CD DRIVE.

OR...

• CLICK THE QUICK ACCESS PANEL BUTTON AND SELECT THE CD FROM THE MENU.

TO SHUFFLE TRACKS:

• CLICK THE NOW PLAYING LIST BUTTON AND SELECT SHUFFLE LIST NOW FROM THE MENU.

OR...

• PRESS CTRL + H.

TO REPEAT A TRACK:

• CLICK THE NOW PLAYING LIST BUTTON AND SELECT REPEAT FROM THE MENU.

OR...

• PRESS CTRL + T.

TO EJECT A CD:

• CLICK THE ACCESS APPLICATION MENUS BUTTON AND SELECT PLAY → EJECT FROM THE MENU.

OR...

• PRESS CTRL + E.

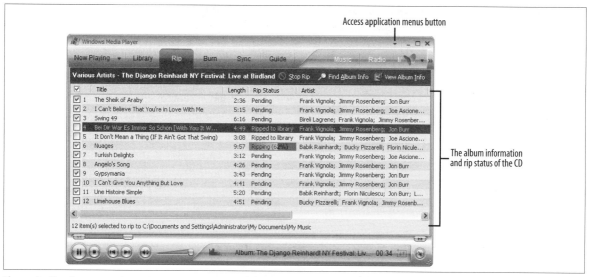

Figure 8-13. The Rip window of the Windows Media Player.

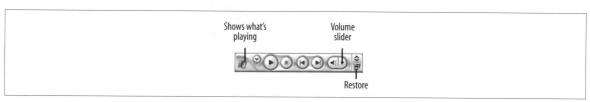

Figure 8-14. The Rip Music tab of the Options dialog box.

You don't always have to insert a CD to play music tracks. With Windows XP Media Player, you can copy, or rip, your favorite CDs directly onto your hard drive, making more of your music available with just a few clicks. Once music tracks are downloaded onto your computer you can create customized playlists, copy tracks to portable music devices, and even burn mixed CDs!

1 Insert a music CD into your computer's CD drive.

The Media Player automatically begins playing your CD. The player can play and copy tracks at the same time, but it's usually a good idea to turn the music off while copying.

2 Click the Rip button on the Features taskbar.

Media Player looks up the album title and track names and lists them in the window.

NOTE *If the Media Player can't find information on your CD, you will have to enter track names and other album information you would like to include manually.*

All the tracks that will be copied to your computer are selected with a checkmark. If you don't want to save a track, uncheck its check box.

3 Uncheck the check box of tracks you don't want to save.

You're ready to begin copying tracks.

4 Click the Rip Music button on the toolbar.

Windows Media Player starts copying the music into your My Music folder and displays the ripping progress.

If for some reason you want to stop the operation, all you have to do is click the Stop Rip button.

When the copying process is complete, you can find your copied tracks in the Media Library and the My Music folder.

You can change the settings for copying music, such as file format and copy location.

5 Click the Access application menus button at the top of the Windows Media Player window.

The menus for the Windows Media Player appear.

6 Select Tools → Options from the menu.

The Options dialog box appears.

7 Click the Rip Music tab.

Here, you can specify the settings for ripping music, such as the location and file format. Notice that the Media Player can rip tracks in several formats, includ-ing MP3. Refer to Figure 1-14 for more information on these settings.

8 Specify the copy settings you want to use. Click OK.

The Options dialog box closes and the copy settings are changed. Move on to the next lesson to find out how to organize these tracks into personal playlists.

TIP *To Edit Track Information, right-click the track title, artist, composer, or genre and select Edit from the shortcut menu.*

QUICK REFERENCE

TO RIP A CD:

I. INSERT A MUSIC CD INTO YOUR COMPUTER'S CD DRIVE.

2. CLICK THE RIP BUTTON ON THE FEATURES TASKBAR.

3. UNCHECK THE CHECK BOX OF TRACKS YOU DON'T WANT TO SAVE.

4. CLICK THE RIP MUSIC BUTTON.

TO CHANGE RIP MUSIC SETTINGS:

I. CLICK THE ACCESS APPLICATION MENUS BUTTON.

2. SELECT TOOLS → OPTIONS FROM THE MENU.

3. CLICK THE RIP MUSIC TAB.

TO EDIT TRACK INFORMATION:

• RIGHT-CLICK THE TRACK, TITLE, ARTIST, COMPOSER, OR GENRE AND SELECT EDIT FROM THE SHORTCUT MENU.

Figure 8-15. The Library window of the Windows Media Player.

Figure 8-16. The new saved playlist.

Once you have saved music files on your computer, Windows Media Player automatically includes them in your Media Library. The Media Library is a master list of your media files. One popular way to organize these files is by creating your very own playlists.

A playlist is a group of media files that you want to watch or listen to as a group. The Media Player generates a temporary playlist when you play a CD, but you can create playlists of ripped music files by mixing and matching songs in the order you want to hear them. You can then burn these playlists onto CDs, or synchronize them to a portable device.

TIP *Right-click a playlist in the Library to rename, edit, or delete it.*

1 Click the **Library button** on the **Features taskbar**.

The Library appears. The Contents pane categorizes your files, such as music, TV, video, or other media. The Details pane displays the category selected in the Contents pane. The List pane displays details about the current playlist, but it can also be used to create a new playlist, burn a playlist, or sync a playlist.

2 Click the Now Playing List button and select New List → Playlist from the menu.

The Now Playing List is cleared.

To create the new playlist, drag the files from the Contents or Details panes into the List pane. Like sifting through folders in Windows Explorer, click a category to expand it and locate the individual file you want to add.

3 Find the track you want to add. Click and drag the track into the List pane.

The selected track appears in the right pane.

4 Repeat Step 4 until all tracks have been added to the playlist.

Don't worry about adding tracks in order. You can rearrange the order of the playlist by clicking and dragging the tracks in the list.

Now you need to save your playlist for future reference.

5 Click the Now Playing List button and select Save Playlist As from the menu.

The Save As dialog box appears.

6 Type a name for your playlist in the File Name text box. Click Save.

The Save As dialog box closes and the new playlist now appears in the My Playlists category of the Media Library.

Congratulations! You have successfully created a playlist. Move on to the next lesson to learn how to burn your own CDs.

QUICK REFERENCE

TO CREATE A PLAYLIST:

1. CLICK THE LIBRARY BUTTON ON THE FEATURES TASKBAR.

2. CLICK THE NOW PLAYING LIST BUTTON AND SELECT NEW LIST → PLAYLIST FROM THE LIST.

3. CLICK AND DRAG THE TRACKS YOU WOULD LIKE TO INCLUDE IN YOUR PLAYLIST INTO THE LIST PANE.

4. CLICK THE NOW PLAYING LIST BUTTON AND SELECT SAVE PLAYLIST AS FROM THE MENU.

5. TYPE A NAME FOR YOUR PLAYLIST IN THE FILE NAME TEXT BOX. CLICK SAVE.

Figure 8-17. The Burn window of the Windows Media Player.

Figure 8-18. The status of burning a CD.

Ever purchase a CD, only to enjoy two of the tracks? We all have. With Windows XP's Media Player you can burn your favorite tracks onto a CD. No more skipping through all those annoying songs; now you can sit back, relax and let the music play.

NOTE *Depending on your computer, you may not have the hardware to burn CDs. If you don't, you won't be able to burn CDs.*

1 Create a playlist of songs you want to burn onto a CD.

Make sure the playlist will fit on the CD. Most CDs store 74 to 80 minutes of music.

2 Click the Burn button on the Features taskbar.

If your playlist is not already shown in the Media Player window, you need to select it.

3 Click the Items to Burn list arrow and select the playlist you want to burn.

The playlist appears in the Items to Burn pane, the left pane of the window. Look over the playlist to make sure it has all the tracks you want.

TIP *It's a good idea to disconnect from the Internet before you begin burning a CD. Having two large programs open at a time can cause delays in the burning process.*

4 (Optional) Click the check boxes of the tracks you do not want to include on the CD.

This removes the track from the list to copy onto the CD, but does not remove it from the playlist saved on your computer.

5 (Optional) Click the Edit Playlist button to add tracks to the selected playlist.

The Edit Playlist dialog box appears. Add tracks to the playlist by clicking them in the Library pane of the dialog box.

When the playlist has all the items you want to burn, insert the blank CD you want to burn to.

6 Insert a blank CD into your CD drive.

Now you need to select the type of CD you want to create.

7 Click the Items on Device list arrow and select Audio CD from the list.

Now you're ready to burn the CD.

NOTE *If "Will not fit" appears in the Status column, this means you cannot fit all of the selected tracks onto your CD. Go through and remove one track at a time until all the selected tracks fit. Create another CD if you can't fit all of your favorite tunes this time around.*

8 Click the Start Burn button.

Almost done! Be patient—the copying process may take a few minutes.

Do not to disturb the Media Player or your CD drive while the CD is burning. Such distractions could cause errors in the copying process, thus causing your tracks to skip.

QUICK REFERENCE

TO BURN A MUSIC CD:

1. CREATE A PLAYLIST OF SONGS.

2. CLICK THE BURN BUTTON ON THE FEATURES TASKBAR.

3. CLICK THE ITEMS TO BURN LIST ARROW AND SELECT THE PLAYLIST YOU WANT TO BURN.

4. (OPTIONAL) CLEAR THE CHECK BOXES OF TRACKS YOU DO NOT WANT TO INCLUDE ON THE CD.

5. (OPTIONAL) CLICK THE EDIT PLAYLIST BUTTON TO ADD TRACKS TO THE SELECTED PLAYLIST.

6. INSERT A BLANK CD INTO YOUR CD DRIVE.

7. CLICK THE ITEMS ON DEVICE LIST ARROW AND SELECT AUDIO CD FROM THE LIST.

8. CLICK THE START BURN BUTTON.

Figure 8-19. The Radio Tuner.

TIP *Some Internet radio stations require a fee with MSN Radio Plus.*

You can use the Windows Media Player to listen to radio stations from around the world that are broadcast, or *streamed,* over the Internet. This means you need a fast and reliable connection to the Internet, such as a DSL or cable modem, to listen to Internet radio.

1 Click the Radio button on the Features taskbar.

Windows Media Player displays the Internet radio stations sorted by category.

To play a station, you must sign in to a MSN Passport account. If you have a Hotmail account, enter your e-mail login information. Otherwise, you'll have to create an MSN Music account.

2 Click Sign In and log in to your MSN Passport account information.

If you don't have an account, click the Create Account button and follow the instructions to create a new account.

3 Click the Expand button to view the stations available in the category. To play a station, click the Play this station button next to the station.

The station begins streaming through your computer.

Table 8-4. Preset Station Lists

Type	Description
Featured Stations	Windows Media Player displays a list of stations that it thinks might interest you.
My Stations	You can put your favorite radio stations in this list.
Recently Played Stations	Windows Media Player displays a list of the radio stations you've listened to most recently.

QUICK REFERENCE

TO LISTEN TO AN INTERNET RADIO STATION:

1. CLICK THE RADIO BUTTON ON THE FEATURES TASKBAR.

2. SIGN IN TO YOUR MSN PASSPORT ACCOUNT.

3. CLICK THE RADIO STATION FROM THE LIST.

4. CLICK THE PLAY THIS STATION BUTTON TO BEGIN THE STREAM.

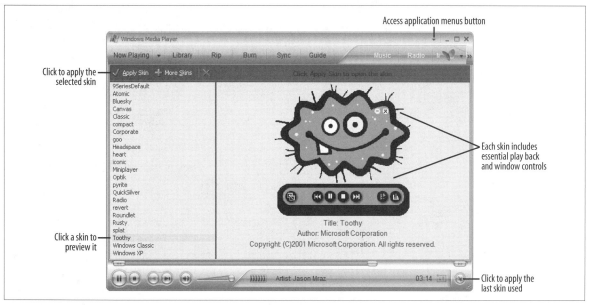

Access application menus button

Click to apply the selected skin

Click a skin to preview it

Each skin includes essential play back and window controls

Click to apply the last skin used

Figure 8-20. The Skin Chooser window of the Windows Media Player.

Are you tired of the plain old Media Player window? Spice things up with the Skin Chooser feature. With the Skin Chooser, you can select from a variety of different options, giving your Media Player a literal face-lift. Makeover your Media Player window and make things a little more fun with a different skin!

1 Click the Access application menus button. Select View → Skin Chooser from the menu.

A list of skins you can use appears in the Media Player window.

Click a skin option to preview it.

2 Select a skin from the list.

A preview of the skin appears in the right pane of the Media Player window, as shown in Figure 8-20. Move on to the next step to apply it to the Media Player.

3 Click the Apply Skin button.

When you apply a skin, Media Player switches to *skin mode*, which only makes basic playback buttons available.

If you need to use other features in the Media Player, you'll have to switch back to full mode.

4 Click the Full Mode button.

The default Media Player window appears once again.

Play around with different skins until you find one you like. Remember that you must be in full mode to change skins. You can also download skins from the Internet if you're not satisfied with the ones currently offered by Windows Media Player.

QUICK REFERENCE

TO APPLY A SKIN:

1. CLICK THE *ACCESS APPLICATION MENUS BUTTON* AND SELECT VIEW → SKIN CHOOSER FROM THE MENU.

2. SELECT A SKIN FROM THE LIST.

3. CLICK THE APPLY SKIN BUTTON.

Figure 8-21. Playing a DVD using Windows Media Player.

If you have a DVD drive, you can use Windows XP's Media Player to play DVD movies right from your computer. This can come in extremely handy when on business trips or family vacations. Who needs an expensive portable DVD player when you have Windows XP?

To play DVDs on your computer you will need something called a software *decoder*. If you bought your system with Windows XP and a DVD drive pre-installed, you most likely have nothing to worry about. If you have an older system, however, you may have to download and install a decoder from the Internet. You can purchase and download a DVD Decoder Pack from Microsoft.com for about $15 U.S. But before you spend any money, make sure to check your computer or DVD-drive manufacturer's Web site for *free* Windows XP DVD updates and downloads.

1 Insert a DVD into your computer's DVD drive.

Depending on your computer, the DVD drive could be the same as your CD drive. The Media Player should open your DVD automatically when it's inserted.

If nothing happens when you insert the DVD, move on to the next step.

2 Click the Access application menus button. Select Play → DVD, VCD or CD Audio from the menu.

If you have a separate DVD drive on your computer, another submenu will appear.

3 Select the DVD title from the menu. Click the Play button.

The DVD begins.

Now, it's great that you can see the movie, but no one wants to watch a movie through a tiny little window. Expand the window so it takes up your whole monitor.

4 Click the Access application menus button. Select View → Full Screen from the menu.

When the DVD is set to full-screen mode, the playback controls appear automatically when you move the mouse. They disappear again after the mouse has been idle for a few seconds.

You can permanently post playback controls on-screen by clicking the thumbtack button located in the top-left corner of the screen. You can also use the keyboard shortcuts listed in Table 8-4.

Table 8-5. DVD Keyboard shortcuts

Action	Shortcut
Play/Pause	Ctrl + P
Stop	Ctrl + S
Rewind	Ctrl + Shift + B
Fast-forward	Ctrl + Shift + F
Previous chapter	Ctrl + B
Next chapter	Ctrl + F
Louder/Quieter	F9 / **F10**
Mute	F8
Eject	Ctrl + E

QUICK REFERENCE

TO PLAY A DVD:

1. INSERT THE DVD INTO THE DVD DRIVE.

2. CLICK THE ACCESS APPLICATION MENUS BUTTON. SELECT VIEW → FULL SCREEN FROM THE MENU.

Lesson Summary

Introduction to the Digital Camera

A **digital camera** lets you take pictures and transfer them to your computer.

The quality, or resolution, of the pictures that a digital camera can take is measured in **megapixels**, or millions of pixels (dots). The more pixels, the better the resolution.

A **Web cam** is a tiny digital video camera that usually sits on top of a computer's monitor. People use Web cams for videoconferencing and to send live images over the Internet.

Transferring Digital Photos to the Computer

Connect your digital camera to your computer with the USB cable or memory card adapter. Select Copy pictures to a folder on my computer and click OK. Click Next to move through the Camera Wizard, step by step. Select the photos you want to transfer to your computer. Name the group of photos and select the folder you want to copy them to. Click Next until you are finished working through the Camera Wizard. Click Finish to close the Camera Wizard.

Viewing and Managing Your Digital Photos

To View Your Digital Photos: Click the Start button and select My Pictures from the menu. Double-click the folder containing your images. Click the Views button and select a view from the list.

To Rename an Image File: Right-click the image you want to rename and select Rename from the shortcut menu.

To Move an Image File: Select the image and click the Move this file task from the File and Folder Tasks menu. Select the drive or folder where you want the file to reside and click Move.

Printing Digital Photos

Click the Start button and select My Pictures from the menu. Double-click the folder containing your photos. Select the Print Pictures task in the Picture Tasks menu and click Next. Make sure the photos you want to print are checked and click Next. Select a printer from the

Printer list and click Next. Choose a printing layout and click Next. Click Finish to close the wizard.

E-mailing Digital Photos

Click the Start button and select My Pictures from the menu. Double-click the folder containing the images you want to send. Select the image(s) and click the E-mail this file task. Click Show more options. Make your selections and click OK. Enter the recipient's e-mail address in the To... field and click Send.

Ordering Prints Online

Click the Start button and select My Pictures from the menu. Double-click the folder containing your photos. Click the Order prints online task in the Picture Tasks menu and click Next. Make sure the photos you want to print are checked and click Next. Select a photo processor and click Next. Select the print size and quality and click Next. Follow the instructions and then click Finish.

Introduction to the Windows Media Player

To Start the Windows Media Player: Click the Start button and select All Programs → Windows Media Player from the menu.

To Exit Windows Media Player: Click the Close button.

Playing a CD

To Play a Music CD: Insert the CD into your computer's disc drive. Or, click the Quick Access Panel button and select the CD from the menu.

To Shuffle Tracks: Click the Now Playing List button and select Shuffle List Now from the menu or press Ctrl + H.

To Repeat a Track: Click the Now Playing List button and select Repeat from the menu or press Ctrl + T.

To Eject a CD: Select Play → Eject from the menu or press Ctrl + E.

Copying a CD to the Hard Drive

To Rip a CD: Insert a music CD into your computer's CD or DVD drive. Click the Rip button on the Features taskbar. Uncheck the check box of tracks you don't want to save and click the Rip Music button.

To Change Rip Music Settings: Click the Access application menus button. Select Tools → Options from the menu and click the Rip Music tab.

To Edit Track Information: Right-click the track, title, artist, composer, or genre and select Edit from the shortcut menu.

Creating a Playlist

Click the Library button on the Features taskbar. Click the Now Playing List button and select New List → Playlist from the list. Click and drag the tracks you would like to include in your playlist into the List pane. Click the Now Playing List button and select Save Playlist As from the menu. Type a name for your playlist in the File Name text box. Click Save.

Burning a Music CD

Create a playlist of songs you want to burn onto the CD. Click the Burn button on the Features taskbar. Click the Items to Burn list arrow and select the playlist you want to burn. (Optional) Clear the check boxes of tracks you do not want to

include on the CD. (Optional) Click the Edit Playlist button to add tracks to the selected playlist. Insert a blank CD into your CD drive. Click the Items on Device list arrow and select Audio CD from the list. Click the Start Burn button.

Listening to Internet Radio Stations

Click the Radio button on the Features taskbar. Sign in to your MSN Passport account. Click the radio station from the list. Click the Play this station button to begin the stream.

Changing Skins

Click the Access application menus button and select View → Skin Chooser from the menu. Select a skin from the list. Click the Apply Skin button.

Playing a DVD

Insert the DVD into the DVD drive. Click the Access application menus button. Select View → Full Screen from the menu.

Quiz

1. What are megapixels?

   A. Cameras that sit on top of your computer.

   B. Millions of pixels (dots).

   C. Hundreds of pixels (tiny triangles).

   D. Dietary supplements.

2. A digital camera lets you take pictures and then transfer them to your computer. (True or False?)

3. In order to transfer digital photos to your computer using Windows XP, you will need: (Select all that apply.)

   A. A USB cable OR memory card adapter.

   B. A MIDI interface.

   C. An external card reader (if your camera was made before the year 2000).

   D. French Fries.

4. Matte photo paper generally produces the richest, most colorful prints. (True or False?)

5. If you see a warning icon when ordering prints

online, what should you do?

   A. Shut down your computer.

   B. Ignore it, it means nothing.

   C. Call the Fire Department.

   D. Choose a different size for the print.

6. What kinds of digital media can you play on the Windows Media player? (Select all that apply.)

   A. Music files.

   B. DVDs.

   C. CDs.

   D. Videos.

7. By default, Windows Media Player creates audio files in ____ format:

   A. MP3

   B. WMA

   C. JPEG

   D. MTV

Homework

1. Open the My Pictures folder and switch to Thumbnails View.

2. Rename one of your images.

3. Open the Windows Media Player.

4. Create a new playlist.

5. Open the Radio Tuner and add a new station to the My Stations list.

6. Change the Media Player's skin to "Canvas."

Quiz Answers

1. B. Megapixels are millions of pixels (dots). The more pixels, the better the resolution of your digital images..

2. True. A digital camera lets you take pictures and then transfer them to your computer via a USB cable or memory card adapter.

3. A and C. You will need a USB cable OR memory card adapter to conect your camera to your computer, and for thoe of you with cameras made before the year 2000, you will need an external card reader as well..

4. False. High-gloss paper generally produces the richest, most colorful prints. Matte paper is best when used for low-contrast images, such as black and white prints.

5. D. When you see a warning icon next to a print size, this means the picture's resolution is not high enough for that particular size. Choose a different size for the best-quality print.

6. All of the above. Windows Media Player can play music files, videos, CDs, and DVDs.

7. B. By default, Windows media Player creates audio files in Windows Media Audio (WMA) format. To create files in the more popular MP3 formate, you will need to download the software from the MP3 utilities Web page.

CHAPTER 9

OPTIMIZING AND MAINTAINING YOUR COMPUTER

CHAPTER OBJECTIVES:

Defragmenting and fixing errors on your hard disk

Backing up and restoring your hard disk

Freeing up space on your hard disk

Scheduling tasks

Installing and removing software

Adding and removing Windows components

Installing a printer

Installing new hardware

Using the Windows XP update feature

Installing and reinstalling Windows XP

Using the Device Manager

Prerequisites

- Know how to use the mouse to click, double-click, drag and drop, and right-click.
- Know how to use menus, toolbars, and dialog boxes.
- Know how to view and navigate the contents of your computer (disk drives and folders).

Cars require maintenance to keep them running at their peak performance. Some car maintenance tasks are simple and routine, such as changing oil every 3,000 miles. Others are more complicated, such as installing a new radio. Computers are no different. Your computer requires routine maintenance to prevent and/or correct problems and to keep it running at its best possible performance.

This chapter explains how to optimize and maintain your computer. You'll learn how to find and correct problems on your computer's hard disk, install and remove software, backup and restore your important files, add new hardware to your computer, and more.

Figure 9-1. The Tools tab of the Local Disk Properties dialog box.

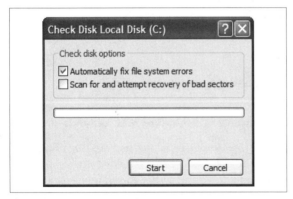

Figure 9-2. The Check Disk Local Disk dialog box.

Over time, errors begin to appear on your computer's hard drive, thus affecting its performance. Fortunately, most of the hard drive damage caused by normal wear and tear is not serious and can easily be diagnosed and fixed by a hard drive repair program. Microsoft Windows XP comes with a hard drive repair program called *Error-checking*. In this lesson, you will learn how to use Error-checking to diagnose and repair any errors on your com-

puter's hard disk—a preventative maintenance task that you should do at least once a month.

1 Click the Start button and select My Computer from the menu.

Next, you need to right-click the drive you want to check.

2 Right-click the (C:) Local Disk icon and select Properties from the shortcut menu.

The Properties for the selected drive appear in the Local Disk (C:) Properties dialog box. Error-checking and several other maintenance tools are located on the Tools tab.

TIP *Turning off your computer without using the Windows XP Shut Down sequence is the biggest cause of hard disk errors.*

3 Click the Tools tab.

The Tools tab appears, as shown in Figure 9-1.

4 Click the Check Now button.

The Checking Disk dialog box appears, as shown in Figure 9-2. The (C:) drive is selected as the drive to be scanned, because it was the drive you right-clicked. Error-checking doesn't have many options, but the ones it does have are important. There are two different types of tests you can have Error-checking run: *Automatically fix file system errors*, and *Scan for and attempt recovery of bad sectors*.

- **Automatically fix file system errors:** Select the "Automatically fix file system errors" check box to have Windows fix disk errors without asking your approval first. If you don't select this check box, Windows XP will prompt you to fix each and every error it finds. All files must be closed to run this program, and the drive is not available to run other tasks while the disk is being checked. If it is in use, you will be asked if you want to reschedule the disk checking for the next time you start your computer.

Checking or unchecking the "Scan for and attempt recovery of bad sectors" box does one of two things:

- **Scan for and attempt recovery of bad sectors unchecked:** Checks only the files and folders on the selected drive(s) for errors. A standard test takes only a minute or two to run, and is the computer-equivalent of a 10-point maintenance check they do on your car during a routine oil change.

- **Scan for and attempt recovery of bad sectors checked:** Checks the files and folders on the selected drive(s) for errors *and* the surface of the hard drive for physical damage. This can take a *long time*—up to several hours if you have a large hard drive. A thorough test is the computer-equivalent of an annual vehicle inspection.

5 Check the Scan for and attempt recovery of bad sectors option.

This will run a thorough test on the (C:) hard drive and will automatically fix any file or folder errors. Remember that you cannot have any files from this disk open, or the program cannot begin.

6 Click Start.

The files and folders on the (C:) drive are checked, and its progress is displayed.

NOTE *Try not to touch Windows while Error-checking is running. No, it won't hurt anything, but any time you make any changes to your computer while Error-checking is running, Error-checking starts all over again.*

If Error-checking reports any bytes in bad sectors (only available if you perform a thorough test), that is not a good sign. Bad sectors are often a sign of an imminent hardware failure. Backup everything on the disk immediately, and then run a thorough Error-checking test every few days. If more bad sectors appear, the drive will likely fail shortly. You shouldn't continue using disks that have bad sectors.

7 Click OK to close the Results window, and click OK to close the Properties window.

That's all there is to using Error-checking. You can also use Error-checking on floppy disks, which are notorious for developing disk errors. If you're checking a floppy disk, make sure you always select the thorough test option.

QUICK REFERENCE

TO USE ERROR-CHECKING:

1. CLICK THE START BUTTON AND SELECT MY COMPUTER FROM THE MENU.

2. RIGHT-CLICK THE DISK YOU WANT TO SCAN, SELECT PROPERTIES FROM THE SHORTCUT MENU, AND CLICK THE TOOLS TAB.

3. CLICK THE CHECK NOW BUTTON.

4. SPECIFY IF YOU WANT ANY ERRORS TO BE AUTOMATICALLY FIXED, AND IF YOU WANT TO SCAN FOR AND ATTEMPT RECOVERY OF BAD SECTORS.

5. CLICK START.

Figure 9-3. The Tools tab of the Local Disk (C:) Properties

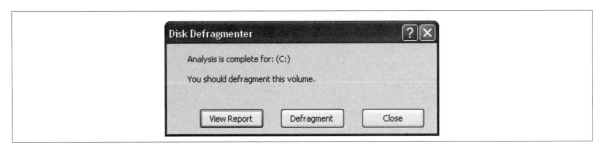

Figure 9-4. Disk Defragmenter reports whether the disk needs to be defragmented.

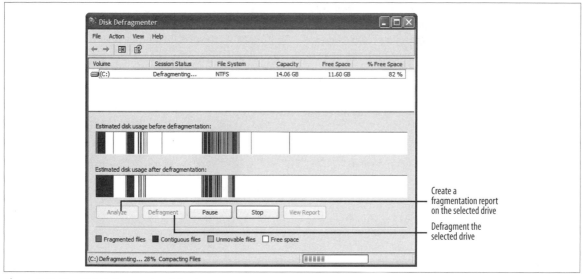

Figure 9-5. The Disk Defragmenter dialog box.

Normally, computers store each file in a single location on their hard drive, just like a song is recorded on a continuous area of a cassette tape. Over time, however, a hard drive can become *fragmented*, and instead of storing a file in one, single location, it begins storing files in pieces, or fragments, in several locations all over the hard drive. When the computer reads a fragmented file, it must read the file from several different areas of the hard drive instead of just one. Defragmenting a hard drive using a special utility program can improve its performance by putting fragmented files back together in one place. Windows XP comes with a disk defragmentation program called, what else? Disk Defragmenter. (In case you haven't noticed by now, Microsoft doesn't give its products very flashy names). You should defragment your computer hard drive about once a month.

Here's how to defragment your hard drive:

1 Click the Start button and select My Computer from the menu.

Next, you need to right-click the Local Disk drive to defragment it.

NOTE *Hard drives are really the only type of drive that benefit from running the Disk Defragmenter.*

2 Right-click the Local Disk (C:) icon and select Properties from the shortcut menu.

The Local Disk (C:) Properties dialog box appears. Defragmentation, and several other maintenance tools, are located on the Tools tab of the Properties dialog box.

3 Click the Tools tab.

The Tools tab appears, as shown in Figure 9-3.

4 Click the Defragment Now button.

The Disk Defragmenter appears, as shown in Figure 9-5. Near the bottom of the window is a row of buttons you will use to defragment your computer.

5 Click the Analyze button.

The Defragment program analyzes the selected hard drive and displays the status of the hard drive in the "Estimated disk usage before defragmentation" color bar.

Eventually a dialog box appears and informs you whether the drive needs to be defragmented.

6 Click Defragment.

The Disk Defragmenter dialog box displays the progress of the defragmentation. Defragmenting a hard drive can take a long time—up to several hours!

NOTE *Don't touch Windows while the hard drive is being defragmented. Just like the Error-checking program, it won't hurt anything, but any changes you make to your hard disk causes Disk Defragmentor to start over.*

When the defragmentating is finally complete, a dialog box appears, asking you if you want to quit Disk Defragmenter.

7 Click Yes to close the Disk Defragmenter.

A few final notes on defragmentation: First, you can't defragment a hard disk that contains errors, so it's usually a good idea to run Error-checking to find and repair errors on your hard drive before you defragment it. Second, the Disk Defragmenter program has been optimized in Windows XP. Not only does it defragment your computer's hard drive, but it also places the programs you use most often at the beginning of the hard drive so they start faster.

Disk Defragmenter
Other Ways to Start Disk Defragmenter:
• Click the Start button and select **All Programs→ Accessories→System Tools→Disk Defragmenter**.

QUICK REFERENCE

TO DEFRAGMENT YOUR HARD DISK:

1. CLICK THE **START** BUTTON AND SELECT MY COMPUTER FROM THE MENU.

2. RIGHT-CLICK THE DISK YOU WANT TO DEFRAGMENT, SELECT PROPERTIES FROM THE SHORTCUT MENU, AND CLICK THE TOOLS TAB.

3. CLICK THE DEFRAGMENT NOW BUTTON.

4. CLICK THE ANALYZE BUTTON, AND CLICK DEFRAGMENT.

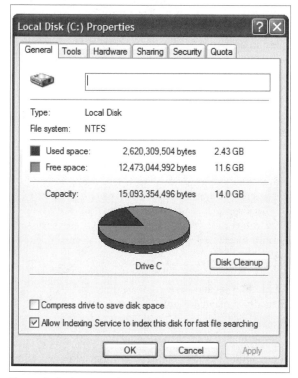

Figure 9-6. The General tab of the Local Disk (C:) Drive Properties dialog box.

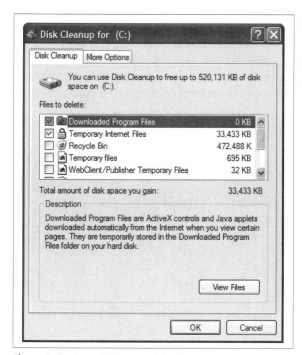

Figure 9-7. The Disk Cleanup dialog box.

As you work at your desk day after day, you create unnecessary paperwork that you eventually throw away to free your desk from clutter. Windows does the same thing as time passes, except instead of paper it creates unnecessary files that don't do anything except waste valuable space on your hard disk. The Disk Cleanup utility program erases these garbage files for you. This lesson explains how to use the Disk Cleanup utility to clear these unnecessary files from your computer.

1 Click the Start button and select My Computer from the menu.

Next, you need to right-click the Local Disk drive.

NOTE *The Local Disk drive is the only drive that uses Disk Cleanup.*

2 Right-click the Local Disk (C:) icon and select Properties from the shortcut menu. Click the General tab.

The Properties for the drive appear, as shown in Figure 9-6.

3 Click the Disk Cleanup button.

Windows analyzes the hard disk and determines how many unnecessary files you can delete and how much space will be freed by deleting these files.

After several seconds, the Disk Cleanup dialog box appears and displays this information, as shown in Figure 9-7.

The files you can safely delete fall into several categories—see Table 9-1 for descriptions of them.

4 Click OK.

Disk Cleanup deletes the selected types of unnecessary files.

That's all there is to using Disk Cleanup to free space on your hard drive. If you find you still need more room on your hard disk, you have several more options. Here are some things you can do to reclaim space on your hard disk:

• **Remove Unnecessary Programs:** One of the best ways to reclaim space on your hard disk is to remove old programs you don't use. Open Add or Remove Programs in the Control Panel to have Windows delete these programs for you.

- **Remove Unnecessary Windows Components:** Although this won't free up a lot of space, you can remove some Windows components by opening Add or Remove Programs in the Control Panel, clicking the Add/Remove Windows Components button, and deselecting the components you want to remove.

Table 9-1. Types of files you can delete to save space

File Type	Description
Downloaded Program Files	Similar to Temporary Internet Files, Downloaded Program Files are small programs (ActiveX controls and Java applets if you want to be technical) that have been downloaded from the Internet when you view certain pages.
Temporary Internet Files	The Internet saves Web pages on your hard disk for quick viewing—so when you return to a Web page, it can fetch it much faster from your hard disk than it can from the Internet. This collection of files used to speed up the Internet is known as a cache. You can safely remove these temporary Internet files from your computer without deleting your Web settings and bookmarks or favorite locations. Disk Cleanup does not normally delete these files, since they help speed up the Internet.
Office Setup Files	To avoid the requirement of inserting a CD whenever you run a Microsoft Office Program, the setup files from program installation may be saved on your computer. Deleting these files is not recommended as they help maintain your Office programs.
Recycle Bin	The Recycle Bin contains files you have deleted from your computer. These files are not permanently removed until you empty the Recycle Bin.
Temporary Files	Programs sometimes store temporary information in a TEMP folder, usually located in the Windows folder. Before a program closes, it usually deletes this information. Turning your computer off without following the Windows shutdown procedure doesn't give the program or Windows time to cleanup after themselves, and these TMP files are leftover. You can almost always safely remove .TMP files.
Temporary Offline Files	If you work over a network, copies of files you've worked on recently are saved on your computer so they can be easily accessed if you are disconnected from the network.
Offline Web Pages	Offline pages are Web pages that are stored on your computer so you can view them without being connected to the Internet. You can safely remove offline Web pages from your computer without deleting your Web settings and bookmarks or favorite locations.
Offline Files	Offline files are local copies of network files that you specifically made available.
Compress Old Files	Compress (or zip) old files into condensed versions to create more space on the hard drive. You can work with a compressed file or folder just as you would an uncompressed file or folder.

QUICK REFERENCE

1. CLICK THE START BUTTON AND SELECT MY
   COMPUTER FROM THE MENU.

2. RIGHT-CLICK THE LOCAL DISK (C:) ICON AND
   SELECT PROPERTIES FROM THE SHORTCUT MENU.
   CLICK THE GENERAL TAB.

3. CLICK THE DISK CLEANUP BUTTON.

4. CLICK OK.

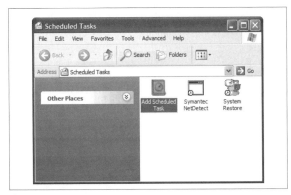

Figure 9-8. The Scheduled Tasks window.

Figure 9-9. Select the program you want to schedule.

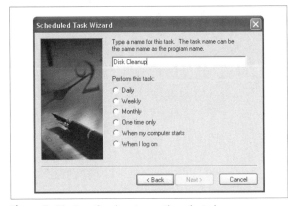

Figure 9-10. Specify when to run the selected program.

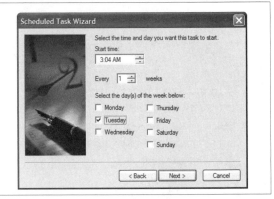

Figure 9-11. Select the time and day the task should start.

To keep your computer in peak condition, you should run maintenance programs regularly. You can have Windows automatically perform these and other tasks on a regular basis for you with the *Task Scheduler*. The Task Scheduler works a lot like TiVo, except instead of recording your favorite television shows while you're away, Task Scheduler automatically runs specified programs. This lesson explains how to use the Task Scheduler to run your programs on a regular basis.

1 Click the Start button and select All Programs → Accessories → System Tools → Scheduled Tasks from the menu.

The Scheduled Tasks window appears, as shown in Figure 9-8.

2 Double-click the Add Scheduled Task icon.

The first screen of the Schedule Tasks Wizard appears.

3 Click Next.

The Scheduled Task Wizard lists all the programs that are installed on your computer. You must select the program you want to schedule from the list. Error-checking, Microsoft Backup, Disk Defragmenter, and Disk Cleanup are all excellent candidates for Scheduled Tasks.

Let's schedule the Disk Cleanup program.

4 Select Disk Cleanup from the list and click Next.

Now you need to specify how often you want the selected program to run, as shown in Figure 9-10.

5 Select Monthly and click Next.

Now you need to specify the time Task Scheduler should run the selected program. You should always try to schedule a time when the computer won't be in use, such as late at night (so long as you don't turn off your computer when you're done with it).

6 Change the Start time to 3:00 AM.

To change the time, you must first select the hour, minute, or AM/PM. Now choose the day you want the program to run.

7 Select the Day option, as shown in Figure 9-11.

The task will run at 3:00 AM the first day of every month.

8 Click Next.

Now enter your user name and password. This makes the task run under your personalized settings.

9 Type your user name and password, confirm the password, and then click Next.

The last screen of the Scheduled Task Wizard appears, reporting that you have successfully added a new scheduled task.

10 Click Finish.

The Scheduled Task Wizard closes and the selected program appears in the Scheduled Tasks window.

When you no longer want a program to be scheduled, just delete it from the Scheduled Tasks window—just like you would delete a file.

Disk Cleanup
Other Ways to Start Disk Cleanup:
• Click the Start button and select **All Programs**→
Accessories→**System Tools**→**Disk Cleanup**.

QUICK REFERENCE

TO SCHEDULE A TASK:

1. CLICK THE START BUTTON AND SELECT ALL PROGRAMS → ACCESSORIES → SYSTEM TOOLS → SCHEDULED TASKS FROM THE MENU.

2. DOUBLE-CLICK THE ADD SCHEDULED TASK ICON.

3. CLICK NEXT.

4. SELECT THE PROGRAM YOU WANT TO SCHEDULE A TASK FOR AND CLICK NEXT.

5. SPECIFY HOW OFTEN YOU WANT THE PROGRAM TO RUN AND CLICK NEXT.

6. SELECT THE TIME AND DAY WHEN YOU WANT THE TASK TO OCCUR AND CLICK NEXT.

7. ENTER YOUR USER NAME AND PASSWORD INFORMATION AND CLICK NEXT.

8. CLICK FINISH.

TO REMOVE A TASK FROM THE TASK SCHEDULER:

• OPEN THE TASK SCHEDULER AND DELETE THE TASK, JUST AS YOU WOULD A FILE OR FOLDER.

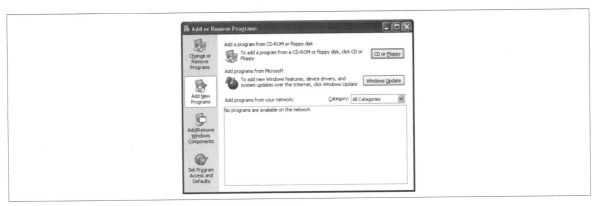

Figure 9-12. The Add or Remove Programs window.

Figure 9-13. Windows searches your floppy drive and CD-ROM drive for the program you want to install.

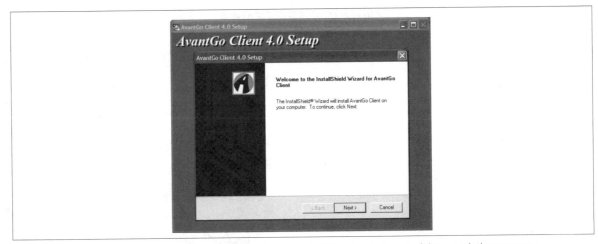

Figure 9-14. The installation program for every software program is different-—but most of them work the same way.

Thanks to the advanced install files and improved operating systems, computer users rarely have to do more than click the mouse a few times to install a program. It's usually just a matter of inserting the program CD, and before you know it, the program is installed on your computer. But if nothing happens after you insert the disk, you may have to start things rolling yourself. This lesson will show you how to install most programs.

1 Find the Program's disk (or disks) and insert it (or the first disk) into the disk drive.

If your software comes on more than one disk, dig through the box until you find a disk labeled Disk 1, Installation, or Setup.

If you're installing a newer program from a CD-ROM, you might not have to do much more—most CD-

ROM's will automatically start the installation program when the CD is inserted. You can move on to Step 8 if this is the case.

2 Click the Start button and select Control Panel from the menu. Click the Add or Remove Programs category and click the Add New Programs button on the left side of the window.

Add New Programs

The Add or Remove Programs window appears, as shown in Figure 9-12. Here you must select where the program you want to install is located.

TIP *Most programs have a special installation program used to install them onto your computer. These programs are usually named Setup, Install, or something similar.*

3 Click the CD or Floppy button and click Next in the Install Program Wizard.

Windows searches your CD-ROM drive for the program you want to install. Most programs come with a special program called SETUP or INSTALL, which installs the main program onto your computer.

4 Select the Setup or Install file and click Finish.

The install wizard for the program begins. All you have to do now is follow the wizard's instructions to finish installing the program.

5 Follow the install wizard instructions to finish installing the program.

If you're installing a finicky program, a program that you've downloaded from the Internet, or a program located on a network, you're probably going to have to install the program yourself.

Here's how to install a program on your own.

6 Click the Start button and select My Computer from the menu.

You have to open the disk drive or folder where the setup program is located. For example, double-click the CD-ROM icon if you're installing from a CD-

ROM. If you're installing a program from a network or that you've downloaded from the Internet, find and open the folder where the file is saved.

7 Navigate to the location of the program install file. Double-click the file name Setup or Install.

The program's install wizard appears.

8 Follow the install wizard instructions to finish installing the program.

The installation process varies between each program, although most set-ups have more similarities than differences. Most programs use a step-by-step Wizard to guide you through the installation process, let you specify where you want to install the program (although they have their own default folder in mind), and let you specify which program components you want to install.

Many installation programs create their own folder and icons in the Start menu, which can be both a blessing and a curse—a blessing because you don't have to manually add an icon to the All Programs menu, and a curse because if you've installed a lot of software onto your computer, your All Programs menu will be cluttered with dozens of folders and programs. You can always reorganize the All Programs menu and reduce the amount of folders and clutter.

QUICK REFERENCE

TO INSTALL SOFTWARE USING THE CONTROL PANEL:

1. FIND THE PROGRAM'S DISK (OR DISKS) AND INSERT IT (OR THE FIRST DISK) INTO THE DISK DRIVE.

2. CLICK THE START BUTTON AND SELECT CONTROL PANEL FROM THE MENU.

3. CLICK ADD OR REMOVE PROGRAMS.

4. CLICK ADD NEW PROGRAMS.

5. CLICK THE CD OR FLOPPY BUTTON AND FOLLOW THE WIZARD INSTRUCTIONS TO LOCATE THE SETUP OR INSTALL FILE.

TO INSTALL SOFTWARE MANUALLY:

1. OPEN MY COMPUTER, FIND THE DISK DRIVE OR FOLDER WHERE THE PROGRAM YOU WANT TO INSTALL IS LOCATED, AND DOUBLE-CLICK THE INSTALLATION PROGRAM (USUALLY CALLED SETUP OR INSTALL).

2. FOLLOW THE ON-SCREEN INSTRUCTIONS TO INSTALL THE PROGRAM.

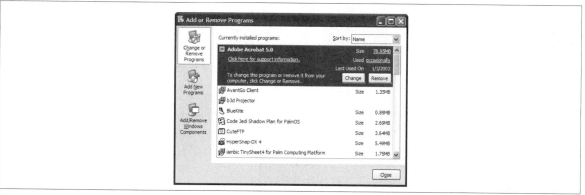

Figure 9-15. The Change or Remove Programs view of the Add or Remove Programs dialog box.

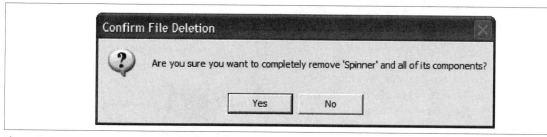

Figure 9-16. The Confirm File Deletion dialog box.

You've finally finished that adventure game you've spent 100 hours on, and since you no longer need the game, you decide to reclaim the 200 megabytes it occupies on your hard drive. So how do you remove, or delete, a program that you no longer need from Windows? You'll learn how in this lesson.

Before Windows 95, removing programs from the computer was a very messy process—so messy, in fact, that most people never removed programs they no longer needed. The unused programs just sat there, taking up valuable space on the hard drive. Times have changed, and removing *most* programs is a breeze with Windows XP. The following steps should remove all but the most obsolete programs from your computer.

1 Click the Start button and select Control Panel from the menu. Click the Add or Remove Programs category.

**Add or Remove
Programs**

The Add or Remove Programs dialog box appears with a list of all the programs on your computer, as shown in Figure 9-15.

Most of the programs installed on your computer should appear on this list, in alphabetical order.

2 Select the program you want to remove from your computer, and click the Remove button.

Be absolutely sure you want to remove the program, as it will be completely erased from your hard disk. If you created any files or documents with the program that you're removing, it's probably a good idea to back them up, but removing a program usually doesn't affect any files it created.

3 Click Yes to confirm the program's removal, and finish removing the program by following the on-screen instructions.

Since every program is different, the steps for removing a program may differ slightly as well. The steps basically confirm that you want to delete the program and may ask you to specify which components of a program you want to delete. You may also have to restart your computer.

After following the prompts and instructions, the selected program is deleted from your computer. Of course, you can always reinstall the program should you ever decide you need it again.

What if the program I want to remove doesn't appear in the list? Sorry, but there is no easy way to remove this type of program. The program was probably written for an older version of Windows, or even MS-DOS, and cannot be automatically removed by Windows. There are still several things you can try to remove the program.

First, check the menu group where the program is located in the Start menu. Usually there are several additional menus or icons. If one of the options says something like "Uninstall Software," you're in luck—you can click that option and remove the program.

Second, you can purchase and install an Uninstall program to remove the program. Uninstall programs are great for removing older Windows programs and they're usually safe to use, too. The disadvantage is that you have to buy them. Before rushing out to your computer store, consider the number of programs you need to remove from your computer. If it is only one or two, then the prospect of paying $30 to $50 for an Uninstall program isn't very appealing.

Third, you can try erasing the program the old-fashioned way—by opening My Computer or Windows Explorer and finding and deleting the folder where the program is located. Be very careful and make sure you know what you're doing when you remove or erase the program yourself—you don't want to delete something that shouldn't be deleted!

QUICK REFERENCE

TO REMOVE A PROGRAM:

1. CLICK THE START BUTTON AND SELECT CONTROL PANEL FROM THE MENU.

2. CLICK THE ADD OR REMOVE PROGRAMS CATEGORY.

3. SELECT THE PROGRAM YOU WANT TO REMOVE FROM YOUR COMPUTER AND CLICK THE REMOVE BUTTON.

4. CLICK YES TO CONFIRM THE PROGRAM'S REMOVAL AND FINISH REMOVING THE SELECTED PROGRAM BY FOLLOWING THE ON-SCREEN INSTRUCTIONS.

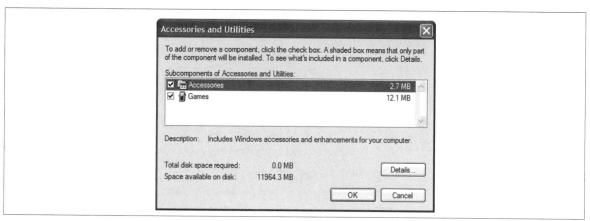

Figure 9-17. The Windows Components Wizard.

Figure 9-18. Details of the Accessories and Utilities component category.

Windows XP is normally not installed with all the components that come on the Windows XP CD. This prevents programs you don't need from taking up hard disk space on the computer. For example, if your computer doesn't have a modem, it doesn't make much sense to install any communication components. So what are these optional Windows components? Take a look at Table 9-2. This lesson will show you how you can add and remove these optional Windows components to and from your computer.

1 Click the Start button and select Control Panel from the menu. Click the Add or Remove Programs category and click the Add/Remove Windows Components button.

**Add/Remove
Windows
Components**

The Windows Components Wizard appears, as shown in Figure 9-17. You can view which components have been installed and which haven't by looking at the Components list.

The Windows components are grouped by category.

An unchecked box (☐) by a category indicates *none* of its components have been installed. A checked box (☑) by a category means *all* of its components have been installed. A shaded check box (☑) by a category means *some* of its components have been installed.

To view which components are in a category, select the category and click the Details button.

2 Scroll down the Components list to view all the components to choose from. Click the Accessories and Utilities category (the word, not the checkbox) to select it, and click the Details button.

The details of the Accessories and Utilities category appear in their own dialog box, as shown in Figure 9-18.

3 Click the Games category. Click the Details button.

Games installed on the computer are checked (☑). To remove a Windows component, simply remove the check mark from a check box (☐).

4 Click Cancel.

We're back to the Games dialog box..

5 Click OK in the Games dialog box, and click OK in the Accessories and Utilities dialog box.

You have returned to the Windows Components Wizard window.

It's not recommended, but you can also remove an entire category by clicking its check box.

6 Click Next.

Windows identifies the component changes.

7 Click Finish.

The Internet Games component is removed from the computer.

Remember, if you remove a component, you can always go back and click the check box to add the component again. But to add a component, you may need to have the Windows XP CD-ROM on hand.

Table 9-2. Windows components

Components	Description
Accessories and Utilities	Install a variety of accessories, including games, small applications, and wallpaper.
Fax Services	Allows faxes to be sent and received.
Indexing Service	Locates, indexes, and updates documents to provide fast full-text searching.
Internet Explorer	Adds or removes access to Internet Explorer from the Start menu and Desktop.
Internet Information Services (IIS)	Includes Web and FTP support, along with support for FrontPage, transactions, Active Server Pages, and database connections.
Management and Monitoring Tools	Includes tools for monitoring and improving network performance.
Message Queuing	Programs for playing sounds, animation, and video on your computer. Also adds additional sound effects.
Online Services	Provides guaranteed message delivery, efficient routing, security, and transactional support.
MSN Explorer	Explore the web, read your e-mail, talk to your online buddies, enjoy online music and video, and more.
Networking Services	Contains a variety of specialized, network-related services and protocols.
Other Network File and Print Services	Shares files and printers on this computer with others on the network.

Table 9-2. Windows components (Continued)

Components	Description
Outlook Express	E-mail client that allows you to send and receive e-mail messages.
Update Root Certificates	Automatically downloads the most current root certificates for secure e-mail, WEB browsing, and software delivery.
Windows Media Player	Plays media files, such as music and video.
Windows Messenger	Allows you to chat with your instant messenger contacts.

QUICK REFERENCE

TO ADD OR REMOVE WINDOWS COMPONENTS:

1. CLICK THE START BUTTON AND SELECT CONTROL PANEL FROM THE MENU.

2. CLICK THE ADD OR REMOVE PROGRAMS CATEGORY.

3. CLICK THE ADD/REMOVE WINDOWS COMPONENTS BUTTON.

4. CLICK THE BOX BESIDE THE COMPONENT CATEGORY YOU WANT TO ADD ☑ OR REMOVE ☐.

5. CLICK NEXT.

6. CLICK FINISH.

TO ADD OR REMOVE A WINDOWS COMPONENT IN A CATEGORY:

1. SELECT THE CATEGORY, CLICK DETAILS, AND THEN CLICK THE BOX BESIDE THE COMPONENT CATEGORY YOU WANT TO ADD ☑ OR REMOVE ☐.

2. CLICK OK.

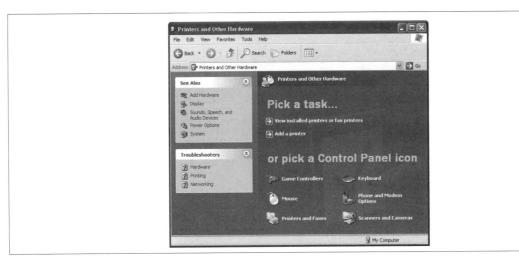

Figure 9-19. The XP Home Printers and Other Hardware window.

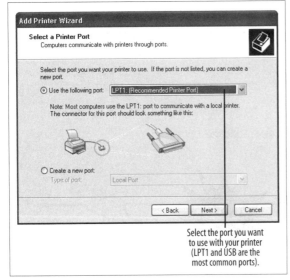

Select the port you want
to use with your printer
(LPT1 and USB are the
most common ports).

Figure 9-20. Selecting a printer port.

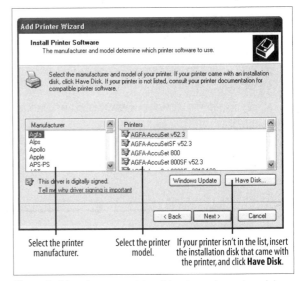

Select the printer
manufacturer.

Select the printer
model.

If your printer isn't in the list, insert
the installation disk that came with
the printer, and click **Have Disk**.

Figure 9-21. Selecting a printer driver by make and model.

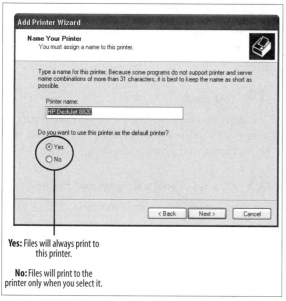

Yes: Files will always print to
this printer.

No: Files will print to the
printer only when you select it.

Figure 9-22. Assigning a name to the printer, and designating
the default printer.

Want to add a printer to your computer? Before you can
use it you need to install it on your computer. This lesson
will show you how to install a printer attached to your
computer.

1 **If at possible, install the printer using the included
software and documentation.**

Hopefully that's all you will have to do and you can
skip the remaining steps in this lesson! If you can't
find the software and/or documentation, read on…

2 **Place the printer near your computer and plug the
printer cable into your computer's USB or parallel port.
Turn your computer and the printer on.**

USB Port

Most printers connect to the USB port at the back of
your computer, but there are still some printers that
connect to the older, much larger, parallel port. Usually, the computer detects the new printer and will
automatically begin installing the printer. If for some
reason this doesn't happen read on.

Parallel Port

3 **Click the Start button and select Control Panel
from the menu. Click the Printers and Other Hardware
category.**

The Printers and Other Hardware window appears, as
shown in Figure 9-19.

4 **Click the Add a printer task.**

The first page of the Add Printer Wizard springs onto
your screen.

The Add Printer Wizard will help you setup your
printer by walking you step-by-step through the
entire installation process.

5 **Click Next.**

The Add Printer Wizard may ask how the printer is
connected to the computer: locally or over a network.
A local printer plugs directly into your computer; a
network printer is located elsewhere on the network.

6 **Select the Local option.**

You can skip ahead by clicking the "Automatically
detect and install my Plug and Play printer" check
box, which attempts to install the printer for you.

7 **Click Next.**

Here you need to specify the port you want to use.

8 **Select the port that your computer uses from the
drop down list.**

If you don't see your port in the list (a common problem if you're using a USB printer) you will probably
need to install the printer using the software that
came with it. If you don't have the software, try downloading it from the manufacturer's Web site.

9 **Click the manufacturer of your printer from the
manufacturer list.**

You may have to scroll down the list. When you click
on the manufacturer's name, a list of printer models

from that manufacturer appears in the model list to the right.

10 Click the model of your printer in the model list.

If you can't find your printer in the list, insert the installation disk that came with your computer and click the Have Disk button. You may have to refer to the instructions that came with your printer to install it.

11 Click Next.

Give the printer a name in the Printer Name box. You must also decide if you want to use the printer being installed as the default. The default printer is where Windows prints all of its files, unless you specify otherwise.

12 Enter a printer name. Click the Yes option to set the default printer.

The Add Printer Wizard assigns a name to the printer and sets it as the computer's default printer.

13 Click Next.

Specify if this printer will be shared by others. If your computer is not part of a network you won't be sharing the printer.

14 Click Next.

Windows asks if you would like to print a test page to make sure your new printer works. This is a good way to verify that your printer is working properly.

15 Click Yes to print a test page and click Next.

Finally, your printer is almost complete.

16 Click Finish.

That's it—your printer is installed and should appear as a new icon in the Printers folder. Don't' forget to see if your test page printed successfully.

QUICK REFERENCE

TO INSTALL A NEW PRINTER:

1. IF AT POSSIBLE, INSTALL THE PRINTER USING THE INCLUDED SOFTWARE AND DOCUMENTATION.

2. CLICK THE START BUTTON AND SELECT CONTROL PANEL FROM THE MENU.

3. CLICK THE PRINTERS AND OTHER HARDWARE CATEGORY.

4. CLICK THE ADD A PRINTER TASK. CLICK NEXT.

5. SPECIFY HOW THE PRINTER IS CONNECTED (LOCAL OR NETWORK). CLICK NEXT.

6. SELECT A PORT TO USE WITH THE PRINTER. CLICK NEXT.

7. SELECT THE PRINTER'S MANUFACTURER AND MODEL. IF YOUR PRINTER DOESN'T APPEAR IN THE LIST, INSERT THE DISK THAT CAME WITH THE PRINTER AND CLICK THE HAVE DISK BUTTON. CLICK NEXT.

8. (OPTIONAL) ASSIGN A NAME TO THE PRINTER AND SET THE PRINTER AS THE DEFAULT. CLICK NEXT.

9. SPECIFY IF THE PRINTER WILL BE SHARED AND CLICK NEXT.

10. IF YOU WANT A TEST PAGE PRINTED AND CLICK NEXT.

11. CLICK FINISH.

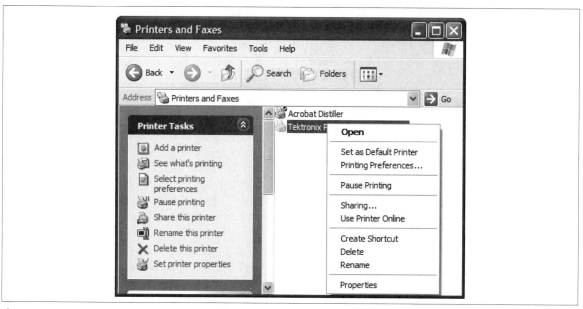

Figure 9-23. Right-click any printer in the Printers folder to change its settings.

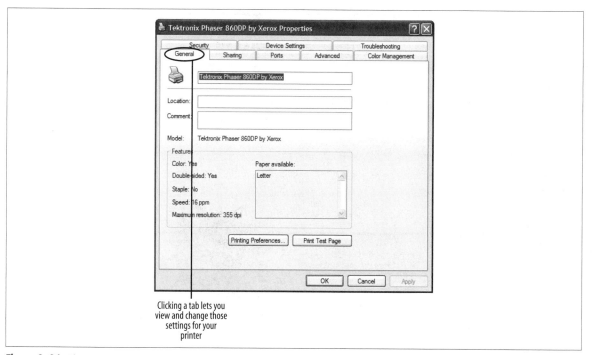

Clicking a tab lets you view and change those settings for your printer

Figure 9-24. The printer Properties dialog box will be different for every printer, depending on the printer's features.

Sometimes you may want to tweak the settings on your printer. For example, perhaps you have more than one printer connected to your computer and want to change the default printer. Maybe you want to take advantage of some of your printer's more advanced features or are having trouble printing and want to look at your printer's settings to find out what's wrong. This lesson will show you how to change which printer your computer uses as the default printer (where your computer prints everything unless you specify otherwise) and how to view and change the default settings for your printer.

1 Click the Start button and select Control Panel from the menu.

The Control Panel appears.

2 Click the Printers and Other Hardware category and click Printers and Faxes.

The Printers and Faxes window appears.

3 Right-click the printer you want to set as the default printer and select Set as Default Printer from the shortcut menu.

The default printer displays a black checkmark (✪). Any documents you print will be sent to the default printer.

You can also view the properties for your printers. Here's how:

4 Right-click the printer and select Properties from the shortcut menu.

The Properties dialog box for your particular printer appears, as shown in Figure 9-24.

Keep in mind that every printer is different, so the Properties dialog box for your printer may look a lot different from the one shown in Figure 9-24. All Printer Properties dialog boxes let you change the default options for your particular printer—what port it uses, its print quality, etc.

5 Click Cancel to close the Properties dialog box, then close the Printers folder.

QUICK REFERENCE

TO CHANGE THE DEFAULT PRINTER:

1. CLICK THE START BUTTON AND SELECT CONTROL PANEL FROM THE MENU.

2. CLICK THE PRINTERS AND OTHER HARDWARE CATEGORY AND CLICK PRINTERS AND FAXES.

3. RIGHT-CLICK THE DESIRED PRINTER AND SELECT SET AS A DEFAULT PRINTER.

TO CHANGE A PRINTERS'S PROPERTIES:

• RIGHT-CLICK THE PRINTER AND SELECT PROPERTIES.

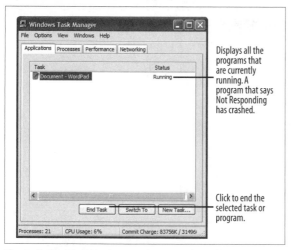

Figure 9-25. The Windows Task Manager window.

Displays all the programs that are currently running. A program that says Not Responding has crashed.

Click to end the selected task or program.

If you haven't already noticed, sooner or later you're going to discover that computers don't always work the way they're supposed to. Nothing is more frustrating than when a program, for no apparent reason, decides to take a quick nap, locks up, and stops responding to your commands. There's usually no way to restore a frozen application, but you can usually shut down the misbehaving program without having to restart your computer.

1 Start the WordPad program.

The WordPad program appears on the screen. There is not a "Crash Program" command anywhere in WordPad, so you'll have to use your imagination. Imagine that you've just finished writing a letter in WordPad. Like a good Windows user, you save your file, and then click the Print button to send the document to the printer. Nothing. Not only does the document fail to print, WordPad decides to go on strike and stops responding to your commands.

When a program freezes, there's nothing you can do except dump the program from your computer's memory (hopefully you've been periodically saving

whatever you've been working on so you won't lose too much of your work). The next step will show you how to forcefully close a program.

2 Press Ctrl + Alt + Delete.

The Windows Task Manager window appears, as shown in Figure 9-25.

All the programs that are running are listed. Any programs that are frozen or locked up will have a "(Not responding)" message after them. WordPad hasn't stopped responding, but for the sake of this lesson we'll pretend it has.

3 Select WordPad and click End Task.

Windows forcibly closes the WordPad program.

Sometimes a program may cause your entire computer to lock-up, and even pressing Ctrl + Alt + Delete won't do anything. What should you do when this happens? There is only one thing you can do—turn your computer off, and restart it.

QUICK REFERENCE

TO SHUT DOWN A FROZEN PROGRAM:

1. PRESS CTRL + ALT + DELETE.

2. SELECT THE PROGRAM AND CLICK END TASK.

Figure 9-26. The Add Hardware Wizard.

Figure 9-27. The Add Hardware Wizard searches for new hardware.

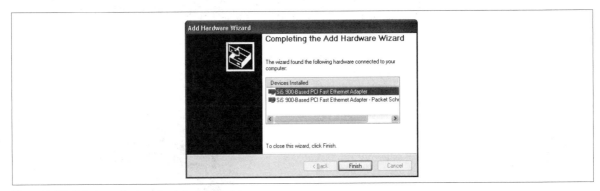

Figure 9-28. Windows displays the detected hardware.

Anytime you add a new hardware gadget to your computer, you need to make sure Windows XP can talk with and operate it. Windows communicates to your computer's hardware components using a small piece of software called a *driver*. A driver is like a computerized operating manual that tells Windows how to communicate and operate all the hardware devices in your computer.

Whenever you install a new piece of hardware to your computer, such as a network card or a removable storage device, you need to install the driver for that particular piece of hardware. If you're lucky, the piece of hardware is a *Plug and Play* device. Plug and Play devices are devices that Windows can automatically detect and set up to work with your computer, making them a breeze to install. Most new devices are Plug and Play.

If the device doesn't automatically install, you'll have to get things going yourself. This lesson will help you install a hardware device either way.

1 **Plug in the hardware device to your computer.**

Your computer can be on or off when you plug in the device, although the computer will have an easier time detecting the device if you plug it in before you turn on the computer.

2 **If Windows XP detects the device, the Found New Hardware icon will appear in the system tray area, followed by the Found New Hardware Wizard. Follow the on-screen instructions.**

Make sure you have the disk or CD-ROM that came with your new hardware device and the Windows XP CD-ROM handy—Windows will probably ask you for them.

If Windows XP doesn't automatically detect your new hardware, try installing the hardware yourself.

3 **Click the Start button and select Control Panel from the Start menu.**

The Control Panel appears.

4 **Select Pritners and Other Hardware.**

Here's how to start the Hardware Wizard:.

5 **Click the Add Hardware task.**

The first screen of the Add Hardware Wizard appears.

6 **Click Next and follow the on-screen instructions to install the new hardware.**

First, Windows looks for new Plug and Play devices on your computer. If it finds any, you will probably be asked to insert the disk or CD-ROM that came with your new hardware device.

Next, Windows searches for hardware that is not Plug and Play compatible, which may take a *long* time. If it finds any, you will be asked to insert the disk or CD-ROM that came with your new hardware device.

If you've followed the above steps and Windows still can't find your new device, or if the device doesn't work after you've installed it, bad news—you might have a *hardware conflict*. Some hardware devices require resources on your computer. These resources are as technical as they sound—IRQs, DMA channels, and I/O ports. All you need to know about them is that there is a limited number of them on your computer (for example, most com-

puters have fewer than two available IRQs), and, for the most part, several hardware components can't share the same resource. For example, if you were trying to install a modem that uses IRQ 3 and your network card is already using IRQ 3, the modem isn't going to work.

So what's the solution? You can change the resource settings for most devices—either through Windows or by moving some pins or switches on the hardware device itself (refer to the hardware's user manual for how to do this).

QUICK REFERENCE

- PLUG IN THE HARDWARE DEVICE TO YOUR COMPUTER.

  WINDOWS SHOULD AUTOMATICALLY DETECT AND INSTALL THE DEVICE FOR YOU. IF NOT, GO ON TO THE NEXT STEP.

1. IF WINDOWS DOESN'T RECOGNIZE THE NEW HARDWARE, CLICK THE START BUTTON AND SELECT CONTROL PANEL FROM THE MENU.

2. CLICK THE PERFORMANCE AND MAINTENANCE CATEGORY AND CLICK SYSTEM.

3. CLICK THE PRINTERS AND OTHER HARDWARE CATEGORY.

4. CLICK THE HARDWARE TASK.

5. CLICK NEXT AND FOLLOW THE ON-SCREEN INSTRUCTIONS TO SEARCH FOR YOUR NEW HARDWARE.

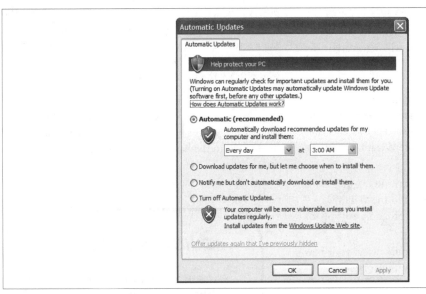

Figure 9-29. The Automatic Updates dialog box.

Windows XP Service Pack 2 is an update that is installed on your computer through automatic updates.

When a manufacturer finds a problem in a product they have made, they call back the product for repairs or to replace it. Microsoft does a similar thing with Windows: when a security vulnerability is found, Microsoft creates a patch to repair the problem. You don't have to bring your computer into a repair shop or send it back to Microsoft, because Automatic Updates downloads critical repairs and updates that are essential for a functional computer onto your computer over the Internet.

TIP *An Internet connection is required to use Automatic Updates.*

1 Click the Start button and select Control Panel from the menu.

The Control Panel appears.

2 Click the Security Center category and click Automatic Updates.

The Automatic Updates dialog box appears, as shown in Figure 9-29.

The options to change Automatic Updates are described in the following table.

Table 9-3. Automatic Update settings

Setting	Description
Automatic (recommended)	Updates are downloaded and installed automatically every day at 3:00 AM. The schedule for checking updates can be changed.
Download updates for me, but let me choose when to install them.	Updates are downloaded but not installed. An icon in the system tray notifies that updates are ready to be installed.
Notify me but don't automatically download or install them.	When updates are available, an icon in the system tray notifies you that updates are available at the Microsoft Web site.
Turn off Automatic Updates.	All responsibility to keep your computer up to date is yours.

QUICK REFERENCE

TO RUN AUTOMATIC UPDATES:

1. CLICK THE START BUTTON AND SELECT
    CONTROL PANEL FROM THE MENU.

2. CLICK THE SECURITY CENTER CATEGORY.

3. CLICK AUTOMATIC UPDATES.

Follow instructions on the Windows Update Screen to install updates on your computer.

Figure 9-30. The Microsoft Windows Update Web page.

🔵 *Windows XP Service Pack 2: Windows Update now includes security patches and updates for Microsoft applications, including SQL, Exchange, and Office, in addition to updates for Windows XP. Windows Update itself has changed, so you may be asked to update Windows Update.*

Keeping your computer up to date is important. If you don't rely on Automatic Updates to do this for you, you are responsible for downloading updates through Windows Update. Windows Update allows you to download critical updates, but it includes more fun updates, like a new Windows Media Player or desktop themes.

1 Click the Start button and select All Programs → Windows Update from the menu.

The Microsoft Windows Update Web page appears with two options:

- **Express Install:** This option installs the same updates as Automatic Updates. Includes critical and security updates necessary for your computer to work properly.

- **Custom Install:** In addition to critical and security updates, you can install and review optional updates, such as new desktop themes.

2 Click the type of install you want to perform.

Windows Update scans your computer to see which updates are available for your computer. When the scan is complete, go ahead and install your updates.

3 If you selected Express Install, click the Install button. If you selected Custom Install, click the check box next to the updates you want to install. Click Go to install updates to install the updates.

The Windows Update service downloads and installs the files you selected. Since you're on the Internet, this can take some time, depending on how many files you selected and how fast your connection to the Internet is. You may have to restart your computer when the download is complete, depending on the changes that have been made to your computer.

QUICK REFERENCE

TO USE WINDOWS UPDATE:

1. ESTABLISH A CONNECTION TO THE INTERNET.

2. CLICK THE START BUTTON AND SELECT ALL PROGRAMS → WINDOWS UPDATE FROM THE MENU.

3. CLICK THE TYPE OF INSTALL YOU WANT TO PERFORM.

4. EXPRESS INSTALL: CLICK THE INSTALL BUTTON.

5. CUSTOM INSTALL: CLICK THE CHECK BOX NEXT TO THE UPDATES YOU WANT TO INSTALL. CLICK GO TO INSTALL UPDATES TO INSTALL THEM.

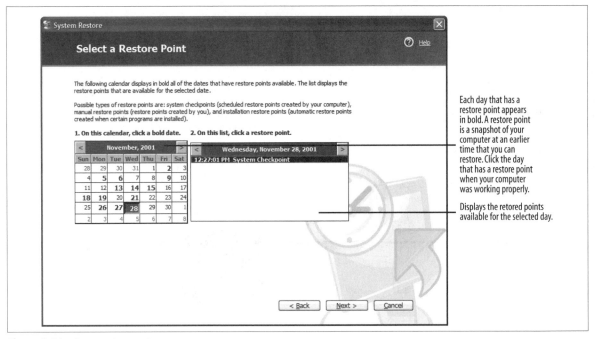

Figure 9-31. The new System Restore program.

If you are experiencing problems with your computer, you can use Windows XP's *System Restore* utility to return your computer configuration to a time before the problems occurred. For example, perhaps your computer doesn't work properly after you installed a junky discount software program. You can use System Restore to return your computer configuration back to the way it was before you installed that junky program, without losing recent work, such as e-mail, documents, or history and favorites lists.

System Restore keeps track of the changes you make to your computer at specific intervals and when you install new hardware and software programs. You can also create your own restore points to record your computer settings at any given time, in case you want to return your computer to that state later.

In this lesson you will learn how to use System Restore.

1 Click the **Start button and select All Programs** → **Accessories** → **System Tools** → **System Restore from the menu.**

The Welcome to System Restore window appears. You can select one of two options:

- **Restore my computer to an earlier time:** This option lets you undo the changes made to your computer by selecting a restore point on a calendar.

- **Create a restore point:** Windows XP automatically creates restore points, but you can also create your own restore points manually by selecting this option. This is useful if you are about to make a major change to your computer, such as installing a new program or new hardware.

Since Windows XP automatically creates restore points for you, most of the time you will select the first option.

2 Make sure the **Restore my computer to an earlier time** option is selected and click **Next.**

The Select a Restore Point window appears, as shown in Figure 9-31.

The calendar displays the current month and the days for which restore points are available. Each day with a restore point appears in **bold**.

The right side of the window displays the restore points that are available for the selected day (if you were making a lot of system changes to your computer, there may be more than one).

3 Select the restore point nearest to the time when your computer was working properly. Click Next.

The next screen appears, asking you to close all open files and programs before restoring your computer.

4 Close all open programs. Click Next.

System Restore returns your computer to the selected restore point configuration. When its it's finished, your computer will automatically restart.

After your computer restarts, you will be greeted by the System Restore window and a message indicating that your computer has been restored to a previous state.

5 Click OK to close the System Restore window.

You can also use System Restore to reverse the changes made when you restored your computer. To undo any restoration, simply repeat Step 1, select the "Undo my last restoration" option in Step 2, and follow the on-screen instructions.

Please note that System Restore does not replace the process of uninstalling a program. To completely remove the files installed by a program, you must remove the program using Add/Remove Programs in the Control Panel or the program's own uninstall program.

QUICK REFERENCE

TO RESTORE YOUR COMPUTER:

1. CLICK THE START BUTTON AND SELECT ALL PROGRAMS → ACCESSORIES → SYSTEM TOOLS → SYSTEM RESTORE FROM THE MENU.

2. MAKE SURE THE RESTORE MY COMPUTER TO AN EARLIER TIME OPTION IS SELECTED. CLICK NEXT.

3. SELECT THE RESTORE POINT NEAREST TO THE TIME WHEN YOUR COMPUTER WAS WORKING PROPERLY. CLICK NEXT.

4. CLOSE ALL OPEN FILES AND PROGRAMS. CLICK NEXT.

5. WHEN THE RESTORE IS COMPLETE THE COMPUTER AUTOMATICALLY RESTARTS.

6. CLICK OK TO CLOSE THE SYSTEM RESTORE WINDOW.

TO CREATE A RESTORE POINT:

1. CLICK THE START BUTTON AND SELECT ALL PROGRAMS → ACCESSORIES → SYSTEM TOOLS → SYSTEM RESTORE FROM THE MENU.

2. SELECT CREATE A RESTORE POINT. CLICK NEXT.

3. ENTER A NAME FOR YOUR RESTORE POINT. CLICK CREATE.

4. CLICK CLOSE TO CLOSE THE SYSTEM RESTORE WINDOW.

Figure 9-32. The Hardware tab of the System Properties dialog box.

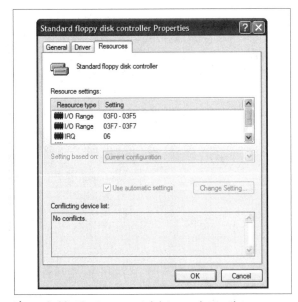

Figure 9-33. The Resources tab lets you change the resources a particular device uses.

Figure 9-34. The Device Manager lists all the hardware devices installed on your computer.

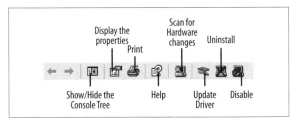

Figure 9-35. The Device Manager toolbar.

The Device Manager lets you:

- View information about your computer's hardware.
- Remove hardware device drivers.
- Change the computer resources a device uses.

If you're trying to install a new hardware device, have carefully followed the instructions that came with the device and the device still doesn't function, there may be one of two problems:

- The device is defective and you'll need to get another one

or

- You have a *resource conflict*. Most hardware devices require resources on your computer. These resources include Interrupt Requests (IRQs), Direct Memory Access (DMA) channels, and Input/Outputs (I/Os). You don't have to know what these resources mean from a technical standpoint, but it is important that you realize that because these resources are limited, your computer may not be able to accommodate very many hardware components.

The most common type of resource conflict is an Interrupt Request (IRQ) conflict, which occurs when there aren't enough IRQs available. For example, if you were trying to install a modem that uses IRQ 3 and your network card is already using IRQ 3, the modem isn't going to work.

So what's the solution? You can change the resource settings for many devices, either by using the Device Manager or by moving some pins or switches on the hardware device itself (refer to the hardware's user manual for how to do this).

This lesson will introduce you to the Device Manager so you can see the hardware devices that are installed on your computer, and how to configure or remove them.

1 Click the Start button and select Control Panel from the menu. Click the Performance and Maintenance category.

The Performance and Maintenance category of the Control Panel appears.

2 Click System.

The System Properties dialog box appears.

3 Click the Hardware tab and click the Device Manager button.

The Device Manager displays your computer's hardware in hierarchical order.

4 Click the Computer plus symbol to expand the category.

Right-click a hardware device to display its properties.

5 Right-click the Network Connection device and select Properties from the shortcut menu.

Here you can see which hardware devices are using which resources.

Most hardware devices have two or three tabs in the Properties dialog box. They are:

- **General:** Displays the status of the hardware and allows you to disable it.
- **Driver:** Displays details about the device driver and allows you to update the driver (provided you have a newer driver).
- **Resources:** Displays the resource currently used by the hardware. It's almost always best to let Windows manage a device's resources automatically. Only manually change a device's resources if instructed by the hardware manual or technical support.

6 Click the Close button and close all open windows to end the lesson.

Table 9-4. Symbols you'll see in the Device Manager

Symbol	Description
?	The device doesn't have any drivers installed, and therefore your computer can't use it. You'll have to install drivers for the device—see the lesson on installing hardware.
!	The device has a problem. This can be caused by a resource conflict (the device is trying to use a resource on your computer that's already in use), an incorrect driver, or a hardware failure. The type of problem will be displayed in the properties for the hardware.

QUICK REFERENCE

TO OPEN THE DEVICE MANAGER:

1. CLICK THE START BUTTON AND SELECT CONTROL PANEL FROM THE MENU.

2. CLICK THE PERFORMANCE AND MAINTENANCE CATEGORY AND CLICK SYSTEM.

3. CLICK THE HARDWARE TAB AND CLICK THE DEVICE MANAGER BUTTON.

TO VIEW OR CHANGE A DEVICE'S PROPERTIES:

- RIGHT-CLICK THE DEVICE AND SELECT PROPERTIES FROM THE SHORTCUT MENU.

TO REMOVE A DEVICE DRIVER:

- SELECT THE DEVICE AND CLICK THE UNINSTALL BUTTON ON THE TOOLBAR.

BE VERY CAREFUL WHEN USING THE DEVICE MANAGER! DON'T REMOVE A HARDWARE DEVICE OR CHANGE ITS SETTINGS UNLESS YOU KNOW WHAT YOU'RE DOING.

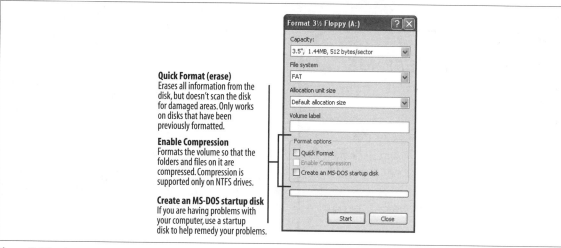

Figure 9-36. The Format Floppy dialog box.

Quick Format (erase)
Erases all information from the disk, but doesn't scan the disk for damaged areas. Only works on disks that have been previously formatted.

Enable Compression
Formats the volume so that the folders and files on it are compressed. Compression is supported only on NTFS drives.

Create an MS-DOS startup disk
If you are having problems with your computer, use a startup disk to help remedy your problems.

Default Printer

Before you can use a disk, you must format it so that you can save information on it. You can also format a disk to erase any files that are saved on it and prepare it for new files. You can save yourself a lot of time by buying pre-formatted disks—just make sure they are formatted in IBM format!

It's true that this type of disk is almost obsolete; some new computers don't even have this type of drive installed. But you may still find a need for them when installing drivers and USB ports. Here's how to format a disk:

1 Connect or insert the disk you want to format into your computer.

NOTE *Formatting a disk completely erases any information stored on it, so make sure the disk you want to format doesn't contain any information you may need.*

2 Click the Start button and select My Computer.

The My Computer window appears.

3 Right-click the drive containing the disk you want to format (usually A:), and select Format from the shortcut menu.

The Format dialog box appears. There are several options you can specify when formatting a disk—see Figure 9-36 to see what they are.

4 Click Start.

The drive whirs as it formats the disk. Formatting a disk usually takes about a minute. When the format is complete, the Format Results dialog box appears with information about the formatted disk.

NOTE *If the Format Results dialog box says your disk has bytes in bad sectors, throw it away. A disk with bad sectors is not reliable and should not be entrusted with your valuable data.*

5 Click Close to close the Results dialog box, and click Close again to close the Format dialog box.

QUICK REFERENCE

TO FORMAT A DISK:

1. CONNECT OR INSERT THE DISK YOU WANT
    TO FORMAT INTO YOUR COMPUTER.

2. OPEN MY COMPUTER, RIGHT-CLICK THE
    DRIVE AND SELECT FORMAT FROM THE
    SHORTCUT MENU.

3. SELECT THE FORMATTING OPTIONS AND
    CLICK START.

Chapter Nine Review

Lesson Summary

Repairing Disk Errors

To Use Error-checking: Click the Start button and select My Computer. Right-click the disk you want to scan, select Properties from the shortcut menu, and click the Tools tab. Click the Check Now button, specify disk options, and click Start.

Defragmenting Your Hard Disk

Click the Start button and select My Computer. Right-click the disk you want to defragment, select Properties from the shortcut menu, and click the Tools tab. Click the Defragment Now button, click Analyze button, and then click Defragment. Or, click the Start button and select All Programs → Accessories → System tools → Disk Defragmenter from the menu.

Freeing Up Space on Your Hard Disk

Click the Start button and select My Computer from the menu. Right-click the hard disk and select Properties from the shortcut menu. Or click the Start button and select All Programs → Accessories → System Tools → Disk Cleanup from the menu. Click the Disk Cleanup button and click OK.

You can also free up hard disk space by removing programs and Windows components that you don't use.

Scheduling Tasks

The Task Scheduler automatically runs specified programs when you tell it to.

To Schedule a Task: Click the Start button and select All Programs → Accessories → System Tools → Scheduled Tasks. Double-click the Add Scheduled Task icon, click Next, select the program you want to schedule from the list, and click Next. Specify how often you want the program to run and click Next. Select the time and day when you want the task to occur and click Next. Enter your user name and password information, click Next, and then click Finish.

Installing New Software

To Install Software Using the Control Panel: Find the Program's disk (or disks) and insert it (or the first disk) into the disk drive. Click the Start button and select Control Panel. Click Add or Remove Programs. Click Add New Programs, click the CD or Floppy button, and then click Next. Follow the on-screen instructions to install the software automatically.

To Install Software Manually: Open My Computer, find the disk drive or folder where the program you want to install is located, and find and double-click the installation program (usually called SETUP or INSTALL). Follow the on-screen instructions to install the program.

Removing Software

Click the Start button and select Control Panel. Click Add or Remove Programs. Click the Change or Remove Programs button, find and select the program you want to remove from your computer, and click the Remove button. Finish removing the selected program by following the on-screen instructions.

Adding and Removing Windows Components

To Add or Remove Windows Components: Click the Start button and select Control Panel → Add or Remove Programs. Click the Add/Remove Windows Components button, and click the box beside the component category you want to add or remove. Click Next, then click Finish.

To Add or Remove a Windows Component in a Category: Select the category, click Details, and then click the box beside the component category you want to add or remove. Click OK when you're finished.

Installing a Printer

To Install a New Printer: If at possible, install the printer using the included software and documentation. If you don't have the software click the Start button and select Control Panel from the menu. Click the Printers and Other Hardware category and click the Add a printer task and click Next. Specify how the printer is connected (local or network) and click Next. Select a port to use with the printer and click Next. Select the printer's manufacturer and model. If your printer doesn't appear in the list, insert the disk that came with the printer and click the Have Disk button and click Next. Assign a name to the printer and set the printer as the default and click Next. Specify if the printer will be shared and click Next.

Specify if you want a test page printed and click Next. Finally, click Finish.

Changing Printer Settings and the Default Printer

To Change the Default Printer: Click the Start button and select Control Panel from the menu. Click the Printers and Other Hardware category and click Printers and Faxes. Right-click the desired printer from the list and select Set as Default Printer from the shortcut menu.

To View/Change a Printer's Default Properties: Right-click the appropriate printer, and select Properties from the shortcut menu.

Shutting Down a Frozen Program

When a program freezes or locks-up, you can close the program by pressing Ctrl + Alt + Delete, selecting the program, and clicking End Task.

Installing New Hardware

Most hardware devices are Plug and Play compliant, so Windows will automatically recognize and install them when you add them to your computer system.

To Add New Hardware to Your Computer: Plug in the hardware device to your computer. Windows should automatically detect and install the device for you. If Windows doesn't recognize the new hardware, click the Control Panel from the Start menu, then click the Hardware task. Click the Printers and Other Hardware category and click the Add Hardware task. Click Next and follow the on-screen instructions to have Windows search for your new hardware.

Using Automatic Updates

You must be connected to the Internet to run Automatic Updates.

To Run Automatic Updates: Click the Start button and select Control Panel from the menu. Click the Security Center category and click Automatic Updates.

Using Windows Update

Establish a connection to the Internet, then click the Start button and select All Programs → Windows Update from the menu. Click the type of install you want to per-

form. If you selected **Express Install**, click the Install button. If you selected **Custom Install**, click the check box next to the updates you want to install and then click Go to install updates to install them.

Restoring Your Computer

To Restore your Computer: Click the Start button and select All Programs → Accessories → System Tools → System Restore from the menu. Make sure the Restore my computer to an earlier time option is selected and click Next. Select the restore point nearest to the time when your computer was working properly and click Next. Close all open files and programs and click Next. When the restore is complete the computer automatically restarts. Click OK to close the System Restore window.

To Create a Restore Point: Click the Start button and select All Programs → Accessories → System Tools → System Restore from the menu. Select Create a restore point and click Next. Enter a name for your restore point and click Create. Click Close to close the System Restore window.

Using the Device Manager:

- **To Open the Device Manager:** Click the Start button and select Control Panel from the menu. Click the Performance and Maintenance category and click System. Click the Hardware tab in the System Properties dialog box, and click the Device Manager button.

To View/Change a Device's Properties: Right-click the device and select Properties from the shortcut menu.

To Remove a Device Driver: Select the device and click the Uninstall button.

Be VERY CAREFUL when using the Device Manager! Don't remove a hardware device or change its settings unless you know what you're doing.

Formatting a Disk

Formatting disk erases any previous files stored on it and prepares the disk so that you can save information on it.

To Format a Disk: Insert the disk you want to format into the drive, open My Computer, right-click the drive, and select Format from the shortcut menu. Select the formatting options you want to use, and click Start.

Quiz

1. Which statement is NOT true about Error-checking?

   A. You can do a standard or thorough disk scan with Error-checking.

   B. Error-checking can automatically repair most disk errors it finds.

   C. Error-checking will find and remove any computer viruses it finds on your disk.

   D. A thorough scan of a hard drive takes a long time—up to several hours.

2. By right-clicking your hard drive and selecting Properties, you can access all of these programs EXCEPT?

   A. Error-checking.

   B. Drive Converter (FAT32).

   C. Disk Defragmenter.

   D. Disk Cleanup.

3. You're a busy person and have better things to do than perform routine maintenance on your computer. What can you do to get out of having to manually run Error-checking, Disk CleanUp, and Disk Defragmenter every week?

   A. Pay someone else to run these programs for you.

   B. Don't use your computer.

   C. Add these programs to the StartUp folder in the Programs menu.

   D. Add these programs to the Task Scheduler.

4. You've finally bought the "Bird Watcher's Encyclopedia" CD-ROM you've been wanting for months. How do you install it on your computer? (Select all that apply.)

   A. Insert the CD-ROM into the drive—Windows XP may automatically install it.

   B. Insert the CD-ROM, open My Computer, look for a program file named "Setup", "Install", or something similar, and double-click it.

   C. Right-click the taskbar, select Properties from the shortcut menu, click the Start Menu Programs tab, and click the Add button.

   D. Open the Control Panel, double-click Add/Remove Programs, and click Install.

5. Which of the following statements is NOT true?

   A. You can remove most programs on your computer by opening the Control Panel, clicking Add or Remove Programs, selecting the program you want to remove, and clicking the Remove button.

   B. Everything included on the Windows XP CD-ROM is installed when you install Windows.

   C. Pressing Ctrl + Alt + Delete opens the Close Program window, which you can use to forcefully end a program that has stopped responding.

   D. The default printer is the printer Windows always uses unless you specify otherwise.

6. The most common printer port is COM1. (True or False?)

7. Which of the following statements is NOT true?

   A. Computers have a limited amount of resources, which are used by hardware devices. If two hardware devices try to use the same resource, you have a *hardware conflict*.

   B. Windows XP should automatically recognize and install any Plug and Play hardware devices that you've added when you first turn on the computer.

   C. You can use the Add Hardware Wizard to install your hardware if Windows XP fails to recognize it.

   D. Plug and Play devices get their name because you spend a lot of time playing around with them to get them to work.

Homework

1. Use Disk Cleanup to clear unnecessary files from your hard disk.

2. Start Error-checking, run a standard scan of your hard disk, and have Windows automatically fix any errors it finds.

3. Open the Task Scheduler. Would you know how to add a task to the Task Scheduler?

4. See which Windows components are currently installed on your computer.

5. Defragment your hard disk.

6. Open the Device Manager.

Quiz Answers

1. C. Error-checking will find and repair most disk errors it finds, but it's oblivious to computer viruses. You will need a virus-scanning program for that.

2. B. Since you don't use the Drive Converter (FAT32) program much (if ever), it's not located under the Disk Properties dialog box.

3. D. Adding programs to the task scheduler runs them on the days and times you specify.

4. A, B, and D. All of these are methods to install software.

5. B. There are many Windows components that are often not installed when you install Windows XP—to save space and because most people would not use them.

6. False. The most common printer port is LPT1.

7. D. Although this statement certainly seems to be true, Plug and Play devices actually get their name because you supposedly can plug them in and start using them.

CHAPTER 10

EXPLORING THE INTERNET

CHAPTER OBJECTIVES:

Understand and connect to the Internet

Find a specific Web page

Browse and search the Web

Add Web pages to Favorites

Change your Home page

Display and clear a history of visited Web pages

Download pictures and software

Understand the Information Bar

Use the Pop-up Blocker

Understand how to secure your computer

Use e-mail

Prerequisites

- **Know how to use the mouse to click, double-click, drag and drop, and right-click.**
- **Know how to start programs in the Start Menu.**
- **Know how to use menus, toolbars, and dialog boxes.**

Unless you've been living on a deserted island for the past ten years, you already know that the Internet is the biggest thing to happen to computers since… well, computers! You can't ignore it—the Internet is not going away and it's already changing the world we live in. Fortunately, for the most part, the Internet is incredibly easy to use. Even the most computer-phobic users seem to feel right at home on the Internet.

This chapter explains the ins and outs of the Internet. If you've ever spent a sleepless night wondering exactly what the Internet is and how it got started, you'll finally learn it all. We'll discuss how to get your computer connected to the Internet, and how to surf the Web using the Windows XP Internet Explorer, especially with the changes in Service Pack 2. You'll also learn some useful tips like how to secure your computer, how to search for information, how to bookmark your favorite Web pages so that you can easily come back to them later, and how to change the Web page that first appears when you connect to the Internet. Finally, you'll learn how to download and how to send and receive e-mail.

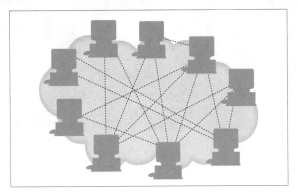

Figure 10-1. The Internet is the largest network in the world.

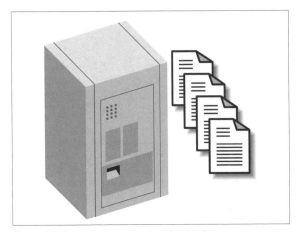

Figure 10-2. Web pages are stored on Web servers.

The Internet is the largest computer network in the world. It consists of millions of computers all over the planet, all connected to each another.

The Internet was born in the 1960s when the United States military worried that a nuclear bomb could destroy its computer systems (there weren't many of them back then). So it placed several computers far apart from each other and connected them with some super-fast telephone lines so that the computers could talk to each other. If a nuclear bomb blew up one computer, another computer could instantly take over; thus, the computer network wouldn't go down. Years passed and other organizations, such as colleges and universities, started connecting their computers to this growing network to share information.

Although the Internet has been around a long time, it wasn't until the 1990s that the *World Wide Web* was born. The World Wide Web is what you probably think of when you think of the Internet, although it's really just a part of the Internet. The Web consists of millions of documents that are stored on hundreds of thousands of computers that are always connected to the Internet. These documents are called *Web pages*, and you can find Web pages on every subject imaginable—from your local newspaper to online catalogs to airline schedules, and much more.

Web pages are stored on *Web servers*. A Web server is a computer, not unlike your own computer, only bigger and faster. There are hundreds of thousands of Web servers located all over the world. Web servers are always connected to the Internet so that people can view their Web pages 24 hours a day.

So what can you do once you're connected to the Internet? Plenty. Table 10-1. shows just a few of the many things there are to do through the Internet.

Table 10-1. What can I do on the Internet?

Task	Description
Send and Receive E-mail	Exchanging electronic mail (or e-mail) is the most popular feature on the Internet. Just like regular paper mail, you can send and receive e-mail with people around the world, as long as they have access to a computer and the Internet. Unlike regular paper mail, e-mail is delivered to its destination almost instantly.
Browse the World Wide Web	The World Wide Web is what most people think of when they think of the Internet—although it's really only a part of the Internet. The World Wide Web is an enormous collection of inter-connected documents stored on Web servers all over the world. The World Wide Web has information on every subject imaginable.
Join online discussions with newsgroups	Newsgroups are discussion groups on the Internet that you can join to read and post messages to and from people with similar interests. There are thousands of newsgroups on topics such as computers, education, romance, hobbies, politics, religion, and more.

Table 10-1. What can I do on the Internet? (Continued)

Task	Description
Chat with other online users	Chatting lets you communicate with people on the Internet instantly—no matter how far away they are! Most chats are text-based, meaning you have to type when you converse with people on the Internet. A growing number of chats have voice and even video capabilities—all without having to pay long distance changes.
Download software	You can download pictures, demo programs, patches and drivers for your computer, and many other types of files and save them to your computer.
Listen to music and watch videos	You can listen to sound on the Web, such as radio stations, or music by your favorite artists.

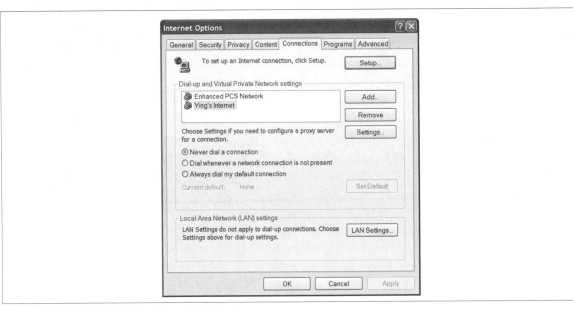

Figure 10-3. Microsoft's Internet Connection Wizard.

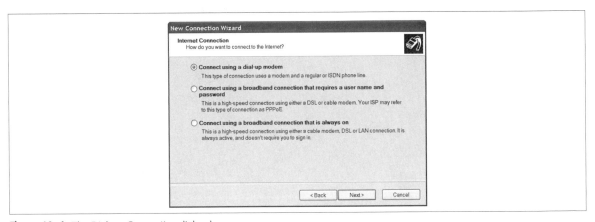

Figure 10-4. The Dial-up Connection dialog box.

Figure 10-5.

There are three things you'll need to connect to the Internet:

- **An Internet Service Provider (ISP):** An Internet Service Provider is a lot like a phone company, except instead of letting you make telephone calls to other people, an Internet Service Provider lets your computer connect to the Internet. Just like your telephone company, Internet Service Providers charge for their services.

- **A Web Browser:** A Web browser is a program that lets your computer view and navigate the World Wide Web. One of the biggest additions in Windows XP is that it comes with a built-in Web browser—Internet Explorer. Another Web browsing program that is very popular is Netscape Navigator.

- **A Phone Line and Modem or Other Connection:** A modem is your computer's very own telephone that lets it talk to other computers through the telephone line. There are slower dial-up modems that connect to the Internet using your phone and much faster cable modems and Digital Subscriber Lines (DSL) as well. DSL is technology that provides high-speed Internet access through standard phone lines. A cable modem connects to the Internet through the cable hookup in your house. Both of these connections are much faster than a dial-up modem and are connected to the Internet 24 hours a day, so you don't tie up any phone lines.

1 Make sure you have an account with an Internet Service Provider.

If you want, you can follow the step-by-step instructions and let the New Connection Wizard help you find an Internet Service PRovider—or you can find your own. Ask a computer-savvy friend or an employee at a local computer store for the name anad number of a local IInternet Service Provider. Once you are set up with an Internet Service Provider, come back and finish the rest of this leson.

2 Click the Start button and select Internet Explorer from the menu.

Since you probably don't have an existing Internet connection, you will probably get an error page when you start Internet Explorer—don't worry about it.

3 Select Tools → Internet Options from the menu, then click the Connections tab.

The Connections tab of the Internet Options dialog box appears, as shown in Figure 10-3. This is where you tell Windows how you want to connect to the internet.

4 Click Setup.

The Welcome to the New Connection Wizard screen appears.

5 Click Next.

You are presented with a few options; we want to use the default Connect to the Internet option.

6 Click Next.

Choose from a list of Internet Service Providers (ISPs): If you don't have an account with an Internet Service Provider, you can select this option to get set up with Microsoft's very limited selection of ISPs.

Set up my connection manually: Although it's not the default option, most of the time, you'll want to set up your connection manually, especially if you already have an account with an ISP. Be ready with your user name, password, and, if you're still using a dial-up connection, phone number.

Use the CD I got from an ISP: If you received a CD from your ISSP, you can insert it, select this option, and click Next...although you can probably install the software just as easily without the help of the new Connection Wizard.

7 Select the Set up my connection manually option and click Next.

More Internet connection choices are included, as shown in Figure 10-4. Here's what they are:

Connect using a dial-up modem: Use this option if you're still using a dial-up modem.

Connect using a broadband connection that requires a user name andpassword: Select this option if you have a DSL or cable modem that requires a user name and password to connect to the Internet.

Connect using a broadband connection that is always on: Most DSL and cable modems always stay on and connect to the Internet; select this option if you have this ttype of connection to the Internet.

You will probably have to refer to your ISP documentation to determine which of these three options is right for you.

8 Select the option that best describes how you want to connect to the Internet and click Next.

The last step will differ, depending on which of the three options you selected; don't worry—the rest of the Wizard should be self-explanatory.

9 Follow the remaining on-screen instructions, entering a name for the Internet connection, your user name, and password when prompted.

NOTE *If you're connected to the Internet through a network at work, an ISDN or DSL line, or a cable modem, you won't hear anything at all since these are all digital connections. It would probably pay off to check if you have access to cable or DSL connections in your area. If so, it's probably worth the extra $10 or $20 a month to get a connection to the Internet that is at least ten times faster than a standard phone connection. Plus, you don't have to worry about tying up the phone when you're using the Internet.*

After a connection to the Internet has been established, Internet Explorer displays your Home page. A *home page* is the page your Web browser displays when it connects to the Internet. The default start page for Microsoft Internet Explorer is Microsoft's start page (what else did you think it would be?), but you can easily change your default start page—more about that in another lesson.

QUICK REFERENCE

TO CONNECT TO THE INTERNET:

1. MAKE SURE YOU HAVE AN ACCOUNT WITH AN INTERNET SERVICE PROVIDER (ISP).

2. CLICK THE START BUTTON AND SELECT INTERNET EXPLORER.

3. SELECT TOOLS → INTERNET OPTIONS FROM THE MENU, THE CLICK THE CONNECTIONS TAB.

4. CLICK SETUP.

5. CLICK NEXT.

6. CLICK NEXT.

7. SELECT THE SET UP MY CONECTION MANUALLY OPTION AND CLICK NEXT.

8. SELECT THE OPTION THAT BEST DESCRIBES HOW YOU WANT TO CONNECT TO THE INTERNET AND CLICK NEXT.

9. FOLLOW THE REMAINING ONSCREEN INSTRUCTION, ENTERING A NAME FOR THE INTERNET CONNECTION, YOUR USER NAME, AND PASSWORD WHEN PROMPTED.

Figure 10-6. The Microsoft Web site.

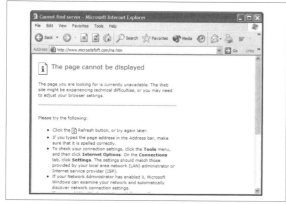

Figure 10-7. When a Web page is unavailable, this screen is displayed in Internet Explorer.

Web addresses are everywhere—on television advertisements, in magazine and newspaper articles, and even on business cards. These www.something.coms you've seen and heard so much about are *URLs* (Uniform Resource Locator). Just like there is a house, office, or building behind a postal address, there is a Web page behind every Web address. Unlike postal addresses, however, through the magic of technology you can instantly arrive at a Web page by typing its Web address, or URL, into your Web browser. Well, hopefully instantly… if you've already been on the Internet for any amount of time, you probably know that sometimes the Internet gets busy and *net congestion* can cause a Web page to come up slowly—if it comes up at all! This lesson will show you how to visit the Web sites behind all the Web addresses you've seen.

1 **Connect to the Internet.**

It doesn't matter where you are on the Internet—you can always enter a Web address in the Address bar.

2 **Click an empty area in the Address bar.**

The text in the Address bar becomes highlighted.

3 **Type the address of the Web page you want to view: type** www.microsoft.com **and press Enter.**

After a moment, the home page of the Microsoft Web site appears.

Web addresses are preceded by *http://*. For example, the address we want is *http://www.microsoft.com*. Technically, you don't need to add the http:// before typing the Web address—save yourself some time and leave it out.

NOTE *If you forget the www in front of a Web address or a .com, an Internet Explorer called IntelliSense® attempts to correct the Web address by adding the www or .com for you. Unfortunately, it's not foolproof: sometimes it works, sometimes it doesn't.*

Let's go to another Web site.

4 **Type** www.yahoo.com **in the Address bar and press Enter.**

Possibly the most famous Web site on the Internet, the Yahoo home page, appears.

Sometimes when you're browsing the Web, you'll see a screen like the one in Figure 10-7. This means the Web site is unavailable. Several things can cause a Web page not to load:

- The computer where the Web page is stored is down.
- Too many users are trying to view the same Web page at the same time.
- You've lost your connection to the Internet.
- The Web page no longer exists, or maybe it never existed in the first place (did you type in the correct Web address?).

For all these cases, try going to the Web site again later. Whatever was causing the problem might be fixed a few minutes or hours later.

QUICK REFERENCE

TO DISPLAY A SPECIFIC WEB PAGE:

- TYPE THE WEB ADDRESS IN THE ADDRESS BAR AND PRESS ENTER.

OR...

- PRESS CTRL + L, TYPE THE WEB ADDRESS, AND CLICK OK.

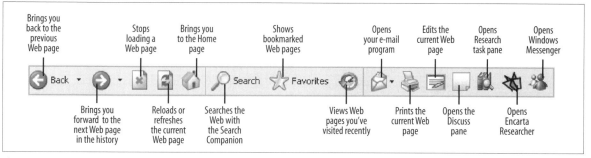

Figure 10-8. The Internet Explorer toolbar. Your toolbar may be different depending on how your computer is set up.

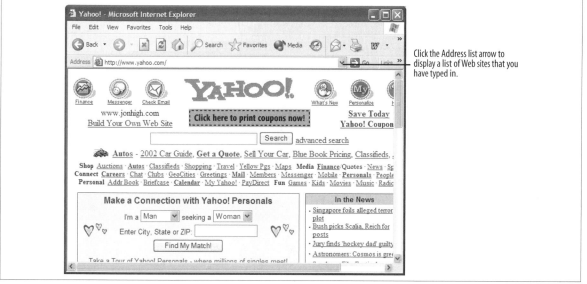

Click the Address list arrow to display a list of Web sites that you have typed in.

Figure 10-9. The Yahoo home page.

Windows XP Service Pack 2: Internet Explorer blocks pop-up windows you don't request. For example, all pop-up windows are initially blocked, but any pop-up windows you request to open will appear. If you are certain you want to view a blocked pop-up window, click the Information Bar and select Temporarily Allow Pop-ups from the shortcut menu.

The World Wide Web is remarkably easy to navigate. It's so easy that most users have an uncanny ability to browse through Web pages without any training, even if they have difficulty with other computer programs. This lesson explains how to find your way through the millions of Web pages that are on the Internet. Even if you already think you have browsing down, you should read this lesson—you might learn a trick or two.

1 Make sure your Web browser is open and that you're connected to the Internet.

Hopefully you know how to do this by now! Let's go to the Yahoo! home page.

2 Click the Address bar, type www.yahoo.com, and press Enter.

The Yahoo home page fills the screen. Many of the underlined words and pictures you see on the Yahoo page are actually *hyperlinks*. When you position the pointer over a hyperlink, it changes to a 🖑. Clicking a hyperlink will automatically:

• Take you to a page within the same Web site.

• Take you to a page in a different Web site.

• Take you to a part of the same Web site.

- Allow you to download a file.
- Send an e-mail to a specified e-mail address.
- Play a video or sound.

3 Position the pointer over any of the links you see.

The pointer changes anytime it is over a link. Links can be either text or pictures.

4 Click the Travel icon or text.

The new Web page appears.

You can easily move back to the previous Web page.

5 Click the Back button on the toolbar.

You're back at the Yahoo home page. The Forward button moves forward through the Web pages you have viewed.

6 Click the Forward button on the toolbar.

You return to the previous page.

Just like a metro highway system at rush hour, the Internet often becomes congested when too many users try to view the same Web site at the same time. When this happens, it may take a long time for the Web page to appear on-screen, or it may not be accessible at all. Here are a few strategies to try if you are having problems displaying Web pages.

7 Click the Address bar, type www.microsoft.com, and press Enter. Before the Microsoft home page completely loads, click the Stop button on the toolbar.

You can also try *refreshing* a sluggish or difficult Web page. There are basically two reasons to refresh a Web page:

- To attempt to view a Web page that is not loading.
- To update a Web page that contains information that is constantly changing, such as headline news stories or financial information.

8 Click the Refresh button on the toolbar.

Refresh button

Another way you can return to previously visited Web sites is to use the Address bar, which remembers every Web address that you've manually typed into it.

9 Click the Address list arrow.

A list of the Web addresses you've previously entered appears below the address bar.

10 Select the http://www.yahoo.com site from the list.

You return to the Yahoo Web site.

QUICK REFERENCE

TO USE A HYPERLINK:

- CLICK THE HYPERLINK WITH THE POINTER.

TO GO BACK TO THE PREVIOUS PAGE:

- CLICK THE BACK BUTTON ON THE TOOLBAR.

TO STOP THE TRANSFER OF INFORMATION:

- CLICK THE STOP BUTTON ON THE TOOLBAR.

TO REFRESH A WEB PAGE:

- CLICK THE REFRESH BUTTON ON THE TOOLBAR.

TO RETURN TO A WEB ADDRESS YOU TYPED IN THE ADDRESS BAR:

- CLICK THE ADDRESS BAR LIST ARROW AND SELECT THE WEB ADDRESS.

Figure 10-10. The Search Companion task pane.

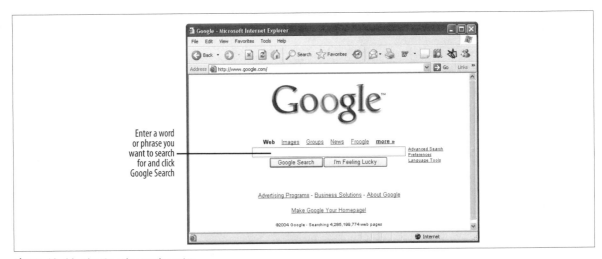

Figure 10-11. The Google search engine.

The Internet's greatest strength is also its greatest weakness: with so much information—literally millions of Web pages—it can be extremely difficult to find what you're looking for. Fortunately, there are many search engines that catalog the millions of Web pages on the Internet so that you can find Web pages on topics that interest you, such as Google and Yahoo!. In this lesson, you'll learn how you can search the Web to find information on the topics you specify.

1 Make sure your Web browser is open and you are connected to the Internet.

2 Click the Search button on the toolbar.

📷 **To:**

Search button

The Search Companion pane appears on the left side of Internet Explorer, as shown in Figure 10-10. This is where you specify what you want to search for.

3 Click the Search box and type your question.

For better search results, use complete sentences or several keywords that describe what you're looking for. For example, typing "Where can I find a good oyster restaurant in Chicago?" would yield better results than simply "oysters".

4 Click Search.

The Search Companion searches the Web for results using the MSN search engine. The results of the search are shown in the window to the right of the task pane, ranked by relevance.

5 Click the Web page you want to view.

Are you finding irrelevant information in your search results? Then you may have to refine your search. For example, a search on the word "Windows" may result in links to "Andersen Windows," "stained glass windows," and "Microsoft Windows," while a search on the phrase "Microsoft Windows" will result in links to

"Microsoft Windows." Some search engines will let you search within your results. For example, you could do a search for "Microsoft Windows" and then further refine your search by searching the results for the word "Networking."

6 Click the Search Companion task pane Close button.

You don't have to use the Search Companion to surf the Web—you can go directly to a search engine's Web site and specify what you want to look for there. Table 10-2 is by no means a definitive inventory of the search engines that are currently available on the Web, but it lists the best and most popular Web search engines and their Web addresses.

Table 10-2. Popular search engines on the Web

Site	Web Address	Description
AOL	search.aol.com	The default search engine for America Online subscribers, the AOL search engine isn't bad, but you're probably better off using Google or Yahoo.
Excite	www.excite.com	Excite once had a powerful, highly-rated search engine, but in recent years it has fallen behind the other search engines in terms of features and popularity.
MSN	www.msn.com	The MSN, or Microsoft Network, is not only the default search engine for Internet Explorer; it's also the default home page (surprise, surprise). Even with that enormous advantage, both Google and Yahoo still manage to be the preferred search engines for most Internet users.
Google	www.google.com	Google is the most popular search engine in the world and it's consistently ranked as having the most relevant search results. However, it doesn't contain many features other than its fantastic Web search.
Yahoo	www.yahoo.com	Yahoo is actually more of a directory service than a search engine, but it makes it very easy to find topics, especially if you're new to the Internet.

QUICK REFERENCE

TO SEARCH THE WEB FOR INFORMATION USING INTERNET EXPLORER:

1. CLICK THE SEARCH BUTTON ON THE TOOLBAR.

2. TYPE THE WORD OR PHRASE YOU WANT TO SEARCH FOR IN THE SEARCH BOX AND CLICK SEARCH.

3. CLICK THE LINK FOR THE WEB PAGE YOU WANT TO VIEW.

4. CLICK THE SEARCH BUTTON ON THE TOOLBAR TO CLOSE THE SEARCH PANEL.

TO SEARCH THE WEB FOR INFORMATION USING A SEARCH ENGINE:

• TYPE THE WEB ADDRESS FOR THE SEARCH ENGINE IN THE ADDRESS BAR AND PRESS ENTER. TYPE THE WORD OR PHRASE YOU WANT TO SEARCH FOR IN THE WEB PAGE'S SEARCH BOX AND PRESS ENTER.

Figure 10-12. The Add Favorite dialog box.

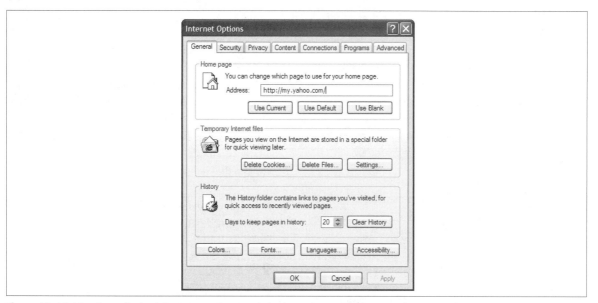

Figure 10-13. Click the Favorites button to view a list of your favorite Web pages.

Figure 10-14. The General tab of the Internet Options dialog box. You can change your home page here.

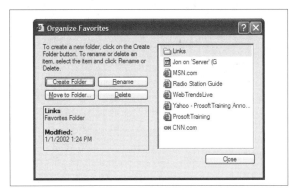

Figure 10-15. The Organize Favorites dialog box.

You have finally found a Web page about hippopotamus food, and you want to return back to it later. What should you do? Well, you don't have to write down the Web address on a Post-It note and stick on your monitor—you can add the Web page to Internet Explorer's Favorites feature so you can always quickly return back to it later. In this lesson, you'll learn how to add your favorite Web sites to the Favorites list. You'll also learn how to change your home page (also called a start page)—the Web page that appears each time you start Internet Explorer.

1 Make sure the Web browser is open and you're connected to the Internet.

2 Go to a Web page that you visit frequently and want to add to your Favorites list.

It doesn't matter how you get to the Web site—type the page's Web address in the Address bar (if you know it) or navigate to it by clicking a hyperlink from another Web site. When the desired Web page appears on your screen, you can add it to your Favorites so you can always easily return to it later.

3 Select Favorites → Add to Favorites from the menu.

The Add Favorite dialog box appears, as shown in Figure 10-12. The name of the Web page appears in the Name box—if you want, you can replace the Web page's default name with one that is more meaningful to you. Clicking the Create In button lets you add shortcuts to a folder.

4 Click OK to add the Web page.

A shortcut to the Web page is added to your list of favorites.

Here's how to display your favorite Web sites:

5 Click the Favorites button on the toolbar.

A list of your favorite Web pages appears in a panel on the left side of Internet Explorer, as shown in Figure 10-13.

Favorites button
Other Ways to View Your Favorite Web Pages:
• Select Favorites from the menu bar and select the Web page.

6 Click the favorite Web page you want to view.

If your favorite Web page is in a folder, just click the folder ( ) and then the favorite Web site. The Web page you clicked appears in the right panel of Internet Explorer.

Is there a Web page that you *really* like and use almost every time you're on the Internet? You might consider making that Web page your *Home page*—the Web page that appears each time you start Internet Explorer. Some of the search engines we discussed in the previous lesson make excellent home pages. Here's how to make a Web page your home page:

7 Go to a Web page that you want to set as your home page and select Tools → Internet Options from the menu. Click the General tab, if necessary.

The Internet Options dialog box appears, as shown in Figure 10-14. The address of your current home page appears in the box in the Home page section.

8 Click the Use Current button to set the Web page that is displayed on your screen as your new home page.

9 Click OK.

The Internet Options dialog box closes. The next time you start Internet Explorer, the Web page you selected will appear as your start page.

If you've added a lot of Web pages to your list of favorites, it can be difficult to find a specific Web page out of all those entries. You can organize your favorites list by creating subfolders to keep related Web pages together—for example, you might create a folder called "Travel" to keep all your travel related Web pages together, and another folder called "Financial" to hold your financial and investment related Web pages. Here's how to organize your list of favorites:

10 Select Favorites → Organize Favorites from the menu.

The Organize Favorites dialog box appears, as shown in Figure 10-15. We don't need to go into detail

here—you can organize your favorites using the same Windows file management techniques you already know (if you don't, review the file management chapter). The Organize Favorites dialog box even provides you with several handy buttons to move, rename, and delete files and shortcuts.

11 Close the Organize Favorites dialog box.

QUICK REFERENCE

TO ADD A WEB PAGE TO YOUR LIST OF FAVORITES:

- GO TO THE WEB PAGE, SELECT FAVORITES → ADD TO FAVORITES FROM THE MENU AND CLICK OK.

OR...

- GO TO THE WEB PAGE, RIGHT-CLICK ANYWHERE ON THE WEB PAGE AND SELECT ADD TO FAVORITES FROM THE SHORTCUT MENU.

TO GO TO A FAVORITE WEB PAGE:

- CLICK THE FAVORITES BUTTON ON THE TOOLBAR AND SELECT THE WEB PAGE FROM THE LEFT SIDE OF INTERNET EXPLORER. CLICK THE FAVORITES BUTTON WHEN YOU'RE FINISHED.

OR...

- SELECT FAVORITES FROM THE MENU BAR AND SELECT THE WEB PAGE.

TO CHANGE YOUR HOME PAGE:

- GO TO THE WEB PAGE, SELECT TOOLS → INTERNET OPTIONS FROM THE MENU AND CLICK THE USE CURRENT BUTTON.

TO ORGANIZE FAVORITES:

- SELECT FAVORITES → ORGANIZE FAVORITES FROM THE MENU.

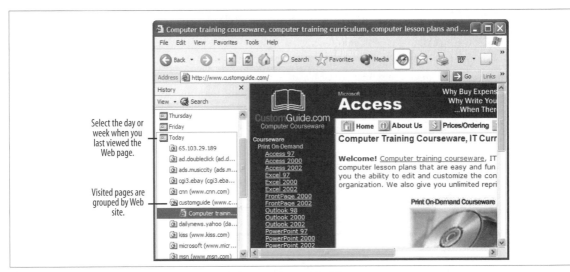

Figure 10-16. Internet Explorer displays a history of previously visited Web sites.

Can't find your way back to that really neat "101 Lutefisk Recipes" Web site you were looking at yesterday? Don't worry—Internet Explorer keeps track of the Web pages you've visited over the past 20 days. This lesson shows you how to access that list.

1 Make sure the Web browser is open and you're connected to the Internet.

2 Click the History button on the toolbar.

History button

A history of all the Web pages you've visited recently appears in the left side of Internet Explorer. The history is grouped chronologically and by Web site—all you have to do is click the day or week you viewed the Web page, the name of the Web site, and the Web page.

3 Click the day or week you viewed the Web page that you want to view.

If you can't remember the day or week off hand, don't worry. Finding the Web page you want to view in the history may take a bit of trial and error, because who really remembers the exact day when they visited a specific Web page?

When you click a day or week, the Web sites you viewed during that day or week appear, organized by Web site folder.

4 Click the Web site you want to revisit.

The Web site's individual Web pages appear.

5 Click the Web page you want to view.

The Web page appears.

6 Click the History button on the toolbar when you're finished working with your history of recently viewed Web pages.

The History pane disappears.

QUICK REFERENCE

TO DISPLAY A HISTORY OF VISITED WEB PAGES:

1. CLICK THE HISTORY BUTTON ON THE TOOLBAR.

2. CLICK THE DAY OR WEEK YOU VIEWED THE WEB PAGE.

3. CLICK THE WEB SITE YOU WANT TO REVISIT.

4. CLICK THE SPECIFIC WEB PAGE YOU WANT TO VIEW.

5. CLICK THE HISTORY BUTTON ON THE TOOLBAR WHEN YOU'VE FINISHED.

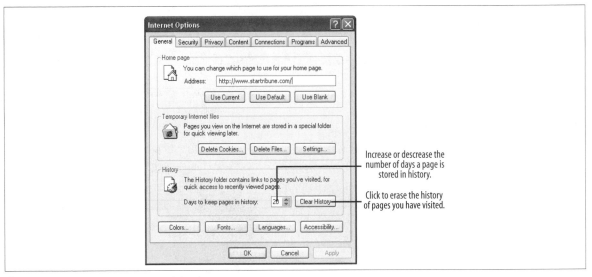

Figure 10-17. The Internet Options dialog box.

You and your spouse have spent weeks planning and researching your surprise family vacation this summer. Unfortunately, since many of your searches and reservations have been made over the Internet, your Web-savvy kids know everything about the trip, thanks to the History feature. You can take control of this feature by erasing the record of your Web activity.

1 Select Tools → Internet Options from the menu.

The Internet Options dialog box appears.

Clearing the history is permanent, so make sure this is something you want to do.

2 Click the Clear History button in the History section of the tab.

A dialog box appears, asking you to confirm the action.

3 Click Yes.

And just like that, the list of saved page links disappears.

You might also notice that you can change the number of days a page is saved in history. By default, pages are saved for 20 days, but you can increase or decrease that number if you want. Setting the number to zero only stores links to pages visited on the current day.

4 Click OK.

One thing to remember is that the history is different from the Back and Forward buttons on the toolbar. The history keeps a record of every Web page that is visited over a period of time. The Back and Forward buttons only remember which pages were visited when the Web browser was open.

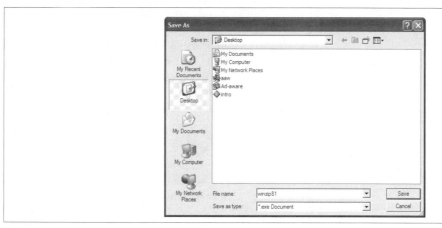

Figure 10-18. Specify where you want the file to be saved on your hard drive.

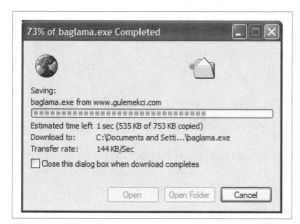

Figure 10-19. Windows displays the progress of a download.

> 🔷 *Windows XP Service Pack 2: Internet Explorer blocks downloads you do not instigate. For example, if Internet Explorer doesn't think you requested a download, or if the download waits too long to begin, it is blocked. If you are certain you want to download the file, click the Information Bar and select Download File from the shortcut menu.*

Another common use of the Internet is to download files from a Web server and save them onto your local hard drive. Some of the most common types of files people download from the Internet include:

- **Images:** You can save any picture that you see on a Web page, print it, use it as your Windows wallpaper, or anything else you can think of.

- **Programs:** Many software companies have demo versions of their programs available on the Internet that you can download and evaluate. In addition, thousands of shareware programs are available for you to download for free!

- **Patches, Fixes, and Drivers:** One of the great things about the Internet is finding fixes for your programs, and drivers for your hardware devices, such as a driver for a discontinued foreign printer.

- **Music:** MP3s are revolutionizing the music industry. MP3 files are sound files that you can listen to on your computer. They have digital CD quality sound, but use compression so that they are 11 times smaller than the CD equivalent and small enough to be easily downloadable from the Internet.

- **Viruses:** Just kidding—the last thing you want to download from the Internet is a computer virus! Since you won't always know where a program or file you want to download comes from, you should make sure your computer has a virus protection program installed before you download anything from the Internet.

Aside from possibly contracting a virus, the only other downside of downloading files from the Internet is that it can take a long time—especially if you use a dial-up connection.

Downloading and saving programs over the Internet is quite simple: just follow the links on the Web site. But you can also save other elements on a Web page, such as images and even the pages themselves.

TIP *Be careful when downloading files. Many downloads are free, but there are also many that require purchase.*

1 Right-click the image you want to save and select Save Picture As from the shortcut menu.

Windows asks where to save the image in the Save As dialog box, as shown in Figure 10-18.

NOTE *Never download an image for free and then profit from its use: it is a copyright violation. If you're looking for images to use in publications or Web sites, there are many Web sites with stock images that you can purchase.*

2 Navigate to the drive and/or folder where you want to save the image, give the image a different name, and click Save.

Windows saves the image in the specified drive and/or folder. If this does not work, the image has probably been protected so that others can't download the picture and use it for free.

You can also save a Web page or file that's on the other side of a hyperlink, the "target" of the link.

3 Right-click the link or file and select Save Target As from the shortcut menu.

Windows asks where to save the image in the Save As dialog box. As with images, you have to specify where you want to save the file.

4 Navigate to the drive and/or folder where you want to save the file, give the file a different name if you want, and click Save.

Windows will download the file and save it to the drive and/or folder you specified. It may take several minutes or several hours to download the file, depending on the file's size and how fast your connection to the Internet is. Windows displays a dialog box that shows the progress of the download, as shown in Figure 10-19.

NOTE *Make sure you remember where you save your files! Many people download software without thinking about where they're saving it, only to be unable to find the file once it's finished downloading. It makes sense to create and use a folder called "Downloads" or something similar where you can save your downloaded files.*

One more note about downloading files and programs off the Internet: many of the programs are stored in *ZIP* files. ZIP files package programs and files together, making them easier to download.

ZIP files do two things:

- **Compress information:** Instead of downloading a 2 MB file, compressing the file will cut the download time in half.

- **Store multiple files together in a single ZIP file:** Instead of downloading 20 or so files that a program requires to run, you only have to download a single ZIP file.

QUICK REFERENCE

TO DOWNLOAD AN IMAGE:

1. RIGHT-CLICK THE IMAGE YOU WANT TO SAVE AND SELECT **S**AVE PICTURE AS FROM THE SHORTCUT MENU.

2. NAVIGATE TO THE DRIVE AND FOLDER WHERE YOU WANT TO SAVE THE IMAGE, GIVE THE IMAGE A DIFFERENT NAME IF YOU WANT, AND CLICK **S**AVE.

TO DOWNLOAD A LINK TARGET:

1. RIGHT-CLICK THE LINK AND SELECT **S**AVE TARGET AS FROM THE SHORTCUT MENU.

2. NAVIGATE TO THE DRIVE AND FOLDER WHERE YOU WANT TO SAVE THE FILE, GIVE THE FILE A DIFFERENT NAME AND CLICK **S**AVE.

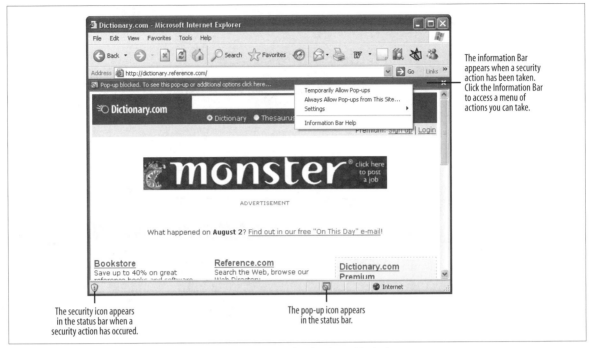

The information Bar appears when a security action has been taken. Click the Information Bar to access a menu of actions you can take.

The security icon appears in the status bar when a security action has occured.

The pop-up icon appears in the status bar.

Figure 10-20. The Information Bar notifying that a pop-up window has been blocked.

Windows XP Service Pack 2: The Information Bar notifies you when a security action has taken place. Click the Information Bar to overrule Internet Explorer or to change the settings.

One of the most noticeable additions to Internet Explorer in Windows XP Service Pack 2 is the Information Bar. The Information Bar notifies you when a security action has taken place in order to protect you from harmful files. For example, it tells you when a suspicious download has been stopped and when an unwanted pop-up window has been blocked. The Information Bar could also appear if a Web site tries to install an ActiveX control or run active content on your computer automatically.

Another benefit of the Information Bar is that it enables you to overrule the block and proceed with the action. Though you can't turn off the Information Bar altogether, you can change how it works with each individual notification by clicking the Information Bar when it appears.

Here are some messages that you might see in the Information Bar:

• To help protect your security, Internet Explorer blocked this site from downloading files on your computer. Click here for options…

• Pop-up blocked. To see this pop-up or additional options click here…

• To protect your security, Internet Explorer stopped this site from installing an ActiveX control on your computer. Click here for options…

• To help protect your security, Internet Explorer has restricted this file from showing active content that could access your computer. Click here for options.

QUICK REFERENCE

TO USE THE INFORMATION BAR:

• CLICK THE INFORMATION BAR AND SELECT AN OPTION FROM THE SHORTCUT MENU.

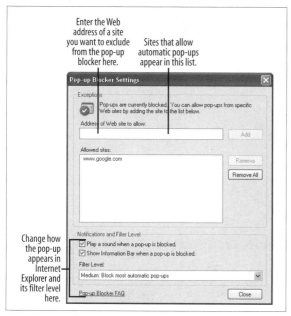

Enter the Web address of a site you want to exclude from the pop-up blocker here.

Sites that allow automatic pop-ups appear in this list.

Change how the pop-up appears in Internet Explorer and its filter level here.

Figure 10-21. The Pop-up Blocker Settings dialog box.

 Windows XP Service Pack 2: Internet Explorer's Pop-up Blocker prevents extra windows from appearing on your screen. You can change how the Pop-up Blocker works by clicking the Information Bar, or under the Tools menu.

Another change included in Service Pack 2 is the pop-up blocker. The pop-up blocker prevents annoying advertisement windows from disrupting your browsing on the Web. Most people will appreciate the pop-up blocker, but if you don't, here's how to change its settings.

1 Select Tools → Pop-up Blocker → Pop-up Blocker Settings **from the menu.**

The Pop-up Blocker Settings dialog box appears, as shown in Figure 10-21.

If you know the Web site you want to allow pop-ups, you can enter the name of the Web site in the dialog box.

2 Type the Web site in the Address of Web site to allow **text box and click** Add.

The address is added to the Allowed sites list in the dialog box.

By default the pop-up blocker is always on, but you can turn it off.

3 Select Tools → Pop-up Blocker → Turn Off Pop-up Blocker **from the menu.**

When the pop-up blocker is off you will probably experience some unwanted advertising windows as you surf the Web. The pop-up blocker has a pretty good filter, so between controlling its settings and making exceptions, you probably won't ever have to turn it off completely.

QUICK REFERENCE

TO CHANGE POP-UP BLOCKER SETTINGS:

I. SELECT TOOLS → POP-UP BLOCKER → POP-UP BLOCKER SETTINGS FROM THE MENU.

2. CHANGE THE POP-UP BLOCKER SETTINGS IN THE DIALOG BOX.

OR...

CLICK THE INFORMATION BAR AND SELECT AN OPTION FROM THE SHORTCUT MENU.

TO TURN OFF THE POP-UP BLOCKER:

I. SELECT TOOLS → POP-UP BLOCKER → TURN OFF POP-UP BLOCKER FROM THE MENU.

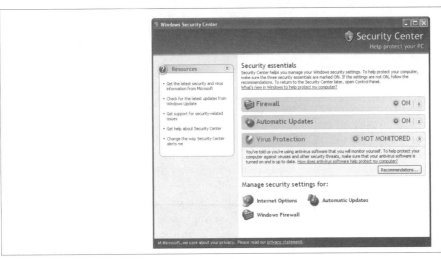

Figure 10-22. Windows XP has new security features in Service Pack 2 that help protect your computer from attackers.

Security is a sensitive issue. We hire security officers to protect our workplaces, analyze national security efforts, and install security systems in our homes. But many people aren't sure of what they can do to secure their computer, even though identity theft is occurring more often now than ever before. Microsoft has added many security improvements to Windows XP in Service Pack 2, and listed below are some security precautions and resources that you can maintain to keep your computer safe.

Install anti-virus software: Every computer that accesses the Internet should have anti-virus software installed on it. This software identifies potentially harmful files, and keeps them from infiltrating your computer.

Update anti-virus software: One of the biggest reasons a computer gets infected is that anti-virus software is not updated. Always download updates for your anti-virus software, and always renew your anti-virus software license.

Update software: Always download updates and repairs for programs. This will prevent attackers from exploiting holes in the software. Windows XP's Automatic Updates keeps your computer's technology safe and current.

Use firewalls: A firewall blocks malicious files or computers from connecting to your computer. A firewall is especially important for computers that connect to the Internet via DSL or cable modems. Windows Firewall has been added in SP2, but you can also choose your own software program.

Be smart with e-mail: Viruses and worms are sent through e-mail messages all the time. Never open an e-mail message from someone you don't know.

In the end, the best defense against a security problem is you. By using common sense and avoiding sites, files and messages that look suspicious, your computer will be safe.

QUICK REFERENCE

INFORMATION SECURITY:

INFORMATION SECURITY IS THE PRACTICE OF PROTECTING YOUR COMPUTER FROM INTRUDERS.

HERE ARE SOME SECURITY PRECAUTIONS THAT HELP PROTECT YOUR SENSITIVE INFORMATION.

- INSTALL ANTI-VIRUS SOFTWARE
- UPDATE ANTI-VIRUS SOFTWARE
- UPDATE SOFTWARE
- USE FIREWALLS
- BE SMART WITH E-MAIL

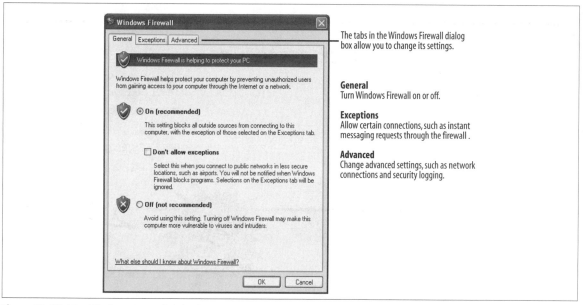

Figure 10-23. The Windows Firewall dialog box.

Windows XP Service Pack 2: Windows Firewall has been added to help keep your computer more secure. It is turned on by default.

You like to spend sunny afternoons out on your backyard patio. Unfortunately, so does your neighbor's slobbery dog. In fact, the offending canine is usually accompanied by its owner, who has a knack for disturbing an otherwise pleasant afternoon. What do you do to keep these uninvited guests out of your yard? Keep them out with a fence or a wall.

Just like your yard, when your computer is on the Internet, it is inundated with connections from other computers. To keep these annoying intruders out, Microsoft has built a firewall for your computer. A *firewall* is a utility that keeps your computer secure by restricting the information that comes into your computer. Its main objective is to prevent intruders, such as hackers, viruses and worms, from getting in to your computer. The firewall is like a monitor of all the information between your computer and the Internet, allowing "good" information through, and rejecting "bad" information.

So what is the difference between good and bad information? Basically, any connection you try to make to another computer, such as viewing a Web page or connecting to another network, is allowed. But when someone tries to make a connection to your computer—an "unsolicited request"—that connection is blocked. Let's take a look at the Windows Firewall.

1 Click the Start button and select Control Panel from the menu. Click the Security Center category.

The Security Center displays the security features that are active on your computer.

2 Click Windows Firewall near the bottom of the screen.

The Windows Firewall dialog box appears. You should always keep Windows Firewall on, unless you have your own firewall software that you want to use.

You can change how the firewall works by changing some of its settings, however. Refer to Figure 10-23 for more information on these settings.

QUICK REFERENCE

WINDOWS FIREWALL:

THIS SECURITY UTILITY KEEPS YOUR COMPUTER SECURE BY RESTRICTING THE INFORMATION THAT COMES INTO YOUR COMPUTER.

TO OPEN WINDOWS FIREWALL:

1. CLICK THE **START** BUTTON AND SELECT CONTROL PANEL FROM THE MENU.

2. CLICK THE **SECURITY CENTER** CATEGORY.

3. CLICK **WINDOWS FIREWALL**.

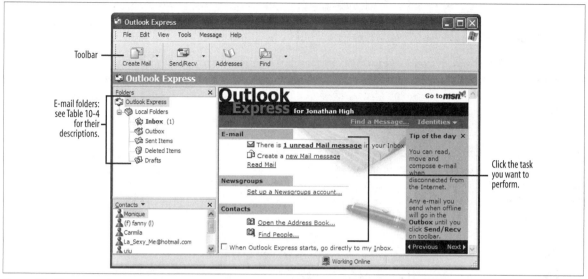

Figure 10-24. Microsoft Outlook Express is the e-mail program that is included with Windows XP.

Figure 10-25. Outlook Express toolbar.

JaneDoe@zipcorp.com

User Name	**Domain Name**
This is the name of the person's email account. It is similar to the person's name on an envelope.	This is the location of the person's account on the Internet. It is similar to the address on an envelope.

Figure 10-26. An Internet e-mail address has two parts: a user name and a domain name, separated by the @ symbol.

📖 *Windows XP Service Pack 2: Outlook Express has undergone improvements in its security settings, including some security features that also appear in Outlook 2003.*

Do you really need an introduction to e-mail? You already know that you can use e-mail to send messages to the staff at the office or to people all over the world. You probably also know that e-mail is fast (almost instanta-neous) and economical (many e-mail accounts are completely free!).

Just like you need to know a person's street address if you want to send them a letter, you need to know a person's e-mail address to send that person an e-mail message. Figure 10-26 is an example of what a typical e-mail address looks like.

Windows XP comes with an e-mail program called *Outlook Express*. Outlook Express is a stripped-down version of Microsoft's full-featured e-mail program *Outlook*, which comes with Microsoft Office. Outlook Express allows you compose, send, and receive e-mail messages over the Internet. The remainder of the lessons in this chapter will show you how to accomplish these tasks.

Move on to the one and only step in this lesson and we'll take a quick look at Outlook Express before we move on and learn how to compose, send, and receive e-mail.

1 Click the Start button. Select All Programs → Outlook Express from the menu.

The main screen of Outlook Express appears, as shown in Figure 10-24. Notice the folders in the left pane of Outlook Express? These folders categorize your messages and work just like the In and Out boxes you've seen at the office. Table 10-3 describes each of these folders.

TIP   *Many people prefer to use Web-based e-mail, such as Hotmail, since you can use it on any computer that has a connection to the Internet.*

NOTE   *The first time you open Outlook Express, you will have to set up your account, such as user name, send and receive server types, e-mail address, and so on.*

Although we'll be working in Microsoft Outlook Express throughout the remaining lessons in this chapter, Outlook Express is by no means the only program you can use to send and receive e-mail. There are many, many different e-mail programs available, such as GroupWise, Lotus Notes, and even America Online that can also send and receive e-mail. In fact, if you're connected to the Internet and have a Web browser, you don't even need an e-mail program at all to send and receive e-mail—you can do it right from the Web!

Web-based e-mail is usually free, and it allows you to compose, send, and receive e-mail using a Web page instead of an e-mail program. Many people actually prefer using Web-based e-mail instead of an e-mail program because it's free and can be accessed anywhere there is a computer with an Internet connection. Hotmail, owned by Microsoft (who else?), is the largest Web-based e-mail program in the world.

Table 10-3. E-mail folders

Folder	Description
	Stores the messages you've received.
	Temporarily stores any messages that you've composed but have not been sent.
	Stores copies of messages you have sent.
	Stores messages that you've deleted.
	Stores draft messages that you haven't completed yet.

QUICK REFERENCE

TO START OUTLOOK EXPRESS:

- CLICK THE START BUTTON AND SELECT ALL PROGRAMS → OUTLOOK EXPRESS FROM THE MENU.

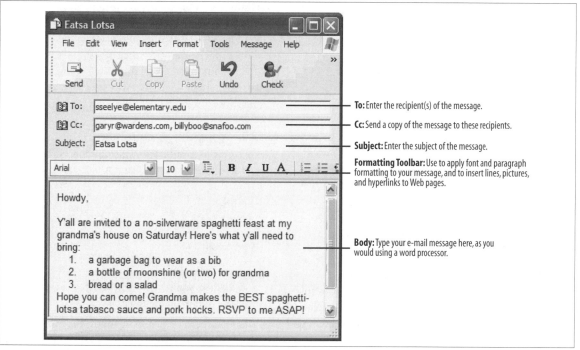

Figure 10-27. The New Message window.

To: Enter the recipient(s) of the message.

Cc: Send a copy of the message to these recipients.

Subject: Enter the subject of the message.

Formatting Toolbar: Use to apply font and paragraph formatting to your message, and to insert lines, pictures, and hyperlinks to Web pages.

Body: Type your e-mail message here, as you would using a word processor.

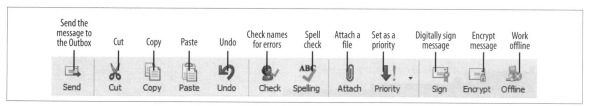

Figure 10-28. The New Message toolbar.

Here's a brief explanation of how to compose and send an e-mail message:

1 Click the Start button and select All Programs → Outlook Express from the menu.

The Outlook Express program window appears.

2 Click the Create Mail button on the Outlook Express toolbar.

The New Message window appears, ready for you to write your e-mail message. The first thing to do is to specify the recipient's e-mail address in the To: field.

You can either type this address in the To: box, or you can click the "Select Recipients from a list" button that appears immediately to the left of the To: box.

3 Type the recipient's e-mail address in the To: field.

To: button

If you need to send a message to more than one person, simply enter all the recipient's e-mail addresses, making sure you separate them with a comma (,) like this: JohnWilson@acme.com, BettyT@yahoo.com.

Skip to Step 7 when you're finished.

4 If the address is in your Address Book, click the To: button.

The Select Recipients dialog box appears.

5 Double-click the name of the recipient in the Name list.

Repeat this step to add more than one recipient from the Name list. '

6 Click OK.

The Select Recipients dialog box closes and the recipient(s) appear in the To: field.

7 (Optional) To send a copy of a message to someone, click in the Cc: field and enter their e-mail address(es).

You can type their name in the field or click the Cc: button to select a name from the Address Book.

So what is (Cc) and (Bcc)? Table 10-4 gives a description of each of these ways to send a message.

Next, enter the subject of the message so your recipient(s) will know what the message is about. The subject will appear in the heading of the message in the recipient's inbox.

8 Click the Subject field and enter a subject for the e-mail.

Now you're ready to type the actual e-mail message.

9 Click the pointer in the body of the message then type the message as you would in a word processor.

Keep in mind that all the generic Windows program commands you've learned—such as cutting, copying, pasting, and formatting text—will work in Outlook Express.

10 (Optional) To check the spelling of your message, select Tools → Spelling from the menu.

Outlook Express checks the spelling in your message, flags each word it can't find in its dictionary, and suggests an alternate word. To replace an unknown word with a suggestion, select the suggestion in the Change To list and click the Change button. To ignore a word the spell checker doesn't recognize, such as the name of a city, click Ignore All.

11 (Optional) To send a file or picture along with your message, click the Attach button on the toolbar and select the file in the Insert Attachment dialog box.

Attach button

12 When you're finished with the message, click the Send button on the toolbar.

The message is sent to the Outbox folder, and will be sent the next time you click the Send and Receive button.

13 Click the Send and Receive All button on the Outlook toolbar.

Send and Receive button

Outlook sends all the messages that are stored in the Outbox folder and retrieves any new e-mail messages it finds on the e-mail server.

Table 10-4. Ways to address an e-mail message

Address	Description
To	Sends the message to the recipient you specify (required).
Carbon Copy (Cc)	Sends a copy of the message to a recipient who is not directly involved, but would be interested in the message.
Blind Carbon Copy (Bcc)	Sends a copy of the message to a recipient without anyone else knowing that they received the message.

QUICK REFERENCE

TO COMPOSE A MESSAGE:

1. OPEN OUTLOOK EXPRESS.

2. CLICK THE CREATE MAIL BUTTON ON THE OUTLOOK EXPRESS TOOLBAR.

3. TYPE THE RECIPIENT'S ADDRESS IN THE TO: FIELD.

OR...

CLICK THE TO: BUTTON, CLICK THE NAME OF THE RECIPIENT IN THE NAME LIST, THEN DOUBLE-CLICK THE NAME. CLICK OK WHEN YOU'RE FINISHED.

1. CLICK THE SUBJECT FIELD AND ENTER THE MESSAGE'S SUBJECT.

2. CLICK THE POINTER IN THE LOWER PANE AND TYPE THE MESSAGE.

3. (OPTIONAL) CHECK THE SPELLING OF YOUR MESSAGE BY SELECTING TOOLS → SPELLING FROM THE MENU.

4. (OPTIONAL) ATTACH A FILE TO THE MESSAGE BY CLICKING THE ATTACH BUTTON ON THE TOOLBAR AND THEN SELECTING THE FILE IN THE INSERT ATTACHMENT DIALOG BOX.

5. CLICK THE SEND BUTTON ON THE TOOLBAR TO SEND THE MESSAGE.

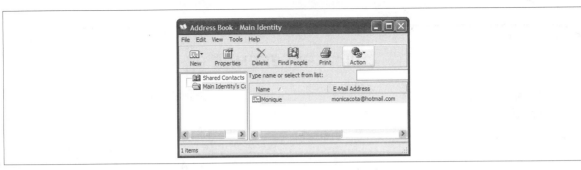

Figure 10-29. The Address Book window.

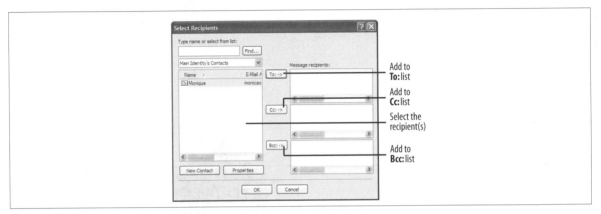

Figure 10-30. The Select Recipients dialog box.

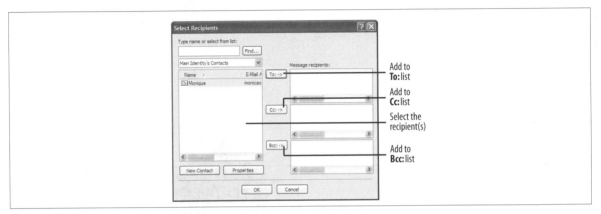

Figure 10-31. The Properties dialog box.

Unless you only write to two or three people, it's almost impossible to memorize the e-mail addresses of everyone you correspond with, especially when they have e-mail addresses that look something like brad.james.train-dept@gold.tc.umn.edu. Fortunately, if you use the Windows Address Book, you don't have to. Simply enter the names and e-mail addresses to whom you regularly send

messages, and you'll never have to remember another obscure e-mail address again.

1 If necessary, open Outlook Express.

2 Click the **Address Book** button on the Outlook Express toolbar.'

Address Book Button
Other Ways to Open the Address Book
• Press **Ctrl+Shift+B**.

The Address Book window appears, as shown in Figure 10-29. Two types of items appear in the Windows Address Book:

- **Contacts:** Contacts are the individual recipients in your Address Book.

- **Groups:** A group allows you to send messages to a group of recipients.

3 Click the New button in the Address Book toolbar. Select New Contact from the list.

New Contact button

The Properties dialog box appears with the Name tab in front, as shown in Figure 10-31.

4 Type the recipient's first and last name in the appropriate fields.

5 Enter the recipient's name in the Display box, then enter the e-mail address.

You can also use the other tabs in the Properties dialog box to add additional information—such as phone numbers and addresses—about the recipient.

6 Click OK to close the Properties dialog box.

You return to the Address Book window, where the new contact appears.

7 Click the Address Book window Close button to close it.

QUICK REFERENCE

TO ADD A NAME TO THE ADDRESS BOOK:

1. CLICK THE ADDRESS BOOK BUTTON ON THE OUTLOOK EXPRESS TOOLBAR.

2. CLICK THE NEW BUTTON ON THE ADDRESS BOOK TOOLBAR AND SELECT NEW CONTACT FROM THE DROP-DOWN LIST.

3. TYPE THE RECIPIENT'S FIRST AND LAST NAME AND ENTER THE RECIPIENT'S E-MAIL ADDRESS.

4. TO ADD ADDITIONAL INFORMATION ABOUT THE CONTACT, CLICK ON OTHER TABS IN THE PROPERTIES DIALOG BOX.

5. CLICK OK, THEN CLOSE THE ADDRESS BOOK.

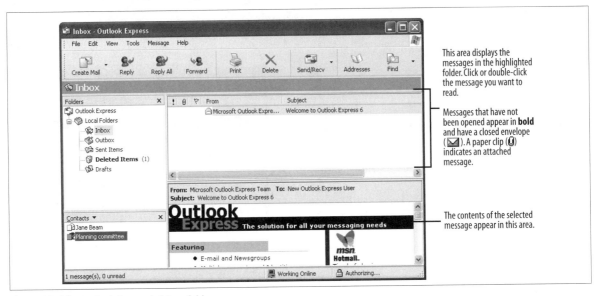

Figure 10-32. Outlook Express's Inbox folder.

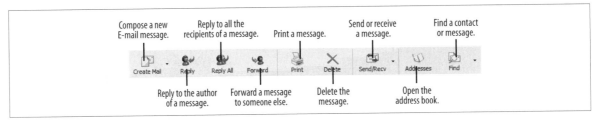

Figure 10-33. Outlook Express's Inbox toolbar.

⚙ *Windows XP Service Pack 2: Outlook Express has added some security settings that affect how you view messages:*

E-mails can now be read in plain-text format instead of HTML. This prevents some security issues that can occur with HTML messages.

Images in HTML messages are blocked. This prevents Spammers from knowing if your address is valid and is also more convenient for dialup users.

This lesson explains how to receive and read your e-mail messages with Outlook Express. You'll find it's a lot easier to retrieve and read e-mail messages than it is to sort through and read postal mail—no envelopes to rip open, no scribbled handwriting to decipher, no junk mail to go through... well that's not quite true. Unfortunately, the online world is plagued with junk mail, called *Spam*, just like the postal world. Oh well.

Send and Receive Button
Other Ways to Send and Receive Messages:
• Press *Ctrl+M*.

1 If necessary, open Outlook Express.

2 Click the Inbox folder in the left pane of the Outlook Express window.

The contents of the Inbox folder appear in the upper-right pane of the Outlook Express window, as shown in Figure 10-32. Let's check and see if you have any new e-mail.

3 Click the Send and Receive button on the Outlook Express toolbar.

Normally, Outlook Express automatically checks your mail server for new messages every 30 minutes. If it finds any new messages on your mail server, it downloads them and saves them to your computer. You can force Outlook to check for new messages by clicking the Send and Receive button. If you connect to the Internet with a modem connection, Outlook Express will automatically dial out and connect to the Internet to establish a connection with your mail server.

Inbox folder

Your new messages are saved in the Inbox folder. Any new, unread messages appear in **bold** and have a closed envelope icon next to them. Here's how to open and read a message.

4 Click the message you want to read.

The contents of the message appear in the lower-right pane of Outlook Express, and the From and Subject information appear at the top of this pane. You can also open a message its own window—this is especially helpful when you want to read a long message. Simply double-click the message you want to read. The message appears in its own window. You can

close the message's window when you're finished reading it by clicking the window's close button.

If a message has one or more files attached to it, a paper clip will also appear in this area. If a message contains an attachment, go to Step 5 to open it. If not, skip ahead to Step 6.

5 (Optional) To open files attached to a message, click the paper clip icon and select the file from the list.

Paper Clip

Sometimes you'll want to print a copy of a message. Here's how to do it:

6 (Optional) To print a message, click the Print button on the toolbar. Click OK to print the message.

Print Button
Other Ways to Print:
• Select File→Print from the menu
• Press *Ctrl+P*.

QUICK REFERENCE

TO RECEIVE AND READ E-MAIL MESSAGES:

1. START OUTLOOK EXPRESS AND CLICK THE INBOX FOLDER.

2. CLICK THE SEND AND RECEIVE ALL BUTTON ON THE OUTLOOK EXPRESS TOOLBAR.

3. CLICK OR DOUBLE-CLICK THE MESSAGE YOU WANT TO READ.

TO OPEN AN ATTACHED FILE:

- FOLLOW THE ABOVE STEPS TO READ THE MESSAGE, THEN CLICK THE PAPER CLIP ICON, AND THEN CLICK THE FILE YOU WANT TO OPEN FROM THE LIST THAT APPEARS FROM THE PAPER CLIP.

TO PRINT A MESSAGE:

- CLICK THE PRINT BUTTON.

OR...

- SELECT FILE → PRINT FROM THE MENU.

OR...

- PRESS CTRL+ P.

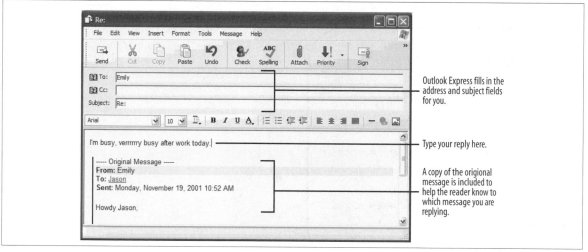

Figure 10-34. You can reply to a message.

You can reply to a message, just like you would answer a letter. This lesson explains how to do it.

1 Find and open the message you want to reply to.

You learned how to open and read messages in the previous lesson. Next, you need to decide who you want to respond to. You have two choices:

- **Reply to Author:** Sends the reply only to the author of the message.

**Reply to Author
button**

- **Reply to All:** Sends the reply to everyone who received the message.

**Reply to All
button**

2 Click the reply option you want to use: Reply to Author or Reply to All.

A window appears where you can type your reply.

3 Type your reply and click the Send button on the toolbar when you're finished.

You can use special characters to express emotion in your e-mail messages, in chat rooms, or elsewhere on the Internet. Table 10-5 has some of the more common ones. Some of them resemble a face if you turn them sideways.

Table 10-5. Expressing emotion in your messages

Abbreviation	Description	Abbreviation	Description
:) or : -)	Smile	FAQ	Frequently asked questions
: (or : - (	Frown	IMHO	In my humble opinion
;) or ; -)	Wink	LOL	Laughing out loud
:)~ or : -)~	Sticking tongue out	ROTFL	Rolling on the floor laughing
: O or : - O	Surprise	FWD	Forwarded message

QUICK REFERENCE

TO REPLY TO A MESSAGE:

1. FIND AND OPEN THE MESSAGE YOU WANT TO REPLY TO.

2. CLICK THE REPLY OPTION YOU WANT TO USE: REPLY TO AUTHOR OR REPLY TO ALL.

3. TYPE YOUR REPLY AND CLICK THE SEND BUTTON ON THE TOOLBAR WHEN YOU'RE FINISHED.

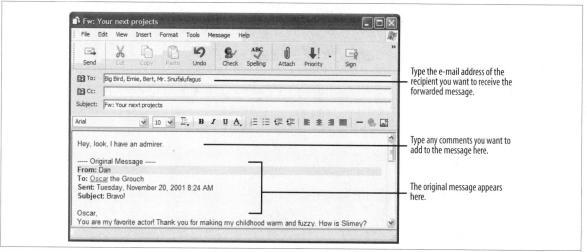

Figure 10-35. You can forward a message.

After you've read a message, you can add your own comments and *forward* it, or pass it along, to someone else. Besides the typical business correspondence, many people especially like to forward e-mails that contain jokes or words of wisdom.

1 Find and open the message you want to forward.

2 Click the Forward button on the toolbar.

Forward button

A window appears with the message you are forwarding. You need to specify to whom you want to send, or forward, the message.

3 Type the recipient's e-mail address in the To: field or use the Address Book to enter the recipient's address.

You can also add your own comments about the message you are forwarding.

4 (Optional) To add your own comments to the message, click the message body area and type your comments.

You're ready to send the forwarded message.

5 Click the Send button on the toolbar to forward the message.

Remember that clicking Send normally only sends it to the Outbox folder. You'll have to click the Send and Receive button to actually send the message.

When you no longer need a message, you can delete it to prevent your Inbox folder from becoming cluttered with dozens of messages. Deleting a message is very, very easy. Here's how to do it:

6 Select the message you want to delete and press the Delete key.

The message is removed from the current folder and is placed in the Deleted Items folder.

QUICK REFERENCE

TO FORWARD A MESSAGE:

1. FIND AND SELECT THE MESSAGE YOU WANT TO FORWARD AND CLICK THE FORWARD MESSAGE BUTTON ON THE TOOLBAR.

2. ENTER THE RECIPIENT'S E-MAIL ADDRESS IN THE TO: FIELD.

3. (OPTIONAL) ENTER YOUR OWN COMMENTS IN THE MESSAGE BODY AREA.

4. CLICK THE **SEND** BUTTON ON THE TOOLBAR.

TO DELETE A MESSAGE:

- SELECT THE MESSAGE YOU WANT TO DELETE AND PRESS THE DELETE KEY.

Chapter Ten Review

Lesson Summary

Introduction to the Internet

The Internet is the largest computer network in the world, with millions of computers all over the world connected to each other.

Web pages are stored on Web servers, which are always connected to the Internet so that people can view their Web pages 24 hours a day.

Some of things you can do using Internet include sending and receiving e-mail, browsing the World Wide Web, posting and reading newsgroup messages, chatting with other Internet users, and downloading software.

Connecting to the Internet

To connect to the Internet you need an Internet Service Provider (ISP), a Web browser program, and a phone line and modem or other connection to the Internet.

To Connect to the Internet: Make sure you have an account with an Internet Service Provider (ISSSP). Click the Start button and select Internet Explorer, then select Tools → Internet Options from the menu, then click the Connections tab. Click Setup, Next, Next. Select the Set up my connection manually option and click Next. Select the option that best describes how you want to connect to the Internet and click Next.

Displaying a Specific Web Page

To Display a Specific Web Page: Type the Web address in the Address bar and press Enter. Or, press Ctrl + L, type the Web address, and click OK.

Sometimes a Web page may not be available for viewing. This can be caused by a Web server being down where the Web page is stored, by Internet congestion, or by the Web page no longer existing. Try returning to the Web page later.

Browsing the Web

A hyperlink is a link to another Web page or file. The pointer changes to a [🖑] whenever it is positioned over a hyperlink.

To Use a Hyperlink: Click the hyperlink with the 🖑 pointer.

To Go Back to the Previous Page: Click the Back button on the toolbar.

To Stop the Transfer of Information: Click the Stop button on the toolbar.

To Refresh a Web Page: Click the Refresh button on the toolbar.

To Return to a Web Address you Typed in the Address Bar: Click the Address bar list arrow and select the Web address.

Searching the Web

To Search the Web for Information Using Internet Explorer: Click the Search button on the toolbar, type the word or phrase you want to search for in the Search the Web for box and click Search, then click the link for the Web page you want to look at. Click the Search button on the toolbar to close the search panel.

To Search the Web for Information Using a Search Engine: Type the Web address for the search engine in the Address bar and press Enter. Type the word or phrase you want to search for in the Web page's Search box and press Enter.

Adding a Web Page to Favorites and Changing your Home Page

To Add a Web Page to Your List of Favorites: Go to the Web page, select Favorites → Add to Favorites from the menu and click OK, or right-click anywhere on the Web page and select Add to Favorites from the shortcut menu.

To Go To a Favorite Web Page: Click the Favorites button on the toolbar and select the Web page from the left side of Internet Explorer, then click the Favorites button when you're finished. You can also go to a favorite Web page by selecting Favorites from the menu bar and selecting the Web page.

To Change Your Home Page: Go to the Web page, select Tools → Internet Options from the menu and click the Use Current button.

To Organize Your Favorites: Select Favorites → Organize Favorites from the menu.

Displaying a History of Visited Web Pages

Click the History button on the toolbar and click the day or week you viewed the Web page. Click the Web site you want to revisit and then the specific Web page. Click the History button on the toolbar when you've finished.

Clearing the History of Visited Web Pages

Select Tools → Internet Options from the menu. Click the Clear History button, click Yes to confirm the deletion and click OK.

Saving Pictures and Files to Disk (Downloading)

To Download an Image: Right-click the image you want to save and select Save Picture As from the shortcut menu, navigate to the drive and folder when you want to save the image, give the image a different name if you want, and click Save.

To Download a File: Right-click the file you want to download, select Save Target As from the shortcut menu, navigate to the drive and folder when you want to save the file, give the file a different name if you want, and click Save.

Many programs and files on the Internet are stored in compressed ZIP files and need to be unpacked using a program called WinZip.

Understanding the Information Bar

The Information Bar notifies you when a security action has taken place.

To Use the Information Bar: Click the Information Bar and select an option from the shortcut menu.

Using the Pop-up Blocker

To Change Pop-up Blocker Settings: Select Tools → Pop-up Blocker → Pop-up Blocker Settings from the menu and change the Pop-up Blocker settings in the dialog box. Or, click the Information Bar and select an option from the shortcut menu.

To Turn Off the Pop-up Blocker: Select Tools → Pop-up Blocker → Turn Off Pop-up Blocker from the menu.

Understanding Information Security

Information security is the practice of protecting your computer from intruders. Here are some security pre-cautions that help protect your sensitive information. Install anti-virus software; Update anti-virus software; Update software; Use firewalls; Be smart with e-mail

Understanding Windows Firewall

This security utility keeps your computer secure by restricting the information that comes into your computer.

To Open Windows Firewall: Click the Start button and select Control Panel. Click the Security Center icon and click the Windows Firewall icon.

Introduction to E-mail

To Start Outlook Express: Click the Start button. Select All Programs → Outlook Express from the menu.

Composing and Sending E-mail

To Compose a Message: Start Outlook Express, click the Create Mail button on the Outlook Express toolbar, type the recipient's address in the To: field or click the To: button to the left of the To: field and double-click the name. Click OK when you're finished. Click the Subject field and enter the message's subject. Click the pointer in the lower pane and type the message. Click the Send button on the toolbar to send the message.

To Check a Message for Spelling Errors: Before you send the message, select Tools → Spelling from the menu.

To Attach a File to a Message: Before you send the message click the Attach button on the toolbar and then select the file in the Insert Attachment dialog box.

You can address a message using To which sends the message to the recipient you specify (required), Carbon Copy (Cc) which sends a copy of the message to a recipient who is not directly involved, but would be interested in the message, and Blind Carbon Copy (Bcc) which sends a copy of the message to a recipient without anyone else knowing that they received the message.

Adding a Name to the Address Book

To Add a Name to the Address Book: Click the Address Book button on the Outlook Express toolbar, and click the New button on the Address Book toolbar and select New Contact from the drop-down list. Type the recipient's first and last name in the appropriate fields and enter the recipient's display name and e-mail address. To add additional information about the contact, click on other tabs in the Properties dialog box. Click OK, and then close the Address Book.

Receiving E-mail

Outlook Express checks your mail server for new messages automatically, but you can also check for new messages by clicking the Send and Receive All button on the Outlook Express toolbar.

To Receive and Read E-mail Messages: Start Outlook Express and click the Inbox folder, click the Send and Receive All button on the Outlook Express toolbar, and click or double-click the message you want to read.

To Open an Attached File: Follow the above steps to read the message, then click the 🖉 paper clip icon and then click the file you want to open from the list that appears from the paper clip.

To Print a Message: Click the Print button, or select File → Print from the menu, or press Ctrl+ P.

Replying to a Message

To Reply to a Message: Find and open the message you want to reply to, click the reply option you want to use: Reply to Author or Reply to All. Type your reply and click the Send button on the toolbar when you're finished.

Forwarding a Message

To Forward a Message: Find and select the message you want to forward and click the 🖼 Forward Message button on the toolbar, enter the recipient's e-mail address in the To: field, enter your own comments in the message body area, and click the 🖼 Send button on the toolbar.

To Delete a Message: Select the message you want to delete and press the Delete key.

Quiz

1. A Web server is:

   A. The world's largest supercomputer that contains and runs the Internet.

   B. A computer that stores Web pages and that is always connected to the Internet.

   C. A computer that acts as a gateway between your office network and the Internet.

   D. A waiter at a restaurant for spiders.

2. A Home page is the first Web page you see when you connect to the Internet. (True or False?)

3. Which button on Internet Explorer's toolbar brings you back to the page you last viewed?

   A. Home

   B. Stop

   C. Refresh

   D. Back

4. What can you do to keep your computer secure?

   A. Install and update anti-virus software.

   B. Use a firewall.

   C. Avoid suspicious e-mail messages.

   D. All of the above.

5. Which of the following statements is NOT true?

   A. Internet Explorer keeps a history of visited Web pages for 20 days.

   B. A search engine lets you search for Web pages by topic.

   C. Eudora is an e-mail program that comes with Windows XP.

   D. You can download and save images from a Web page onto your computer.

6. When you've finished writing a letter in Outlook Express, clicking the Send button on the toolbar will instantly send the message to its destination. (True or False?)

7. Which of the following statements is NOT true?

   A. When you reply to a message, Outlook Express includes the content of the original message to make it easy for the recipient to know which message you're replying to.

B. E-mail messages can contain files, such as pictures and word processing documents called *attachments*.

C. You can send anonymous e-mail using the Blind Carbon Copy (Bcc) field.

D. You can save a list of Web pages you visit frequently in Internet Explorer's Favorites list.

8. What is a firewall?

A. A security device that keeps your computer secure by restricting the information that comes into your computer.

B. What you put around your cubicle after doing something wrong.

C. There is no such thing.

D. A fire prevention tactic used by firefighters.

Homework

1. Get a connection to the Internet.

2. Open Internet Explorer.

3. Go to the Yahoo Web site (www.yahoo.com).

4. Search the Internet for information on Russia.

5. Spend at least 30 minutes browsing the Web on whatever topics you want.

Quiz Answers

1. B. A Web server is a computer that holds Web pages and is connected to the Internet 24 hours a day so that people can view those Web pages.

2. True.

3. C. The Back button returns you to the Web page you just left.

4. D. You should install and update anti-virus software, use a firewall, and avoid suspicious e-mail messages to keep your computer secure.

5. C. Eudora *is* a popular e-mail program, but it doesn't come with Windows XP: Outlook Express does.

6. False. This was a tricky question—when you click the Send button, you save the message to the Inbox folder. To send any messages that are in the Inbox, click the Send and Receive button on the toolbar.

7. C. Adding a recipient to the Blind Carbon Copy field allows them to receive a message without seeing who else received the message.

8. A. A firewall is a device that keeps your computer secure by restricting the information that comes into your computer. Windows has been updated with a Firewall in Service Pack 2.

CHAPTER 11

PASSWORDS, LOGONS, AND USER ACCOUNTS

CHAPTER OBJECTIVES:

Understand a workgroup and a domain

Understand the differences between Windows XP Home and Professional

Create and edit user accounts

Change the logon process

Log on and off Windows

Change your password

Prerequisites

- **Know how to use the mouse to click, double-click, drag and drop, and right-click.**
- **Know how to start programs in the Start Menu.**
- **Know how to use menus, toolbars, and dialog boxes.**

Passwords have been used as a first-line of defense against intruders for thousands of years. A password assures an individual's identification: once they pass a test of identification—whether it's a secret knock or a spoken word—entrance is granted.

Technology has easily adapted this common-sense approach of ensuring a user's identity, only on computers we gain access to a user account, not a secret hideout or speakeasy. For example, to log on to an Internet e-mail account, you must identify yourself with a user name, then prove who you are by entering a password.

This chapter will show you how to use and manage your own account to make sure it is secure. You will also learn how to create and edit user accounts for everyone who shares a computer.

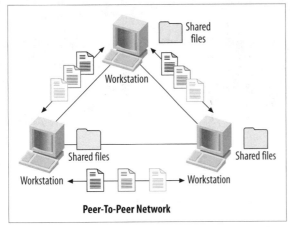

Figure 11-1. In a peer-to-peer network, everyone stores their files on their own computer. Anyone on the network can access files stored on any other computer.

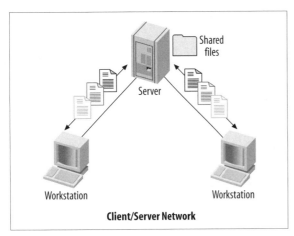

Figure 11-2. In a client/server network, everyone stores their files on a central computer called a server. Everyone on the network can access the files stored on the server.

Figure 11-3. The domain levels of an e-mail address.

There are two versions of Windows XP: Home and Professional. In most ways, the versions are not at all different. But because Home users are less likely to be part of a big network, or *domain*, Microsoft made some actions different, like creating user accounts on the computer. This lesson explains the difference between a *workgroup*, which is applicable to Windows XP Home users, and a *domain*, which is applicable to Windows XP Professional users.

Workgroup (Windows XP Home)

This is an example of a peer-to-peer network, so there is no hierarchy of computers. Workgroups share resources with each other, such as printers and folders, but there is no centralized power. A network you might set up at home would be considered a workgroup.

If you do not have a home network, your computer is stand-alone and you can create and manage user accounts on your computer the same as in a workgroup.

Domain (Windows XP Professional)

This is an example of a client/server network, which means computers are connected to each other through a main server computer. All the computers within a domain work as a unit under the same rules and procedures.

Domains and computers within the domain also have a specific identification on the Internet, called an IP address. All devices sharing part of that address are in the same domain. For example, in the e-mail address: janedoe@zipcorp.com, zipcorp is the name of the domain that Jane Doe's computer is a part of. The .com also identifies the zipcorp domain as a business.

There is much more to learn about the basic differences between a workgroup and a domain in the Networking with Windows chapter in this book. But for the purposes of lessons in this chapter, if you are on a workgroup, or small network, follow the lessons for a workgroup. If you are part of a domain, or larger corporate network, follow the lessons for a domain.

QUICK REFERENCE

WORKGROUP:

- WINDOWS XP HOME USERS ARE CONFIGURED TO BE PART OF A WORKGROUP.

IF YOU USE WINDOWS XP HOME BUT ARE NOT PART OF A NETWORK, YOUR COMPUTER IS STAND-ALONE AND FOLLOWS THE SAME PROCEDURES AS A WORKGROUP.

DOMAIN:

1. WINDOWS XP PROFESSIONAL USERS ARE CONFIGURED TO BE PART OF A DOMAIN

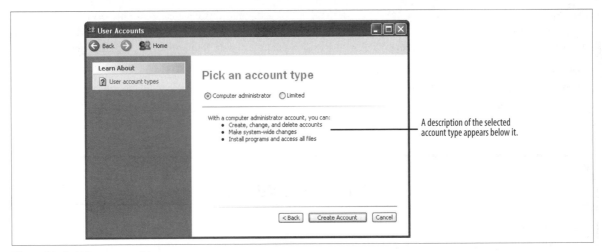

Figure 11-4. Pick an account type.

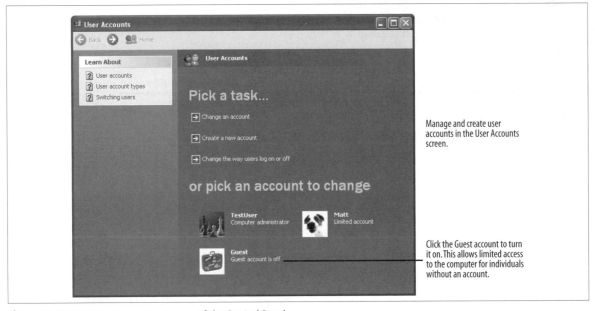

Figure 11-5. The User Accounts category of the Control Panel.

TIP *Creating a new user account on your computer is not adding a computer to a network. See the chapter on Networking with Windows for this information.*

Many home computers aren't used by just one, but several family members. If you share your computer with several people, you may want to create a new user account for each person so they can have personalized settings on the computer. Each user account allows settings for:

- **Permissions:** These have to be set up by a network administrator. Permissions provide access to some areas of the network, while restricting access to others.

- **Background and screen colors:** Each user can personalize their desktop with the background and Windows screen colors that suit their own personal tastes.

- **Start menu and shortcuts:** Each user account has its own personalized Start menu and Desktop. For example, a shortcut added to the Desktop in Joe Schnook's account won't appear on Mary Johnson's Desktop.

NOTE *To create a new user account you must be logged on to Windows XP as an administrator (or know the administrator password).*

This lesson will show you how to add new user accounts to a computer using Windows XP Home.

1 Make sure you are logged on to an account with Administrator status.

Only administrators can create new accounts on a computer.

2 Click the Start button and select Control Panel.

The Control Panel appears.

3 Click the User Accounts category. Click the Create a new account task.

User Accounts

The User Accounts dialog box appears.

First, create a name for the user. This name will appear in the Welcome screen when the user logs in to their account.

NOTE *User names cannot be the same as any other user or group name, and can contain up to 20 uppercase or lowercase characters including spaces. User names cannot contain the following characters: \ / : ★ ? " | + ★ ?*

4 Type the user name in the User name box. Click Next.

Now assign a permission level to the user. There are two levels to choose from:

- **Computer Administrator:** This type of account grants the user access to system settings, installing programs, and files. This user can also create, edit and delete other user accounts. This is a good permission level for parents or the owner of the computer.

- **Limited:** This type of user has access to programs on the computer, but cannot change system settings or delete important files. This is a good level for children or users that do not need to maintain the computer.

5 Choose the access level for the user. Click Create Account.

The new user account appears in the User Accounts dialog box.

That's all there is to adding a new user account to your Windows XP Home computer, if you have administrator status, that is! Now that the account is created you can explore more account management tasks, such as creating a password, in a later lesson.

QUICK REFERENCE

TO CREATE A NEW USER ACCOUNT USING WINDOWS XP HOME:

1. LOG ON TO A COMPUTER ADMINISTRATOR ACCOUNT.

2. CLICK THE START BUTTON AND SELECT CONTROL PANEL.

3. CLICK THE USER ACCOUNTS CATEGORY.

4. CLICK THE CREATE A NEW ACCOUNT TASK.

5. ENTER A USER NAME FOR THE ACCOUNT. CLICK NEXT.

6. SELECT THE ACCESS LEVEL FOR THE USER (COMPUTER ADMINISTRATOR OR LIMITED). CLICK CREATE ACCOUNT.

Figure 11-6. Enter a User name and the Domain the user is in.

Figure 11-7. Specify the level of access you want to give the new user.

Figure 11-8. The new user account appears in the Users tab of the User Accounts dialog box.

If your computer uses Windows XP Professional, you can create an account on your computer for other users in the domain. This is different from creating an account in Windows XP Home, because the user already has to be in the domain: if Windows doesn't recognize the account name you're trying to create, it won't let you create the account.

NOTE *To create a new user account you must be logged on to Windows XP as an administrator or know the administrator password. However, network policy settings may still prevent you from completing this procedure.*

Here's how to create new accounts on a computer that uses Windows XP Professional.

1 Make sure you are logged on to an account with Administrator status.

Only administrators can create new accounts on a computer.

2 Click the Start button and select Control Panel.

The Control Panel appears.

If your account has administrator status you can add users to the computer. Otherwise, you may have to call your organization's computer support department.

3 Click the User Accounts category. Click User Accounts.

User Accounts

The User Accounts dialog box appears.

You're ready to start entering the new user account.

4 Click Add.

The Add New User dialog box appears.

5 Type the user name in the User name box.

Because the user is already in the domain, you don't have to make up a new user name. Just make sure the user name you type is the same as the user name in the domain.

Now enter the domain that the user is in.

6 Type the domain in the Domain box. Click Next.

The last step in adding a new user account is assigning their level of access. You have three options:

- **Standard user:** Users can modify the computer and install programs, but cannot read or modify files that belong to other users.

- **Restricted user:** Users can operate the computer and save documents, but cannot install programs or make changes to the system files and settings.

- **Other:** Select from other types of user access, such as *Administrators*, who can read or modify files that belong to other users, share folders on your computer, and create user accounts.

7 Select the level of access you want to grant to the new user and click Finish.

The new user account appears in the User Accounts dialog box.

8 Click OK to close the User Accounts dialog box.

That's all there is to adding a new user account to your Windows XP Professional computer, if you're able to log on as an administrator, that is! You may want the new user to log on to the computer using their domain user name and password to make sure everything works okay.

QUICK REFERENCE

TO CREATE A NEW USER ACCOUNT USING WINDOWS XP PROFESSIONAL:

1. CLICK THE START BUTTON AND SELECT CONTROL PANEL.

2. CLICK THE USER ACCOUNTS ICON. CLICK USER ACCOUNTS.

3. CLICK ADD.

4. ENTER THE USER'S DOMAIN USER NAME.

5. ENTER THE DOMAIN THE USER IS ON. CLICK NEXT.

6. SELECT THE TYPE OF ACCESS YOU WANT TO GRANT THE NEW USER AND CLICK FINISH.

7. CLICK OK.

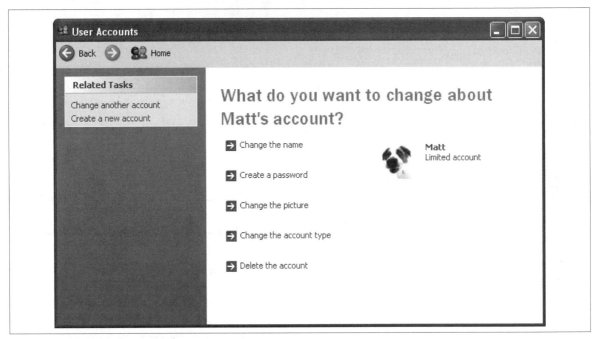

Figure 11-9. Editing account tasks in the User Accounts dialog box.

When a user account is created, only basic settings like the user name and account type are established. But you can also change many of the account's settings, such as the password, account type, or the name. Once a user account has been created, it's easy to edit its settings.

1 Click the **Start button and select Control Panel.**

The Control Panel appears. You must have administrator status to edit user accounts.

2 Click the **User Accounts category.**

User Accounts

The User Accounts dialog box appears.

3 Click the **user account you want to change.**

The User Accounts dialog box appears with a list of tasks that change the account.

To perform a task, just click it and enter the information requested on the screen. Review the following table for more information on each task.

Table 11-1. Change Account tasks

Task	Description
Change the name	Change the name that appears in the account.
Create a password	Increase security by requiring the user to enter a password when logging in to the account. Other users can see the account password hint in the Welcome screen.
Change the picture	Select from a number of available images, or select your own image, that appears with the account name in the Welcome screen and Start menu.
Change the account type	Changes the account from Limited to Computer Administrator, or vice versa.
Delete the account	Delete the account from the computer. This deletes the user's customized settings such as e-mail messages or Internet favorites, but you can save the items on the user's desktop.

QUICK REFERENCE

TO CHANGE A USER ACCOUNT IN WINDOWS XP HOME:

1. CLICK THE **START** BUTTON AND SELECT CONTROL PANEL.

2. CLICK THE **USER ACCOUNTS** ICON.

3. CLICK THE ACCOUNT YOU WANT TO CHANGE.

4. CLICK A TASK TO CHANGE THE ACCOUNT SETTINGS.

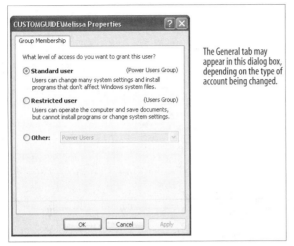

> The General tab may appear in this dialog box, depending on the type of account being changed.

Figure 11-10. The Group Membership tab of the User Account Properties dialog box.

Over time, you may find that a user needs more or less access to the computer. When a domain user account is created, basic settings like the user name and password are already established on the domain, you're just giving that user permission to use your computer. The user has control over their user name and password, but you can change the level of access the user has on your computer.

1 Click the **Start** button and select **Control Panel**.

The Control Panel appears. You must have administrator status to edit user accounts.

2 Click the **User Accounts** category. Click **User Accounts**.

The User Accounts dialog box appears.

3 Select the user account you want to change from the list of users. Click **Properties** and click the **Group Membership** tab if necessary.

The Group Membership tab of the Account Properties dialog box appears.

Remember when you gave the user a level of access to the computer? This is where you can change that status.

4 Select the level of access you want to grant to the user and click **OK**.

The user's account now belongs to a different access group.

Select **Log Off** to log off Windows XP.

Figure 11-11. To log off your account, click the Start button and select Log Off.

The Switch User option does not appear if the Welcome screen is turned off.

Figure 11-12. Select a Log Off option.

When you're finished using the computer, log off your account so that it's ready for the next person. Windows XP Home also has the unique option of switching user accounts, instead of logging off. This allows you to switch easily between open user accounts without logging on and off.

1 Save all your work and exit all your programs.

There really isn't a lot of difference between logging off your computer and shutting it down. Save any files you've been working on and consider backing up any vital information on a removable storage device.

2 Click the Windows **Start button** and select **Log Off**.

The Log Off Windows dialog box appears, as shown in Figure 11-12. Click one of the following options:

- **Switch User:** Keeps the current user account and its programs open so you can switch to another account in the Welcome screen. This option is not available if the Welcome screen has been turned off.
- **Log Off:** Logs off the user account.

3 Click **Log Off**.

Windows logs you off the system and displays the Welcome to Windows dialog box, or the Welcome screen, allowing another person to log on to Windows to use the computer.

QUICK REFERENCE

TO LOG OFF WINDOWS XP HOME:

1. SAVE ALL YOUR WORK AND EXIT ALL YOUR PROGRAMS.

2. CLICK THE **START** BUTTON AND SELECT LOG OFF.

3. CLICK LOG OFF.

   OR...

   CLICK **SWITCH USER** TO KEEP THE ACCOUNT OPEN, AND LOG ON TO A DIFFERENT ACCOUNT.

Select **Log Off** to log off Windows XP

Figure 11-13. To log off your account, click the Start button and select Log Off.

Figure 11-14. Windows XP asks if you are sure you want to log off.

In Windows XP Professional, there are several security reasons for logging off your computer.

- **To secure your computer from unauthorized access:** If your computer contains sensitive information you may want to log off Windows when you step out of the office to prevent unauthorized users from using your computer.

- **You share the same computer with another user:** If you share your computer with one or more people, you can create and log on to different user accounts so that each person can use their own personalized files and settings.

- **To gain administrative rights to a shared folder or printer:** Some critical or confidential areas of your computer or network may be restricted so that only authorized users can access them. User accounts with *administrative rights* pretty much have access to everything on your computer. You must be logged on as an administrator or a user with administrative rights to add or change user accounts and to share folders on your computer.

In this lesson you will learn the complex task of logging off Windows XP Professional.

1 Save all your work and exit all your programs.

There really isn't a lot of difference between logging off your computer and shutting it down. Save any files you've been working on and consider backing up vital information on a removable storage device.

2 Click the Start button and select Log Off.

The Log Off Windows dialog box appears.

3 Click Log Off.

Windows logs you off the system, allowing another person to log on to the domain to use the computer.

QUICK REFERENCE

TO LOG OFF WINDOWS XP PROFESSIONAL:

1. SAVE ALL YOUR WORK AND EXIT ALL YOUR PROGRAMS.

2. CLICK THE **START** BUTTON AND SELECT LOG OFF.

3. CLICK **LOG OFF**.

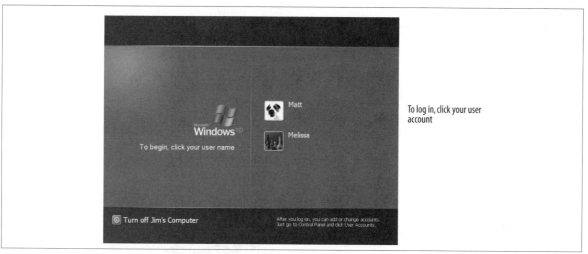

Figure 11-15. The Welcome screen is the default log in screen.

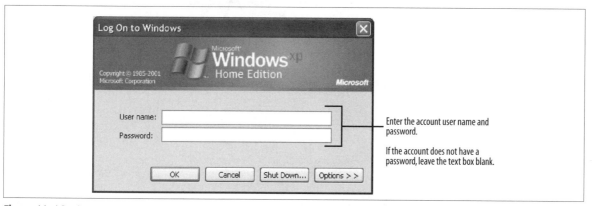

Figure 11-16. The Log On to Windows dialog box appears if the Welcome screen has been turned off.

The procedure for logging back on to Windows XP really isn't any different from turning your computer on—except that you don't have to wait as long.

The default log in screen is the Welcome screen, as shown in Figure 11-15.

1 Click your account user name.

If your account has a password, you will be prompted to enter it.

Logging on to Windows couldn't be easier.

If the Computer Administrator wants to increase security and has turned off the Welcome screen, logging in will be a little different, as shown in Figure 11-16.

1 Enter your user name and password. If your account doesn't have a password, leave the text box blank.

Remember that when you enter your password, Windows will display a series of ••••••••s to protect your password from prying eyes.

2 Press Enter or click OK.

Windows logs in using your account settings.

QUICK REFERENCE

TO LOG ON TO WINDOWS XP HOME USING THE WELCOME SCREEN:

- CLICK YOUR ACCOUNT USER NAME. ENTER YOUR ACCOUNT PASSWORD IF PROMPTED.

TO LOG ON TO WINDOWS XP HOME WITHOUT THE WELCOME SCREEN:

1. ENTER YOUR USER NAME AND PASSWORD. IF YOUR ACCOUNT DOESN'T HAVE A PASSWORD, LEAVE THE TEXT BOX BLANK.

2. PRESS ENTER OR CLICK OK

Figure 11-17. The Welcome to Windows XP dialog box.

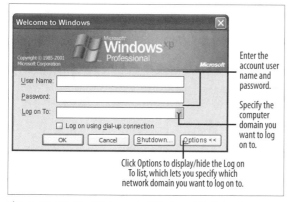

Enter the account user name and password.

Specify the computer domain you want to log on to.

Click Options to display/hide the Log on To list, which lets you specify which network domain you want to log on to.

Figure 11-18. The Welcome to Windows XP dialog box.

Logging on to a computer using Windows XP Professional is a little different because you are logging in to a network, not just a computer, so security needs to be tight.

The first screen is a defense against hackers or worms that might try to hack into your computer while you're not using it.

1 Press Ctrl + Alt + Delete.

The Log on to Windows dialog box appears, as shown in Figure 11-16.

2 Enter your user name and password.

Remember that when you enter your password Windows will display a series of •••••••s to protect your password from prying eyes.

3 If necessary, click Options and click the Log on To list arrow to select the domain name that you want to log on to.

This setting probably won't ever change, but you should be aware that it is required to log in to the domain.

4 Press Enter or click OK.

Presto! You're logged on to Windows XP and are ready to get back to work.

QUICK REFERENCE

TO LOG ON TO WINDOWS XP PROFESSIONAL:

1. PRESS CTRL + ALT + DELETE.

2. ENTER YOUR USER NAME AND PASSWORD.

3. MAKE SURE YOU ARE LOGGING IN TO THE CORRECT DOMAIN.

4. PRESS ENTER OR CLICK OK.

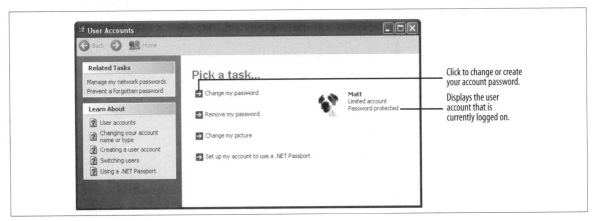

Figure 11-19. User Account tasks.

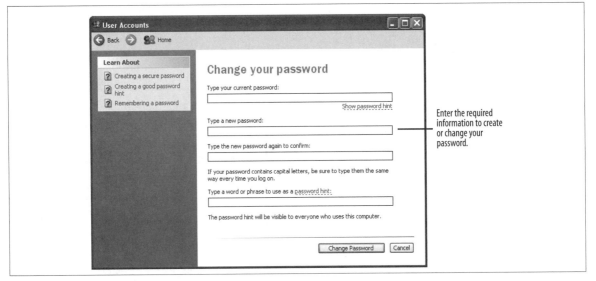

Figure 11-20. Changing or creating your password.

TIP *The most secure passwords combine letters and numbers.*

Windows XP Home accounts don't require passwords, but you can add one to your account for more privacy. Change your password regularly to ensure your account is secure.

1 Click the Start button and select Control Panel.

The Control Panel appears.

2 Click the User Accounts icon.

The User Accounts screen appears.

3 Click your account. To create a password, click the Create a password task. To change a password, click the Change my password task.

The information required to create and change a password is very similar.

4 Enter the information required to create or change your password.

5 Click Create password or Change password to confirm the password.

Now the new or changed password will be required whenever you log in to the account.

QUICK REFERENCE

TO CHANGE OR CREATE YOUR PASSWORD ON WINDOWS XP HOME:

1. CLICK THE **START** BUTTON AND SELECT **CONTROL PANEL**.

2. CLICK THE **USER ACCOUNTS** ICON.

3. CLICK YOUR ACCOUNT.

4. CLICK THE **CREATE A PASSWORD** TASK.

   OR...

   CLICK THE **CHANGE MY PASSWORD** TASK.

5. ENTER THE REQUIRED INFORMATION TO CHANGE OR CREATE THE PASSWORD.

6. CLICK **CREATE PASSWORD** OR **CHANGE PASSWORD**.

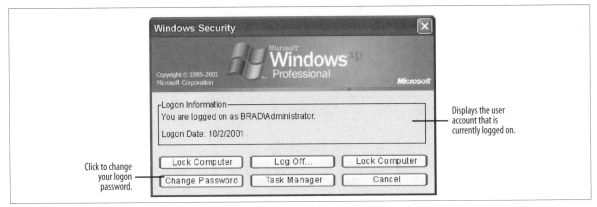

Figure 11-21. The Windows Security dialog box.

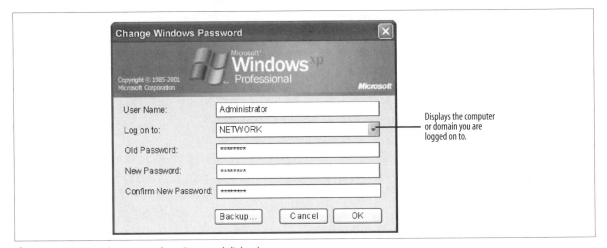

Figure 11-22. The Change Windows Password dialog box.

TIP *The most secure passwords combine letters and numbers.*

As a domain user, you were probably assigned a user name and password the first time you logged in to your computer. But you have control over your own password, and it's a good idea to change passwords regularly for security purposes.

1 Press Ctrl + Alt + Delete.

The Windows Security dialog box appears.

2 Click the Change Password button.

The Change Password dialog box appears, displaying your user name and the domain that you are logged on to. First, tell Windows XP your old password.

3 Type your current password in the Old Password box and press Tab.

Now enter your new password.

4 Type your new password in the New Password box, press Tab, and type your new password again in the Confirm New Password box.

When you pick a password, don't use words or numbers that are easily associated with you, such as the name of your dog or your birthday.

5 Click OK.

A dialog box appears, confirming that your password has been changed.

6 Click OK. Click Cancel to close the Windows Security dialog box.

That's all there is to changing your password. Make sure you write it down so that you don't forget it next time you have to log on to Windows XP!

QUICK REFERENCE

TO CHANGE YOUR ACCOUNT PASSWORD ON WINDOWS XP PROFESSIONAL:

1. PRESS CTRL + ALT + DELETE.

2. CLICK THE CHANGE PASSWORD BUTTON.

3. TYPE YOUR OLD PASSWORD IN THE OLD PASSWORD BOX AND PRESS THE TAB KEY.

4. TYPE YOUR NEW PASSWORD IN THE NEW PASSWORD BOX, PRESS TAB AND TYPE YOUR NEW PASSWORD AGAIN IN THE CONFIRM NEW PASSWORD BOX.

5. CLICK OK TO CLOSE THE DIALOG BOX, CLICK OK TO CONFIRM THE NEW PASSWORD AND CLICK CANCEL TO CLOSE THE WINDOWS SECURITY DIALOG BOX.

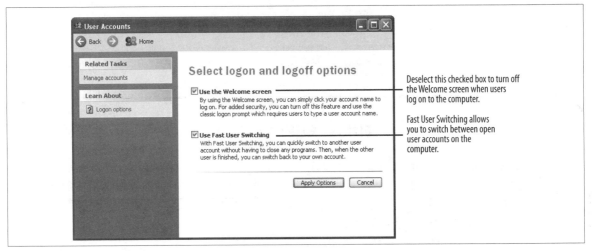

Figure 11-23. Change the way users log on or off.

TIP *You must be logged in as a computer administrator to change the logon process.*

When logging in, Windows XP Home users are greeted with a Welcome screen that displays all the accounts on the computer. But if you want to increase security, you can change the logon process so that instead of a Welcome screen that lists all the user accounts, a blank dialog box appears, so that the user must enter their own account information.

This lesson shows you how to turn off the Welcome screen and log on to the computer using the standard Log On to Windows dialog box.

1 Click the Start button and select Control Panel.

The Control Panel appears.

2 Click the User Accounts category.

The User Accounts screen appears.

3 Click the Change the way users log on or off task.

Another dialog box appears with controls on how users begin and end their sessions with Windows.

As you can see, by default the "Use the Welcome screen" check box is selected. To turn off the Welcome screen, uncheck this option.

4 Click the Use the Welcome screen check box so it is not selected. Click Apply Options.

The Home page of the User Accounts category appears.

The Welcome screen will no longer appear when users log on to their accounts. Instead of clicking their account name on the Welcome screen, they will have to type their account information, such as user name and password, in the Log On to Windows dialog box. This is similar to the dialog box that appears when logging on to computer in a domain.

QUICK REFERENCE

TO CHANGE THE LOGON PROCESS ON A WORKGROUP:

1. CLICK THE START BUTTON AND SELECT CONTROL PANEL.

2. CLICK THE USER ACCOUNTS CATEGORY.

3. CLICK THE CHANGE THE WAY USERS LOG ON OR OFF TASK.

4. CLICK THE USE THE WELCOME SCREEN CHECK BOX SO IT IS NOT SELECTED.

5. CLICK APPLY OPTIONS.

Lesson Summary

Workgroup vs. Domain

Workgroup: Windows XP Home users are configured to be part of a workgroup. If you use Windows XP Home but are not part of a network, your computer is stand-alone and follows the same procedures as a workgroup.

Domain: Windows XP Professional users are configured to be part of a domain.

Creating a New User Account on a Workgroup Computer

To Create a New User Account Using Windows XP Home: Click the Start button and select Control Panel. Click the User Accounts category and click the Create a new account task. Enter a user name for the account and click Next. Select the access level for the user (Computer Administrator or Limited) and click Create Account.

Creating a New User Account on a Domain Computer

To Create a New User Account Using Windows XP Professional: Click the Start button and select Control Panel. Click the User Accounts icon and click User Accounts. Click Add. Enter the user's domain User name. Enter the domain the user is on and click Next. Select the type of access you want to grant the new user and click Finish. Click OK.

Editing a User Account on a Workgroup

To Change a User Account in Windows XP Home: Click the Start button and select Control Panel. Click the User Accounts icon. Click the account you want to change and click a task to change the account settings.

Editing a User Account on a Domain

To Change a User Account in Windows XP Professional: Click the Start button and select Control Panel. Click the User Accounts icon and click User Accounts. Select the user account you want to change, click Properties, and click the Group Membership tab if necessary. Select the level of access you want to grant to the user and click OK.

Logging Off Windows on a Workgroup

To Log Off Windows XP Home: Save all your work and exit all your programs. Click the Windows Start button and select Log Off. Click Log Off, or click Switch User to keep the account open, and log on to a different account.

Logging Off Windows on a Domain

To Log Off Windows XP Professional: Save all your work and exit all your programs. Click the Windows Start button and select Log Off. Click Log Off.

Logging On to Windows on a Workgroup

To Log On To Windows XP Home Using the Welcome Screen: Click your account user name. Enter your account password if prompted.

To Log On To Windows XP Home Without the Welcome Screen: Enter your user name and password. If your account doesn't have a password, leave the text box blank. Press Enter or click OK.

Logging On to Windows on a Domain

To Log On to Windows XP Professional: Press Ctrl + Alt + Delete. Enter your user name and password. Make sure you are logging in to the correct domain. Press Enter or click OK.

Changing Your Password on a Workgroup

To Change or Create Your Password on Windows XP Home: Click the Start button and select Control Panel. Click the User Accounts icon and click your account. Click the Create a password task, or if you already have a password, click the Change my password task. Enter the required information to change or create the password. Click Create password or Change password.

Changing Your Password on a Domain

To Change Your Password on Windows XP Professional: Press Ctrl + Alt + Delete and click the Change Password button. Type your old password in the Old Password box and press the Tab key. Type your new password in the New Password box, press Tab and type your new password again in the Confirm New Password box. Click OK to close the dialog box, click OK to confirm the new password and click Cancel to close the Windows Security dialog box.

Changing the Logon Process on a Workgroup

To Change the Logon Process for Windows XP Home: Click the Start button and select Control Panel and click the User Accounts category. Click the Change the way users log on or off task. Click the Use the Welcome screen check box so it is not selected and click Apply Options.

Quiz

1. What is the difference between a workgroup and a domain? (Select all that apply.)

   A. A workgroup has centralized file and account maintenance. A domain is not centralized.

   B. A workgroup is a network of computers that share resources, but does not have a presence on the Internet. A domain has an identification on the Internet, called an IP address.

   C. A workgroup is more common in organizations and businesses. A domain is more suitable for home users.

   D. A workgroup is a peer-to-peer network. A domain is a client/server network.

2. What kind of network is Windows XP Home configured for?

   A. A domain.

   B. A workgroup.

   C. A client/server network.

   D. It isn't configured for a network. You must purchase networking software to create a network with Windows XP Home.

3. Which settings are personalized in a user account?

   A. Permissions.

   B. Start menu.

   C. Desktop background.

   D. All of the above.

4. When you create a user account on your domain computer, the user must already be part of the domain. (True or False?)

5. Which of the following statements is NOT true?

   A. When you create a user account, you can limit the user's access on the computer by choosing the account type.

   B. You must be logged in to an administrator account to create a user account on a computer.

   C. User accounts on Windows XP Home require a password.

   D. User accounts on Windows XP Professional use the user name and password they use to log on to a domain.

6. The Guest account in Windows XP Home gives unlimited access to individuals without an account on the computer. (True or False?)

7. Which of the following statements are NOT true? (Select all that apply.)

   A. You can change the picture associated with an account in Windows XP Professional.

   B. Changing your account password regularly helps keep your account secure.

   C. You can change the picture associated with an account in Windows XP Home.

   D. Only an administrator can change an account password.

8. Why should you log off your account when you're finished using the computer? (Select all that apply.)

   A. Log off so the computer is ready for the next user.

   B. Don't log off, just shut down the computer.

   C. Log off to prevent an unauthorized user from accessing your account or network.

   D. All of the above.

9. You can change how users log on or off their accounts in Windows XP Home by turning off the Welcome screen. (True or False?)

CHAPTER 12

NETWORKING WITH WINDOWS XP

CHAPTER OBJECTIVES:

Understanding networks

Browsing the network

Mapping a network drive

Connecting to a network printer

Sharing your files and printer with other users on the network

Changing access permissions to a shared folder

Specifying security options to a shared folder

Prerequisites

- **Know how to use the mouse to click, double-click, click and drag, and right-click.**
- **Know how to use menus, toolbars, and dialog boxes.**
- **Know how to view and navigate the contents of your computer (disk drives and folders).**
- **Know how to maintain and optimize your computer.**

A network is a group of computers that are connected so that they can share equipment and information. If you're using Windows XP you are almost certainly connected to a large network, because Microsoft was thinking of large business networks when it designed Windows XP. Computers running Windows 95 and 98 can also be connected to a network, but they don't have the built-in security features that Windows XP does.

Networking is an enormous topic—network engineers often spend at least a year and half studying for six tests that are every bit as hard as a CPA or bar exam. This chapter won't make you a Microsoft Certified System Professional, but it will explain how to perform several common networking tasks, such as how to browse the network, connect to a network printer, and share files and folders on your computer with other users on the network. We'll leave the more complicated networking tasks for your network administrator.

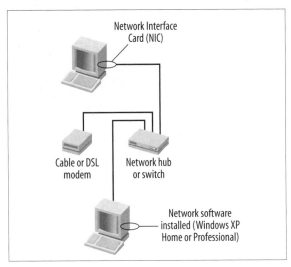

Figure 12-1. The basic components of a peer-to-peer network.

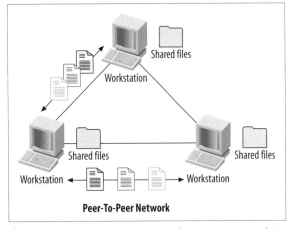

Figure 12-2. In a peer-to-peer network, everyone stores their files on their own computer. Anyone on the network can access files stored on any other computer.

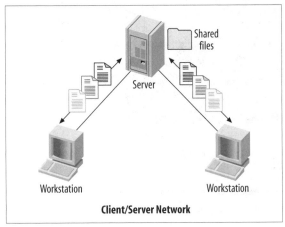

Figure 12-3. In a client/server network, everyone stores their files on a central computer called a server. Everyone on the network can access the files stored on the server.

OK, so what exactly *is* a network? A network is several computers, printers, and other devices that are connected together with cables or radio signals. This allows the computers to "talk" with each other and share information and resources (usually files and printers). Networks vary in size; they can be as small as two computers connected to each other by a cable, or they can span the entire globe—the Internet is actually the world's largest network.

So what are the benefits of networking? Plenty:

- **Share Information:** Networks allow you to share files and programs. Before networks, people had to save their files on floppy disks in order to exchange information. This wasted a lot of time—especially if the computers were located in opposite ends of the building!

- **Share Equipment:** Computers connected to a network can share equipment to reduce costs. For example, rather than buying a printer for each computer, everyone can share one central network printer.

- **Use Network Software:** Software designed for networks lets people send and receive electronic mail (e-mail) with other users on the network, schedule meetings with other users on the network, and share databases. When you're browsing the Web, you're actually using software designed for a network!

A Network can be distributed over a small or large area:

- **Local Area Networks (LAN):** A network that connects computers in the same geographic area or building, using cables. Local Area Networks are what most people think of when they think of a network—and what we'll be discussing throughout the chapter.

- **Wide Area Networks (WAN):** A network that connects computers across a large geographic area using telephone lines or satellites. The Internet is actually a huge Wide Area Network.

Local Area Networks (LANs) are subdivided into two types of network subcategories: peer-to-peer (or workgroups) and client/server (or domains), as shown in Figure 12-2 and Figure 12-3:

- **Peer-to-Peer Network:** In a peer-to-peer network, everyone stores their files on their own computer, and anyone on the network can access files stored on any other computer. Because you don't need any additional software (Windows XP includes peer-to-peer networking), peer-to-peer networking is an inexpensive way to connect computers in a small office or home. The disadvantages of a peer-to-peer network are that it doesn't offer as much security as client/server networks, and it can be difficult to find files that are stored on many different computers. Windows XP Home is designed for use in small home and office peer-to-peer networks.

- **Client/Server Network:** In a client/server network, everyone stores their files on a central computer called

a server. Everyone on the network can access the files stored on the server. Client/server networks are more secure, easier to administer, and much more powerful than peer-to-peer networks. That's why they are used to connect computers in most businesses. The disadvantages of client/server networks are that they require special, expensive software, such as Windows NT or NetWare, and they are more complicated to install and configure than peer-to-peer networks. Windows XP Professional is designed for use in larger client/server networks.

And, if that weren't enough, there are two basic ways that you can connect to a network:

- **Ethernet:** An Ethernet network lets you connect computers in the same geographic area or building using cables. Its high speed, reliability, and simplicity have made Ethernet easily the most popular way to connect computers and devices in a network.

- **Wireless or WiFi:** A wireless, or *WiFi* (stands for *wireless fidelity*) network lets you connect computers anywhere in your home or office without wires. A wireless network uses the same technology found in cordless phones and allows computers to "talk" to each other through radio waves.

QUICK REFERENCE

NETWORK BENEFITS:
- SHARE INFORMATION
- SHARE EQUIPMENT
- USE NETWORK SOFTWARE

NETWORK DISTRIBUTION:
- LOCAL AREA NETWORK (LAN)
- WIDE AREA NETWORK (WAN)

BASIC TYPES OF NETWORKS:
- PEER-TO-PEER
- CLIENT/SERVER

BASIC NETWORK CONNECTION TYPES:
- ETHERNET
- WIRELESS OR WIFI

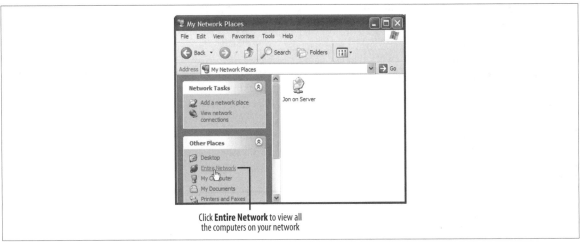

Figure 12-4. The My Network Places window gives you access to folders and files on your computers.

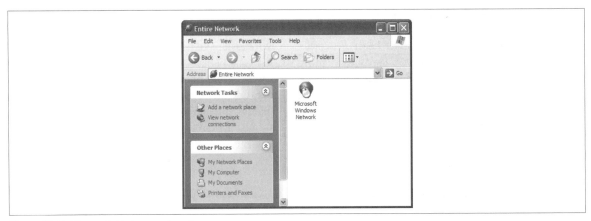

Figure 12-5. The available types networks.

Figure 12-6. The available domains and workgroups on your network.

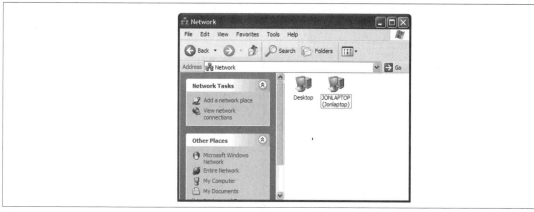

Figure 12-7. The computers connected to a network domain or workgroup.

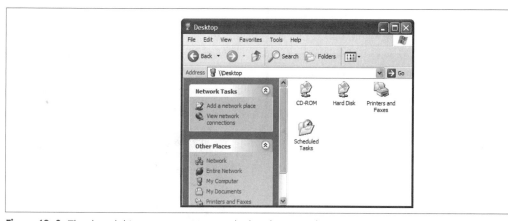

Figure 12-8. The shared drive on a computer attached to the network.

If your computer is connected to a network, you can easily browse through the shared folders and files on the network. The procedure for browsing the contents of the network is no different than browsing through the contents of your computer—double-click a folder or file to open it. You can also create, copy, move, rename, and delete files and folders on the network, just like you would on your computer's hard drive (if your network administrator has given you enough rights to the network, that is!). To browse the network, first we need to open *My Network Places*.

1 Click the Start button and select My Network Places from the menu.

My Network Places

The My Network Places window appears, displaying all the computers on the network. Obviously, your network has its own computers and resources, so your window will differ from the one shown in Figure 12-4.

2 Select the Entire Network task in the Other Places menu.

Windows XP displays all the types of networks to which your computer is connected, as shown in Figure 12-5. For example, your organization may have both a Novell network and a Microsoft network. If this weren't confusing enough, computers may be (and often are) connected by several different types of networks.

3 Double-click the network you want to browse.

Windows XP displays all of the network domains and workgroups to which your computer is connected, as shown in Figure 12-6. You can think of a network domain or workgroup as a neighborhood where computers reside. Network domains and workgroups are often organized by departments.

4 Double-click the network domain that contains the computer you want to browse.

Since most large organizations may have dozens—if not hundreds—of network domains and workgroups, you will need to know the name of the network domain or workgroup where the computer you want to browse resides. If you need guidance, ask your helpful network administrator.

When you double-click a network it displays all the computers connected to it, as shown in Figure 12-7.

5 Find and double-click the computer that contains the files or folders you want to use.

The computer's shared folders appear in the window, as shown in Figure 12-8 (although the folders you see will undoubtedly be different). You know what to do from here: double-click the folder you want to open—no different than in My Computer or Windows Explorer. If nothing appears in the window when you double-click a computer, either the computer doesn't have any shared folders or your network administrator hasn't given you the rights to view those shared folders.

If a shared folder is password protected, a password dialog box will appear when you double-click the folder. Simply type the password and click OK. If you want Windows to remember your password for the network folder, check the "Save this password in your password list" box—and you won't have to retype the password the next time you try to open the folder.

6 Find and double-click the shared drive or folder.

If you have the proper permission you will be able to view, open, and possibly modify and delete the files on the shared drive or folder.

QUICK REFERENCE

TO BROWSE THE NETWORK:

1. CLICK THE START BUTTON AND SELECT MY NETWORK PLACES FROM THE MENU.

2. SELECT THE ENTIRE NETWORK TASK IN THE OTHER PLACES MENU.

3. DOUBLE-CLICK THE TYPE OF NETWORK YOU WANT TO BROWSE.

4. DOUBLE-CLICK THE NETWORK DOMAIN THAT CONTAINS THE COMPUTER YOU WANT TO BROWSE.

5. FIND AND DOUBLE-CLICK THE COMPUTER THAT CONTAINS THE FILES OR FOLDERS YOU WANT TO USE.

6. FIND AND DOUBLE-CLICK THE SHARED DRIVE OR FOLDER.

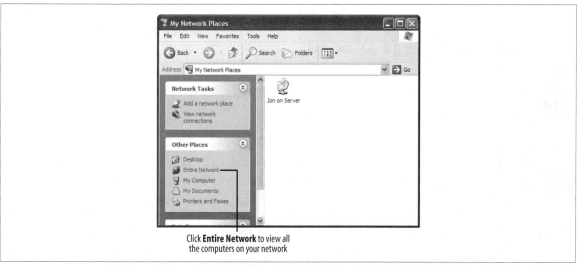

Figure 12-9. The My Network Places window displays all the computers on your network.

Figure 12-10. To map to a network drive, right-click the folder and select Map Network Drive from the shortcut menu.

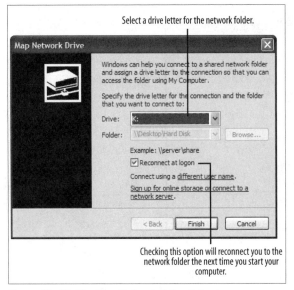

Select a drive letter for the network folder.

Checking this option will reconnect you to the network folder the next time you start your computer.

Figure 12-11. The Map Network Drive dialog box.

If you frequently access a specific network folder, you should consider *mapping* the network folder. When you *map* a network folder, you assign it a drive letter, like (G:), so that it appears as a drive in My Computer, Windows Explorer, and in your programs Open and Save dialog boxes. Once a network folder has been mapped and assigned a drive letter, you can open and access it just like any other drive on your computer—which is much faster than having to browse through the network again and again to find it. First you need to open the shared drive or folder you want to map…

**My Network
Places**

1 Click the Start button and select My Network Places from the menu.

The My Network Places window appears, displaying all the computers on the network, as shown in Figure 12-9.

2 Select the Entire Network task in the Other Places menu.

Windows XP displays all the types of networks to which your computer is connected. For example, your organization may have both a Novell network and a

Microsoft network. If this weren't confusing enough, often computer may be (and often are) connected by several different types of networks.

3 Double-click the type of network you want to browse.

Windows XP displays all the network domains and workgroups to which your computer is connected.

4 Double-click the network domain or workgroup that contains the computer to want to browse.

Since most large organizations may have dozens of network domains and workgroups, you will need to know the name of the network domain or workgroup where the computer you want to browse resides. Ask your helpful network administrator.

When you double-click a network icon it displays all the computers connected to the network.

5 Find and double-click the computer that contains the files or folders you want to use.

The computer's shared folders appear in the window, as shown in Figure 12-10 (although the folders you see will undoubtedly be different). You know what to do from here: double-click the folder you want to open—no different than in My Computer or Windows Explorer. If nothing appears in the window when you double-click a computer, it either means that computer doesn't have any shared folders or else your network administrator hasn't given you the rights to view those shared folders.

If a shared folder is password protected, a password dialog box will appear when you double-click the folder. Simply type the password and click OK. If you want Windows to remember your password for the network folder, click the "Save this password in your password list" check box—and you won't have to retype the password the next time you try to open the folder.

If you access the same network folder frequently, it makes sense to map it and assign it a drive letter, so you don't have to spend as much time finding and opening the folder every time. Here's how to map a network drive:

6 Right-click the network folder you want to map and select Map Network Drive from the shortcut menu.

The Map Network Drive dialog box appears, as shown in Figure 12-11. You have to assign a drive letter, such as H:, to the network folder. Clicking the Drive list arrow lets you select from those drive letters that aren't currently in use. Checking the "Reconnect at login" check box will re-map the network folder to its assigned drive letter whenever you start your computer. If the "Reconnect at login" check box is left blank, then the network folder will only be mapped to its assigned drive letter until you turn off your computer.

Once a network folder has been mapped, it appears as a drive in My Computer.

7 Select a drive letter from the Drive list, and check the Reconnect at login check box if you want to permanently map the network folder.

Decide you don't need to be mapped to a network folder anymore? Then here's how to disconnect a mapped network drive.

8 Right-click the network drive you want to disconnect, and select Disconnect Network Drive from the shortcut menu.

QUICK REFERENCE

TO MAP A NETWORK DRIVE:

1. CLICK THE START BUTTON AND SELECT MY NETWORK PLACES FROM THE MENU.

2. SELECT THE ENTIRE NETWORK TASK IN THE OTHER PLACES MENU AND FIND THE COMPUTER AND FOLDER YOU WANT TO MAP.

3. RIGHT-CLICK THE FOLDER AND SELECT MAP NETWORK DRIVE FROM THE SHORTCUT MENU.

4. SELECT A DRIVE LETTER FROM THE DRIVE LIST, AND CHECK THE RECONNECT AT LOGIN CHECK BOX IF YOU WANT TO PERMANENTLY MAP THE NETWORK FOLDER.

TO DISCONNECT A MAPPED NETWORK DRIVE:

• RIGHT-CLICK THE NETWORK DRIVE YOU WANT TO DISCONNECT, AND SELECT DISCONNECT NETWORK DRIVE FROM THE SHORTCUT MENU.

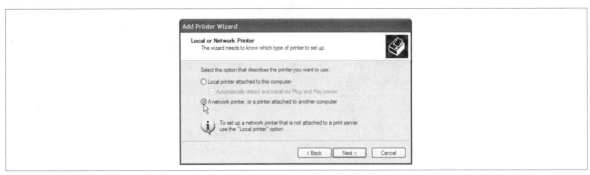

Figure 12-12. The Add Printer Wizard asks if you want to connect to a local or network printer.

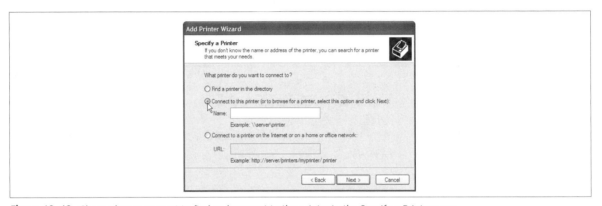

Figure 12-13. Choose how you want to find and connect to the printer in the Specify a Printer page.

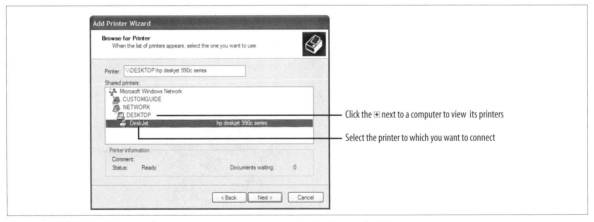

Click the ⊞ next to a computer to view its printers

Select the printer to which you want to connect

Figure 12-14. Select the network printer you want to connect to in the Browse for Printer page.

Connecting your computer to a network printer isn't much different from installing a local printer to your computer. In fact, if you already know how to install a local printer to your computer you can probably install a network printer without even having to look at this lesson. Still, here's how to do it if you want the step-by-step procedure.

1 Make sure you're logged on to the network.

Network Printer
Other ways to Start the Add Printer Wizard:
1. Click the Start button and select Printers and Faxes from the menu.
2. Click the Add a Printer task in the Printer Tasks menu.

Obviously, you won't be able to install a network printer if your computer isn't connected to the network.

2 Click the Start button and select Control Panel from the menu. Click the Printers and Other Hardware category.

The Printers and Other Hardware category appears.

3 Click the Add a printer task.

The first page of the Add Printer Wizard springs onto your screen.

4 Click Next.

The Add Printer Wizard may ask how the printer is connected to the computer: whether it's a local printer or a network printer.

5 Select A network printer or Local printer attached to this computer option and click Next to continue.

Next the Add Printer Wizard asks you how you want to find and connect to the network printer. You have several choices:

- **Find a printer in the directory:** If you're on a domain that uses Microsoft's Active Directory (chances are you're not) you can easily search the entire network for a specific printer.

- **Connect to this printer:** If you know the printer name and the computer or server name, you can enter it in the Network path or queue route box like this: \\Computer Name\Printer Name. More than likely you won't know the printer name and will have to move on to the next step and browse for the printer on the network. Since most networks don't use Microsoft's Active Directory yet, this is the option that you usually use to connect to a network printer.

- **Connect to a printer on the Internet or on a home or office network:** If you know a printer's URL and

if you have permission to use that printer, you can connect to a printer on the Internet by typing the printer name and the computer or server name like this: //Computer Name/Printer.

6 Click the Connect to this printer option and click Next.

The Browse for Printer page appears, as shown in Figure 12-14. First you will have to specify the network domain or workgroup where the network printer is located.

7 If necessary, click the + next to the desired network domain or workgroup to display its computers.

All the computers with shared printers on the network domain or workgroup should appear—all you have to do is select the computer and printer to which you want to connect.

8 Click the + next to the desired computer or server to display its printer(s), click the desired printer, and click Next.

Windows wants to know if you want to use the printer as your default printer.

9 Specify whether or not you want the selected network printer to be your default printer and click Next.

Windows XP correctly identifies the make and manufacturer of your printer. Move on to the next step to finish adding the network printer.

10 Click Finish.

Windows may ask you to insert the Windows XP CD-ROM or the printer driver software.

11 If prompted, insert the printer driver CD-ROM and click OK.

Windows copies the necessary files onto your computer.

That's it—you're connected to the network printer, which appears as an icon in the Printers folder.

QUICK REFERENCE

TO CONNECT TO A NETWORK PRINTER:

1. CLICK THE **START** BUTTON AND SELECT **CONTROL PANEL** FROM THE MENU. CLICK THE **PRINTERS AND OTHER HARDWARE** CATEGORY.

2. CLICK THE **ADD A PRINTER** TASK.

3. CLICK **NEXT**.

4. SELECT THE **A NETWORK PRINTER, OR A PRINTER ATTACHED TO ANOTHER COMPUTER** OPTION AND CLICK **NEXT**.

5. SELECT THE **CONNECT TO THIS PRINTER** OPTION AND CLICK **NEXT**.

6. CLICK THE + NEXT TO THE DESIRED NETWORK DOMAIN OR WORKGROUP.

7. CLICK THE + NEXT TO THE DESIRED COMPUTER OR SERVER, CLICK THE DESIRED PRINTER AND CLICK **NEXT**.

8. SPECIFY WHETHER YOU WANT TO USE THE PRINTER AS THE DEFAULT PRINTER AND ASSIGN A DIFFERENT NAME TO THE PRINTER IF YOU WANT. CLICK **NEXT**.

9. CLICK **FINISH**

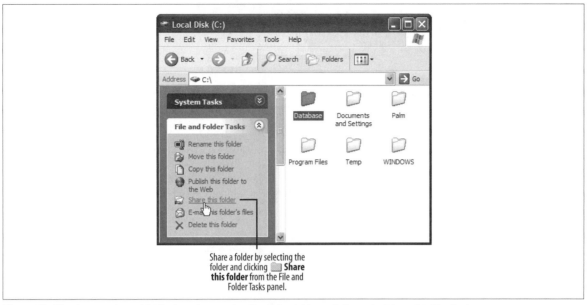

Share a folder by selecting the folder and clicking ▦ **Share this folder** from the File and Folder Tasks panel.

Figure 12-15. Share a selected folder by selecting the Share this folder task from the File and Folder Tasks menu.

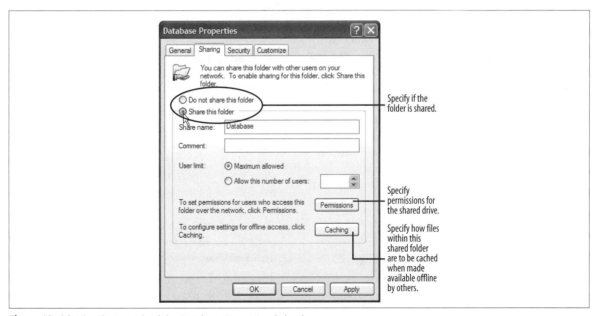

Specify if the folder is shared.

Specify permissions for the shared drive.

Specify how files within this shared folder are to be cached when made available offline by others.

Figure 12-16. The Sharing tab of the Database Properties dialog box.

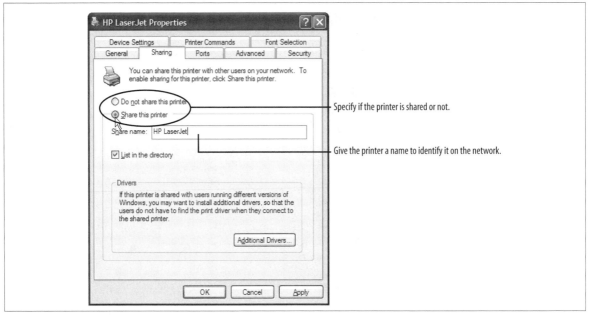

Figure 12-17. The Sharing tab of the Printer Properties dialog box.

Sharing enables other computers on the network to access the files and folders saved on your computer's hard drive, and a printer connected to your computer. You can specify exactly what information you want to share with people on the network and which users have permission to access that information. For example, you might want to share only a particular folder rather than the entire contents of your computer's hard drive. This lesson explains how to share your computer's files so other users can read and modify them. This lesson also explains how to share a printer, so other users can use it to print their files.

Your user account must have administrative privileges in order for you to share a folder. If you don't have administrative rights, have your network administrator log on for you.

1 Make sure that you are logged on to Windows XP with a user account that has administrative privileges.

Only user accounts with administrative rights can share folders on a computer—so you will need to make sure that you're logged on to Windows XP using the Administrator account or a user account with administrative privileges.

2 Click the Start button and select My Computer from the menu.

The My Computer window opens.

3 Find and select the drive or folder you want to share, and click the Share this folder task in the File and Folder Tasks menu.

Shared folder

Now you have the option of entering a new name for your shared folder.

4 Click the Share this folder option and, if you want, enter a new name for the shared folder in the Share Name text box.

Unless you specify otherwise, Windows uses the drive letter or folder name as the default share name.

5 Click OK.

A hand appears under the drive or folder, indicating it is being shared and is accessible to other users on the network (provided they have the proper permissions—more on that in a later lesson). To stop sharing a folder or drive, all you need to do is repeat Steps 2-5 and select the Not Shared option in Step 4.

Sharing a computer's printer so that other computers on the network can use it is not much different than sharing a drive or folder. Here's how to do it:

6 Click the Start button and select Printers and Faxes from the menu.

The Printers and Faxes window appears.

7 Select the printer you want to share and click the Share this printer task in the Printer Tasks menu.

Shared printer

The Sharing tab of the Printer Properties dialog box appears, as shown in Figure 12-17.

8 Click the Shared this printer option and, if you want, enter a name for the shared printer in the Share Name text box.

Unless you specify otherwise, Windows uses part of the printer's name as its default share name.

9 Click OK to share the printer.

A hand appears under the printer, indicating it is being shared and is accessible to other users on the network. To stop sharing a printer, all you need do to is repeat Step 6-9 and select the Not Shared option in Step 8.

QUICK REFERENCE

TO SHARE A DRIVE OR FOLDER:

1. MAKE SURE THAT YOU ARE LOGGED ON TO WINDOWS XP WITH A USER ACCOUNT THAT HAS ADMINISTRATIVE PRIVILEGES.

2. OPEN MY COMPUTER, FIND AND SELECT THE FOLDER YOU WANT TO SHARE AND CLICK THE SHARE THIS FOLDER TASK IN THE FILE AND FOLDER TASKS MENU.

3. CLICK THE SHARE THIS FOLDER OPTION AND, IF YOU WANT, CHANGE THE NAME FOR THE SHARED FOLDER IN THE SHARE NAME TEXT BOX.

4. (OPTIONAL) CLICK THE PERMISSIONS BUTTON AND SPECIFY ANY PERMISSIONS.

5. CLICK OK.

TO SHARE A PRINTER:

1. CLICK THE START BUTTON AND SELECT PRINTERS AND FAXES FROM THE MENU.

2. SELECT THE FOLDER YOU WANT TO SHARE AND CLICK THE SHARE THIS PRINTER TASK IN THE PRINTER TASKS MENU.

3. CLICK THE SHARE THIS PRINTER OPTION AND, IF YOU WANT, CHANGE THE NAME FOR THE SHARED PRINTER IN THE SHARE NAME TEXT BOX.

4. (OPTIONAL) CLICK THE PERMISSIONS BUTTON AND SPECIFY ANY PERMISSIONS

5. CLICK OK.

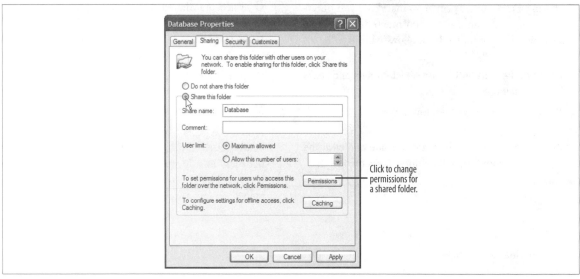

Figure 12-18. The Database Properties dialog box.

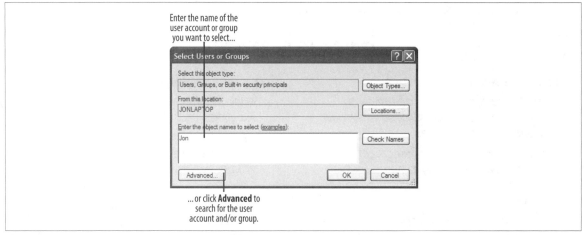

Figure 12-19. The Select Users or Groups dialog box.

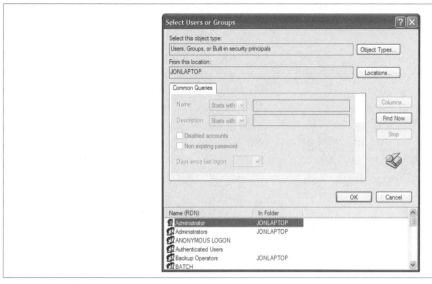

Figure 12-20. The Advanced Select Users or Groups dialog box.

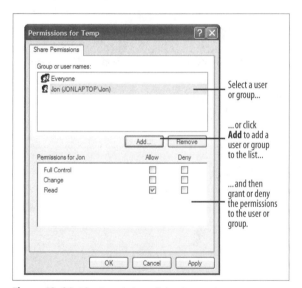

Select a user or group...

...or click **Add** to add a user or group to the list...

...and then grant or deny the permissions to the user or group.

Figure 12-21. The Permissions dialog box.

You can specify which particular users can access your shared folders and/or printer by granting or removing their permissions. This lesson explains how.

1 Make sure that you are logged on to Windows XP with a user account that has administrative privileges.

Your company may not allow you to log on to Windows XP as an administrator, in which case you will have to contact your company's real network adminis-

trator and ask them to change your permission settings for you.

2 Click the Start button and select My Computer from the menu.

The My Computer window opens.

3 Find and select the drive or folder you want to share and click the Share this folder task in the File and Folder Tasks menu.

The Properties dialog box appears, as shown in Figure 12-18.

NOTE *You must first share a folder or printer before you can change its permissions. See the lesson on "Sharing Your Files and Printers on the Network" to do this.*

4 Click Permissions.

The Permissions dialog box appears, as shown in Figure 12-21. Here you can specify who has access to the folder and the type of access they have (for shared folders).

First, select the user account or group to which you want to assign or deny permissions. If the user account or group isn't listed you will have to enter it—which can be a little tricky the first few times you try it. Here's how to select a user account or group.

5 If the user account or group you want to assign permissions to is listed, skip ahead to Step 7. Otherwise, click Add.

The Select Users or Groups dialog box appears, as shown in Figure 12-19. This is where you can enter the name of the user account or group that you want to grant or deny permission to the shared folder.

6 If you know the name of the user account(s) or group(s), enter it/them in the text box and click OK.

If you don't know the exact name of the user account(s) or group(s), click Advanced to open the Advanced Select Users or Groups dialog box (shown in Figure 12-20) and click Find Now to browse all available user accounts and groups. Select the user account(s) or group(s) and click OK, OK when you're finished.

Great! Now you can grant or deny permissions for the user account or group.

7 Select the group or user account whose permissions you want to modify and then check or uncheck the permissions you want to grant or deny. Repeat for all the groups and/or user accounts.

Refer to Table 12-1 for more information about the different types of access. Move on to the next step when you have specified the permissions for all the groups and/or user accounts.

8 Click OK, OK to close the remaining dialog boxes.

If you no longer want a user, group, or computer listed in the Permissions dialog box, you can remove them by selecting their name and clicking Remove.

Table 12-1. Types of access

Access Level	Description
Full Control	Users can open, create, change, move, and delete files in the folder, and may also be able to share folders and change permissions.
Change	Users can open, create, change, move, and delete files in the folder.
Read	Users can open but not change or delete files in the folder.
No Access	Users cannot see the shared folder.

QUICK REFERENCE

**TO CHANGE PERMISSIONS TO A SHARED
FOLDER OR PRINTER:**

1. MAKE SURE THAT YOU ARE LOGGED ON TO
   WINDOWS XP WITH A USER ACCOUNT THAT HAS
   ADMINISTRATIVE PRIVILEGES.

2. FIND AND SELECT THE DRIVE OR FOLDER YOU WANT
   TO SHARE AND CLICK SHARE THIS FOLDER FROM
   THE FILE AND FOLDER TASKS PANEL.

3. CLICK PERMISSIONS.

4. IF THE USER ACCOUNT OR GROUP YOU WANT TO
   ASSIGN PERMISSIONS TO IS LISTED, SKIP AHEAD
   TO STEP 7. OTHERWISE, CLICK ADD.

5. IF YOU KNOW THE NAME OF THE USER ACCOUNT(S)
   OR GROUP(S), ENTER IT/THEM IN THE TEXT BOX AND
   CLICK OK.

IF YOU DON'T KNOW THE EXACT NAME OF THE USER
ACCOUNT(S) OR GROUP(S), CLICK ADVANCED TO OPEN
THE ADVANCED SELECT USERS OR GROUPS DIALOG
BOX AND CLICK FIND NOW TO BROWSE ALL
AVAILABLE USER ACCOUNTS AND GROUPS. SELECT
THE USER ACCOUNT(S) OR GROUP(S) AND CLICK OK,
OK WHEN YOU'RE FINISHED.

1. REPEAT STEP 5 FOR EACH USER OR GROUP YOU
   WANT TO HAVE ACCESS. CLICK OK WHEN YOU'RE
   FINISHED.

2. SELECT THE GROUP OR USER ACCOUNT WHOSE
   PERMISSIONS YOU WANT TO MODIFY AND THEN
   CHECK OR UNCHECK THE PERMISSIONS YOU WANT
   TO GRANT OR DENY. REPEAT FOR ALL THE GROUPS
   AND/OR USER ACCOUNTS.

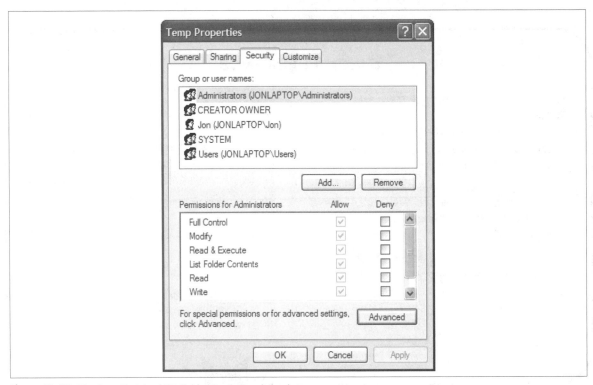

Figure 12-22. The Security tab of the Folder Properties dialog box.

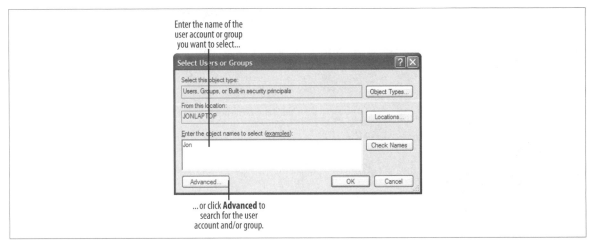

Figure 12-23. The Select Users or Groups dialog box.

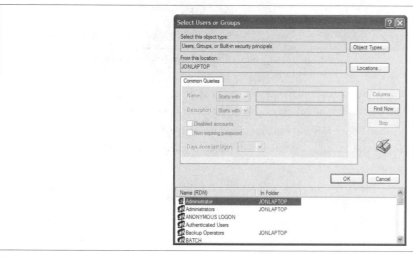

Figure 12-24. The Advanced Select Users or Groups dialog box.

Security and permissions to shared folders and printers can be a little confusing at first, so think of a computer running Windows XP as the Pentagon. That's right—the headquarters for the United States military. Visitors can walk right into the Pentagon's lobby, and there are even tours of low security areas of the Pentagon. But to work in most areas of the Pentagon, you need a security clearance. And to gain access to the top-secret rooms where the government conceals the wreckage of crashed UFOs and files on who really shot president Kennedy, you need top secret security clearance.

Security clearance levels in Windows XP are called *permissions*. By assigning permissions, you are restricting what a user can and can't do.

1 Make sure that you are logged on to Windows XP with a user account that has administrative privileges.

Only user accounts with administrative rights can change a folder's security options.

2 Select the drive or folder you want to share, click the Share this folder task in the File and Folder Tasks menu, and click the Security tab.

The Security tab of the Folder Properties dialog box appears, as shown in Figure 12-22.

3 If the user account or group you want to assign permissions to is listed, skip ahead to Step 5. Otherwise, click Add.

The Select Users or Groups dialog box appears, as shown in Figure 12-23. This is where you can enter the name of the user account or group that you want to grant or deny permission to the shared folder.

4 If you know the name of the user account(s) or group(s), enter it/them in the text box and click OK.If you don't know the exact name of the user account(s) or group(s), click Advanced to open the Advanced Select Users or Groups dialog box (shown in Figure 12-24) and click Find Now to browse all available user accounts and groups. Select the user account(s) or group(s) and click OK, OK when you're finished.

Great! Now you can grant or deny permissions for the user account or group.

5 Select the group or user account whose permissions you want to modify and then check or uncheck the permissions you want to grant or deny. Repeat for all the groups and/or user accounts.

Refer to Table 12-2 for more information about the different types of permissions. Move on to the next step when you have specified the permissions for all the groups and/or user account.

6 Click OK to close the Folder Properties dialog box.

Table 12-2. Types of security permissions

Permission	Description
Full Control	**Users May:** View, open, create, and modify files, run programs (executables), delete files and folders, and change the folder's permissions.
Modify	**Users May:** View, open, create, and modify files, and run programs (executables). **Users May Not:** Delete files and folders or change the folder's permissions.
Read & Execute	**Users May:** View and open files and run programs (executables). **Users May Not:** Create, modify, or delete files or folders or change the folder's permissions.
List Folder Contents	**Users May:** View files. **Users May Not:** Open, create, modify, or delete files or folders, run programs (executables), or change the folder's permissions.
Read	**Users May:** View and open files. **Users May Not:** Open, create, modify, or delete files or folders, run programs (executables), or change the folder's permissions.
Write	**Users May:** Create and modify files and folders. **Users May Not:** View, open or delete files or folders, run programs (executables), or change the folder's permissions.
Special Permissions	Varies, depending on user specified options.

QUICK REFERENCE

TO CHANGE SECURITY PERMISSIONS:

1. MAKE SURE THAT YOU ARE LOGGED ON TO WINDOWS XP WITH A USER ACCOUNT THAT HAS ADMINISTRATIVE PRIVILEGES.

2. FIND AND SELECT THE DRIVE OR FOLDER YOU WANT TO SHARE, CLICK THE SHARE THIS FOLDER TASK IN THE FILE AND FOLDER TASKS MENU, AND CLICK THE SECURITY TAB.

3. IF THE USER ACCOUNT OR GROUP YOU WANT TO ASSIGN PERMISSIONS TO IS LISTED, SKIP AHEAD TO STEP 6. OTHERWISE, CLICK ADD.

4. IF YOU KNOW THE NAME OF THE USER ACCOUNT(S) OR GROUP(S), ENTER IT/THEM IN THE TEXT BOX AND CLICK OK.

IF YOU DON'T KNOW THE EXACT NAME OF THE USER ACCOUNT(S) OR GROUP(S), CLICK ADVANCED TO OPEN THE ADVANCED SELECT USERS OR GROUPS DIALOG BOX AND CLICK FIND NOW TO BROWSE ALL AVAILABLE USER ACCOUNTS AND GROUPS. SELECT THE USER ACCOUNT(S) OR GROUP(S) AND CLICK OK, OK WHEN YOU'RE FINISHED.

1. REPEAT STEP 4 FOR EACH USER OR GROUP YOU WANT TO HAVE ACCESS. CLICK OK WHEN YOU'RE FINISHED.

2. SELECT THE GROUP OR USER ACCOUNT WHOSE PERMISSIONS YOU WANT TO MODIFY AND THEN CHECK OR UNCHECK THE PERMISSIONS YOU WANT TO GRANT OR DENY. REPEAT FOR ALL THE GROUPS AND/OR USER ACCOUNTS.

Chapter Twelve Review

Lesson Summary

Introduction to Networks

A network allows all connected users to share information, equipment, and software.

In a peer-to-peer network, everyone stores their files on their own computer. Anyone on the network can access files stored on any other computer.

In a client/server network, everyone stores their files on a central computer called a server. Everyone on the network can access the files stored on the server.

To connect computers to a network you need: a network interface card, cables, a network operating system, and a hub (depending on the type of cables you're using).

Browsing the Network

To Browse the Network: Click the Start button and select My Network Places from the menu. Select the Entire Network task in the Other Places menu, and double-click the type of network you want to browse. Double-click the network domain that contains the computer you want to browse, then find and double-click the computer that contains the files or folders you want to use. Find and double-click the shared drive or folder.

Mapping a Network Drive

To Map a Network Drive: Click the Start button and select My Network Places from the menu. Click the Entire Network task in the Other Places menu and find the computer and folder you want to map. Right-click the folder and select Map Network Drive from the shortcut menu. Select a drive letter from the Drive list, and check the Reconnect at login check box if you want to permanently map the network folder.

To Disconnect a Mapped Network Drive: Right-click the network drive you want to disconnect from and select Disconnect Network Drive from the shortcut menu.

Connecting to a Network Printer

First make sure you are logged on to the network. Click the Start button and select Control Panel from the menu. Click the Printers and Other Hardware category. Click the Add a printer task and click Next. Select the A network printer, or a printer attached to another computer option and click Next. Select the Connect to this printer option and click Next. Click the + next to the desired network domain or workgroup. Click the + next to the desired computer or server and click Next. Specify whether you want to use the printer as the default printer and assign a different name to the printer if you want. Click Next and click Finish.

Sharing Your Files and Printer on the Network

When you share a folder or printer on your computer, you allow other computers on the network to use it.

To Share a Drive or Folder: Make sure that you are logged on to Windows XP with a user account that has administrative privileges. Open My Computer, find and select the folder you want to share, and click the Share this folder task from the File and Folder Tasks menu. Click the Shared this folder option and, if you want, change the name for the shared folder in the Share Name box. (Optional) Click the Permissions button and specify any permissions. Click OK.

To Share a Printer: Click the Start button and select Printers and Faxes from the menu. Select the folder you want to share and click the Share this printer task in the Printer Tasks menu. Click the Shared this printer option and, if you want, change the name for the shared printer in the Share Name text box. (Optional) Click the Permissions button and specify any permissions, then click OK.

Changing Access Permissions to a Shared Folder

By changing permissions to a shared folder or printer you determine which users have access to the shared folder or printer and what kind of access they have.

To Change Permissions to a Shared Folder or Printer: Make sure that you are logged on to Windows XP with a user account that has administrative privileges. Find and select the drive or folder you want to share and click the Share this folder task in the File and Folder Tasks menu. Click Permissions to open the Permissions dialog box. If the user account or group you want to assign permissions to is listed, select the group or user account whose permissions you want to modify and then check or uncheck the permissions you want to grant or deny.

If the user account or group you want to assign permissions to isn't listed, click Add. If you don't know the exact name of the user account(s) or group(s), click Advanced to open the Advanced Select Users or Groups dialog box and click Find Now to browse all available user accounts and groups. Select the user account(s) or group(s) and click OK, OK when you're finished.

Repeat for all the groups and/or user accounts.

There are several types of access:

- **No Access**

  Users cannot see the shared folder.

- **Read**

  Users can open but not change or delete files in the folder.

- **Change**

  Users can open, create, change, move, and delete files in the folder.

- **Full Control**

  Users can open, create, change, move, and delete files in the folder, and mayalso be able to share folders and change permissions.

Specifying Security Options to a Shared Folder

To Change Security Permissions: Make sure that you are logged on to Windows XP with a user account that has administrative privileges. Find and select the drive or folder you want to share, click the Share this folder task in the File and Folder Tasks menu, and click the Security tab. If the user account or group you want to assign permissions to is listed, select the group or user account whose permissions you want to modify and then check or uncheck the permissions you want to grant or deny.

If the user account or group you want to assign permissions to isn't listed, click Add. If you don't know the exact name of the user account(s) or group(s) click Advanced to open the Advanced Select Users or Groups dialog box and click Find Now to browse all available user accounts and groups. Select the user account(s) or group(s) and click OK, OK when you're finished.

Repeat for all the groups and/or user accounts.

Quiz

1. A large corporation would probably use a peer-to-peer network as its network. (True or False?)

2. What are the benefits of networking? (Select all that apply).

   A. A network allows you to share information, such as files and folders.

   B. A network allows you to share equipment, such as printers.

   C. A network allows you to use software designed for networks, such as e-mail and multi-user databases.

   D. A network allows you to share electricity and conserve power.

3. In a peer-to-peer network, everyone stores their files on their own computer. (True or False?)

4. You plug your new computer into the office network, double-click the My Network Places to browse the network, but there's nothing there! What could be wrong? (Select all that apply).

   A. The Workgroup name in the Network dialog box (found by right-clicking My Network Places and clicking the Identification tab) is incorrect.

   B. Your computer's voltage output is too high.

   C. Your computer doesn't have the right network protocol installed.

   D. Who cares? Give the network administrator a call—it's their job to fix these kinds of problems!

5. In order to change access permissions for a shared folder, you must be logged on to Windows XP with a user account that has administrative privileges. (True or False?)

Homework

1. Open My Network Places.

2. Browse the contents of the shared folders on the computers connected to the network.

3. Map a folder on the network as a network drive—don't check the Reconnect at login option.

4. Open the Network dialog box by right-clicking the My Network Places icon and selecting Properties from the shortcut menu. Click the Identification tab to see what the names of your computer and network are. Close the dialog box when you're finished.

Quiz Answers

1. False. Larger organizations almost always use a Client/Server network.

2. A, B, and C. Networking has nothing to do whatsoever with electrical consumption.

3. True. In a peer-to-peer network, everyone stores their files on their own computer.

4. A and C. You should right-click My Network Places and see if your computer is using the same network protocol as everyone else and if the workgroup name is correct.

5. True. Only user accounts with administrative rights can change a folder's access permissions.

CHAPTER 13

SETTING UP A NETWORK

CHAPTER OBJECTIVES:

A look at common network hardware

Understand Ethernet and wireless networks

Installing Ethernet and wireless networks

Connecting to a wireless network

Troubleshooting a network

Installing a network card

Managing network protocols and components

Understanding and configuring TCP/IP

Prerequisites

- **A good understanding of Microsoft Windows XP.**
- **Know how to view and navigate the contents of your computer (disk drives and folders).**
- **Know how to install and work with hardware devices.**

First, a disclaimer and a warning: if your computer is connected to a large client/server network, you should skip most of this chapter, with the possible exception of how to connect to a wireless, or WiFi, network. Your network is probably a lot more complicated than what is discussed in the other lessons. Leave the networking to your company's network administrator or computer guru.

If you have two or three computers at home or in a small office that you want to connect to share files, printers, and Internet connection, read on. This chapter will introduce you to the fundamentals of networking. You won't be a certified network engineer after you finish this chapter, but you will be able to create a small peer-to-peer network that connects the two or three computers at your office or home.

This chapter covers both Ethernet and newer wireless (WiFi) types of networks. You'll learn how to connect to both types of networks and what to do if you're having problem getting connected. You'll also learn the fundamentals of networking: the terms 802.11B, WEP, and DHCP, and TCP/IP probably mean nothing to you now, but you'll have a good understanding of these terms and more by the time you've finished this chapter.

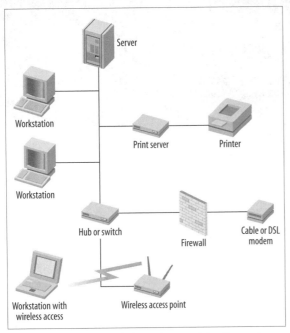

Figure 13-1. The network shown here contains the most common components on a small network.

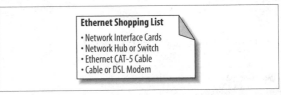

Ethernet Shopping List
• Network Interface Cards
• Network Hub or Switch
• Ethernet CAT-5 Cable
• Cable or DSL Modem

Figure 13-2. What you'll need to set up a small Ethernet network.

WiFi Shopping List
• WiFi Network Cards
• WiFi Access Point or Router
• Cable or DSL Modem

Figure 13-3. What you'll need to set up a small wireless or WiFi network.

So you've decided you want to set up a small home network to share your printer, files, and Internet access? Great—let's go shopping! The biggest networking decision you will have to make is if you want an Ethernet-based network or a wireless (WiFi) one. Both have their own set of pros and cons, which we'll cover in detail a little later. This lesson will give you a broad overview of the most common network devices and terms that you may come across.

Table 13-1. Common home network hardware devices

Network Device	Description
Workstation	Workstations are simply the computers that are connected to the network that everyone uses.
Server	A server is a central computer where users on the network can save their files and information. Servers are dedicated to network use and are normally not used to run applications or browse the Internet—and therefore you normally won't find a server in most home networks!
Cable or DSL Modem	A modem connects computers to the Internet through an existing phone line or cable connection. Cable modems and DSL modems are both very fast and can connect entire networks to the Internet.

Table 13-1. Common home network hardware devices (Continued)

Network Device	Description
 Firewall	A firewall is a system that prevents unauthorized access to or from a network. Firewalls can be hardware or software based, or a combination of both. Firewalls are often built-in to other products; for example, many cable or DSL modems may come with their own built-in firewall. Windows XP also comes with a software-based firewall.
 Hub or Switch	A hub is a device where all the cables on a network connect, similar to an electrical surge protector. A switch is an "intelligent hub" and manages network traffic, ensuring that information gets to the correct destination.
 Ethernet Cable	An Ethernet cable is the wire that physically connects the computers, printers, and other equipment on a network. When you buy an Ethernet cable make sure that it's CAT-5.
 PCI Desktop Network Adapter	A network interface card (NIC) is a device that physically connects each computer to the network and allows your computer to "talk" to other computers and devices on the network. Most desktop computers already have a built-in network adapter, but if yours doesn't you can install a PCI network adapter.
 PCMCIA Notebook Network Adapter	A network interface card (NIC) is a device that physically connects each computer to the network and allows your computer to "talk" to other computers and devices on the network. Most notebook computers already have a built-in network adapter, but if yours doesn't, you can install a PCMCIA network adapter.
 Print Server	A print server lets you connect a printer directly to a network instead of a computer so that everyone on the network can use it.
 Wireless Access Point	A wireless access point normally plugs into a wired Ethernet network and acts as the network's "radio station," broadcasting and receiving information to WiFi-enabled computers and devices on the network. Most wireless access points create a 100-foot diameter *hotspot* where computers can connect to the wireless network.
 Wireless Router	Very useful if you are setting up a wireless network from scratch, a wireless router is a single device that contains: 1) A port to connect to a cable or DSL modem, 2) a firewall, 3) an Ethernet hub, 4) a router, and of course, 5) a wireless access point.

Table 13-1. Common home network hardware devices (Continued)

Network Device	Description
PCI Desktop WiFi Adapter	Although desktop computers usually come with a built-in Ethernet card, they almost never come with built-in WiFi capability, so you'll almost certainly have to buy and install a PCI WiFi adapter if you want to connect a desktop computer to a wireless network.
PCMCIA Notebook WiFi Adpater	Many notebook computers already have a built-in WiFi adapter, but if yours doesn't you can install a PCMCIA WiFi adapter.
WiFi Print Server	A WiFi print server lets you connect a printer directly to a network without cables so that everyone on the network can use it.

Photos courtesy of LinkSys, a Division of Cisco Systems, Inc.

QUICK REFERENCE

HARDWARE REQUIREMENTS FOR AN ETHERNET NETWORK:

- NETWORK INTERFACE CARDS
- NETWORK HUB OR SWITCH
- ETHERNET CAT-5 CABLE
- CABLE OR DSL MODEM

REQUIREMENTS FOR AN WIRELESS OR WIFI NETWORK:

- WIFI NETWORK CARDS
- WIRELESS ACCESS POINT OR ROUTER
- CABLE OR DSL MODEM

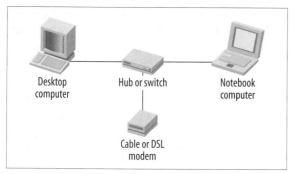

Figure 13-4. A diagram of a very simple Ethernet network.

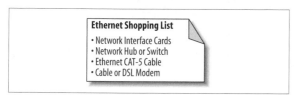

Figure 13-5. What you'll need to set up an Ethernet network.

Ethernet Shopping List
- Network Interface Cards
- Network Hub or Switch
- Ethernet CAT-5 Cable
- Cable or DSL Modem

A hub or switch connects all
the computers and devices on
a network.

Developed in the early 1970s (yes, it's really that old!), Ethernet is one of the most simple, reliable, and long-lived networking protocols ever designed. Its high speed, reliability, and simplicity have made Ethernet easily the most common and popular way to connect computers and devices in a network.

To get an idea of how Ethernet works, imagine several people trying to talk in an unmediated meeting. There isn't a schedule of when each person can get a chance to speak; people can simply stand up and talk whenever there is silence in the room. And, if two or more people stand up and talk at the same time, a *collision* occurs. When that happens, both parties sit back down for a very brief, random amount of time, then one of them will stand up and try talking again—hopefully without any interruptions or collisions this time. And, obviously the number of collisions on a network will increase as more computers and network traffic are added. (An Ethernet *switch* can greatly reduce the number of collisions on an Ethernet network by intelligently managing network traffic.)

Here are some of the basic pros and cons of going with an Ethernet network:

A network PCMCIA adapter for
a notebook computer

Ethernet Advantages

- **Reliability:** Ethernet has been around for a long, long time and nothing beats it for its dependability.

A network PCI adapter for
a desktop computer

- **Support:** Most computers—desktops and laptops alike—already have an Ethernet card built right into them!

- **Speed:** Ethernet is fast; most Ethernet networks can transfer information at up to 100 Mbps—usually more than twice as fast as the best wireless networks. And the new Gigabit Ethernet standard can handle a jaw-dropping 1,000 Mbps of network traffic.

- **Security:** Because it doesn't broadcast network information over the airwaves like WiFi, Ethernet is theoretically more secure—someone would have to tap into the network's lines in order to access it (something called the Internet).

Ethernet Disadvantages

- **Wires, wires, wires:** The computers in an Ethernet network must be physically connected by cables that resemble a fat telephone cord. It's not a big deal if you want to connect two computers that are sitting right next to each other, but it is a pain to run all that Ethernet cable if you want to connect a computer in your office upstairs with another computer in the basement.

What You Need to Create an Ethernet Network

Besides the rather obvious and most important part of the network, which are the actual computers, you'll need a few things to create a small Ethernet network, including:

- **Network Hub or Switch:** A hub is a device where all the cables on a network connect, similar to an electrical surge protector. A switch is an "intelligent hub" that manages network traffic, ensuring that information gets to the correct destination.

- **Ethernet Cable:** An Ethernet cable is the wire that physically connects the computers, printers, and other equipment on a network. When you buy an Ethernet cable make sure that it's CAT-5.

- **Ethernet Network Interface Cards:** A network interface card (NIC) is a device that physically connects each computer to the network and allows your computer to talk to other computers and devices on the network. Most computers already come with a network adapter built-in, but if yours doesn't you can install one; a PCI network adapter for desktops or a PCMCIA network card adapter for laptops.

- **Cable Modem or DSL Modem (Optional):** A modem connects computers to the Internet through an existing phone line or cable connection. Cable modems and DSL modems are both very fast and can connect all the computers in a home or small office network to the Internet. If you subscribe to a high-speed Internet service they will almost certainly set up the cable modem or DSL modem for you.

Ethernet devices are available in a number of speeds (although the vast majority uses the 100 Base-T standard). The following table describes common Ethernet speeds.

Table 13-2. Ethernet speeds

Standard	Speed	Description
10 Base-T	10 Mbps	Ten years ago, 10 Base-T was the standard speed of most Ethernet networks, but it's all but obsolete now. You may still find 10 Base-T Ethernet on older network devices, or on devices that simply don't require any more bandwidth, like a cable or DSL modem.
100 Base-T (Fast Ethernet)	100 Mbps	100 Base-T Ethernet is by far the most common Ethernet standard in use. It's fast—ten times faster than 10 Base-T, yet it can still communicate with 10 Base-T network devices; at only 10 Mbps, however.
Gigabit Ethernet	1,000 Mbps	Gigabit Ethernet is a new Ethernet standard that works just like 10 Base-T Ethernet, only ten times faster. Gigabit Ethernet can still talk to 100 Base-T and even 10 Base-T network devices. Because it's so new, Gigabit Ethernet devices are still quite expensive.

QUICK REFERENCE

ETHERNET ADVANTAGES:

- RELIABILITY
- WIDELY SUPPORTED
- SPEED
- SECURITY

ETHERNET DISADVANTAGES

- WIRING CAN BE DIFFICULT TO SET UP.

COMMON ETHERNET SPEEDS

- 10 MBPS (10 BASE-T)
- 100 MBPS (100 BASE-T)
- 1,000 MBPS (GIGABIT)

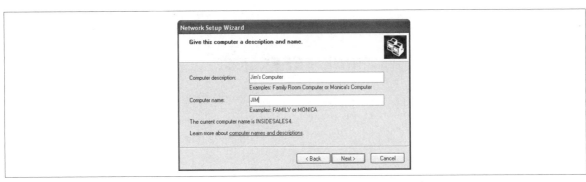

Figure 13-6. You have to give your computer a name and description to connect to a network.

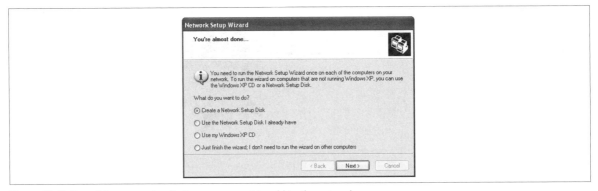

Figure 13-7. Remaining computers that you may want to add to the network.

So you want to network the two or three computers at the office or at home. Good for you—networking your computers is easier than you might think. In order to network your computers, you need to obtain the proper hardware: Ethernet network cards (if your computers don't already have them), Ethernet cables, and a network hub or switch. You can actually buy networking start-up kits that contain all these items, which can be a lot easier than buying everything separately.

TIP   *Most new computers come with network cards already installed.*

1   If necessary, install the network cards in all the computers you want to connect to the network.

You're going to have to follow the instructions that came with the network card here. To install a network card, you have to open your computer, find an empty expansion slot, and insert the network card into that slot.

2   Plug the Ethernet cables into each computer's network card and into the hub or switch.

Now that the hardware components of your Ethernet network are ready, you'll have to configure Windows XP's networking settings.

3   Turn on your computer and connect to the Internet. If Windows XP automatically detects the network card, follow the onscreen instructions.

Windows will automatically detect and install your network card if it is plug-and-play compliant. Make sure you have the software that came with the network card handy—Windows will probably ask you for it.

4   If Windows doesn't detect your network card, see Lesson 13-10: *Installing a Network Card.*

Once your network hardware is installed, connected, and working properly you will have to run the Network Setup Wizard on *every* computer in the network.

NOTE   *Windows XP works fine on a network with computers that have older versions of Windows (Windows 98/ME/NT/2000) installed.*

5 Click the Start button and select Control Panel from the menu. Click the Network and Internet Connections category and click the Network Setup Wizard.

The Network Setup Wizard appears.

6 Click Next, Next to skip past the first two pages of the Network Wizard.

First you need to tell Windows how your computer is connected to the Internet.

7 Select the appropriate Internet connection method (click the View an example link if you're not sure) and click Next.

Next, you need to give your computer a name in order to identify it on the network.

NOTE *If you have an existing network connection that is simply disconnected, Windows XP will inform you of this. Make sure your network cables are plugged in and click Next.*

8 Enter the Computer description and Computer name and click Next.

Your computer name must be unique, can contain up to 15 characters, and cannot include blank spaces.

Next, you need to identify the network to which you want to connect.

9 Enter the Workgroup name and click Next.

Just like the computer name, the workgroup name can contain up to 15 characters. Unlike the computer name, the workgroup name must be the same for all the computers on the network. So if you type "Network" in the workgroup box in one computer, make sure you type "Network" for any other computers attached to the network—otherwise the computers won't be able to see each other.

Now specify whether you want to give other computers on the network the ability to access your computer's files and/or printer.

10 Specify whether you want to share your computer's files and printer then click Next.

Time to review all your network settings…

11 Review your network settings and click Next.

The Network Setup Wizard does its magic and connects your computer to the network. You will have to run the Network Setup Wizard on each computer you want to add to your network, so the last page of the Wizard relates to how you want to deal with the other computers. You have a few options, mostly concerning whether or not any of the remaining network computers are using an earlier version of Windows (98/ME/NT/2000).

- **Create a Network Setup Disk:** Select this option if the next computer you want to add to the network uses an earlier version of Microsoft Windows.

- **Use the Network Setup Disk I already have:** Select this option if the next computer you want to add uses an earlier version of Microsoft Windows *and* if you have already created a Network Setup Disk for the computer.

- **Use my Windows XP CD:** You can also use the Windows XP CD-ROM to add computers using older versions of Microsoft Windows to the network.

- **Just finish the Wizard:** Select this option if all the remaining computers on the network use Windows XP (the most common option).

12 Select one of the options, depending on the Windows version installed on the *next* computer that you want to run the Network Setup Wizard on.

Finally, you'll have to run the Network Setup Wizard on the remaining network computers.

13 Repeat this process on the remaining network computers. If the computer uses an earlier version of Windows, use the Network Setup Disk or Windows XP CD to connect it to the network.

QUICK REFERENCE

TO INSTALL A SMALL HOME ETHERNET NETWORK:

1. ENSURE THAT THE NETWORK INTERFACE CARDS ARE INSTALLED AND WORKING IN ALL COMPUTERS BEING ADDED TO THE NETWORK.

2. CONNECT THE COMPUTERS TO THE HUB OR SWITCH WITH AN ETHERNET CABLE.

3. CLICK THE START BUTTON AND SELECT CONTROL PANEL FROM THE MENU.

4. CLICK THE NETWORK AND INTERNET CONNECTIONS CATEGORY AND CLICK THE NETWORK SETUP WIZARD.

5. CLICK NEXT, NEXT.

6. SELECT THE APPROPRIATE INTERNET CONNECTION AND CLICK NEXT.

7. CLICK NEXT, NEXT.

8. ENTER THE COMPUTER DESCRIPTION AND COMPUTER NAME AND CLICK NEXT.

9. ENTER THE WORKGROUP NAME AND CLICK NEXT.

10. REVIEW YOUR NETWORK SETTINGS AND CLICK NEXT.

11. SELECT ONE OF THE OPTIONS, DEPENDING ON THE WINDOWS VERSION INSTALLED ON THE NEXT COMPUTER.

12. REPEAT THIS PROCESS ON ALL REMAINING COMPUTERS IN THE NETWORK.

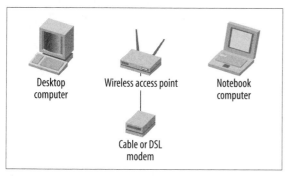

Figure 13-8. A diagram of a very simple wireless or WiFi network.

WiFi Shopping List

• WiFi Network Cards

• Wireless Access Point or Router

• Cable or DSL modem

Figure 13-9. Here's what you'll need to set up a WiFi network.

One of the hottest new technologies in the computer world is wireless networking or *WiFi*, which lets you connect computers without any wires. Wireless networks allow computers to "talk" to each other by broadcasting and receiving radio waves. Wireless networks are often simply part of a larger, Ethernet network.

Wireless router and access points

Of course, WiFi networking has its own set of pros and cons:

Wireless Networking Advantages

• **Simplicity:** Wireless networks are often very simple to set up because there aren't any messy wires involved.

• **Public Availability:** If you have a laptop with WiFi capability you can browse the Internet and check your

e-mail from thousands of wireless hotspots in coffee shops, airports, and hotels.

A wireless network (WiFi) PCMCIA adapter for a notebook computer

• **Convenience:** Wireless networks are downright cool—nothing is more amazing than browsing the Web on your laptop while you're sitting in the living room in front of the television or outside on the porch.

Wireless Networking Disadvantages

A wireless network (WiFi) PCMCIA adapter for a desktop computer

• **Security:** …or lack thereof. WiFi broadcasts information just like a radio transmitter, so it can be easy for an unauthorized computer to listen in and gain access to your network. There are a number of ways to secure a wireless network; the problem is that many people simply don't know how to do it.

• **Interference:** A wireless network shares the same crowded frequency as other wireless networks—and cordless phones too! All those devices can cause a lot of interference and as a result many wireless networks are quite unreliable.

• **Hotspots and Access** Points

You can find wireless network *hotspots* that let you browse the Internet and check your e-mail in many places outside the home or office. A hotspot is a place where you can connect to a wireless network. There are many wireless hotspots now available in such places as restaurants, hotels, coffee shops and airports.

Wireless Security

Wireless network hotspots can be open or secure. If a hotspot is open, then anyone with a wireless network card can access the hotspot. If the hotspot is secure, then the user will usually need to know the *WEP* key to connect to it. WEP stands for Wired Equivalent Privacy, and it is a way to encrypt the information that a wireless network sends through the air. There are two variations of WEP: 64-bit encryption (really 40-bit) and 128-bit encryption (really 104-bit). 40-bit encryption was the original standard but it was easily broken. 128-bit encryption is more secure and is what most wireless networks use.

What You Need to Add a Wireless Hotspot to an Existing Network

If you already have several computers connected by an Ethernet network you can easily add a WiFi hotspot to the mix. Here's what you'll need:

- **Wireless Access Point:** A wireless access point normally plugs into a wired Ethernet network and acts as the network's "radio station", broadcasting and receiving information to and from WiFi-enabled computers and devices on the network. Try to get an access point that uses the 802.11g wireless standard, described in Table 13-3.
- **Wireless Network (WiFi) Cards:** Any computers you want to connect to a wireless network must have a wireless network or WiFi card. WiFi is already built in to many newer laptops. If your laptop doesn't have WiFi you can buy a PCMCIA card or an external USB port adapter. For desktop computers, you'll need a PCI

card that you install inside the machine, or an external USB port adapter. Try to get cards that use the 802.11g wireless standard, described in Table 13-3.

In a typical home or office, your new hotspot will cover about 100 feet in all directions, although walls and floors do dramatically reduce this range.

What You Need to Create a Wireless Network from Scratch

Even if you're starting at the very beginning, there's no need to get discouraged. Here's what you'll need:

- **Wireless Access Point or Wireless Router:** If you're building a network from scratch you will probably want to use a wireless router instead of a wireless access point. A wireless router is a single device that contains: 1) A port to connect to a cable or DSL modem, 2) a firewall, 3) an Ethernet hub, 4) a router, and of course, 5) a wireless access point.
- **Wireless Network (WiFi) Cards:** Once again, any computers you want to connect to a wireless network must have WiFi networking cards or adapters installed.
- **Cable Modem or DSL Modem (Optional):** A modem connects computers to the Internet through an existing phone line or cable connection. Cable modems and DSL modems are both very fast and can connect all the computers in a home or small office network to the Internet. If you subscribe to a high-speed Internet service they will almost certainly set up the cable modem or DSL modem for you.

If wireless networking wasn't complicated enough, there are several different wireless standards out there that you have to be aware of. Table 13-3 briefly describes these standards.

Table 13-3. WiFi network standards

Standard	Speed	Range	Description
802.11b	10 Mbps	150 feet	802.11b was the first version to reach the market. It is the most common, inexpensive, and, at only 10 Mbps, the slowest of all wireless standards.
802.11a	54 Mbps	100 feet	802.11a was a short-lived standard that was much faster (54 Mbps) than 802.11b but had a shorter range. 802.11a is incompatible with the 802.11b standard, so don't expect to find it in your local coffee shop.

Table 13-3. WiFi network standards (Continued)

Standard	Speed	Range	Description
802.11g	54 Mbps	150 feet	802.11g combines the best of both worlds: It has the range of 802.11b and the speed of 802.11a. Best of all, 802.11g is fully compatible with the very common 802.11b standard. If you get any wireless network equipment make sure it conforms to the 802.11g wireless standard.

QUICK REFERENCE

WIRELESS NETWORKING ADVANTAGES:

- SIMPLE TO SET UP
- PUBLIC AVAILABILITY
- CONVENIENT TO USE

WIRELESS NETWORKING DISADVANTAGES

- MORE SECURITY ISSUES AND PROBLEMS.
- INTERFERENCE AND RELIABILITY PROBLEMS.

WIRELESS (WIFI) STANDARDS

- 802.11B

  SPEED: 10 MBPS

  RANGE: 150 FEET

  AVAILABILITY: VERY COMMON

- 802.11A

  SPEED: 54 MBPS

  RANGE: 100 FEET

  AVAILABILITY: RARE

- 802.11G

  SPEED: 54 MBPS

  RANGE: 150 FEET

  AVAILABILITY: COMMON - ALSO COMPATIBLE WITH THE MORE COMMON 802.11B STANDARD

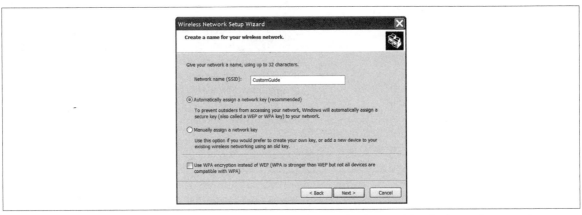

Figure 13-10. Enter a network name (SSID) and select an encryption standard and network key for the wireless network.

Figure 13-11. Most wireless routers and access points can be configured by entering their IP address in any Web browser.

This lesson will help get you started installing a wireless network. Let's get started!

1 If necessary, install the WiFi cards in all the computers you want to connect to the wireless network.

You're going to have to follow the instructions that came with the WiFi card. To install a network card, you have to open your computer, find an empty expansion slot, and insert the WiFi card into that slot.

2 Turn on your wireless router or access point and, if necessary, connect it to your DSL or cable modem.

Next you have to configure Windows XP's networking settings.

3 Turn on your computer. If Windows XP automatically detects the network card, follow the onscreen instructions. If Windows doesn't detect your network card, see Lesson 13-10: *Installing a Network Card*.

Now you're ready to configure your wireless network. Microsoft Windows XP SR2 contains a new Wireless Network Wizard that can make setting up a wireless network *a little bit* easier. Unfortunately, the Wireless Network Wizard isn't very magical—it won't configure your wireless network for you—but it *can* be very useful in helping you come up with a wireless network name (SSID) and network key that you can use to set up your wireless network.

4 Click the Start button and select Control Panel from the menu. Click the Network and Internet Connections category and click the Wireless Setup Wizard.

The Wireless Setup Wizard appears.

5 Select the Set up a new wireless network option and click Next.

Now you need to give your wireless network a name (known as an SSID) and specify the type of network key you want to use to secure your wireless network from unauthorized users. You have two options for the wireless network key:

- **Automatically assigned network key:** Select this option if you want Windows to automatically assign a network key to your wireless network. Unless you specify differently by checking the "Use WPA encryption" box, the network key will use the more common but less secure WEP wireless security standard. Learn more about wireless security in Table 13-4.

- **Manually assign a network key:** Select this option if you want to specify the network key yourself or if you want to create an open, or unsecured, wireless network that anyone can access.

6 Enter a Network name (SSID), specify the type of network key you want to use with your wireless network, and click Next.

If you decided to go with a manual network key you will have to enter the network key you want to use on the wireless network.

7 If you chose a manual network key in the previous step, enter it in the Network key and Confirm network key fields and click Next.

There are a few guidelines you must follow for the network key:

- **WEP:** The network key must be *exactly* 5 or 13 characters or *exactly* 10 or 26 alphanumeric characters.

- **WPA:** The network key must be between 8 and 63 characters (longer WPA keys are more secure) or *exactly* 64 alphanumeric characters.

- **Open:** If you are sure you want to create an unsecured wireless network that anyone with a com-

puter and WiFi card can access, just leave both the Network key and Confirm network key fields blank.

The Wireless Network Wizard provides two ways of creating the wireless network:

- **Use a USB flash drive:** This option lets you save your wireless network settings (the wireless network name or SSID and network key) to a USB flash drive that you can use to add additional computers to the wireless network.

- **Set up a network manually:** This option creates a printout of your wireless network settings (the wireless network name or SSID and network key) that you can use to manually set up the remaining computers. Although it's *not* Microsoft's recommended choice this is the better of the two options, as you have more control entering the SSID and network key in other computers (which have USB ports) *and* in your wireless access point or router (which doesn't).

8 Select the method you want to use to create the wireless network, click Finish, and follow the remaining onscreen instructions.

Next you will need to use the printout in order to enter the wireless network name (SSID) and network key in your wireless router or access point.

9 Configure the wireless router or access point using the manufacturer's software and/or documentation.

Most wireless routers and access points can be configured by connecting them and a computer to a hub or switch with an Ethernet cable, turning the computer or wireless router or access point on, and entering the wireless router or access point's IP address in the computer's Web browser.

When you configure the wireless router or access point, make sure you include: a) The network name or SSID, b) the encryption method (open, WEP, or WPA), and c) the network key from the printout you created in Step 7.

Once you've got the wireless router or access point up and running, it's time to configure the remaining computers you want to connect to the wireless network.

10 Go back to Step 4 and repeat this process on the remaining computers in the network.

QUICK REFERENCE

INSTALLING A WIRELESS HOME NETWORK:

1. ENSURE THAT ALL WIFI CARDS ARE INSTALLED AND WORKING IN EACH COMPUTER YOU WANT TO ADD.

2. TURN ON YOUR WIRELESS ROUTER OR ACCESS POINT AND, IF NECESSARY, CONNECT IT TO YOUR DSL OR CABLE MODEM.

3. CLICK THE START BUTTON AND SELECT CONTROL PANEL FROM THE MENU. CLICK THE NETWORK AND INTERNET CONNECTIONS CATEGORY AND CLICK THE WIRELESS SETUP WIZARD.

4. FOLLOW THE ONSCREEN INSTRUCTIONS TO CREATE A NETWORK NAME (SSID), ENCRYPTION STANDARD, AND NETWORK KEY.

5. IN THE FINAL STEP OF THE WIZARD, SELECT SET UP A NETWORK MANUALLY AND CLICK FINISH.

6. PRINT A COPY OF THE WIRELESS NETWORK CONFIGURATION AND USE IT TO HELP YOU CONFIGURE YOUR WIRELESS ROUTER OR ACCESS POINT (USING THE MANUFACTURER'S SOFTWARE AND/OR DOCUMENTATION).

7. RUN THE WIRELESS NETWORK WIZARD ON THE REMAINING COMPUTERS IN THE NETWORK. USE YOUR WIRELESS NETWORK CONFIGURATION PRINTOUT TO HELP YOU CONFIGURE THEM.

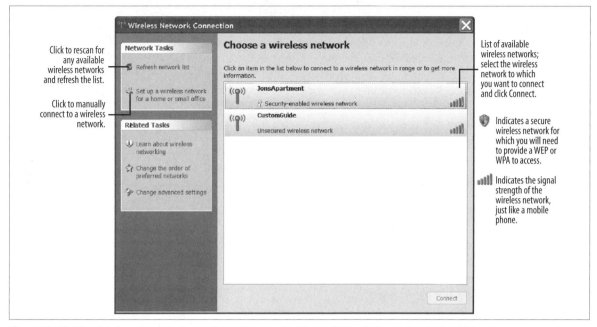

Figure 13-12. The Wireless Network Connection dialog box lists the available wireless networks to which you can connect.

You've decided to take your laptop to the local coffee shop to get some work done away from the distractions at home or the office. You've just turned on your computer and are beginning to enjoy your café latte when you notice the "Free Wireless Internet" sign. Wow – since you have a newer WiFi enabled notebook computer, you decide to check your e-mail. But how do you connect to the coffee shop's wireless network—or any wireless network, for that matter—to access the Internet? This lesson explains how.

NOTE *Most WiFi network cards come with their own proprietary software, which may configure and manage your wireless network settings instead of Windows and therefore the procedures for using and configuring your wireless network settings may differ from those shown here.*

1 Click the Start button and select Control Panel from the menu. Click the Network and Internet Connections category. Then click Network Connections.

Windows displays a list of all your network connections.

Wireless Network Connection

2 Select the Wireless Network Connection icon then select the View Available Wireless Networks task from the Network Tasks menu.

A list of wireless networks within range appears, as shown in Figure 13-12.

- **Wireless Security Indicator:** Wireless network hotspots can be open or secure. If a hotspot is open, anyone with a wireless network card can access the hotspot. If the hotspot is secure, a icon will appear next to it and you will usually need to know the *WEP* key to connect to it. WEP stands for Wired Equivalent Privacy, and it is a way to encrypt the information that a wireless network sends through the air. Table 13-4 describes the more common wireless encryption standards you'll come across.

- **Signal Strength Indicator:** These bars indicate the signal strength of the wireless network, just like a mobile phone does. And, just like a mobile phone, a full set of bars means you'll get a stronger and more reliable connection, fewer bars means a weaker, slower, and more unreliable connection.

3 Select the desired wireless network from the list that appears and click Connect.

A couple of things can happen now, depending on whether or not the wireless network is open or secure. If the wireless network is open, Windows XP should be able to connect to it.

If the network key is provided automatically by your network the connection will be made automatically, otherwise you will need to enter and confirm the WEP or WPA key. If you don't have the key you won't be able to connect to the wireless network.

4 If prompted, enter and confirm the WEP or WPA key and click Connect.

If the signal strength is strong enough, if you've entered the right WEP or WPA key, and if your computer and the network are using compatible wireless standards (see Table 13-4 for a description of these) you should be connected to the wireless network. That's a lot of "ifs", which means there is a good chance something could go wrong when you're connecting to a wireless network. If you are having problems connecting to the wireless network, check the following:

- Is your WiFi card turned on?
- Does your WiFi card support the same wireless network standard as the network? For example, if you have a 802.11b WiFi card you won't be able to connect to a 802.11a wireless network. See Table 13-4 for a list of wireless network standards.
- Did you enter the correct WEP or WPA key?
- Is the WiFi signal strong enough? If the Signal Strength Indicator only displays a single bar, you may have problems connecting to the wireless network.

More and more wireless networks are encrypted, as they should be, to prevent unauthorized users from eavesdropping. The following table lists some of the more common WiFi encryption standards in use.

Table 13-4. Common WiFi encryption standards

Security Standard	Description
Open	An open wireless network has no security whatsoever, therefore anyone with a WiFi card can access it. Open wireless networks or "hotspots" can be found in a growing number of coffee shops, hotels, and other public areas.
WEP / Shared	WEP stands for Wired Equivalent Privacy and is the most common way to encrypt the information that a wireless network sends through the air. There are two variations of WEP: 64-bit encryption (really 40-bit) and 128-bit encryption (really 104-bit). 40-bit encryption was the original standard but it was easily broken. 128-bit encryption is more secure and is what most wireless networks use. You must have the right WEP key or "pass phrase" to gain access to a WEP protected network.
WPA	WPA stands for WiFi Protected Access and is a new security wireless standard that addresses some of the shortcomings of WEP and has better authentication and encryption features. The problem with WPA is it's so new that some older WiFi devices don't support it.
WPA-PSK	A variation of WPA is called WPA-SPK stands for WiFi Protected Access – Pre Shared Key. WPA-PSK is a simplified but still powerful form of WPA suitable for home wireless networks.

QUICK REFERENCE

TO CONNECT TO AN EXISTING WIRELESS NETWORK OR HOTSPOT:

1. CLICK THE START BUTTON AND SELECT CONTROL PANEL FROM THE MENU. CLICK THE NETWORK AND INTERNET CONNECTIONS CATEGORY THEN CLICK NETWORK CONNECTIONS.

2. SELECT THE WIRELESS NETWORK CONNECTION ICON THEN SELECT THE  VIEW AVAILABLE WIRELESS NETWORKS TASK FROM THE NETWORK TASKS MENU.

3. SELECT THE DESIRED WIRELESS NETWORK AND CLICK CONNECT.

4. IF PROMPTED, ENTER AND CONFIRM THE WEP OR WPA KEY AND CLICK CONNECT.

WIRELESS (WIFI) ENCRYPTION STANDARDS:

- OPENNO SECURITY; ANYONE CAN CONNECT TO THE NETWORK.

- WEP/SHAREDMOST COMMON ENCRYPTION STANDARD.

- WPAA NEWER, MORE SECURE ENCRYPTION STANDARD BUT NOT AS WIDELY SUPPORTED AS WEP.

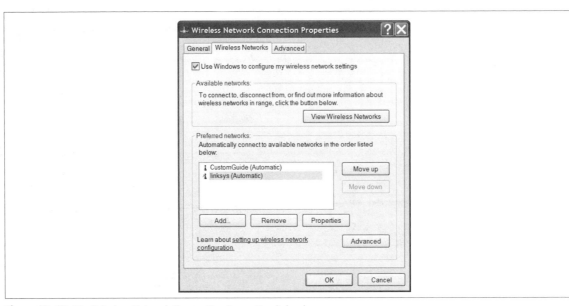

Figure 13-13. The Wireless Network Connection Properties dialog box.

Figure 13-14. The Wireless Network Properties dialog box.

Normally a wireless network will broadcast its name, known as an SSID, so that any nearby WiFi enabled computers will know that the wireless network is there—although, if the wireless network is secure, they won't be able to connect to it unless they know the network key.

Because security is a growing concern many system administrators may choose *not* to broadcast the network name or SSID so that WiFi enabled computers won't see the network name when they scan for any available wireless networks.

You can still manually connect to the wireless network, provided you know the network name or SSID and the network security key. This lesson explains how.

NOTE *Most WiFi network cards come with their own proprietary software, which may configure and manage your wireless network settings instead of Windows and therefore the procedures for using and configuring your wireless network settings may differ from those shown here.*

1 Click the Start button and select Control Panel from the menu. Click the Network and Internet Connections category then click Network Connections.

Windows displays a list of all your network connections.

2 Click the Wireless Network Connection icon then click the View Available Wireless Networks task from the Network Tasks menu.

A list of available wireless networks within range of your computer will appear, as shown in Figure 13-12.

3 Click the ☆ Change the order of preferred networks task from the Related Tasks menu.

Wireless Network Connection

The Wireless Network Connection Properties dialog box appears, as shown in Figure 13-13.

4 Click Add.

The Wireless Network Properties dialog box appears, as shown in Figure 13-14. This is where you enter the information about the wireless network to which you want to connect.

5 Type a name for the wireless network in the Network name (SSID) field.

In case you're wondering, SSID stands for Service Set Identifier. It's more commonly called the network name because it simply identifies a wireless network.

If the network you want to connect to is open and doesn't have any wireless encryption enabled you can skip ahead to Step 9, otherwise move on to the next step.

6 If you are connecting to a secure wireless network where the network key is automatically provided, ensure that the The key is provided for me automatically box is checked. If the wireless network key is not automatically provided (more common), make sure the The key is provided for me automatically box is not checked.

For example, a network key might be automatically provided on the wireless network adapter that your network administrator gave to you.

7 If you are connecting to a secure wireless network and know what the wireless network key is, click the Network Authentication list arrow and select the desired authentication method. If necessary, click the Data encryption list arrow and select the desired encryption method.

Table 13-3 describes the available wireless authentication methods.

8 Enter the network key in both the Network key and Confirm network key fields.

That should be all the information Windows XP needs in order to connect to the wireless network.

9 Click OK, OK.

That's it! If everything is working properly, you should now be able to connect to the wireless network. If you are having problems connecting to the wireless network, check out the usual suspects:

- Is your WiFi card turned on?
- Does your WiFi card support the same wireless network standard as the network? For example, if you have a 802.11b WiFi card you won't be able to connect to a 802.11a wireless network. See Table 13-4 for a list of wireless network standards.
- Did you specify the correct encryption method and enter the correct WEP or WPA key? See Lesson 13.4: *Common WiFi Encryption Standards* for more details on wireless authentication methods.
- Is the WiFi signal strong enough? If the Signal Strength Indicator only displays a single bar, you may have problems connecting to the wireless network.

If the wireless network that you are adding does not have an access point or a router, select the "This is a computer-to-computer (ad hoc) network; wireless access points are not used" check box.

QUICK REFERENCE

TO MANUALLY CONNECT TO A WIRELESS NETWORK:

1. CLICK THE START BUTTON SELECT CONTROL PANEL FROM THE MENU. SELECT NETWORK AND INTERNET CONNECTIONS FROM THE LIST, THEN SELECT NETWORK CONNECTIONS.

2. SELECT THE WIRELESS NETWORK CONNECTION ICON AND THEN SELECT THE VIEW AVAILABLE WIRELESS NETWORKS TASK FROM THE NETWORK TASKS MENU.

3. SELECT THE ☆ CHANGE THE ORDER OF PREFERRED NETWORKS TASK FROM THE RELATED TASKS MENU.

4. CLICK ADD.

5. IN THE NETWORK NAME (**SSID**) FIELD, TYPE A NAME FOR THE WIRELESS NETWORK.

6. CHECK OR UNCHECK THE THE KEY IS PROVIDED FOR ME AUTOMATICALLY BOX, DEPENDING ON WHETHER OR NOT YOUR NETWORK KEY IS AUTOMATICALLY PROVIDED.

7. IF YOU ARE CONNECTING TO A SECURE WIRELESS NETWORK AND KNOW WHAT THE WIRELESS NETWORK KEY IS, CLICK THE NETWORK AUTHENTICATION LIST ARROW AND SELECT THE DESIRED AUTHENTICATION METHOD. IF NECESSARY, CLICK THE DATA ENCRYPTION LIST ARROW AND SELECT THE DESIRED ENCRYPTION METHOD.

8. ENTER THE NETWORK KEY IN BOTH THE NETWORK KEY AND CONFIRM NETWORK KEY FIELDS.

9. CLICK OK, OK.

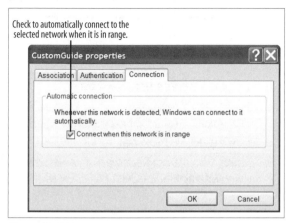

Figure 13-15. The Connection tab of the Wireless Network Properties dialog box.

When you bring your WiFi enabled notebook to a brand new hotspot it makes sense that you will have to search for, find, and connect to the wireless network. It doesn't make sense for you to go through all that work to simply connect to the wireless network in your home or office, however. Don't worry—you can tell Windows to automatically connect to any network whenever it's in range..

NOTE *Most WiFi network cards come with their own proprietary software, which may configure and manage your wireless network settings instead of Windows and therefore the procedures for using and configuring your wireless network settings may differ from those shown here.*

1 Click the Start button and select Control Panel from the menu. Click the Network and Internet Connections category and then click Network Connections.

Windows displays a list of all your network connections.

Network Connection

2 Select the Wireless Network Connection icon then click the ⁽ᵗᵖ⁾ View Available Wireless Networks task from the Network Tasks menu.

A list of available wireless networks within range of your computer will appear, as shown in Figure 13-12.

3 Select the wireless network that you want to connect to. Click the Change advanced settings task in the Related Tasks menu.

The wireless Network Connection Properties dialog box appears..

4 Click the Wireless Networks tab.

Select the network forom the list of preferred networks.

5 Select the network you want to connect to automatically. Click Properties.

The Properties dialog box for the network appears.

6 Click the Connection tab.

The Connection tab of the Properties dialog box, shown in Figure 13-15, is where you can specify if you want Windows to automatically connect to the selected wireless network.

7 Ensure that the Connect when this network is in range box is checked and click OK. Click OK.

That's all you need to do. Windows will automatically connect to the selected wireless network whenever it is in range.

QUICK REFERENCE

TO AUTOMATICALLY CONNECT TO A WIRELESS NETWORK:

1. CLICK THE START BUTTON AND SELECT CONTROL PANEL FROM THE MENU. CLICK THE NETWORK AND INTERNET CONNECTIONS CATEGORY, THEN CLICK NETWORK CONNECTIONS.

2. CLICK THE WIRELESS NETWORK CONNECTION ICON AND THEN CLICK THE VIEW AVAILABLE WIRELESS NETWORKS TASK FROM THE NETWORK TASKS MENU.

3. SELECT THE DESIRED WIRELESS NETWORK AND CLICK CHANGE ADVANCED SETTINGS TASK IN THE RELATED TTASKS MENU.

4. CLICK THE WIRELESS NETWORKS TAB

5. SELECT THE NETWORK YOU WANT TO CONNECT TO AUTOMATICALLY AND CLICK PROPERTIES

6. CLICK THE CONNECTION TAB.

7. ENSURE THAT THE CONNECT WHEN THIS NETWORK IS IN RANGE BOX IS CHECKED AND CLICK OK.

Figure 13-16. Make sure that the network card is firmly plugged all the way into its expansion slot.

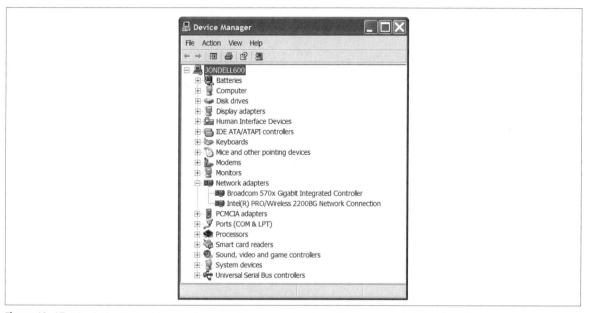

Figure 13-17. Check the Device Manager to ensure that your network card is properly installed and working.

Networking Wizards, built-in network cards, and Plug and Play hardware have made it possible for the average computer user to install and maintain a small network; but it's often not a painless process. Networking is still an enormous and very technical topic, and college degrees and thousands of books have been devoted to the subject.

Nothing can be more frustrating and confusing than network problems. It would take an entire volume of books to list everything that can go wrong with a network and we obviously don't have time for that; but we can devote the next several lessons to the most common network problems and what you can do to fix them. Let's start with the basics.

1 Are other computers connected to the network working?

If none of your computers can connect to the network, it may indicate a bad network hub or switch or wireless access point.

2 Check the physical connections.

Make sure that the network card is firmly plugged all the way into its expansion slot. If you're trying to connect to an Ethernet network, make sure that the Ethernet cable is securely plugged into your computer and into the network hub or switch. Most network cards and hubs or switches have LED indicator lights to show successful connections and network activity. Another problem could simply be a bad Ethernet cable. If you have an extra Ethernet cable, try using it instead and see if it fixes the problem.

If the Ethernet cable seems to be connected and working properly, the next thing to check is if the network card and its driver are properly installed and working.

3 Ensure that your network card is installed using the Device Manager. Click the Start button and select Control Panel from the menu. Click the Performance and Maintenance category and click System. Click the Hardware tab and click the Device Manager button.

The Device Manager window appears, as shown in Figure 13-17. The Device Manager lists the hardware on your computer in an outline. We're looking for a few things:

- **Network Adapters:** Find the Network Adapters category and, if necessary, expand it by clicking the ⊞ next to it.

- **Device Problem:** If this icon appears on a network adapter it means the adapter has a problem. This can be caused by a resource conflict (the device is trying to use a resource on your computer that's already in use), an incorrect driver, or a hardware failure. Try fixing this problem by reinstalling its driver: Right-click the adapter icon and select Update Driver… from the shortcut menu. Make sure you have the software for the network adapter in the CD-ROM drive or readily available.

- **Disabled Device:** If this icon appears on a network adapter it means the adapter has been disabled for some reason. Right-click the adapter icon and select Enable from the shortcut menu to enable it.

- **Unknown Device:** A yellow question mark icon indicates a hardware device that Windows doesn't recognize. To fix this problem you will need to locate and install the driver and software for the device. If you don't have the software, see if you can download it at the manufacturer's Web site. For more specific information, refer to Lesson 13-10: *Installing a Network Card*. Or, better yet, refer to the documentation that came with your network card!

4 Make sure you have the necessary network protocols and components correctly installed.

Lesson 13-1 explains how to check for and install network protocols and components. Most home and small networks require that the 🖥 Client for Microsoft Networks component and 🖧 TCP / IP are installed.

5 Make sure that your TCP/IP settings are correct.

Lesson 13-12: *Understanding and Configuring TCP/IP* explains how to view and change your TCP/IP settings. If you are connecting to an existing network or cable/DSL modem, you will need to know if your computer should use a static or dynamic IP address. Here's the difference between the two.

- **Static IP Address:** Every device on the network is assigned its own unique IP address that never changes. If you give your computer a static IP address, make sure it uses the same scope as the other devices on the network. (For example, if the IP address for your cable modem is 192.168.0.1, then your computer's IP address should be 192.168.0.x, where x is a value between 1-254, excluding 1.)

- **Dynamic IP Address:** Your network will need a *DHCP* (stands for Dynamic Host Configuration Protocol) server to assign and keep track of IP addresses. Many servers, cable modems, and DSL modems have a DHCP server built-in to them to take care of this task. If you are having problems obtaining a dynamic IP address, try assigning a static IP address to your computer with the same scope as the other devices on the network and see if that fixes the problem.

6 If you are trying to connect to a wireless network check the following:

- Is your WiFi card turned on?

- Does your WiFi card support the same wireless network standard as the network? If you have an 802.11b WiFi card you can't connect to an 802.11a network. See Table 13-3 for a list of wireless network standards.

- Did you enter the correct encryption method network key? See Table 13-3 for more information.

- Is the WiFi signal strong enough? If not, you may have problems connecting to the wireless network.

QUICK REFERENCE

BASIC NETWORK TROUBLESHOOTING:

1. ARE OTHER COMPUTERS CONNECTED TO THE NETWORK WORKING?

2. CHECK THE PHYSICAL CONNECTIONS: NETWORK CARDS AND ETHERNET CABLES ARE FIRMLY PLUGGED IN.

3. ENSURE THAT YOUR NETWORK CARD IS INSTALLED USING THE DEVICE MANAGER. CLICK THE START BUTTON AND SELECT CONTROL PANEL FROM THE MENU. CLICK THE PERFORMANCE AND MAINTENANCE CATEGORY AND CLICK SYSTEM. CLICK THE HARDWARE TAB AND CLICK THE DEVICE MANAGER BUTTON.

4. MAKE SURE YOU HAVE THE NECESSARY NETWORK PROTOCOLS AND COMPONENTS CORRECTLY INSTALLED.

5. IF YOU ARE TRYING TO CONNECT TO A WIRELESS NETWORK CHECK THE FOLLOWING:

   - IS YOUR WIFI CARD TURNED ON?

   - DOES YOUR WIFI CARD SUPPORT THE SAME WIRELESS NETWORK STANDARD AS THE NETWORK?

   - DID YOU SPECIFY HAVE THE RIGHT ENCRYPTION METHOD NETWORK KEY?

   - IS THE WIFI SIGNAL STRONG ENOUGH?

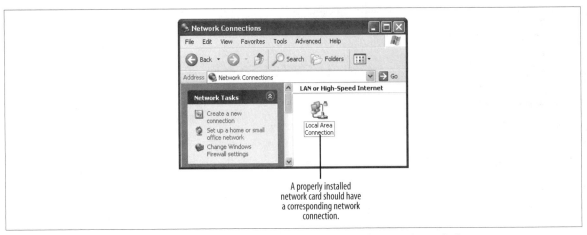

A properly installed
network card should have
a corresponding network
connection.

Figure 13-18. Check your Network Connections to ensure that your Network card is properly installed.

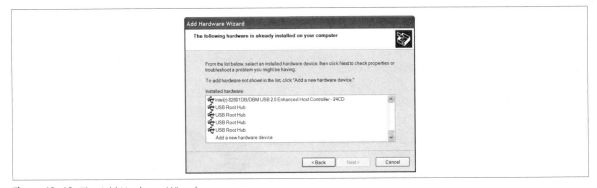

Figure 13-19. The Add Hardware Wizard.

If your computer already has a network card that is working properly or if you have successfully installed a Plug and Play network card without any problems, you can skip this lesson. If you're having problems getting your computer to connect to the network, one of the first things to check is if your network card is installed and working properly.

Let's start out by checking the obvious...

1 Click the Start button and select Control Panel from the menu. Click the Network and Internet Connections category and then click Network Connections.

Windows displays a list of all your network connections. You should see one or both of these network connection icons, depending on your computer's setup:

- **Local Area Connection:** Indicates an Ethernet network interface card is installed on your computer.

- **Wireless Network Connection:** Indicates a wireless network (WiFi) interface card is installed on your computer.

If you are missing the network connection icon (for example, you are trying to connect to an Ethernet network and don't see a Local Area Connection icon), you will need to install the software and drivers for the network interface card. Here's how to do that...

2 Ensure that the network card is physically installed properly into the computer.

Make sure your computer is turned off before you install anything!

If you have a desktop computer and a PCI network card, make sure that the card is firmly inserted into an expansion slot. If you have a laptop and a PCMCIA network card, ensure the card is pushed all the way into the PC Card slot.

3 Turn on your computer. If Windows XP automatically detects the device, the Found New Hardware icon will appear in the notification area, followed by the Found New Hardware Wizard. Follow the onscreen instructions.

Make sure you have the disk or CD-ROM that came with your new hardware device handy—Windows will probably ask you for it. If Windows doesn't automatically detect your new hardware, move on to the next step.

4 Click the Start button and select Control Panel from the menu. Click the Printers and Other Hardware category and then clickAdd Hardware.

The first page of the Add Hardware Wizard appears.

5 Click Next. Select Yes when prompted (since the network card is already plugged in) and click Next.

If you see your ⬛ network card and it doesn't have a ⚠ problem icon next to it, this means Windows thinks your network card is working properly.

6 If you can't find your ⬛ network card in the list, scroll to the end of the list, select Add a new hardware device and click Next.

The next page of the Add Hardware Wizard appears.

7 Ensure Search for and install the hardware automatically option is selected and click Next.

Windows will search for any new hardware devices on your computer. If it finds any, you will probably be asked to insert the software that came with your network card. If it has problems identifying the network card it will ask you if you know the specific hardware model you want to install.

8 Click Next, scroll down and select Network adapters and click Next.

Now you will need to insert the CD-ROM that came with your network card. Can't find it? Then you will need to go to the manufacturer's Web site and hopefully find and download the software or driver required.

9 Click Have Disk, navigate to the drive or folder where the network driver is located, and click OK.

Keep your fingers crossed; hopefully you have the right network driver.

10 Select the driver for your adapter and click Next. Click Next to confirm the installation.

You may get a rather frightening-looking warning about installing software without a Microsoft digital signature. Don't worry about it—just click Yes to install the driver.

11 If a digital signature warning message appears, click Yes to install the software anyway and then click Finish.

Hopefully Windows will see your network card—if not, you may have a bad network card. Try installing a new network card and see if that solves the problem.

QUICK REFERENCE

TO SEE IF WINDOWS RECOGNIZES A NETWORK CARD:

1. CLICK THE START BUTTON AND SELECT CONTROL PANEL FROM THE MENU. CLICK THE NETWORK AND INTERNET CONNECTIONS CATEGORY AND THEN SELECT NETWORK CONNECTIONS.

2. ENSURE THAT THERE IS A NETWORK CONNECTION PRESENT FOR YOUR NETWORK CARD.

TO INSTALL A NETWORK CARD:

1. TURN ON YOUR COMPUTER. IF WINDOWS XP AUTOMATICALLY DETECTS THE DEVICE, THE FOUND NEW HARDWARE ICON WILL APPEAR IN THE NOTIFICATION AREA, FOLLOWED BY THE FOUND NEW HARDWARE WIZARD. FOLLOW THE ONSCREEN INSTRUCTIONS.

2. CLICK THE START BUTTON AND SELECT CONTROL PANEL → PRINTERS AND OTHER HARDWARE → ADD HARDWARE FROM THE MENU.

3. CLICK NEXT. SELECT YES WHEN PROMPTED AND CLICK NEXT AGAIN.

4. IF YOU CAN'T FIND YOUR NETWORK CARD IN THE LIST, SCROLL TO THE END OF THE LIST, SELECT ADD A NEW HARDWARE DEVICE AND CLICK NEXT.

5. CLICK NEXT, SCROLL DOWN AND SELECT NETWORK ADAPTERS AND CLICK NEXT.

6. SELECT THE DRIVER FOR YOUR ADAPTER AND CLICK NEXT. CLICK NEXT TO CONFIRM THE INSTALLATION.

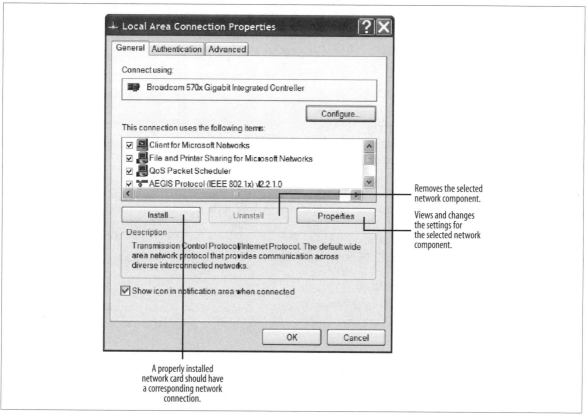

Removes the selected
network component.

Views and changes
the settings for
the selected network
component.

A properly installed
network card should have
a corresponding network
connection.

Figure 13-20. The Local Area Connection Properties dialog box.

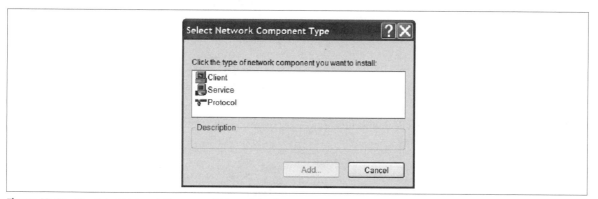

Figure 13-21. The Select Network Component Type dialog box.

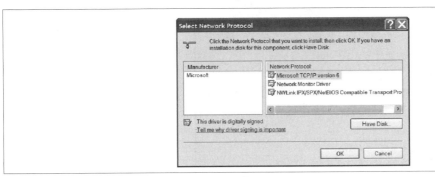

Figure 13-22. The Select Network Protocol dialog box.

Networking components lets your computer access other computers, other computers access your computer, and more. Windows XP comes with the most common networking components already installed and configured, so you probably will never need to add or remove any network components. Still, if you have to do any network troubleshooting, you will probably want to check your networking components to make sure the default network components, listed in Table 13-5 are all there.

1 Click the Start button and select Control Panel from the menu. Click the Network and Internet Connections category and then click Network Connections.

Windows displays a list of all your network connections.

Network Connection

2 Right-click the desired Network Connection icon and select Properties from the shortcut menu.

The Local Area Connection Properties dialog box appears, as shown in Figure 13-20. Here's how to add a networking component...

3 Click Install.

The Select Component Type dialog box appears, as shown in Figure 13-21. You must select one of the following types of network components:

- **Client:** The basic networking software that allows you to use files and printers shared on the network.

- **Protocol:** The language a computer uses to communicate over a network. Computers must use the same protocol to communicate with each other. Every network adapter must have its own protocol(s) installed. So if you have two or more network adapters installed, each of them needs to have their own protocols installed and *bound* to them.

- **Services:** Gives your computer special abilities on the network. Some services enable you to share your files and printers with other people on the network, automatically back up your system, and make your computer a Web server.

Table 13-5 lists the most common networking components.

4 Select the type of networking component you want to install, click Add.

Next, you will need to select the specific network component. Networking components are listed by manufacturer, as shown in Figure 13-22.

5 Select the manufacturer, select the networking component, click OK.

If you're installing a networking component that's not listed in Table 13-5 you will have to click the Have Disk button and specify where Windows should look to install the software.

6 If you want to remove a network component, select the networking component you want to remove and click Remove.

NOTE *Be very careful about removing networking components—if you remove the wrong thing you can easily lose your network connection.*

7 Click OK.

If you're having problems with your network, check your network components and ensure the items listed as installed by default in Table 13-5 are all there.

Table 13-5. Common network components

Component	Description
Client for Microsoft Networks	Supports a network connection to Windows for Workgroups 3.11, Windows 95/98, Windows NT, and Windows NT Server and access to all shared resources. **Installed by default.**
Client Service for NetWare	Supports a network connection to Novell NetWare 3.x and 4.x. With the IPX protocol, you can use the Novell file system and print to Novell printers.
File and Printer Sharing for Microsoft Networks	Lets you share your computer's files and printer with other users on the network. **Installed by default.**
TCP / IP	The most popular network protocol and the one used by the Internet. TCP/IP uses numbers, such as 255.304.649.3, instead of names to identify computers and equipment on the network. **Installed by default.**
NWLink IPX / SPX	The protocol used by NetWare-based networks.

QUICK REFERENCE

TO ADD A NETWORK COMPONENT:

1. CLICK THE **START** BUTTON AND SELECT CONTROL PANEL FROM THE MENU. CLICK THE NETWORK AND INTERNET CONNECTIONS CATEGORY AND THEN CLICK NETWORK CONNECTIONS.

2. RIGHT-CLICK THE DESIRED NETWORK CONNECTION ICON AND SELECT PROPERTIES FROM THE SHORTCUT MENU.

3. CLICK **INSTALL**.

4. SELECT THE TYPE OF NETWORKING COMPONENT YOU WANT TO INSTALL AND CLICK **ADD**.

5. SELECT THE MANUFACTURER, SELECT THE NETWORKING COMPONENT, AND CLICK **OK**.

TO REMOVE A NETWORK COMPONENT:

*   SELECT THE NETWORKING COMPONENT YOU WANT TO REMOVE AND CLICK **REMOVE**.

TYPES OF NETWORK COMPONENTS:

*   CLIENT
*   PROTOCOL
*   SERVICES

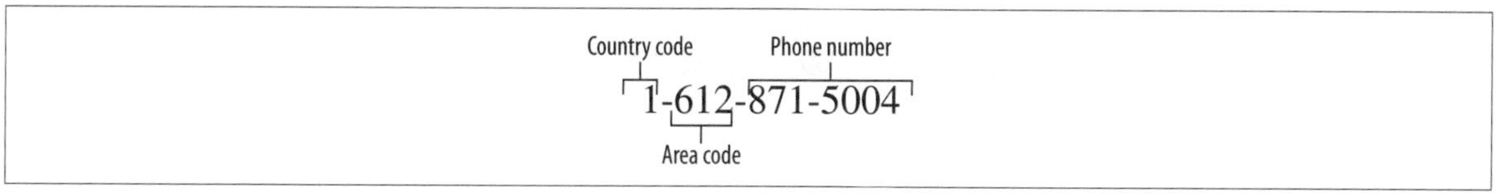

Country code   Phone number

1-612-871-5004

Area code

Figure 13-23. The first part of a phone number contains information about the phone's location.

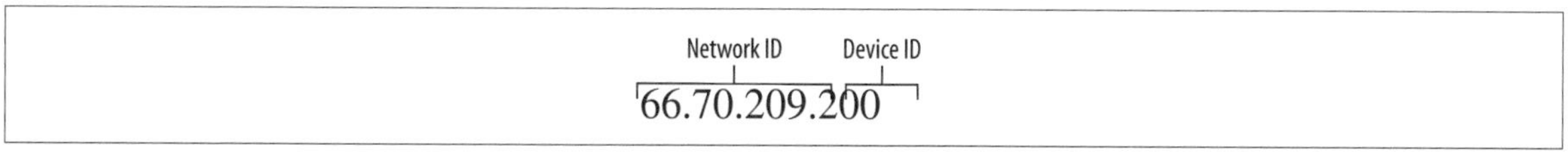

Network ID   Device ID

66.70.209.200

Figure 13-24. The first part of an IP address contains information about the network (a simplification that applies to small networks).

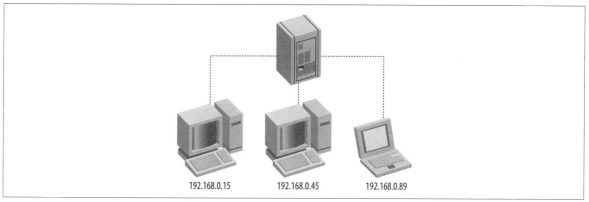

192.168.0.15   192.168.0.45   192.168.0.89

Figure 13-25. A computer that has a dynamic IP address will automatically be assigned one by a DHCP server when it connects to the network.

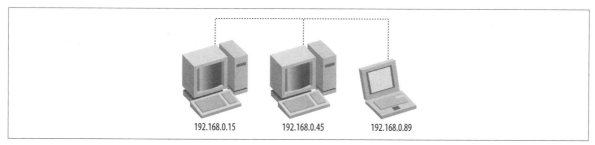

192.168.0.15   192.168.0.45   192.168.0.89

Figure 13-26. A static IP address assigned to a computer doesn't change.

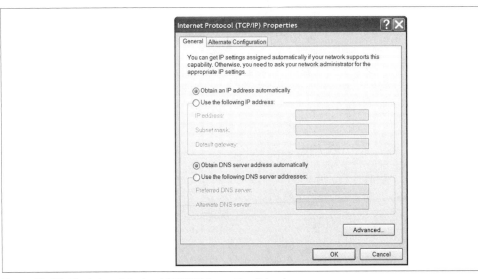

Figure 13-27. The Internet Protocol (TCP/IP) Properties dialog box.

Developed way back in the 1970s by the U.S. Department of Defense, TCP/IP (Transmission Control Protocol/Internet Protocol) is a set of several network protocols, the two main ones being TCP and IP. TCP/IP was originally designed as a wide-area-network (WAN) that could continue to function even if large parts of the network were damaged or destroyed.

Today, TCP/IP is the most popular and widely used network protocol in the world, and is what holds the Internet together. There is a lot to know about TCP/IP; entire books and certification tests are based solely on it. You don't probably don't need to pass a TCP/IP certification test, but knowing some TCP/IP basics can definitely help you configure and troubleshoot a home or small office network.

Each device connected to a TCP/IP network, from laptops to networked printers, has a unique IP address. IP addresses are normally broken up into 4 parts and are similar to phone numbers. The first numbers in an IP address have the broadest scope and may refer to a network's entire country. From there, the remaining numbers narrow things down designating various wide area networks (WANs), local area networks (LANs) all the way down to a specific computer or device on the network. Network engineers will grind their teeth at this oversimplification, but in most small networks the first three numbers of an IP address designate the network, while the last number designates a specific computer or device on the network.

Probably the biggest decision you'll need to make with TCP/IP is whether to use a dynamic or static IP address. Here's the difference between the two:

- **Static IP Address:** You can assign each computer and device on the network its own unique IP address that never changes. This method is fine for small networks, as it's fairly easy to remember the IP addresses that have been used, but it becomes a big management problem as you connect more devices to the network.

- **Dynamic IP Address:** You can automatically assign IP addresses to devices as they log on to the network. Your network will need a *DHCP* (stands for Dynamic Host Configuration Protocol) server to assign and keep track of which IP addresses have been assigned. Many servers, cable modems, and DSL modems have a DHCP server built-in to them to take care of this task. Because it's much easier to manage, most networks use DHCP to dynamically assign IP addresses.

Ready to get your hands dirty? Then roll-up your sleeves and let's take a quick look at how to configure TCP/IP in Windows XP.

1 Click the **Start** button and select **Control Panel** from the menu. Click the **Network and Internet Connections** category and then click **Network Connections**.

Windows displays a list of all your network connections.

2 Right-click the desired Network Connection icon and select Properties from the shortcut menu.

The Local Area Connection Properties dialog box appears. Next you have to find and configure the TCP/IP protocol for the network connection.

3 In the This connection uses the following items: list, find and select Internet Protocol (TCP/IP) and click Properties.

The Internet Protocol (TCP/IP) Properties dialog box appears, as shown in Figure 13-27.

4 If you want to obtain an IP address automatically, select the Obtain an IP address automatically option and then skip ahead to Step 7.

5 If you want to enter your own IP address, select the Use the following IP address option.

You'll have to enter the following information:

- **IP Address:** The IP address you want to assign to your computer. Unless you have a compelling reason NOT to, ensure that the first numbers of the IP address are the same as the other devices on the network.
- **Subnet Mask:** The part of the address mask that identifies an individual network within a larger network. This number is usually 255.255.255.0.
- **Gateway:** In a home or small office the gateway is usually the IP address for the router or modem that connects your network to the Internet.

6 Enter the desired IP Address, Subnet Mask, and Gateway numbers in the appropriate areas.

Hopefully, this will be all the work you will have to do with TCP/IP.

7 Click OK, OK.

If you're having problems connecting to the network or Internet, make sure that the DHCP server is up and running (for automatic IP addresses) and that you've entered the correct IP address, subnet mask, and gateway values (for static IP addresses).

QUICK REFERENCE

TO CONFIGURE TCP/IP:

1. CLICK THE START BUTTON AND SELECT CONTROL PANEL FROM THE MENU. CLICK THE NETWORK AND INTERNET CONNECTIONS CATEGORY AND THEN CLICK NETWORK CONNECTIONS.

2. RIGHT-CLICK THE DESIRED NETWORK CONNECTION AND SELECT PROPERTIES FROM THE SHORTCUT MENU.

3. IN THE THIS CONNECTION USES THE FOLLOWING ITEMS: LIST, FIND AND SELECT INTERNET PROTOCOL (TCP/IP) AND CLICK PROPERTIES.

4. IF YOU WANT TO ENTER YOUR OWN IP ADDRESS, SELECT THE USE THE FOLLOWING IP ADDRESS OPTION AND ENTER THE DESIRED IP ADDRESS, SUBNET MASK, AND GATEWAY NUMBERS

OR...

- IF YOU WANT TO OBTAIN AN IP ADDRESS AUTOMATICALLY, SELECT THE OBTAIN AN IP ADDRESS AUTOMATICALLY OPTION.

- CLICK OK, OK.

TYPES OF IP ADDRESSES:

- STATIC IP ADDRESS
- DYNAMIC IP ADDRESS

Lesson Summary

A Look at Common Network Hardware

The four basic hardware requirements for an Ethernet network are network interface cards, a network hub or switch, an Ethernet CAT-5 cable, and a cable or DSL modem.

The three basic hardware requirements for a wireless or WiFi network are WiFi network cards, a wireless access point or router, and a cable or DSL modem.

Ethernet Networks

The four main advantages of Ethernet networks are reliability, support, speed, and security. One disadvantage is that the wiring can be difficult to set up.

The three most common Ethernet speeds are 10 Mbps (10 Base-T), 100 Mbps (100 Base-T), and 1,000 Mbps (Gigabit).

Installing an Ethernet Home Network

Ensure that the network interface cards are installed and working properly in all computers being added to the network. Connect the computers to the hub or switch with an Ethernet cable. Click the Start button and select Control Panel from the menu. Click the Network and Internet Connections category and then click Network Connections. Click the 🖳 Set up a home or small office network task from the Network Tasks menu. Click Next, Next, then select the appropriate Internet connection and click Next. Click Next, Next, enter the computer description and computer name and click Next. Click Next, enter the workgroup name, then click Next again. Review your network settings and click Next. Select one of the options, depending on the Windows version that is installed on the next computer to be added to the network. Repeat this process on all remaining computers in the network.

Wireless Networks

The three main advantages of wireless networking are simplicity, public availability, and convenience. Two disadvantages are security and interference/reliability.

Three wireless network standards are **802.11b** (Speed: 10 Mbps, Range: 150 ft., Availability: Very common), **802.11a** (Speed: 54 Mbps, Range: 100 ft., Availability:

Rare), and **802.11g** (Speed: 54 Mbps, Range: 150 ft., Availability: Common—also compatible with the more common 802.11b standard).

Installing a Wireless Home Network

Ensure that all WiFi cards are installed and working in each computer you want to add. Turn on your wireless router or access point and, if necessary, connect it to your DSL or cable modem. Click the Start button and select Control Panel from the menu. Click the Network and Internet Connections category and then click Network Connections. Click the 🖳 Set up a wireless network for a home or small office task from the Network Tasks menu. Follow the onscreen instructions to create a network name (SSID), encryption standard, and network key. In the final step of the Wizard, select Set up a network manually and click Finish. Print a copy of the wireless network configuration and use it to help you configure your wireless router or access pointer (using the manufacturer's software and/or documentation). Repeat this process on every computer you want to add to the network. Use your printout to help you configure them.

Connecting to a Wireless Network

Click the Start button and select Control Panel from the menu. Click the Network and Internet Connections category and then click Network Connections. Click the 🖳 View Network Connections task from the Network Tasks menu. Select the Wireless Network Connection icon and then select the ⁽ᵗᵖ⁾ View Available Wireless Networks task from the Network Tasks menu. Select the desired wireless network and click Connect. If prompted, enter and confirm the WEP or WPA key and click Connect.

The three most common wireless (WiFi) encryption standards are **Open** (no security; anyone can connect to the network), **WEP/Shared** (most common encryption standard), and **WPA** (a newer, more secure encryption standard but not as widely supported as WEP).

Manually Connect to a Wireless Network

Click the Start button and select Control Panel from the menu. Click the Network and Internet Connections category and then click Network Connections. Click the Wireless Network Connection icon and then click the ⁽ᵗᵖ⁾

View Available Wireless Networks task from the Network Tasks menu. Click the ☆ Change the order of preferred networks from the Related Tasks menu and click Add. In the Network name (SSID) field, type a name for the wireless network. Check or uncheck the The key is provided for me automatically box, depending on whether or not your network key is automatically provided. If you are connecting to a secure wireless network and know what the wireless network key is, click the Network Authentication list arrow and select the desired authentication method. If necessary, click the Data encryption list arrow and select the desired encryption method. Enter the network key in both the Network key and Confirm network key fields, then click OK, OK.

Automatically Connect to a Wireless Network

Click the Start button and select Control Panel from the menu. Click the Network and Internet Connections category and then click Network Connections. Click the Wireless Network Connection icon and then click the ⁽ᵠ⁾ View Available Wireless Networks task from the Network Tasks menu. Select the desired wireless network and click Connect, then click the Connection tab. Ensure that the Connect when this network is in range box is checked and click OK.

Basic Network Troubleshooting

Are other computers connected to the network working?

Are other computers connected to the network working?

Ensure that your network card is installed using the Device Manager. Click the Start button and select Control Panel from the menu. Click the Performance and Maintenance category, click System, click the Hardware tab and click the Device Manager button.

Make sure you have the necessary network protocols and components correctly installed.

If you are trying to connect to a wireless network check the following: a) Is your WiFi card turned on? b) Does your WiFi card support the same wireless network standard as the network? c) Did you specify have the right encryption method network key? d) Is the WiFi signal strong enough?

Installing a Network Card

To See if Windows Recognizes a Network Card: Click the Start button and select Control Panel from the menu. Click the Network and Internet Connections category and then click Network Connections. Ensure that there is a network connection present for your network card.

To Install a Network Card: Turn on your computer. If Windows XP automatically detects the device, the Found New Hardware icon will appear in the notification area, followed by the Found New Hardware Wizard. If Windows XP does not automatically detect the device, click the Start button and select Control Panel from the menu. Click the Printers and Other Hardware category and click Add Hardware. Click Next, select Yes when prompted, and click Next again. If you can't find your network card in the list, scroll to the end of the list, select Add a new hardware device and click Next. Select the driver for your adapter and click Next. Click Next again to confirm the installation.

Managing Network Protocols and Components

To Add a Network Component: Click the Start button and select My Network Places from the menu. Click the ⬤ View Network Connections task from the Network Tasks menu. Right-click the desired Network Connection icon and select Properties from the shortcut menu. Click Install, select the type of networking component you want to install and click Add. Select the manufacturer and select the networking component, then click OK.

To Remove a Network Component: Select the networking component you want to remove and click Remove.

Three types of network components are **Client** (allows you to use files and printers shared on the network), **Protocol** (the language a computer uses to communicate over a network), and **Services** (gives your computer special abilities on the network).

Understanding and Configuring TCP/IP

To Configure TCP/IP: Click the Start button and select My Network Places from the menu. Click the ⬤ View Network Connections task from the Network Tasks menu. Right-click the desired Network Connection icon and select Properties from the shortcut menu. In the This connection uses the following items: list, find and select Internet Protocol (TCP/IP) and click Properties. If you want to enter your own IP address, select the Use the following IP address option and enter the desired IP address, subnet mask, and gateway numbers. If you want to obtain an IP address automatically, select the Obtain an IP address automatically option. Click OK, OK.

With a **static IP address** you can assign each computer and device on the network its own unique IP address that never changes. With a **dynamic IP address** you can automatically assign IP addresses to devices as they log on to the network.

Quiz

1. Which is NOT a required part of an Ethernet OR wireless network?

    A. A network hub or switch.

    B. A network administrator.

    C. A network interface card (NIC).

    D. An access point.

2. If you are having trouble connecting to a wireless network, what might be the problem? (Select all that apply.)

    A. Your computer's serial number does not match the network name.

    B. Your WiFi card is not turned on.

    C. Your WiFi card does not support the same wireless network standard as the network you are trying to connect to.

    D. The WiFi signal strength is not strong enough.

3. Which of the following are types of network compo-

nents? (Select all that apply.)

    A. Clients

    B. Services

    C. Modems

    D. Protocols

4. TCP/IP is what holds the Internet together. (True or False?)

5. What are some of the advantages of an Ethernet network? (Select all that apply.)

    A. Because Ethernet has been around for quite some time, it is very reliable.

    B. Ethernet cables are very convenient.

    C. Because it doesn't broadcast information via airwaves, Ethernet is extremely secure.

    D. You can browse the Internet using *hotspots* found in most coffee shops.

Homework

1. Check the signal strength of any and all available wireless networks within range of your computer.

2. View the components of a specific network connection.

Quiz Answers

1. B. Your friendly network administrator certainly makes it easier to work with the network, but he or she is not a required part of the network.

2. B, C, and D. If you are having problems connecting to a wireless network, don't panic! The solution is most likely right under your nose.

3. A, B, and D. Client, Protocol, and Services are the three types of network components.

4. True. Transmission Control Protocol/Internet Protocol is the most popular and widely used network protocol in the world.

5. A and C. Ethernet is extremely reliable, secure, and fast. And if that weren't enough, most computers already have an Ethernet card built right into them. How's that for convenience!

INDEX

Symbols

- (minus symbol) next to folder names 113
+ (plus symbol) next to folder names 113
: (or : - ((frowning faces) 343
:) or : -) (smiley faces) 343
:)~ or : -)~ (sticking tongue out) 343
: O or : - O (surprised face) 343
;) or ; -) (winking) 343

Numerics

10 Base-T Ethernet 406
100 Base-T Ethernet 406
1024 by 768 resolution 187
1280 by 1024 resolution 187
16-bit resolution 190
24-bit resolution 190
256 colors, no longer supported in Windows XP 190
32-bit resolution 190
640 by 480 resolution 187
800 by 600 resolution 187
802.11a standard 412
802.11b standard 412
802.11g standard 413

A

access levels
    choosing for new users 355
    for new users on domain computer 357
    types of 392
access permissions to shared folders, changing 391–393
Accessories and Utilities component 280
Accessories menu 33
active windows 46
Add Hardware Wizard 289, 429
Add or Remove Programs window 275
Add Printer Wizard 283
Address bar 36
    jumping to root directory of any drive 104
Address Book feature, adding names to 338–339
Address list arrow
    view list of computer drives and current folder 104
    view previously entered Web addresses 314
adjacent files/folders, selecting 124

Adjust Date/Time command 20
advanced folder options 203–204
aligning paragraphs 84
All Programs menu, selecting programs from 33
alphabetically sorting icons 121
Alt + Tab keys, switching between windows with 46
Alt key 22–24
animated character (Search Companion), changing/
        hiding 129
anti-virus software, installing/updating 330
AOL search engine 317
arranging icons automatically 121
arrow keys 23
ASCII files 119
assigning access permissions 391–393
attachments
    opening attached files in messages 341
    sending in e-mail 336
AutoComplete, turning on/off 130
Auto-hide the taskbar check box 153
Automatic Updates feature xv, 290, 330
automatically assigned network keys 415, 421
"Automatically fix file system errors" check box 264
.avi file extension 127

B

Backgammon, Internet 223
Backspace key 23, 63
bad sectors reported by Error-checking program 265
balloon tips, toggling in Search Companion 130
Bcc (blind carbon copy) field 336
blocking
    pop-up windows 313, 328
        changing settings for 329
    unrequested downloads 325, 328
.bmp file extension 119
    searching for 127
bold font, formatting text with 81
borders of window, dragging 18
broadcasting radio over the Internet 255
Browse button in Run dialog box 164
browsers, Web 309
browsing networks 379–380

About CustomGuide

CustomGuide (*www.customguide.com*) is a leading provider of training materials and e-learning for organizations; their client list includes Harvard, Yale, and Oxford universities. CustomGuide was founded by a small group of instructors who were dissatisfied by the dry and technical nature of computer training materials available to trainers and educators. They decided to write their own series of courseware that would be fun and user-friendly; and best of all, they would license it in electronic format so instructors could print only the topics they needed for a class or training session. Later, they found themselves unhappy with the e-learning industry and decided to create a new series of online, interactive training that matched their courseware. Today employees, students, and instructors at more than 2,000 organizations worldwide use CustomGuide courseware to help teach and learn about computers.

CustomGuide Staff and Contributors

Jonathan High	President	Jeremy Weaver	Senior Programmer
Daniel High	Vice President of Sales and Marketing	Luke Davidson	Programmer
		Lisa Price	Director of Business Development
Melissa Peterson	Senior Writer/Editor	Soda Rajsombath	Office Manager and Sales Representative
Kitty Rogers	Writer/Editor		
Kelly Wardrop	Writer/Editor	Stan Guimont	Senior Sales Representative
Steve Meinz	Writer/Editor	Megan Diemand	Sales Representative
Stan Keathly	Senior Developer	Hallie Stork	Sales Representative
Jeffery High	Developer	Sarah Saeger	Sales Support
Chris Kannenman	Developer	Julie Geisler	Narrator

Colophon

Our look is the result of reader comments, our own experimentation, and feedback from distribution channels. Distinctive covers complement our distinctive approach to technical topics, breathing personality and life into potentially dry subjects.

Jamie Peppard was the production editor and proofreader for *Windows XP Personal Trainer*. Marlowe Shaeffer, Mary Brady, and Claire Cloutier provided quality control. Judy Hoer wrote the index.

The cover image of the comic book hero is an original illustration by Lou Brooks. The art of illustrator Lou Brooks has appeared on the covers of *Time* and *Newsweek* eight times, and his logo design for the game Monopoly is used throughout the world to this day. His work has also appeared in just about every major publication, and it has been animated for MTV, Nickelodeon, and HBO.

Emma Colby designed and produced the cover of this book with Adobe InDesign CS and Photoshop CS. The typefaces used on the cover are Base Twelve, designed by Zuzana Licko and issued by Emigre, Inc., and JY Comic Pro issued by AGFA Monotype.

Melanie Wang designed the interior layout. David Futato designed the CD label. This book was converted by Andrew Savikas and Joe Wizda to FrameMaker 5.5.6 with a format conversion tool created by Erik Ray, Jason McIntosh, Neil Walls, and Mike Sierra that uses Perl and XML technologies. The typefaces are Minion, designed by Robert Slimbach and issued by Adobe Systems; Base Twelve and Base Nine; JY Comic Pro; and TheSansMono Condensed, designed by Luc(as) de Groot and issued by LucasFonts.

The technical illustrations that appear in the book were produced by Robert Romano using Macromedia FreeHand MX and Adobe Photoshop CS.

PowerPoint 2003 Personal Trainer
By CustomGuide, Inc.
ISBN 0-596-00855-4, Includes CD-Rom
336 pages, $29.95

Excel 2003 Personal Trainer
By CustomGuide, Inc.
ISBN 0-596-00853-8, Includes CD-Rom
496 pages, $29.95

Coming Winter 2005

Access 2003 Personal Trainer, *ISBN 0-596-00937-2, $29.95*
Outlook 2003 Personal Trainer, *ISBN 0-596-00935-6, $29.95*
Word 2003 Personal Trainer, *ISBN 0-596-00936-4, $29.95*

**Windows XP Home Edition:
The Missing Manual,
2nd Edition**

By David Pogue
ISBN 0-596-00897-X
600 pages, $24.95

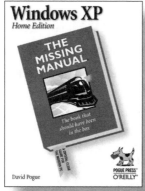

**Windows XP Pro:
The Missing Manual,
2nd Edition**

*By Craig Zacker, Linda Zacker
& David Pogue*
ISBN 0-596-00898-8
680 pages, $29.95

Related Titles Available from O'Reilly

Windows Users

Access Cookbook, *2nd Edition*

Access Database Design & Programming, *3rd Edition*

Excel Hacks

Excel Pocket Guide

Outlook 2000 in a Nutshell

Outlook Pocket Guide

PC Annoyances

Windows XP Annoyances

Windows XP Hacks

Windows XP Home Edition: The Missing Manual

Windows XP in a Nutshell

Windows XP Pocket Guide

Windows XP Power User

Windows XP Pro: The Missing Manual

Windows XP Unwired

Word Hacks

Word Pocket Guide, *2nd Edition*

O'REILLY®

Our books are available at most retail and online bookstores.
To order direct: 1-800-998-9938 • *order@oreilly.com* • *www.oreilly.com*
Online editions of most O'Reilly titles are available by subscription at *safari.oreilly.com*

Keep in touch with O'Reilly

1. Download examples from our books

To find example files for a book, go to:

www.oreilly.com/catalog

select the book, and follow the "Examples" link.

2. Register your O'Reilly books

Register your book at *register.oreilly.com*

Why register your books?
Once you've registered your O'Reilly books you can:

- Win O'Reilly books, T-shirts or discount coupons in our monthly drawing.
- Get special offers available only to registered O'Reilly customers.
- Get catalogs announcing new books (US and UK only).
- Get email notification of new editions of the O'Reilly books you own.

3. Join our email lists

Sign up to get topic-specific email announcements of new books and conferences, special offers, and O'Reilly Network technology newsletters at:

elists.oreilly.com

It's easy to customize your free elists subscription so you'll get exactly the O'Reilly news you want.

4. Get the latest news, tips, and tools

www.oreilly.com

- "Top 100 Sites on the Web"—PC Magazine
- CIO Magazine's Web Business 50 Awards

Our web site contains a library of comprehensive product information (including book excerpts and tables of contents), downloadable software, background articles, interviews with technology leaders, links to relevant sites, book cover art, and more.

5. Work for O'Reilly

Check out our web site for current employment opportunities:

jobs.oreilly.com

6. Contact us

O'Reilly & Associates
1005 Gravenstein Hwy North
Sebastopol, CA 95472 USA

TEL: 707-827-7000 or 800-998-9938
(6am to 5pm PST)

FAX: 707-829-0104

order@oreilly.com
For answers to problems regarding your order or our products. To place a book order online, visit:

www.oreilly.com/order_new

catalog@oreilly.com
To request a copy of our latest catalog.

booktech@oreilly.com
For book content technical questions or corrections.

corporate@oreilly.com
For educational, library, government, and corporate sales.

proposals@oreilly.com
To submit new book proposals to our editors and product managers.

international@oreilly.com
For information about our international distributors or translation queries. For a list of our distributors outside of North America check out:

international.oreilly.com/distributors.html

adoption@oreilly.com
For information about academic use of O'Reilly books, visit:

academic.oreilly.com